Goodbye,
Eastern Europe

Goodbye, Eastern Europe

An Intimate History of a Divided Land

Jacob Mikanowski

Pantheon Books
New York

Pantheon Books and colophon are registered trademarks of Penguin Random House LLC.

Library of Congress Cataloging-in-Publication Data
Name: Mikanowski, Jacob, author.
Title: Goodbye, Eastern Europe : an intimate history of a divided land / Jacob Mikanowski.
Description: First edition. New York : Pantheon Books, 2023.
Includes bibliographical references and index.
Identifiers: LCCN 2022037756 (print). LCCN 2022037757 (ebook).
ISBN 9781524748500 (hardcover). ISBN 9781524748517 (ebook).
Subjects: LCSH: Europe, Eastern—History. Europe, Eastern—
Civilization. National characteristics, East European.
Classification: LCCDJK9.M55 2023 (print) |
LCC DJK9 (ebook) | DDC 947—dc23/eng/20220805
LC record available at https://lccn.loc.gov/2022037756
LC ebook record available at https://lccn.loc.gov/2022037757

www.pantheonbooks.com

Jacket photographs: (left) mccool / Alamy; (right) by Akos Major
Jacket design by Jenny Carrow
Maps by Mapping Specialists, Ltd.

Printed in the United States of America

First Edition

2 4 6 8 9 7 5 3 1

To my parents,
the start of everything.

and

To Nik,
who made it all possible.

Contents

Eastern Europe, c. 1648

0   300 miles
0   300 kilometers

MUSCOVY

Baltic Sea

LIVONIA
Riga
COURLAND

Moscow

Vitebsk

Vilnius
Gdansk
LITHUANIA
Minsk

Berlin

MAZOVIA
Warsaw
POLISH-
LITHUANIAN
COMMONWEALTH
Lublin
VOLHYNIA
Kiev

Prague

HABSBURG
EMPIRE
Kraków
GALICIA
Lviv
PODOLIA
ZAPOROZHIAN
COSSACKS
Kamianets-Podilskyi
Stara Sich
Vienna

Buda
Iaşi
CRIMEAN
KHANATE

Belgrade
Black Sea

Sarajevo
Adriatic Sea

O
T
T
O
M
A
N
Sofia

Salonika
Istanbul
E
M
P
I
R
E

Tyrrhenian
Sea

Ionian
Sea

Aegean Sea

Mediterranean Sea

Eastern European Empires in 1815

300 miles

300 kilometers

Baltic Sea

RUSSIAN EMPIRE

•Vilnius

•Minsk

P R U S S I A

Berlin•

•Warsaw

VOLHYNIA

•Kiev

SILESIA

Prague•

BOHEMIA

Kraków• GALICIA •Lviv

PODOLIA

MORAVIA

Vienna•

BUKOVINA

RUTHENIA

H A B S B U R G

Budapest•

(A U S T R I A N)

HUNGARY

MOLDAVIA

E M P I R E

TRANSYLVANIA

CROATIA-SLAVONIA

BANAT

Belgrade•

WALLACHIA

•Bucharest

BOSNIA   SERBIA

•Sarajevo

Black Sea

DALMATIA

Adriatic Sea

O T T O

M A

N

Sofia•

MONTENEGRO

Istanbul•

•Voskopojë

E M P I R E

Tyrrhenian Sea

Ionian Sea

Aegean Sea

Mediterranean Sea

Eastern Europe, 1921–1939

0   300 miles
0   300 kilometers

NORWAY
Oslo
SWEDEN
Stockholm

FINLAND
Helsinki
Leningrad

Baltic Sea

ESTONIA
Tallinn

DENMARK
Copenhagen

LATVIA
Riga

Moscow

LITHUANIA
Kaunas
Vilnius

UNION OF
SOVIET
SOCIALIST
REPUBLICS

EAST
PRUSSIA

Minsk
BELARUSIAN
S.S.R.

GERMANY
Berlin

Warsaw

POLAND

Kiev

Prague

CZECHOSLOVAKIA

Lwów/
Lviv

UKRAINIAN S.S.R.

Vienna

AUSTRIA

SUBCARPATHIAN
RUS'
Czernowitz/
Cernăuţi

Budapest

HUNGARY

BESSARABIA

Zagreb

YUGOSLAVIA

ROMANIA

Timişoara

Belgrade

Bucharest

ITALY

Adriatic Sea

Black Sea

Rome

Sofia

BULGARIA

Tirana
ALBANIA

Istanbul

Ankara

Tyrrhenian
Sea

GREECE

TURKEY

Sicily

Ionian
Sea

Aegean Sea

Athens

Malta

Mediterranean   Sea

Crete

Cyprus

Eastern Europe, 1949–1990

0   300 miles

0   300 kilometers

NORWAY

Oslo

SWEDEN

Stockholm

FINLAND

Helsinki

Tallinn

Leningrad

DENMARK
Copenhagen

Baltic Sea

Riga

Moscow

WEST
GERMANY

Berlin

EAST
GERMANY

Vilnius

Minsk

UNION OF
SOVIET
SOCIALIST
REPUBLICS

POLAND

Warsaw

Lublin

Prague

CZECHOSLOVAKIA

Kraków

Lviv

Kiev

Vienna

Bratislava

AUSTRIA

Budapest

HUNGARY

Cluj-Napoca

Zagreb

Timișoara

ROMANIA

YUGOSLAVIA

Belgrade

Bucharest

ITALY

Adriatic Sea

Black Sea

Rome

Sofia

BULGARIA

Tirana

ALBANIA

Istanbul

Ankara

Tyrrhenian
Sea

GREECE

Smyrna

TURKEY

Sicily

Ionian
Sea

Athens

Aegean Sea

Malta

Mediterranean Sea

Crete

CYPRUS

Eastern Europe in 2022

Prologue

This is a history of a place that doesn't exist.

There is no such thing as Eastern Europe anymore. No one comes from there. People come from countries: Slovakia, Latvia, Bulgaria. Or they come from cities: Sarajevo, Łódź, Mariupol. Sometimes they say they come from regions or landscapes: the pine woods of Mazovia, the rain-soaked hills of Maramureş, the bare rock of the Albanian Alps.

But wherever they come from, people don't identify as Eastern Europeans. The phrase Eastern Europe is an outsider's convenience, a catchall used to conceal a nest of stereotypes. Some of these stereotypes—poverty, gangsterism, ethnic strife—are genuinely damaging. Others are merely sad. A friend of mine, a professor of Polish and German history, once had a student ask, in all seriousness, whether it was true that Eastern Europe was "a gray place, where no one ever laughed."

With dour connotations like these, it is no wonder that people want to escape being associated with Eastern Europe. Even in the world of international relations, Eastern Europe is losing ground. In the past thirty years, country after country has shed the label. Even before the fall of the Berlin Wall, Czechia, Slovakia, Hungary, and Poland all declared themselves part of Central Europe. The Baltic states of Lithuania, Latvia, and Estonia opted for a northern alternative and would now prefer to be thought of as members of a "Nordic" zone. On both sides of the Balkans, countries from Montenegro to Romania identified themselves with maritime communities formed around either the Adriatic or Black Sea.

With this many defections, Eastern Europe is pretty much a dead letter. And yet not too long ago its existence was self-evident. I am old enough to remember when Eastern Europe was an instantly recognizable reality. In 1986, getting off the tarmac at Chopin Airport in Warsaw meant stepping into a different world from the one I left behind in suburban Pennsylvania. Like the rest of the lands behind the Iron Curtain, this was a world that operated according to its own rules. In Warsaw at that time, you couldn't find ham in a store, but people waited in lines to purchase new translations of foreign fiction. No one voted, but politics was on everybody's lips. Even the smell in the air was different: brown coal burning in winter, the cool exhalation of unwashed landings in summer. Today either of these smells instantly transports me to the lost domain of my childhood.

In those days, the thing that made Eastern Europe a tangible presence, and the glue that held it together, was Communism. Before the epochal transformation wrought by the revolutions of 1989 through 1991, the whole vast stretch of the continent from Estonia in the north to Albania in the south, from Ukraine in the east to Czechoslovakia in the west, belonged to the empire of the Red Star.

But the roots of the region's unity reach much deeper.

There is something distinctive about Eastern Europe, something that sets it apart from Western Europe on one side and the rest of Eurasia on the other. That essential, defining characteristic is diversity—diversity of language, of ethnicity, and above all, of faith.

It was as a religious borderland that Eastern Europe first gained definition as a place different from the rest of Europe. Paganism lasted longer here than it did anywhere else on the continent, and it left a deep imprint on folklore and popular belief. When Christianity did arrive, around A.D. 1000, it came in two different forms—Latin and Greek—creating the first of the region's many religious fissures. Islam arrived a few centuries later, spread by invading Ottoman Turks and Tatars. By 1492, the whole Balkan Peninsula belonged to the Dar al-Islam, and mosques could, and still can, be found as far north as Vilnius in Lithuania.

That same year, when Ferdinand and Isabella of Spain expelled their kingdom's Jews, the last in a long series of such banishments from the Christian nations of the West, the Ottoman Empire invited them to settle in its greatest cities. By then, the East was the cradle of European Jewry. As Western European countries expelled their Jews one after another, Eastern European kingdoms welcomed them in.

For much of its history, Eastern Europe was a frontier society, pushing into territories that had been previously uncultivated or that had been depopulated by long-running frontier wars. Multiple waves of settlement gave much of it a character quite unlike Western Europe (or most of Russia for that matter). In Eastern Europe, it was common to see Catholic and Orthodox Christians living in close proximity with Jews and Muslims. This overlapping of multiple religions made it hard to enforce the dogma of any individual faith. Eastern Europe thus became a haven for religious misfits and heretics. Groups such as the Bogomils, Hussites, Frankists, and Alevis left a deep imprint on the region's culture. So did a welter of magicians, alchemists, and occultists, whose combined presence made Eastern Europe the continent's premier training ground for the dark arts.

Today most of the Jews are gone, and the Islamic presence is much diminished. Working alchemists are even harder to find. Still, in many places, it is possible to feel the weight of their legacies. For years, I've traveled everywhere from the Sufi shrines of Dobruja in Romania to the last wooden synagogues of Samogitia in Lithuania, in search of traces of this vanishing religious plurality. For me, this was a personal quest. My family background—half-Jewish and half-Catholic—encapsulates a fragment of this past diversity.

This book is not a family history, but my family's history forms a braid running throughout it. The Polish poet Czesław Miłosz wrote that "awareness of one's origins is like an anchor line plunged into the deep" without which "historical intuition is virtually impossible."[1] And so it is for me; my ancestors are at the root of everything I write.

As a member of a very small community of Polish-speaking Jews, I was born into a culture that has all but disappeared. This was the world of the secular Jewish intelligentsia, who were passionately attached to Poland's literary heritage but wary of its marriage of Catholicism and nationalism. Their idols were poets and short story writers rather than generals or saints, and their bookshelves were packed with the yellowed spines of émigré journals sent from Paris.

But this is only half of my family's story. The other, Christian half was made up of competing strands, divided by class and trade. Some were peasants and some were craftspeople. A few were even aristocrats, and worked as servants to kings. Even though these ancestors had roots in places as disparate as Hungary, Lithuania, Germany, and the Czech lands, all of them considered themselves to be Poles. The process by which this collective awareness was forged took centuries.

The defining cleavages in my family were between Jew and Christian, commoner and noble, Pole and non-Pole. These were all symptoms of a single overarching pattern. To a degree unknown in much of the rest of the world, in Eastern Europe religion, ethnicity, and class all worked together to delineate boundaries of profession and caste. It was common for landowners, tenants, and townspeople to all speak different languages and belong to different faiths. Because of this, people could live side by side, and yet belong to completely different social worlds. Neighbors stayed strangers, so long as old taboos remained in force.

These patterns of exclusion and animosity combined to create a world of incredible variety. No matter its size, no community in Eastern Europe was ever unmixed, or "pure." Even in the smallest village, a ten-minute walk might take you past temples devoted to three different religions, whose priests all spoke in different tongues. If you were to spend any time on the road, you might encounter whole different sets of languages and beliefs, belonging to the regions' numerous nomads, itinerant salesmen, and other professional wanderers.

For centuries, the traditional societies of Eastern Europe most often resembled a multicolored tapestry. Diversity was not a by-product of this system; it was woven into the whole. But all this proximity of different faiths and languages did not necessarily lead to harmony. This old order depended on the maintenance of strict divisions between classes and among religions. When these divisions broke down in the twentieth century, people gained a new measure of freedom, but they were also exposed to new dangers. In my own family, the mixing of Christian and Jew, farmer and aristocrat was only made possible by the total disaster of World War II. Even then, boundary-crossing was no easy thing; I grew up on stories of family members who were shunned or hadn't seen one another for decades. This, too, is a common enough story in Eastern Europe. Countless families have been split by new borders, old religions, or allegiances to rival causes.

My own divided heritage has provided me with a complicated inheritance. Because of it, I am inclined to see the story of Eastern Europe less as one of nations and states and more as one of competing systems of belief. Political debates in Eastern Europe often revolve around battles over the sacred. During the twentieth century, fascism, Communism, and nationalism provided people with powerful sources of meaning-making. Wherever these ideologies were adopted by large numbers, religious models were not far behind, either as a model or as a competitor.

For centuries, Eastern Europe has been a place of seekers. Less economically developed than the West, but open to a wealth of religious and messianic traditions, its people have long dreamed of a sudden, transformative leap into the future. They also yearned for a more earthly sort of liberation.

For many revolutionaries, empire loomed as an even bigger threat than poverty. To them, freedom meant ruling in the language of their own people, over their own territory. Achieving this goal was rarely easy, for at least two reasons. One was that hardly any region of Eastern Europe was home to a single people. The other was that most of these peoples were rather small, while the empires in which they found themselves were very large. More often than not, then, the fight for independence required a fratricidal struggle against impossible odds.

Eastern Europeans have rarely been in full control of their destiny. Over the centuries, much of their history was written in the imperial capitals of Vienna, Istanbul, and St. Petersburg, and later Berlin and Moscow. But those capitals were not where that history was lived. To me, the history of Eastern Europe is everything that happened in between those centers of power. It is, above all, a land of small states with complicated fates. Its story is not one of kings and emperors, or Axis and Allied armies, but rather one of peasants, poets, and country clerks—people who experienced the clash of empires and ideologies directly, in the flesh.

The storms of the twentieth century destroyed the age-old fabric of Eastern European life. Today only traces remain of the multilingual and multiconfessional world inhabited by my grandparents. Since I feel like a very small part of what remains, I have been drawn to reconstructing that vanished diversity that stands at the center of what it means to be Eastern European. For me, it is less a single identity than a collection of shared affinities, structured around a shared memory of coexistence.

But amid all our differences, Eastern Europeans share one other legacy in common, and that is a gift for seeing comedy amidst tragedy. Prolonged acquaintance with history at its most extreme has given us an extraordinary fluency in the absurd. This can be seen in the region's fiction, and even more in the stories people tell about their own lives.

Hasidic Jews used to say that the best way to get to know their wonder-working rabbis was through the tales their disciples told about them. So it is with Eastern European history. To live in Eastern Europe, especially in the twentieth century, was to undergo a bewildering series of calamities and transformations. A straightforward historical account-ing would turn this dizzying experience into little more than a list of rulers and events. But tales—stories, rumors, and folksongs—expose what these events meant. They can get to the heart of what it was like to experience the horrors of the fascist anti-utopia, the brief elation and prolonged terror of Stalinism, the stasis and scarcity of late socialism, and the sudden evaporation of solid values that accompanied the arrival of capitalism.

To me, these tragicomic stories, abounding in sudden catastrophes, unexpected reversals, and miraculous escapes, are the true lingua franca of Eastern Europe—the common tongue of its otherwise diffuse iden-tity. I have been collecting them for years. I began during my years in Poland and continued through my library and archival research and throughout my many trips to the region. They are the best reminder that Eastern Europe is not just a place of suffering but a civilization of its own, containing endless fascination and wonder.

Here are a few stories culled from my notebooks.

From a movie:[2] One day some Romanian newspaper editors looked at an official photo of Nicolae Ceaușescu with Valéry Giscard d'Estaing and were horrified to see that the Romanian dictator was much shorter than the French president and, worse, wasn't even wearing a hat. To fix this potentially damning mistake, the editors pasted a hat onto Ceaușescu's head, only to realize too late that he was already holding a hat in his hand. Police rushed out at once to intercept and destroy all the issues of the paper that made it into print.

From a biographical dictionary: After the Communist takeover, a scholarly Albanian poet named Sejfullah Malëshova rose to become his country's minister of culture, only to quickly run afoul of the terrifying minister of the interior. Sentenced to years of imprisonment in a notorious prison camp, the poet was freed after the interior minister was himself sentenced to death in a subsequent purge. But the price for the poet's freedom was his voice. He could no longer publish. He could not even speak. For the next twenty years, he worked as a stock clerk in a provincial town, without saying a word the entire time. If someone tried to say something to him, he mimed, pinching his lips to remind them of his vow of silence. Everyone in the town knew his poems, but no one dared recite them aloud, and when the poet died, no one dared attend his funeral. He was buried in the presence of his sister, a gravedigger, and two secret police agents.[3]

And finally, a story from my mother's aunt Jadwiga, told to me on the day I got engaged: Aunt Jadwiga and Uncle Turnowski had tried to marry three times. The first time was in Minsk, in 1940. With difficulty, they put together the money for the fee. On the way to the civil status bureau, they met a friend of theirs, Icek, who was panting from running after them. He needed to borrow money right away; teakettles had just shown up in the stores. They gave him the money they had saved for the marriage license. It had to be done. A marriage could always be postponed, but you never knew when a teakettle would be on sale again.

The second time they tried to get married was two years later, in Tajikistan. This time they had money, and they already lived together, in a small town where everyone knew everybody else. When they went to the civil status bureau, the Soviet bureaucrat in charge expressed surprise that they weren't already married, since they were living together. He said that the order was wrong—they should have gotten married first and only started living together afterwards—and so he denied them a marriage license.

The third time was in Warsaw after the war. Uncle Turnowski had his two witnesses (one of them was Icek, who had needed the teakettle), and they arrived at the scheduled time at the ministry. Jadwiga was missing—she couldn't get the day off at the publishing house where she worked. But this time—finally, after six years—they pulled it off. The official in charge agreed to sign the marriage license in the absence of a bride.

For me, this last story captures my great-aunt Jadwiga and her whole generation. They were born into the dislocation and promise that followed the First World War, they survived the devastation of the Second, and somehow they never lost their perspective or their sense of humor. They measured their days in teakettles and missed appointments as much as they measured them in revolutions, invasions, and capitulations. What follows is written in the shadow of their gigantic lives.

Part I

Faiths

Pagans and Christians

Wet Monday tricksters
(*dziady śmigustne*). Dobra, Poland. 1916.

A great forest, bristling with dangers and the occasional gleam of treasure: that is how the territories of Eastern Europe must have appeared to the average Roman in the time of the emperor Marcus Aurelius. To them, the lands north of the imperial frontiers were largely a mystery. Marcus himself traveled north of the Danube in A.D. 170, to fight a war against a confederation of barbarian tribes. He began writing his *Meditations* there, camped out with his solders by the banks of the River Hron, in what is now Slovakia. This work, a classic of Stoic philosophy, might be the first piece of literature written in Eastern Europe. Marcus did not mention his surroundings even once, but that should not strike us as too surprising. The territories north of the Roman Empire were empty of cities, writing, temples, or any of the other markers that would have indicated the presence of civilized life to someone arriving there from the shores of the Mediterranean. As far as the Romans were concerned, these cold and rather frightening lands were sources of two things and two things alone: inexhaustible hordes of enemies, and a lightweight precious stone called *electrum*, or amber.

I used to have a cigar box that belonged to my grandfather. It was full of the rough orange pebbles of raw amber that he had gathered with my father on Polish beaches. All along the shores of the southern Baltic, from Denmark to Estonia, amber is just that easy to find: you just have to go to the beach after a storm, or know where to dig in the sand. The routes that brought this precious stone, so mysteriously radiant and light, to the shores of the Mediterranean were already old by the time Marcus Aurelius arrived. A century earlier, during the reign of the emperor Nero, a Roman knight had set out north from a frontier post in what is now Austria. He had orders to bring back as much amber as he could buy; the emperor needed it to decorate his new Colosseum. The knight traveled north hundreds of miles, to the shores of the Baltic. To everyone's amazement, he returned with wagonloads of the stuff, pieces the size of pumpkins, enough to decorate the whole amphitheater, down to the knobs on the nets that protected spectators from the wild animals raging within.[1]

The trade in amber between the Baltic and the Mediterranean dates back at least to the Bronze Age. But in this case, commerce did not foster connection. These voyages left only the faintest mark in Eastern Europe—at most, a few fragile traces: buttons from an equestrian's uniform found next to a Polish lake, a cavalry helmet in a Lithuanian tomb. And Roman coins—a profusion of coins. These were not used as money in the countries in which they were received. They were treasure in a truer, purer sense—tokens from another world. In the Russian enclave between Poland and Lithuania (an area that's especially rich in amber), there are ancient cemeteries in which every grave contains at least one shiny brass *sestertius*. These coins were placed next to the head of the deceased, in vessels made from the bark of the sacred birch tree, intended as payment for a Baltic ferryman to the underworld whose name has been lost to time.[2]

—

A flash of silver unearthed by a plow: that is how the ancient world appears in most of the countries of Eastern Europe. Otherwise, silence. History arrives only with the advent of Christianity and, with it, the written word. Before then, we know hardly anything for certain. Here, the Dark Ages were truly dark: north of the old Roman frontier, almost impenetrably so. But even to the south, the gloom is difficult to penetrate. When the Slavs arrived, in the desperate decades of war, famine, and plague that followed the fall of the Western Roman Empire in 476, they seemed to come from nowhere, and then, all of a sudden, to be everywhere at once.

Today Slavic languages are spoken in a vast chunk of Europe, from Bulgaria and the former Yugoslavia in the south to Poland and all of Russia to the north.[3] This is a vast territory, but only some of it seems to have been inhabited by Slavic-speakers from an early date. The first mentions of the Slavs in ancient sources came toward the end of the sixth century. By the year 1000, they were present everywhere from northern Greece to the edge of Finland.

But where did the Slavs come *from*? This question vexes historians, since it has no solution but many competing claims. For many decades, the answer depended on who you were. Russians insisted that the Slavs came from Russia, Ukrainians said they came from Ukraine, and Poles said they came from Poland. Then for a time, a loose consensus emerged placing the Slavic homeland in Polesia, a region of endless wetlands stretching along the length of the border between Ukraine and Belarus. I used to imagine them emerging out of a bog wearing great leather waders, with water dripping down their mustaches, ready to conquer Thessaloniki as soon as they toweled off.

This is no longer the preferred view. Today, the cutting-edge theory is that the Slavs came from what is now Romania, rather paradoxically, since there are no Slavic-speakers there today (Romanian is a Romance language). According to this interpretation, they coalesced as a result of the Eastern Roman Empire's bottomless need for manpower to staff the forts lining the Danubian frontier. There is much to recommend this view, but we will never know for sure. The early Slavs had few notable leaders and no great chroniclers. They came not as a flood but in a series of smaller streams. In the words of one historian, theirs was an "obscure progression," visible only in sporadic moments, illuminated by a dull and flickering flame.[4]

A similar murkiness clings to Slavic beliefs. We know very little about their mythology or rituals—only that they were pagans and worshipped a pantheon of gods. But when the Christian priests arrived to drive out the old ways, no one thought it worthwhile to record them. One of the paradoxes of religious history in Eastern Europe is that paganism lasted so long there, yet we know so little about it. There is no Slavic equivalent to the great compendium of Norse myth preserved in the Icelandic *Edda*, or the Celtic tales contained in the Welsh *Mabinogion* or the Irish *Táin*. All we have are fragments, recorded by hostile witnesses.

One of the first such testimonies comes from, of all places, Sicily. Around A.D. 700, a Slavic raiding party was taken prisoner by the local militia. An enterprising bishop asked its members what they believed in. By means of a translator, they replied that they worshipped "fire, water, and their own swords."[5] Almost seven hundred years later, the Grand Duchy of Lithuania was still being ruled by practicing pagans who believed something very similar. A vast realm that incorporated much of today's Belarus and Ukraine, Lithuania was the last country in Europe to give up the old faith. In 1341, when Grand Duke Gediminas died, he was buried in the full, cruel splendor of the pagan rite: burned to ash on a giant pyre, along with his favorite weapons, slaves, dogs, and horses, and a few German Crusaders thrown in for good measure. When the whole thing caught fire, Gediminas's fellow pagan lords cried out in sorrow and pelted the flames with the claws of lynxes and bears.

Two hundred years later, hardly anything of this pagan faith remained. At most, Polish and Lithuanian chroniclers could recall a few hallowed names. During the Renaissance, humanist scholars amused themselves by inventing ever more elaborate pantheons for their pagan ancestors. To the old gods of thunder, cattle, and grain, they added deities in charge of hogs and wives, a god (and goddess) of beekeeping, as well as humbler spirits to watch over everything from hazelnuts to yeast.

None of these, of course, were genuine. Almost everything that has ever been written about the ancient religion of the Balts and Slavs is false. Most of it is based on a few late observations and the testimonies of outsiders. Beyond the names of a few deities and a few scant archaeological remains, nothing is clear. So what can we say about these gods with certainty? Only three things: they lived in trees, they spoke through horses, and they savored the smell of freshly baked bread.

The paganism of the Balts and Slavs was an "outdoor religion."[6] The forest was its true temple. Most shrines were simply groves, or great trees that held special renown in and of themselves. On an island in the Dnieper River there stood a huge oak tree that passersby honored with sacrifices of arrows, meat, and bread. Until recently, women in Polesia still offered specially baked bread to the setting sun every Easter, and they prayed before a sacred tree to ensure a good harvest.[7] This echo of a thousand-year-old custom lasted until 1986, when the Chernobyl disaster tainted the land and drove its inhabitants to seek refuge elsewhere.

The pagan Prussians (a Baltic people who predated the Germans in what would become East Prussia) worshipped in groves of holy oak trees. Each grove had its own priests and sacrifices. It was a meeting place, a sanctuary, and an oracle. While the cult of the gods was still alive, its adherents would ask the trees and the lakes they worshipped questions, most often about their enemies. Gods spoke through the landscape they inhabited, but the easiest way to ask them a question directly was to seat their spirit astride a horse. When the Slavs who lived by the mouth of the Oder River considered going to war, they would consult a sacred horse by walking it past a series of spears planted in the ground. If the horse left the spears alone, they rode to battle.[8]

As Christianity drew ever nearer, the pagans of the southern Baltic had many occasions to ride to war. For two centuries, from roughly 1200 to 1400, the southeastern shores of the Baltic played host to a blood-thirsty Christian Crusade. It was led by the Teutonic Knights, an order of (mostly) German knights, freshly returned from the Holy Land, searching for a new arena in which to fight a holy war. From northern Poland to Estonia, they preached the word of God with "tongues of iron," to borrow a phrase from Charlemagne. Everywhere the fighting was brutal. In Prussia, it amounted to a war of extermination that ended with the disappearance of the Prussians as a people and the extinction of their language.

Here Christianization really amounted to a form of colonization. In a foretaste of what would happen one day in the New World, the whole social system of medieval Europe was transplanted to the east by force. Eastern European paganism was a local religion, intimately tied to place. Its laws stretched only as far as the course of a single stream or the shade of a certain tree. Christianity, by contrast, was a missionary faith. It tried to remake the whole world in its image. It attacked in waves. First the missionaries came to cut down the holy groves. Then came the Crusaders to break the power of the ancient chiefs and massacre their followers. When their work of slaughter was done, Christian landowners arrived to reduce the baptized survivors to the status of serfs.

The *Chronicle* of Henry of Livonia is our best source for what this war must have felt like to those involved. Henry was a Saxon priest attached from an early age to the household of Bishop Albert of Buxhoeveden, one of the leaders of the conquest of what is now Latvia. In 1200 Albert set out from Hamburg with a fleet of ships and soldiers and landed on the site of present-day Riga. This was to be Albert's bishopric, if he could conquer and convert it.

Henry's *Chronicle* is the story of this conquest. It is told in the first person, covering two decades in the lands that are now Latvia and Estonia. His story is set among virgin woods, frozen rivers, and deep snows. It is punctuated by terrible violence: beheadings, behandings, disembowelments. Men are burned alive, and their hearts eaten to gain their owners' life force. Even among the converts to Christianity, things are touch-and-go. As soon as the Christian fleet that converted them leaves, one group of pagans plunges into the nearest river to scrub off the baptism they just received. They then cut down what they take to be the idols of the Christians and set them afloat on a raft to join their departed masters. Elsewhere, in Estonia, pagans revolted and threw off the rule of the priests. Immediately they rushed to the churchyards, dug up their dead, and incinerated them according to their ancient custom.

The old cult of the trees proved to be especially difficult to eradicate. In Estonia, when priests razed the lovely forest dedicated to the god Tharapita, the locals were amazed that the trees didn't bleed like human beings. In northern Poland, when missionaries tried to do the same thing, the Prussians cut off their heads. In Pomerania, near the border between Poland and Germany, the local tribes considered two trees especially sacred: a gorgeous old nut tree, and a gigantic leafy oak with a spring beneath it. The pagans managed to convince the priests to spare them from being cut down by promising to convert. They solemnly swore that from then on, they would never worship the trees again; they would simply rest in their shade and savor their beauty.[9]

For all the violence wielded by the Crusaders, the old ways never fully went away but were driven underground, or else they found Christian disguises. In some places, pagans made a deal with their conquerors to keep their traditions intact. In western Latvia, a group of local free farmers who came to be known as the Curonian Kings struck a bargain with the Teutonic Knights. In exchange for help fighting their pagan brethren, the Kings were granted two privileges. The first was that they could keep cremating their dead, a habit long denounced by the Christian friars. The second was that they didn't have to chop down their holy grove. This forest, shared in common by seven villages, was kept inviolate. No brushwood could be gathered there, and hunting there was allowed only once a year, at the winter solstice. All the game taken then was shared in common at a great feast, at which great quantities of beer were drunk and the dancing continued through the night. This was a wild hunt, whose trophies belonged to the gods.[10]

Traces of the specific forest where the Curonian Kings held their feast remain to this day. One fragment, called the Elka Grove, is located a few miles south of the town of Kuldīga, in Latvia. Deep into the twentieth century, it was still prohibited to light fires or break branches in this once-sacred grove. Anyone who violated the taboo risked causing either a fire or a death. However, after a funeral in the village, the rule was reversed. Everyone would go to the grove and break off a branch, singing, "Don't die, you people, there's no more room on the hill [i.e., cemetery]!"

Today the seven villages of the Curonian Kings are greatly depopulated, as a result of Soviet land reforms and mass emigration to the West. Their last holy grove still exists, however. It is a small patch of woods on both sides of the highway between Kuldīga and Aizpute. Hoping to find a material trace of the beliefs they had clung to so tenaciously for so many centuries, I went in search of it on one intermittently drizzly day in July. A combination of constant rains and long northern days cooperated to make the landscape an unearthly, bryophytic green. When the sun came out after the third shower in as many hours, steam rose from the road and from the tall trees crowning the nearby hills. A pair of cranes preened by the edge of a field of crop stubble, while storks, walking in calm rows, patrolled for food in freshly plowed furrows.

I wish I could say that, standing within the grove, I felt the presence of the ancient gods of field, wood, rock, and stream, but that would be a lie. The grove itself is small, covering just a few scant acres. Its trees, a mix of stout lindens and scrawny birches, look like a backyard thicket. The Aizpute highway runs through it like a wound. But from a distance, it still makes a powerful impression. The Elka woods stand on a rise that, though slight, makes them look as if they are floating above the surrounding landscape. Seen from the nearest village, the crowns of the trees seem to merge into the clouds. Who can say for certain what voice speaks when the wind blows through their leaves?

In what is now Estonia, Latvia, northern Poland, and the former East Prussia, Christianity was imposed by force. The one exception among the Baltic countries was Lithuania, where local dukes managed to fight the crusading knights to a standstill and held on to their native faith until the close of the fourteenth century. They finally converted in 1387, a year after Jogaila, the Grand Duke of Lithuania, married Queen Jadwiga of Poland, initiating the Polish-Lithuanian union, which would last until 1795, when both countries would be wiped off the map by their imperial neighbors.

For Jogaila, becoming Christian was the price of an alliance. Christian Poland and pagan Lithuania shared a common enemy in the Teutonic Knights. The old crusading order had long since gone rogue, fighting wars purely for conquest, without regard to whether their enemies were Christian or pagan. When he became king, Władysław Jagiełło (Jogaila's new Christian name) was able to muster enough manpower to break the military power of the knights at the Battle of Grunwald in 1410.

Lithuania's conversion to Christianity was a political decision. In earlier centuries, the same could have been said for the Poles, the Czechs (as Bohemians and Moravians), the Hungarians, the Bulgarians, and the Serbs. Unlike most of the pagan Balts, these peoples had strong states, too powerful and too far from their Christian neighbors to be converted by force. And yet between 800 and 1000, they all in turn accepted Christianity. Mojmir of Moravia converted in 831; Khan Boris of Bulgaria in 864; Bořivoj of Bohemia in 884; and Mieszko of Poland in 966. Saint Stephen of Hungary, already a Christian, defeated a pagan relative in 997 to impose Christianity on all of his domains. For all these rulers, becoming Christian was a way of waging politics on a European scale. It was a signal to rival kingdoms to treat them as equals in the checkerboard of marriage pacts and military alliances that made up the great game of European diplomacy. But where did these early kings and dukes get their power in the first place?

In most Eastern European countries, written history begins at the moment of conversion. The lies began there as well. Hired chroniclers—usually Western monks—spun pious myths about where their masters got their crowns. There was wise Queen Libuše, who ruled the Czechs by prophecy and foretold the future beauty of Prague. She heard lawsuits and dispensed justice from the comfort of her sumptuous bed. Although she was wise and just and could see the future, the men of the tribe nonetheless grew dissatisfied with her rule. They wanted a man. Libuše mocked the Czechs for their small-mindedness but ultimately agreed. She would marry a great king and defer to his judgment. Being a prophetess, she told the tribesmen exactly where they could find him.

Her future husband was named Přemysl; he was to be found plowing a field in the middle of the woods with two oxen. When Libuše's messengers found him, he invited them into his hut for a meal of moldy bread and stale cheese. Summoned to the queen's bed, the two were wed, after which they got drunk and had sex. The dynasty they started together lasted for four hundred years. Now a prince, Přemysl the plowman never forgot where he came from. He kept his worn cork shoes forever close to him in his treasury at Vyšehrad.

For their part, the Poles, before they received their own founding dynasty, suffered under the rule of King Popiel, who was so wicked that his subjects chased him into a tower, where he was devoured by mice. He was replaced on the throne by a hospitable wheelwright named Piast. His claim to fame was that he gave ale to some parched travelers and invited them to a party. His descendants also ruled Poland for the next four centuries.

A tankard of ale, a piece of moldy bread, a crust of cheese: these are the Slavic Excaliburs. There is something appealingly democratic in these stories of humble peasants and craftsmen giving rise to kings. By contrast, the Turkic dynasty that ruled over the Bulgarians traced its ancestry back to Attila the Hun, while the similarly non-Slav Árpáds of Hungary claimed to descend from a giant mythological bird. Sadly, however, these stories are all nonsense. The real historical origins of the Eastern European kingdoms isn't written in chronicles; it is recorded in the soil. It is a story that is still coming to light.

In 2000 archaeologists working alongside the expansion of the A1 highway running north from Warsaw stumbled onto a cemetery. They dated it to the late tenth or early eleventh century, the very years when Poland became Christian and its rulers entered onto the European stage. The excavators noticed something odd about the individual burials. The bodies hadn't been cremated, as was normal in pagan cemeteries, but they also weren't pointed to the east, as they would have been in a Christian one. Instead, they were oriented north-south, something previously seen only in Viking burials. The women were buried with fine jewelry, beads of glass mixed with gold evidently crafted in the royal workshops of Baghdad and Byzantium. The men were armed with splendid foreign weapons, like Frankish broadswords and Khazar hatchets. Studies on their skeletons confirmed that most of the dead came from Scandinavia, though some came from farther afield as well—central Russia to the east, and northern Italy to the west.[11]

Who were these men? Most likely, they were members of the Polish royal guard. Arabic sources report that the earliest Polish kings lavished them with favors. And well they might have. The guards were the support and foundation of their rule. The kings needed hired muscle because the real source of their wealth came not from taxing peasants but from the intracontinental slave trade, the greatest source of wealth in the ninth and tenth centuries. It is no coincidence that just as Bohemia, Moravia, and Poland were coming into existence as states, this trade was at its height. Its agents were variously Christian, Jewish, and Muslim, and the captives were mostly pagan. The buyers came mainly from the silver-rich Islamic caliphates of Iraq and Andalusia. There, slaves from different realms were in endless demand. Slavs were highly esteemed, prized for their skill as household laborers. Eunuchs were considered best. According to a contemporary manual, an uncastrated Slavic slave would always stay coarse and simple-minded, but a castrated one was capable of every refinement.[12]

For the most part, the history of the Slavic slave trade was not recorded in written sources; it must be read in the ground. Hoards of Arab silver, buried everywhere from Sweden to Bohemia, trace the fluctuations in the long-distance networks that brought northern captives south to the markets of Baghdad and Córdoba.

Two competing trade routes, both dealing in human cargo, seem to have functioned at the same time. One led south from Novgorod in northern Russia toward the Caspian and Black seas. The other went overland from the Baltic to the great slave market of Prague. In Russia, slaves were loaded onto dugout canoes and paddled downriver toward the Crimea and the southern reaches of the Volga. In Poland and Bohemia, since no rivers crossed the Carpathians, prisoners had to be marched overland. Following this later route south, archaeologists realized something that had been staring them in the face for decades. The function of the giant fortifications, seemingly empty of dwellings, had long puzzled them. These were holding pens, built to house slaves in great numbers before the season came for the caravan to march south.

Poland, Bohemia, and Moravia were made on these caravan trails. Their first rulers were entrepreneurs of violence, who built their wealth by raiding surrounding communities and exporting their people—in chains—to the great emporia of the Mediterranean and the Middle East. No wonder their propagandists invented stories of honest plowmen and humble wheelwrights, when the real foundation of their power lay in enslaving their own people and selling them on the great markets of Venice and Córdoba, much as the first princes of Rus made their fortunes organizing the same trade to Baghdad and Constantinople.

Russia, Poland, and the Czech lands all became states by wedding armed force to commerce. By contrast, the first chieftains of Hungary and Bulgaria engaged in plain pillaging. Both peoples were originally nomadic, hailing from the steppes of southern Russia. Confederations of mounted warriors, they arrived in Europe like a thunderbolt. Beginning in the seventh century, the Bulgarians raided deep into the Byzantine Empire, eventually establishing their own tribal kingdom south of the Danube.

The Hungarians (or Magyars) first appeared in the Balkans some two hundred years later. Initially allies of the Bulgarians, they soon began conducting devastating raids deep into Western Europe. They were a frightening bunch. A chronicler describes one of their first dukes smashing his enemies' heads as if they were "ripe gourds."[13] Even the Magyars' queens were fierce: an early one is said to have been a "hard drinker, who rode like a knight, and killed a man with her bare hands." But these seasoned warriors also eventually followed their pagan brethren into the Christian fold.

For the various pagan chieftains who became Eastern Europe's first Christian kings, conversion was a pragmatic choice, but it carried real spiritual consequences. Just how complicated this transition could be can be seen in a letter sent by the Khan Boris of the Bulgars to Pope Nicholas I in 866. By then, the Bulgars had already been living in Europe for over two hundred years. Over that time, they had gradually merged with their Slavic, agriculturalist neighbors, but they still clung fiercely to the old ways of the steppe—among them, paganism. As Khan Boris was contemplating which church to sign up with, Roman or Byzantine, he wanted to understand the details. He drew up a list of questions for the pope. Could men still wear trousers as Christians? Could women? How many wives could a man take? Was sex allowed after pregnancy or during Lent? Could men bathe on Fridays? Should turbans be worn in church? Was it still all right to heal one's wounds with a magic stone?[14]

The pope responded to Khan Boris's questions point by point: trousers, baths, and turbans were all fine; magic stones and polygamy less so. These responses seem to have pleased the khan more than the answers he received to the same question from the Orthodox Patriarch in Constantinople. Nonetheless, he ultimately decided to side with the Greeks. The deciding factor was a strategic one. The Byzantine emperors were closer, and better armed, than the Romans. Similar calculations shaped the Christianization of the whole region. In the ninth century, the Serbs followed the Bulgarians into the Byzantine orbit.

In 987 the princes of Kiev joined them. For these half-Viking and half-Slavic warlords, the attraction of Byzantine Christianity was aesthetic as much as it was political. Allowed entrance into the churches of Constantinople, the princes of Rus were struck dumb with wonderment. A later chronicler recorded that upon entering the Hagia Sophia, they did not know whether "they were on heaven or on earth," and knew at once that "God dwells there."[15]

The princes of Rus thus chose to side with beauty, although it certainly helped that Constantinople was also their main trading partner. Elsewhere, more mundane prerogatives ruled the day. For the Czechs, Croats, and Poles, the greatest threat to their independence came from the West, in the form of the Frankish Empire and its successor, the German-dominated Holy Roman Empire. Both entities followed the Catholic faith. For the Slavic kingdoms, appealing directly to Rome was a defensive action. It gave them a chance to develop their own Christian institutions, instead of having them imposed from above by a German emperor.

These choices, shaped by the particular circumstances of ninth- and tenth-century politics, had far-reaching consequences. Because of them, Eastern Europe would become a borderland between the rival Christendoms of Rome and Byzantium. The dividing line between Orthodox and Catholic ran right through the heart of many states, creating centuries of strife. Even into the twentieth century, the tensions generated by this schism led nations to disintegrate and combust. But for the first Christian rulers of Eastern Europe, this all lay in an unimaginable future. Their immediate concern was how to incorporate Christianity into their subjects' everyday lives.

In order for Christianity to be lasting, it first had to become local. The easiest way to make this come about was to find some homegrown saints and build a cult around them. It was good if these saints left behind some relics that could pass into royal hands, and even better if they were royal family members themselves. This had the double advantage of conferring legitimacy on the dynasty internally, while making a good show of faith to the wider Christian world.

In Hungary, the founding saint was the first Christian king, Saint Stephen, who earned his sainthood by killing his pagan uncle. Similarly in Serbia, the great Saint Sava was a royal son who escaped from his duties as a provincial governor to become a monk on Mount Athos and, in time, a polyglot scholar and genius of the holy word. In Bohemia, the honor went to a royal youth, a member of the ruling dynasty named Václav (or Wenceslas).

Václav's hagiographers remembered him as an exceptionally devout child. Many nights he would rise from his chambers in the royal castle to wander secretly in the nearby fields. There he reaped grain by moonlight, which he ground, milled, and sifted into flour, out of which he baked wafers for the holy mass. Other nights Václav would go out for midnight strolls in the castle vineyard to gather grapes, which he would then make into wine for mass.[16] These nocturnal perambulations lasted until Václav was twenty-eight, when he was assassinated by his brother, Boleslav the Cruel.

Saint Adalbert (Wojciech in Polish, Vojtěch in Czech), the first patron saint of Poland, was another highborn Czech. Trained for the priesthood from an early age, Vojtěch soon began moving in the highest circle of the clergy. Still in his thirties, he became Bishop of Prague, where he quickly made himself unpopular by preaching against polygamy and the Czech habit of enslaving Christians. Soon Adalbert had to flee back to the German imperial court, from which he had just arrived. There no one was sure what to do with him. Adalbert spent his days praying and studying. At night, he would rise while everyone was still asleep and shine the shoes of the entire imperial court, an act that was endearing in its humility but not exactly designed to bolster his prestige.[17] Finally, it was decided that Adalbert should be a missionary. In 997 he went north to the Baltic to minister to the pagan Prussians. They found him overbearing, as well as difficult to understand, and chopped off his head. The king of Poland ransomed his body for its weight in gold, after which his ghost began performing useful miracles.[18]

Pious insomniacs, cruelly murdered: such were the saints of early Catholic dominion, chosen for their closeness to power and for the numinous power their relics could bestow on an otherwise pagan landscape. Canonized for the sake of politics, they never inspired more than lukewarm devotion. Farther south, in the Orthodox Christian world of the Balkans, the cult of the saints was far more powerful, in large part because saints held a deeper connection to the pagan past. They took over many of the functions of the gods they had replaced.

Saint Elijah, known as the Thunderer, brought lightning and storms, much as Zeus or the Slavic Perun had done in ages past.[19] Saint Theodore helped to bring about the summer every year by driving the chariot of the sun with his twelve horsemen.[20] Saint Bartholomew did the same when fall turned into winter. In this way, the saints were crucial mediators in the yearly unfolding of the seasons, the great drama structuring the lives of all agricultural societies.

Every year the sun grew big and hot in the sky and made the crops ripen, and every year, by midwinter, it grew so small and cold that it seemed life would never come back to the frozen fields. And yet everything depended on its return, which was far from a given. The sun, and spring, had their enemies. They needed champions. Every year, in winter, a dragon tried to swallow the sun, and so every year, Saints Elijah and George had to travel to the underworld to free it.

In summer, various supernatural forces banded together to try to rob plants of their fertility, steal crops, or ruin them with hail. These infernal opponents could take the shape of snakes, dragons, werewolves, or witches. Sometimes saints battled against them, but more often, they thought it best to fight fire with fire.

Behind the sun and beneath the earth, monster fought monster for possession of the soil and the sky. Across Eastern Europe, "good werewolves" and "good dragons" (usually in human form) watched over their communities and protected them from the forces of evil that threatened them from outside. This made sense when seen through the prism of traditional belief; it was harder to explain to members of the Christian elite.

In 1691, a man named Thiess was put on trial for heresy in the Latvian town of Jaunpils. Thiess was over eighty years old and well respected in his village. He was also a werewolf. That he freely admitted it shocked his judges. Thiess, however, explained that he wasn't a bad werewolf who stole people's crops; he was a good werewolf—one of the "hounds of God" who fought with sorcerers from nearby countries, like Russia or Estonia, to protect the village's crops. These battles took place in Hell, the entrance to which was in a nearby swamp, every year around Christmastime. The werewolves didn't always win, but this year, Thiess said, they had. They brought back much barley and rye from Hell and threw it high into the air so that it might fall on the fields of rich and poor alike.[21]

The judges didn't accept Thiess's explanation and sentenced him to be flogged and banished. To them, it didn't seem possible that a person could be a werewolf *and* a good Christian. Maybe if they had a better sense of history, they would have changed their minds; Livonia had long been famous for its werewolves. As recently as the sixteenth century, werewolves were well known to be out in the twelve days after

Christmas. Elsewhere in Eastern Europe, these were commonly called the "dog days" or "heathen days." In the ancient agricultural imagination of Old Europe, this time of year was the most dangerous—when the membrane between this world and the next is at its thinnest, and everything held its breath to see if the sun would reappear from its prison.

The citified Lutherans listening to Thiess at court no longer knew about this tradition. So the trial transcript makes for fascinating reading. At one point, Thiess said he and his werewolf companions organized a pig roast. The judges wanted to know how they could have done this when they "had wolves' heads and paws."[22] The answer, naturally, was that the werewolves tore the meat and put it on a spit as wolves, but they ate it as human beings.

Historians now think Thiess was describing a form of shamanism. The combat he spoke about took place in a trance or a dream. We know of a very similar custom from around the same time in Hungary—except there it involved dragons instead of werewolves, and some of the most powerful shamans were women.

In Eastern European mythology, dragons took many forms: there were dragons who stole crops, and there were also dragons who protected them. Hungary's dragon magicians, known as *táltos*, harnessed the power of good dragons for the benefit of their communities. They had the power of second sight: they could heal the sick, tell the future, or find hidden treasure. Above all, though, the *táltos* were protectors, tasked with defending their village or region from supernatural assault.

Like the Livonian werewolves, the *táltos* often fell afoul of religious authorities. When they did, they were often mistaken for witches. What the *táltos* thought of themselves, and how their neighbors viewed them, can be gleaned from the records of their trials. Usually, the relationship was one of awe. In 1626, when the *táltos* Erszébet Ormos appeared before a Hungarian court, one of the other witnesses at the trial said of her simply, "The dragons are her company." This was a great power, and even the humblest *táltos* knew it. Erszébet Tóth, who came from a small town a little bit east of Budapest and went on trial in 1728, felt that she was in command of tremendous forces. She could speak with the other world by means of a double. This double could roam as far as Turkey, yet her husband would think she was right beside him.

Erszébet Tóth could detect treasure and identify thieves. At night, she roamed around town, aware of what was going on behind every door. She protected her hometown against earthquakes, but her responsibilities were bigger than that. According to her, a "third of Hungary would have been lost" if not for intervention. She was a protector, but she could also be fierce in her own self-defense: "I am the daughter of God. If somebody threatens me, I look into the eyes of that person, and they have to die."[23]

In traditional belief, the dead were everywhere, obscured under thresholds and hidden in whirlpools and at crossroads. Their blessing guaranteed the health of crops. Their dissatisfaction carried the force of a curse. At certain times, they were more present than at others. All Souls' Day, on November 2, remains the great Catholic festival of the dead, but there were others. Christmas Eve was a night, for instance, when deceased family members returned home. So, sometimes, were the days before Easter.[24] On Holy Wednesday, bonfires were lit to warm the souls of the dead.[25]

Often the dead came of their own accord, unbidden. One name for these returning dead was *upiór*, or vampire. While the word *upiór* seems to have a Polish origin, the belief in a specific kind of returning, malevolent dead was common to most of Eastern Europe. Indeed, it was present in every Eastern European country except Estonia and almost absent from any of its surrounding neighbors, aside from Greece. Eastern Europe can be said, in a way, to *be* vampire Europe—bound by an invisible web of beliefs about what the dead might claim from the living, and how they could be warded off.

The West learned of vampires as a result of the great vampire plague that affected the Austrian military frontier in the 1720s and '30s. The frontier, which ran along the borders of the Habsburg and Ottoman empires in what is today Croatia and Serbia, was an odd place: a heavily fortified no-man's-land, patrolled by Slavic refugees from Turkish rule who served under the command of German officers. This is where the Enlightenment first encountered the world of Balkan folk belief. Summoned to remote villages, periwigged army doctors, their pockets bulging with treatises by Newton and Voltaire, arrived to discover things they had never dreamed of: whole cemeteries dug up, grave by grave, revealed that the least corrupted bodies were pierced through the heart with hawthorn stakes. The Slavic villagers blamed the plague on the work of the unquiet dead. Staking them was a way of forcing them to rest, and a torrent of blood issuing from a corpse was a sign that they had identified the culprit correctly. All this was deeply shocking to the Austrian physicians, whose reports brought the vampire into general European circulation. From there, the vampire metamorphosed into his Western iteration, as a blood-hungry immortal, noctambulist, ravisher, and fulfiller of forbidden dreams.

This version has almost nothing to do with reality; it is a phantasm of a phantasm. Eastern European vampires are very different from their Western equivalents. These vampires do not have fangs, and only rarely do they drink blood. They are nocturnal, but sunlight does not harm them. They also differ from place to place: vampirism is not a discrete condition but a spectrum. In Bulgaria, it is believed that the vampire is a shadow, and this shadow is his soul. In Macedonia, they are imagined to be like wineskins full of blood, with eyes that gleam like coals. Since they have no bones, a single prick is enough to kill them. Cut them once, and the blood will run out of them like air out of a balloon. In Serbia, it was thought that a vampire is born with "a belly filled with blood," but if they stay afoot for thirty years, they can become fully solid once more. At this point, they appear quite human.[26]

Often, *upiórs* tried to fit themselves back into the lives they left behind. They envied the living, but they also sought to rejoin them.

Sometimes these reanimated beings embraced their new lives as opportunities to become gainfully employed. In Kosovo one vampire, banished from his home village, left for a nearby city, where he opened a shop and ran it successfully for many years before being caught and killed by an angry mob. A Bulgarian vampire from Nikodin, only seventeen when he died, went to a foreign city, where he became a very successful butcher's apprentice.[27] A Bulgarian vampire from Dospej, in the Samokovsko region, similarly left his home and got a job in Istanbul. Many years later, his wife spotted him traveling. She let everyone know that he wasn't who he claimed to be, but rather the reanimated corpse of her spouse. Taking heed of her words, her relatives set him on fire in a hay shed.

Pitiful shades! I find it hard not to be moved by the story of these quarrymen and butcher's boys who, given a chance at immortal life, simply moved down the road and did more or less the same thing they had always done. They remind me of a story told by a Polish witch at her trial. Offered anything she wanted by the Devil, she asked for two hours in a Toruń tavern—such is the cost of limited horizons.[28]

As tragicomic as these stories are, they contain a kernel of truth about the essential nature of the Eastern European vampire. These were not, primarily, figures who came back from the dead to prey on the living. Rather, they were the dead who forgot to die. Instead of shuffling off to the underworld, they did their best to continue living as they had, sleeping with their wives, bothering their children, taking occasional revenge against those who had harmed them. The great hysteria of the 1730s added countless layers of myth and romantic fantasy around the figure of the vampire, obscuring its true nature. To see what a vampire was before Dracula, bats, and garlands of garlic stole the show, we must go back a bit earlier, before the legends crystallized.

In 1718, a man was buried in the town of Stará Ľubovňa, in what is now Slovakia. His name was Michael Kasparek. He was a Pole—a wine merchant, a swindler, and something of a womanizer as well. Nothing was amiss in the burial: Kasparek was interred in a churchyard, with all necessary ceremony, in a coffin covered in red silk, leaving his wife to grieve and to deal with his creditors.

Eight days after the funeral, Kasparek returned. He appeared to his servant at night. He picked fights, bit, beat, and choked people. He pushed a hops seller into the River Poprad. He barged into a wedding and demanded that he be fed fish. When the wedding party refused him wine, he downed a bottle, smashed all the drinking glasses, and rode away on a white horse. The townsmen were alarmed. They filed a complaint with the magistrate. A priest begged the bishop in Kraków for advice as the town belonged to Hungary, but its churches were Polish and most of its people were German—a typical Eastern European mess.

Meanwhile Kasparek was still on the prowl. He slept with his own widow and impregnated her. He did the same thing to four other women. Then, he vanished. People breathed a sigh of relief. Three weeks later, reports came back from abroad that he was seen in Warsaw, settling old debts and making new ones. At last, after months, the bishop approved an inquest and a trial. It was difficult to arrange, since Kasparek was still ostensibly buried in the churchyard. So they dug him up, cut off his head, and burned the rest of him. Just for good measure, a priest excommunicated him as well.

Again, he returned. Fires broke out across Stará Ľubovňa. Magistrates interrogated Kasparek's brother and widow. They swore that Michael neither made a pact with the Devil nor possessed a magic ring. Meanwhile, the arsons continued. People thought Kasparek was taking revenge for his posthumous execution. "You've burned me, I'd better burn you," someone heard him say. Finally, his widow made a confession. She knew why Kasparek kept coming back. He told her that the devils would not let him into Hell, nor God into Heaven, because they had burned not his own heart but a stranger's. Here was the solution to the riddle: the heart in his corpse had belonged to a sheep. The real one was found, hidden under a dung heap, and ceremoniously burned at the Stará Ľubovňa town hall.[29]

Kasparek's few months back among the living were a reign of terror for this small Slovak town. Still, there was something irrepressible, almost comical, about him. This crooked wine-seller seemed simply to have too much life force to be contained by the grave. Death could not keep him from lying, swindling, scheming, and fucking. And what could be said of him could be said of many others. The dead do not disappear after death. They persist, in their own minds as well as in ours. Again and again they return: sometimes envious, sometimes aggrieved, often just desperate for warmth. The message they bring back is always, in essence, the same: *We live. We live. Our hearts burn.*

Slavic deity, Velestino hoard. Seventh century.

2

Jews

Jewish family. Poland, 1918–1939.

In 1912 the Jewish playwright and folklorist S. Ansky set out on an expedition into the neglected heartlands of Eastern European Jewry. His voyage of exploration would traverse some of the least-visited corners of the Pale of Settlement. For over a century, the Pale had been the only part of the Russian Empire in which Jews were allowed to settle, and was by now home to some 5 million Jews, making it the single largest Jewish community in the world.

During his travels, Ansky paused at every forgotten village and market town, collecting legends and documenting local customs. He was also interested in Jewish monuments and the tales associated with them. In the small Ukrainian town of Kaminka, he went to see the grave of rabbi Shmuel Kaminker, a famous Hasidic holy man who had been renowned in the early nineteenth century for his ability to exorcise possessing ghosts, or *dybbukim*. Shmuel's powers lingered on after his death.

It was said that Shmuel's grave protected Kaminka from fires and flood. But when the cemetery caretaker took Ansky to see Shmuel's ancient tomb and peeled away some of the moss covering the nameplate, he discovered to his surprise that it said, "Moshe, son of Moshe." It was not Shmuel's tomb at all; it had just been remembered that way.[1]

A cry of distress tore through Kaminka. Rabbis, laypeople, women, and children all streamed into the cemetery to view the scandalous discovery. In a moment, their world had been shattered. The holy man who had protected them from danger was snatched away from them. Seeing the people's distress, Ansky delicately backpedaled. He told the townspeople that, in his experience, tombstones sometimes moved; a piece might be chipped off one tomb, then reappear on another one, and over time a whole inscription might migrate in this fashion. It was therefore entirely likely that the revered rabbi Shmuel was indeed buried under the grave of "Moshe, son of Moshe." The townspeople accepted this news with great eagerness, for it meant that they could hold on to what was most precious to them: the memory of the blessed man and the continued use of his wonder-working powers.

Nine hundred years earlier, from a Jewish perspective, Eastern Europe was home to no graves and no ghosts. Some early visitors found it nearly devoid of people as well. One of the first Jewish travelers to record his impressions of the region was an Arabic-speaking merchant from Catalonia, Ibrāhīm ibn Ya'qūb, who visited Poland and Bohemia around 965. He wrote of traveling for weeks through dense forests and sodden marshlands. The few settlements he saw were wooden forts surrounded by palisades of pointed stakes. The only city of any consequence he came across was Prague. Merchants traveled there from far and wide to trade in tin, fur, and most of all, slaves.[2]

To its earliest Jewish inhabitants, Eastern Europe seemed like a wild frontier, a green and empty land without prior associations in history or memory. Jews, coming from the Mediterranean and Western Europe, where they had lived for a millennium, needed a way to inscribe it in their own mental geography. They started with a name, anointing the sparsely settled, largely Slavic lands "Canaan," after the biblical name for the Holy Land before the arrival of the Israelites. For centuries, these early Jewish settlers spoke a language with Slavic vocabulary written in Hebrew script called Knaanic, or the "language of Canaan." By the late

Middle Ages, however, it was nearly extinct, subsumed by the German-derived Yiddish of new arrivals from Ashkenaz, the Jewish name for the lands surrounding the Rhine. Knaanic left hardly any traces, except for inscriptions on coins and glosses in works of rabbinical literature.

The Ashkenazi Jews, driven out of Germany by massacres and expulsions, went first to the Czech lands of Moravia and Bohemia, then slowly trickled into Hungary, Poland, and Lithuania. Poland-Lithuania proved to be especially congenial to Jewish settlement. Following the marriage of the pagan duke Jogaila of Lithuania to the Christian princess Jadwiga of Poland in 1386, these two countries shared a single ruler. Combined, they formed an enormous realm that included the territory of most of today's Poland, Lithuania, and Belarus, as well as much of Ukraine and parts of Latvia. This vast realm was underdeveloped and undersettled. Best of all, it was a tolerant place, especially in matters of religion. In this joint monarchy (later renamed the Polish-Lithuanian Commonwealth), Catholic, Protestant, and Orthodox believers could all rub shoulders. Muslims and Jews were also welcome, the former serving as mounted soldiers, and the latter working for wealthy noblemen as merchants and tradesmen.

Jews flourished in their new home. The Ashkenazi population in the commonwealth grew at such a rate that modern-day demographers still can't quite account for it. The Jews themselves had a simple explanation for their success: it was foreordained. A beautiful story, oft retold, spoke of the Jews of Ashkenaz and their long persecution by many kings. Once, when they despaired of ever finding a tranquil home, a note fell from Heaven. On it were written the words "Go to Poland." The Jews went there and were received with every honor. They were given gold and places to settle and were protected from their enemies. They prospered and spread throughout the land. Near Lublin, they came upon a forest where a tractate of the Gemara, the rabbinic commentaries on Jewish law, was carved into every tree, so they knew that Jews had settled there before. Once they saw it, they knew why this land was called Polin, which means "lodge here" in Hebrew.[3]

By 1600, Poland, largely free from religious persecution and abounding in trade, had gained a reputation as the Paradisus Judaeorum, the "Paradise of the Jews." Poland-Lithuania was the ark from which Jews populated much of the rest of Eastern Europe. In addition to Poland

and Lithuania, most of the Jews living in Russia, Ukraine, Belarus, Latvia, Romania, Czechoslovakia, and Hungary in 1900 could trace their roots back to lands that had once been ruled by the Polish crown. Today the influence of this founder effect is even stronger and reaches around the globe. About 80 percent of the Jews alive today can trace their ancestry back to the Polish-Lithuanian Commonwealth.[4]

The Slavic "lands of Canaan" became, in time, the cradle of the Ashkenazim. This does not mean, however, that Eastern Europe was home only to Ashkenazi Jews. The Balkans were home to two other groups of Jews. The Romaniotes were speakers of Yevanic, which used Greek vocabulary but was written in Hebrew letters. These ancient communities had roots stretching all the way back to Roman times. The Romaniotes were the founding groups of Balkan Jewry, but at the end of the fifteenth century they were largely overwhelmed by newcomers from the West. When Spain expelled its Jews in 1492, a great number found refuge in the growing Ottoman Empire. Speakers of a Spanish-derived language called Ladino, these Sephardim—from Sepharad, the Hebrew name for Spain—quickly became the dominant Jewish community in the southern Balkans. Until the twentieth century, most of the Jews of Bulgaria, Macedonia, Bosnia, and Serbia were Sephardim. Romania, Ashkenazic in the north and Sephardic in the south, straddled the two communities.

The presence of both Ashkenazi and Sephardic Jews in Eastern Europe didn't just contribute to the region's linguistic diversity. Like two widely separated electrodes, it also created a charge, a current of energy that animated the religious life of both groups. Their mutual influence helped make Eastern Europe a great arena for religious innovation and creativity—especially in the face of crisis. A crucial example comes from the middle decades of the seventeenth century.

In 1648 a catastrophe struck the Jews of the Polish-Lithuanian Commonwealth. It began with a quarrel between two noblemen, one Polish and one Ukrainian. The Pole, an influential figure with the crown, took the Ukrainian's house, stole his wife, and beat his son. The Ukrainian, a man named Bohdan Khmelnytsky, ran east to a Cossack stronghold in the badlands of the Ukrainian steppe, where he incited a revolt against the crown. Khmelnytsky's revolt was conducted in the name of the Ukrainian people and the Orthodox faith. But if its targets were mainly the Catholic rulers of Poland, its victims, by and large, were the Jews. Resented for their role as merchants in a mostly rural economy and largely defenseless, the Jews of the Ukrainian part of Poland-Lithuania were subjected to every imaginable atrocity. Nathan Hannover, a rabbi practicing in Ukraine at the time of the rebellion, titled his chronicle of these events *The Abyss of Despair*. It is a catalog of unimaginable horrors: victims skinned alive, arms and limbs chopped off, children impaled on spears, cats sewn into the bellies of pregnant women, babies killed in their mothers' laps.[5]

To the people who lived through them, the Khmelnytsky massacres seemed like the end of the world. A decade later refugees were still turning up or being ransomed from their captors as far away as Amsterdam and Cairo.[6] Meanwhile in Poland, calamity followed upon calamity: after devastating Cossack raids came invasions of Swedes, Tatars, Russians, and even Transylvanians. By 1660, the country was in ruins.

These wars drove Polish Jews from their homes and destroyed their livelihoods. They also wounded their sense of security; never again would they see themselves as a chosen few. Across the Jewish world, would-be messiahs began to catch the ears of expectant crowds, in particular one from Izmir in Turkish Anatolia who called himself Sabbatai Zevi. Thousands flocked to this new redeemer, in a shudder of apocalyptic enthusiasm that embraced both East and West. The fervor lasted until the fateful year 1666, when Sabbatai, given the choice between converting to Islam or being made a pincushion of arrows for his faith, chose to convert. Even after Sabbatai's apostasy, some in Poland-Lithuania continued to believe in his divine election.

The Khmelnytsky massacres had shaken something loose in the world of Polish and Lithuanian Jewry. They needed help in Heaven, someone to plead their case before the divine throne. In Sabbatai Zevi they had sought a foreign messiah for deliverance; when this failed, they turned to more local sources of intercession.

The person who did the most to capitalize on these yearnings was a figure who has come to be remembered by the honorific Baal Shem Tov. He is arguably the most pivotal figure in the history of Eastern European Jewry. Even before he died, the Baal Shem was already a figure of folklore, a mystical giant, the hero of a hundred tales. Within a generation, these stories obscured whatever truth there was to his life.

We have little reliable information about the Baal Shem Tov's youth. He seems to have been born around the year 1700, in a region of the Polish-Lithuanian Commonwealth called Podolia. Now part of Ukraine, it was a true borderland, sitting at the exact intersection of the Catholics, Eastern Orthodox, and Islamic worlds. Less than a generation earlier, Podolia had been won back from the Ottoman Empire. In the Baal Shem's time, the land was still ravaged by war. Its forests teemed with bandits, bears, and the occasional werewolf; its roads (all of them terrible) carried cattle from Moldavia and spices from Istanbul. High in the mountains, Orthodox monks practiced ecstatic meditation in cliffside caves.

In some ways, Podolia resembled the Appalachian Mountains and the Mississippi Valley of North America, another frontier that was being settled at just about the same time in the eighteenth century. Both places previously lay far from prying eyes—fertile ground for the birth of legends and tall tales. The stories that survive about the early deeds of the Baal Shem Tov recall the stories told about Paul Bunyan and Davy Crockett. He tamed wild bears and beat up werewolves. He befriended gentile bandits like the great Oleksa Dovbush, Ukraine's answer to Robin Hood. His carriage could travel impossible distances, and it was said that he could drink a jug of the strongest Romanian plum brandy without getting drunk. How many other heroes of Torah study could say that?

Like Davy Crockett (and unlike Paul Bunyan), the Baal Shem was a real person. We have letters in his own hand and know details of his private life. Once he settled down, around 1740, in the Ukrainian town of Medzhybizh, he paid taxes and was counted by the census. He worked jobs—rather humble ones. Early in his life, he was a grade school teacher and a kosher butcher. For a time, he dug clay to be sold for pottery making. Later, his wife ran a tavern while he meditated in the woods on the secret names of God. In time, he mastered the art of manipulating words and letters to make effective charms in a kind of folk kabbalah, much practiced at the time. Indeed, the name Baal Shem Tov means "Master of the Good Name." It was a function, not a personal name. (He was born Yisroel ben Eliezer.) Many different Baal Shems were active in Poland and Lithuania. Some were established rabbis, while others were travelers, appearing at times in the guise of magicians and mountebanks, selling amulets and dispensing cures.

In his hometown of Medzhybizh, the Baal Shem Tov did much the same thing. He was the town's resident kabbalist, a practical mystic who could diagnose illnesses and trace their source back to unacknowledged sins. Most of his miracles took place in our world, a place of empty purses, runny noses, and jealous neighbors. He busied himself with the affairs of innkeepers, adulterers, noblemen, priests, and thieves. He recovered stolen horses, cured eye ailments, settled wills, negotiated leases, and even played pranks—sometimes rather cruel ones. He was quick with advice and had a good eye for judging livestock.

Whether by virtue of charisma or effectiveness, the Baal Shem Tov stood apart from the other small-town mystics and faith healers who thronged the Polish-Lithuanian borderlands. He was more than just an individual healer or mystic; he was someone people could trust to take really big requests up to Heaven. From his surviving letters, we know that he claimed credit for averting an attack of Cossacks and stopping the spread of the plague, in much the same way that the *táltos* Erszébet Tóth had boasted that she saved a third of Hungary from an earthquake. Like her, the Baal Shem was a protector of the entire community. He satisfied the intense craving people had for an intermediary, someone who could cut through Heaven's red tape and place a request directly before God's throne. Indeed, this is the singular innovation for which the Baal Shem deserves credit as the spiritual inventor of Hasidism. The Baal Shem Tov created, in his person, the role of the *tzaddik,* the righteous man and teacher who doubled as direct conduit for his followers' prayers.

When the Baal Shem Tov died in 1760, he dissolved into his tales. Passed from disciple to disciple by word of mouth, these tales contained the essence of his legacy, which was a kind of democratized mysticism. One of the central teachings of Hasidism was that one did not need to be schooled in the arcana of Jewish thought in order to touch the divine mysteries. Religious ecstasy belonged to everyone. Joy was as much a way of serving God as asceticism. God could be reached through fervent prayer but also through dance, song, and celebration. Or through the telling of tales.

Storytelling was an integral part of the lives of the Hasidim. The Hasidic tale is the signal literary achievement of Eastern European Judaism. As a literary form, it is infinitely flexible. It can have the pungency of a well-told anecdote, the pathos of a short story, or the mystery of a Zen koan. Some are earthy to the point of being crude; others possess the most refined spirituality. Taken together, they form a cosmos. If one overarching drama animates the Hasidic tales, it is the endless striving to reconcile the ways of man and God. There were two main ways to approach this task in Jewish thought: one was to raise the faithful upward, until Heaven was in reach. The other was to grab Heaven and pull it down, until it touched us here on earth.

At least initially, the position of spiritual leader among the Hasidim was not hereditary; it had to be won. *Tzaddiks* attracted followers based on the strength of their teaching and the power of their prayer. Some inspired confidence by their ability to predict the future. Others used humor and warmth to draw disciples toward themselves. Others still— and these inspired the most fervent devotion—scourged their followers with words of fire.

Menahem Mendel of Kotzk, later known as the Kotzker Rebbe, was one such leader. The core of his teaching was a striving after truth, which was to be achieved by ruthless introspection, unadorned by false piety. It was a hard path, with little of the joy traditionally associated with Hasidism. Nonetheless, it exerted a magnetic pull on Hasidim from all over Poland. Even established masters of Torah left their homes and houses of study to be near it, but they did not get much tenderness from the Kotzker Rebbe.[7] He mocked his followers, scorned them, and flayed their souls. They loved him for it.

Menahem Mendel's fervor was contagious, and soon messianic expectations began to swirl around his rabbinic court. In a period of decadence and spiritual softness, the hard path he advocated seemed like a step forward and a promise of more breakthroughs to come. But in a single night in 1839, it all came crashing down.

The story of the Kotzker Rebbe's downfall remains wreathed in legend. No two accounts are the same, and none come from eyewitnesses. Some say he profaned the Sabbath in full view of his congregation, in dramatic defiance of the holy law. Some say he began to preach a doctrine so radical, and so close to heresy, that his own followers felt they had to shout him down. Others insist that spies from the rival court at the Belz stirred up the trouble—they claimed to have seen him lighting a pipe on the Sabbath while visiting his doctor in Lviv.[8] No matter what happened, though, it clearly affected Menachem Mendel profoundly. After this break, he confined himself to a solitary, towerlike room on the top floor of his house. He remained there, alone and unseen, for the next twenty years. According to legend, his only companions in those decades were huge tame rats and old gray frogs that jumped around the rabbi like trained dogs.

Today the house with the tower still stands in Kotzk, a sleepy market town thirty miles north of Lublin. The wooden planks covering its exterior have turned black with age. Whoever lives there now owns a nice satellite dish and a big angry dog. The tower is smaller than the stories would lead you to believe; it seems to barely have space for a single attic room. And yet the Kotzker Rebbe spent the last nineteen years of his life up there. From his windows he would have had a view of the whole town, from the main square to the palace of the Jabłonskis, the home of his patron, a beautiful Polish noblewoman who donated the land for his synagogue.

Outwardly, not much has changed in Kotzk in the past century and a half. The central square is still covered in cobblestones. The Jabłonski Palace still has its fine view of the River Wieprz, framed by neoclassical columns and an alley of old chestnut trees, though today the palace is a home for the mentally ill. Besides the rebbe's house and a mass grave outside town, nothing remains of the Jewish community. Nor is there anything to explain why the Kotzker Rebbe felt the need to imprison himself. Was it a psychotic break? Or, as some of his followers continued to believe after his death, was he driven into seclusion by something deeper—an apprehension of a hidden world, whose existence he felt he had to keep secret?

By the time of the Kotzker Rebbe's death in 1859, Jewish Poland was almost entirely in the hands of the Hasidim. In Lithuania, the religious landscape looked quite different. Jewish Lithuania belonged to the opponents of the Hasidim, the upholders of the old orthodoxy and habits of scholarship called the *misnagdim*. The spiritual leader of the *misnagdim* was a prodigy of learning, born in 1720, named Elijah Zalman. Better known by his honorific, the Vilna Gaon, Elijah was a rabbinic genius whose like is seen only once a millennium. During the Gaon's life and afterward, Vilnius hummed with Talmudic scholarship. Men of every class were expected to excel in religious knowledge. Among the tailors of Vilnius, a man who studied only the religious code *Hayye adam* was considered an ignoramus.

Lithuanian Jews, or Litvaks, considered themselves the most learned Jews of the Polish-Lithuanian Commonwealth, if not the world. This did not endear them to many in neighboring Poland. Jews in Warsaw, who admired devotion more than learning, mocked Lithuanian Jews for their rigid piety and their funny accents. Even my grandfather, who grew up close to the border between the two territories, thought they sounded strange. To Polish Hasids, Litvaks were all brain and no heart. To Litvaks, Polish Hasids were ignorant, superstitious, and dissolute— revelers who would rather get drunk at their *tzaddik's* table than study Torah.

The split between the Hasidim and *misnagdim* divided the Jews of Poland and Lithuania. It also split individual families in two. Yekhezkel Kotik was born in 1847 into a prosperous orthodox family in Kamenets, a shtetl near the city of Brest in Belarus. His grandfather was the wealthiest and most powerful man in town; he held the richest leaseholds, was in charge of the local vodka monopoly, and had all the most important Russian officials in his pocket. Kotik's father, Moshe, was meant to inherit his business, but at thirteen, just before he was due to marry, he ran off to join the court of the nearest Hasidic rabbi. In some families, like that of Moshe's father-in-law, when a child did this, the parents would rend their clothes and sit shiva, as if the child had died.

This type of living death was very nearly pronounced on Moshe. Somehow, through family pressure, father and son were mostly reconciled. Still, the rift between the two never fully healed. From that time on, Grandfather Kotik and the rest of the family celebrated holidays in the main synagogue. Moshe did the same separately, with the men of his prayer house. The high point of Moshe's year was not the family Passover but his annual trip to the rabbi's court, where he stayed for weeks while entirely neglecting his business affairs. It was an act of rebellion. In turn, Moshe's son Yekhezkel rebelled against him. Despite his father's highest hopes, he found that he could not become a Hasid and ultimately left his shtetl for the life of a wandering laborer.

Eventually, Yekhezkel settled in Warsaw and began a quite modern career as a café owner and proprietor of one of the city's first telephones. Memories of his childhood remained with him, however. When he began writing his memoirs in 1912, those memories took center stage. Already then, the shtetl life of his youth seemed like a lost world, long since erased by anti-Semitism, industrialization, and mass emigration to America. The emotional high point of Yekhezkel's recollections is his description of Yom Kippur as it was observed in the 1850s. This was the one day of the year when the quarrels between sons and fathers, rich and poor, Hasidim and *misnagdim,* were all set aside as the community came together to repent their sins as one:

> Oh, those Days of Atonement of long ago. Good Lord, what went on then! The congregants in the synagogue during the Kol Nidre prayer seemed to be gripped by a sense of excitement and fear.... Each one poured out his heart amid a river of tears to his Creator. The heartrending wails from the women's section penetrated down to that of the men, who joined their womenfolk and broke into a chorus of wailing themselves.... The very walls wept, the stones in the streets sighed, and the fishes in the water trembled. How fervently those people prayed—the very same Jews who fought one another viciously throughout the year over a single groshen for their livelihood! No hatred and no envy, no greed and no cunning, no cursing or evil gossip, no food and no drink. All hearts and eyes were turned heavenward, and there was only spirituality—mere bodiless souls.[9]

On days like this, it was possible to forget, however briefly, that the Jews were a people in exile, and that they lived in a land that was not their own. That thought was not impossible to hold, especially in the shtetls and small towns of Poland-Lithuania, whose populations were most often *majority* Jewish, in some cases overwhelmingly so. Christian lords lived in their manors, and Christian peasants worked in the fields, but in town, among the Jewish brewers, cobblers, tailors, innkeepers and tavernkeepers, students, beggars, and watchmakers, one could squint and imagine that the gentile world did not exist at all.

Shtetl is the Yiddish word for "town"; it descends from the more commanding German word *Stadt.* In theory, any collection of houses larger than a village could be a shtetl, although a self-respecting one would at least have a market square. In practice, shtetls had their idiosyncrasies. For one, Jews made up the majority of the population. This made shtetls unlike virtually any other place in the Diaspora. If in most of the world Jews were like passengers traveling across hostile seas, in the shtetl—however poor—they had their feet on the ground. Shtetls were islands of Jewishness, surrounded by archipelagoes of the same.

Thousands of shtetls once dotted Poland, Lithuania, Belarus, and Ukraine. They were also common in the neighboring lands of Slovakia, Hungary, and Romania. This prevalence and density of Jewish settlement made Eastern Europe unique in the world. Nowhere else was Jewish life as plentiful, as varied, or as thickly interwoven with its surroundings. For centuries, shtetl life was everywhere. And then all at once, it was gone for good.

Wooden synagogue. Naroulia, Belarus.

My paternal grandfather, Czesław Berman, grew up in one of these vanished shtetls, a place called Zambrów, a small town which straddled the main route from Warsaw to Białystok. Before the Second World War, it was home to some seven thousand people, half of them Jews.

Only a handful survived. Their world disappeared with the dead. Growing up in the Poland of the 1950s, my parents barely knew it existed. Their Jewish past was obscured so completely that I didn't even know my grandfather's real name. I learned after his death that he had been born not Czesław, but Bezalel, after the craftsman who fashioned the Ark of the Covenant.

Bezalel-Czesław led an eventful life. He spent time in Soviet prison camps and saw Berlin burn under mortar fire, some of which he personally directed. And yet toward the end of his life, he would return again and again in memory to the world of his earliest childhood. He was aided in his reminiscences by *The Zambrów Memorial Book*, written in Yiddish, published in Israel in 1963, and imported from there God knows how. I remember him scanning through it, searching for the names of dead relatives and stories that reached back to his great-grandparents' time, in the mid-nineteenth century. These events were recent enough for him to have heard about them firsthand, yet remote enough to seem as if they had come from ancient Babylonia.

In my mind's eye, the *Memorbuch* was a huge volume, printed in Hebrew letters with gilt lettering on the spine. It pains me to think how little I understood of what it contained. There, culled from the memories of people who emigrated from Zambrów in the 1930s, are the nicknames of the personalities who walked its streets before the First World War: Myshel the Cripple, Bayrakh the Mute, and Katchkheh the Duck; Crazy Zundl, who was always lost in thought; One-eyed Sabbath, who really only had one eye; and Chashkeh the Lady Carpenter, who always knew how best to avert the evil eye.

Shtetls had nicknames as well. Around Zambrów there were the *gartl*-wearers of Czyżew, the Ostrów bullies, the Jabłonka goats, and the Stawka cymbal-players.[10] People from Zambrów itself were known as the gangsters. Until Poland declared its independence in 1918, the town sat in Russia, close to the German border, and it had a reputation for horse smuggling. So did practically every other border town in the Russian Empire. Cities in the Pale were all famous either for their rabbis or for their thieves—unless, like Dvinsk in Latvia, they were famous for both.

Many years after I first saw my grandfather's memorial book, I visited Zambrów myself. Not much there remains from this past. The old streets are gone. Just about the only thing left in town from before the war are the old brick barracks built by the last czar and a Jewish cemetery overgrown with nettles and missing practically every headstone. At a loss, I did what I usually do in the remains of a shtetl: I headed toward the nearest stream.

If you are ever looking for the Jewish quarter of an Eastern European town, head to the central square, then walk downhill until you get your feet wet. Water was never far from the holy in the lives of Eastern European Jews. To pray one needed to be clean, and to be clean one required access to a ritual bathhouse, or *mikvah*, for immersion. Keeping a *mikvah* filled required having a pond or a small stream, and synagogues were typically located next to these small bodies of water.

Atonement also required water. Every Rosh Hashanah, Jews would cast away the previous year's sins. This had to be done over a lake or a stream; you would empty out your pockets while reciting a special prayer, the *tashlich*. In Dvinsk, ten thousand people would gather every year by the banks of the mighty Daugava River to hurl away their transgressions. In Zambrów, people did the same. Today all the city's synagogues are gone too. The main square, once home to my great-grandfather's house, is bisected by a highway and barely recognizable in its present form. But below it, the town stream, the Jabłonka, or "Little Apple," still flows. The waters remain; they are a trace.

.   .   .

In the shtetls of Poland-Lithuania, Jews performed every imaginable occupation, from barbering to bassoon-playing. In the surrounding Slavic-Christian countryside outside the towns, Jews generally worked as itinerant peddlers, or most commonly, manned country inns and taverns. Until the end of the nineteenth century, Jews in Poland-Lithuania were forbidden by law from owning larger parcels of land—effectively barring them from agriculture. Instead, they were forced to take on the role of commercial intermediaries, linking the world of the peasantry and the great noble estates to wider currents of exchange. They managed properties, delivered grain to market or milled it into flour. Above all, they supervised the aristocrats' most precious asset: their monopoly on the production of alcohol. Each monopoly was effectively a license, which permitted certain landowners, and no one else, to distill their surplus wheat and rye into potent—and easily transportable—vodka. The landowners could then sell the vodka back to their own peasants in taverns that they owned and on which they also held a monopoly.

Until the close of the nineteenth century, most of the taverns in Poland-Lithuania were operated by Jews. As outsiders, they were beholden to noble masters and could be relied on not to extend credit too far to their gentile neighbors. The Jewish tavern thus became a fixture of village life, a combination of inn, wedding hall, and company store. Famously dirty, with low ceilings and dirt floors, and stinking of pipe smoke, vinegar, and sweat, the tavern was the one place peasants could go to escape from the fields, celebrate a wedding, or listen to a song.[11] Taverns were good places to get truly drunk, and they were also often the only places to buy essential items such as sugar or nails—another way landowners goosed their profits. A better tavern might serve borscht, kvass, and pierogi; a lesser one, nothing but pickled herring. The pairing of vodka and herring, cherished by all true vodka lovers, finds its origin here.[12]

Shtetl life was never far removed from that of the surrounding countryside. It too followed the rhythms of the seasons. For many Jews, a "green calendar" marched in step with the religious one. It started in spring, when the storks arrived back from their winter homes in Africa, and observant Jews blessed the trees that were just then coming into bloom.

As summer faded into fall, it was time for the wheat harvest. Jews needed special wheat for Passover matzah. Many bought small parcels of land from gentile farmers to gather it themselves. (My grandfather's family was exceptional in that they grew their own wheat and gave it away for free.) Soon after the harvest was done, the blackberries called "Little Diaspora Apples" began to appear. Their juice was dark enough for writing Torah scrolls, which was how they received their name: they recalled the blackness of exile. Then came the true apples: the sweet ones eaten on Rosh Hashanah, the sour ones called "Apples of Sodom," and the wild ones called "Apples of the Cemetery." Miniature Kol Nidre pears, which grew wild in the woods, arrived just in time for Yom Kippur. After that, it was time to put up the sauerkraut for the winter, which had to be done before the first deep frost.[13]

Jews and Christians might share a drink in the neutral space of the tavern, but when it came time to go to church or temple, they regarded each other with a mixture of suspicion and contempt. In Christian eyes, Jews were forever the opponents of Christ. Their presence might be necessary for trade, but their religion, strange language, and unclear rites seemed to contain a threatening and morbid mystery. Jews, in turn, lived in constant dread of blood libel trials and the riots that accompanied them. The notion that Jews needed blood to make their Passover bread had roots deep in the Middle Ages. Panics sparked by suspicion of a Jewish abduction or murder cost many lives.

The separation between the two religions was enshrined in custom and strengthened by law. Before the nineteenth century, if a Christian converted to Judaism, the punishment was death. If a Jew converted to Christianity, he or she would only be dead to their family, but if they then reneged and returned to Judaism, they likewise faced execution.

Despite the risks, the boundary between the two communities was often breached. Jews often worked for Christian employers; they also employed Christian maids. Sometimes, their contacts even blossomed into love. Known cases of gentile-Jewish romance are rare, in part because they usually had to be kept secret. Most of what we know of it in the premodern era comes from instances where things went wrong.

One such case occurred in October 1748, in the city of Mogilev in Belarus. A Jewish man named Abraham was accused before the court of committing an unlawful union with a Ukrainian Christian woman named Paraska. Both were interrogated, and both gave statements about how they had come to be together.

Abraham had originally been married to a Jewish woman named Gisia, but he left her shortly after the wedding because she appeared to be insane. Fleeing to a nearby town, he went to work for a Christian landowner. Paraska was his maid. Abraham and Paraska became intimate, and Paraska became pregnant. They left town together to search for a new place to live. On the way, Paraska gave birth—in the middle of a field. The baby was a girl; an hour later she was dead. They buried her in that same field and kept moving.

When they arrived at the next town, Abraham told Paraska to stay silent and pretend that she was mute; he had a plan. He found work with a Jewish brewer named Herszko. He told Herszko that Paraska was Jewish and that she was his wife. She had been born mute, which explained why she couldn't speak Yiddish or a word of Hebrew. Herszko's own wife began to look after Paraska, taking her to synagogue, teaching her prayers, and cutting her hair short as was fitting for a Jewish wife. According to Abraham, he never pressured Paraska into embracing Judaism. He left the decision of whether to convert in her hands. The most important thing was that they had both promised "not to abandon one another" even though they were not officially married.[14]

This was Abraham's version of events. Paraska's story matched his in most details except one, which proved to be fatal. She admitted that when their daughter was born, she was not stillborn but alive. They had left her that day in the field. Leaving a newborn out to die was a common practice in this time and place, and across the rest of Europe as well. The usual punishment was whipping. This time, however, the judge ordered that Paraska be executed and Abraham burned at the stake. At the last moment, he converted to Christianity to be spared the torment. On December 23, 1748, both he and Paraska were beheaded on the Vilna Road.

Across Eastern Europe, Jews and Christians lived side by side but apart, divided by barriers of custom, religion, and law. Yet both groups also shared a pervasive belief in the supernatural and in the ability of properly applied magic to influence health, safety, and wealth. Jews and Christians frequently relied upon one another's folk remedies. In Poznań, when demons took possession of an abandoned house, the Jewish community called on the local Jesuits for help.[15] Hasidic tales frequently mention Jewish women consulting gentile faith healers for help with childbirth and other ailments. The Baal Shem Tov himself confessed in his surviving letters to seeking cures from passing Roma.[16] Even the Vilna Gaon was said to have learned herbal remedies from Lithuanian Christian women. Christians, in turn, often went to rabbis and other Jewish healers. They drank from springs sanctified by the Baal Shem Tov, and they consulted wonder-working rabbis for help with infertility and advice about the future.

As the quintessential outsiders in Christian communities, Jews could either summon curses or provide spiritual protection. Jews faced many of the same perils as their Christian neighbors, but within the closed world of the shtetl, they most commonly had to handle them on their own. Wandering exorcists handled cases of possession by spirits of the dead known as *dybbukim*. They badgered and cajoled the recalcitrant ghost to leave the body of the possessed. When the exorcist was a great rabbi like Shmuel from Kaminka, it was sure to work; otherwise there were no guarantees. In a memorable case from Warsaw in 1818, reported by many eyewitnesses, an offending spirit flat-out refused to leave a child, saying that if it did so, it "would never be free" from its torments.[17]

The exorcists worked one on one with the dead. However, when an entire community was threatened, whether by war or, worst of all, by the plague, more extreme measures were needed. At that point, the dead had to be called upon as a group. In a Black Wedding, or *shvartze khasene*, two members of the community were married off to ward off a major disaster. The bride and groom typically were among the poorest in town. Often one or both were crippled, mute, or in some other way "unmarriageable." Community members banded together to raise a dowry and provide them with the necessary garments and trousseau.[18] The wedding ceremony would be performed in the cemetery. Thousands would attend. White cloth would be used to measure out the boundary of the cemetery fence, marking the border between the afflicted shtetl and the outside world.

The Black Wedding had a double purpose. One was appeasement: the celebration in the cemetery was a gift to the dead, who in gratitude could then be relied on to assist the living. The other purpose was etiquette: a wedding procession traditionally took precedence over a funeral cortège, so as long as it was going on, it would halt the stream of plague victims awaiting burial. In the language of an ethnographic report, it all seems impossibly remote. Black Weddings sound like something out of fiction, but they really did take place—even in my grandfather's shtetl of Zambrów.

My grandfather's mother, Dina, married a suspenders maker who took her to Warsaw after the First World War. Dina's father was Yankl, a merchant in grain, a dealer in wood products, and a member of a large clan of Jewish farmers named Golombek. According to *The Zambrów Memorial Book*, Yankl was "among the most refined and idealistic of the householders in the shtetl," "full of the love of Zion and very straight."[19] His house was full of people all week long, as his many employees would come by at all hours to drink coffee with milk, eat biscuits, and discuss the affairs of the day. Two of the most frequent guests were Yankl's brother Meir and his wife, Reizl.

In the memorial book, Meir describes an incident that occurred in the plague year of 1893, when cholera swept through Russia and Poland. The outbreak in Zambrów was terrible, claiming dozens of lives. To try to stop it, people tried everything they could think of. They stopped work and recited psalms, organized free massages, and even took a dam off the town stream, in the hopes that its unimpeded flow would sweep the sickness out of the city. It didn't. Then they attempted stronger measures. First, they gathered together all the discarded and damaged remnants from prayer books and held a funeral for them at night in the town cemetery, complete with burning candles and a beadle saying Kaddish. Still, the illness raged on. Desperate, the town played its final card: it held a Black Wedding.[20]

For the bride, they chose a crippled pauper girl named Chana-Yenta, and for the groom, the old bachelor Velvel, also a cripple, who made his living begging door to door. At its own expense, the community dressed them in the finest clothes and rented a house for them, fully furnished. The most esteemed of the town's housewives took charge of planning the wedding ceremony. They baked rolls, cooked meat and fish, and set up the wedding canopy—in the cemetery, of course. On the day of the wedding, a lively throng accompanied the bride and groom to their *huppah*. On their way back from the cemetery, they danced and, despite the shadow of the plague, "made merry for the bride and groom, just as it is supposed to be." Beseeched by the placated dead, God relented and the plague ceased. From then on, Chana-Yenta, the Black Wedding's bride, became known as the "City's Daughter-in-Law." She was given the job of municipal water carrier, and her husband was given an official beggar's license.

From that moment on, Chana-Yenta was a person of consequence in Zambrów. She was considered one of the devout in the shtetl and was always spoken of with respect since, as Meir wrote, "many believed that she did something substantive in deterring the plague." For her part, Chana agreed. She knew as well as anyone that she had saved the town from calamity. As she went from house to house carrying her heavy water buckets, she had a reason to feel proud: she had done the dead a favor, and now all the living were in her debt.

3

Muslims

Muezzin calling faithful to prayer. Bulgaria, c. 1912.

For much of its history, Eastern Europe was on the edge of Europe. In the early Middle Ages, the reason was simple: Europe was Christendom, and Christendom ended wherever the last pagan ruler still held sway. As the pagans were swept away by the Christian tide, Eastern Europe became a frontier in a more specifically Christian sense: it was the place where the Catholic Church met its Orthodox counterpart. It was the border between Rome and Constantinople, Latin and Greek, Gothic spires and wooden domes.

It was a point of tension but not an uncrossable chasm. Beginning in the fourteenth century, with the first Ottoman Turkish invasions of the Balkan Peninsula, Eastern Europe became home to the most important religious fault line on the continent—the division between Christians and Muslims. As the Islamic presence expanded, it profoundly affected many Eastern Europeans' conceptions of themselves. Many Christian rulers deliberately took on the role of defenders of the faith and presented themselves as the last bastion against the Muslim onslaught. This myth of the Antemurale Christianitatis, the "bulwark of Christendom," was taken up by Poland, Albania, Serbia, Croatia, Hungary, and nearly every other country that found itself at some point engaged in battle with a Muslim opponent.

The Antemurale idea was propaganda, but it also had physical reality in the form of castles, walls, boundary posts, and watchtowers. The Baal Shem Tov, the founder of Hasidism, was born around 1700, in present-day Ukraine, in Okopy Świętej Trójcy, whose name means "Ramparts of the Holy Trinity." At the time, the town was literally that—a fortress, right on the boundary between Poland-Lithuania and Turkey. It is characteristic of Eastern Europe that the childhood of this Jewish mystic would unfold inside a Polish-Catholic citadel, among Orthodox Ukrainians, in view of Turkish minarets.

But despite the protestations of nationalist historians, Eastern Europe was never just a rampart: it was also a gate. If Muslims and Christians fought there, they also met, mingled, and rubbed off on each other. Al-Andalus, Islamic Spain, retains a reputation as the one place in Europe where Muslims and Christians lived together and learned from each other. But long after the last Muslim kingdom in Spain was snuffed out by Ferdinand and Isabella's armies in 1492, much of Eastern Europe remained part of the Islamic world. It is still home to the largest and oldest concentrations of Muslims on the continent.

Today Bosnia-Herzegovina and Albania remain Muslim-majority nations (as does Kosovo), while Bulgaria, Montenegro, and North Macedonia are home to sizable Muslim minorities. Traces of a centuries-long Muslim presence are visible in Poland, Romania, Lithuania, and Belarus. Eastern Europe, then, is not so much the edge of Europe as an Islamic periphery, one of the many fringes of a Muslim belt that stretches from West Africa all the way to Southeast Asia. To see it as such requires a radical shift in orientation. We need to stop looking south from Budapest and east from Vienna, and start looking west from Istanbul and north from Cairo.

Muslim travelers began arriving in Eastern Europe in the tenth century, searching for furs and slaves. The written testimonies they left behind are some of our best sources for what Poles, Czechs, and Magyars were like before their rulers converted to Christianity.

Back then Baghdad, the capital of the Abbasid Caliphate, was at the center of a trading network that ran from Morocco to China, and whose tentacles reached as far as Siberia and Scandinavia. Muslim geographers divided the world into seven horizontal bands, or "climes." All these northern lands belonged to the seventh, and coldest, clime—a region of appalling filth and barbarity. From the perspective of Islamic scholars living in the sophisticated garden cities of Persia and Mesopotamia, the Slavs who inhabited these frigid wastelands were only a step above wild beasts.

Their opinion of the Slavs' neighbors to the east, the Turks, was not much better. Most of them were then still pagan. In a few brief centuries, however, these Central Asian nomads would not only convert to Islam but become masters of the Islamic heartland in the Middle East. Not resting there, they would then bring Muslim hegemony to the farthest extent it would ever reach in Europe, all the way to the Adriatic Sea and the gates of Vienna.

Islam arrived in Europe because of trade, but it stayed there because of conquest. The process began with the arrival of the first Turkish soldiers in the Balkans in 1345, and it continued until the Ottoman conquest of Podolia in 1672. Over the course of those three centuries, the Ottoman Empire developed into the most formidable war machine in continental Europe, bringing the entire Balkan Peninsula under its sway, as well as parts of Ukraine, Romania, and much of Hungary.

This extraordinary conquest transformed a vast and varying swath of Eastern Europe into an armed borderland. There was never an Iron Curtain between the domains of Islam and Christianity. Instead of a hard border, there was a zone of limited sovereignty, which soon filled up with every sort of frontier fighter and mercenary. On the Islamic side, the *ghazi* knights were fighting for their faith and their sultan—and hoping to get fat grants of land. In addition, groups of footloose pastoralists, such as the Kipchak and Nogai Tatars, who lived on horse-back, fought for Islam but also for themselves, conducting destructive raids deep into Ukraine and Romania in search of captives and booty.

On the Christian side, the border fighters came in a range of flavors. There were the *uskok* pirates of the Croatian coast, the *pandur* and *grenzer* troops of the Habsburg military frontier, and the *hajduks* of Hungary. All these groups exploited the instability of the border, justifying their raiding, plundering, and slave trading by their faith. None of them, however, had a more sustained reputation for savagery, or for more fiercely guarding their independence against all comers, than the Cossacks of the Ukrainian steppes.

The Cossacks' origins are mysterious. They seem to have begun life as runaways. In the badlands of southern Ukraine, serfs from Russia and Poland-Lithuania could start new lives as free men. The price was constant vigilance: without the protection of a state, they had to become a law unto themselves. Gradually, they adopted the ways of neighbor-ing Turkic tribes and became a society of independent mounted war-riors, loosely organized in "hosts" or armies. The Cossacks mounted spectacular raids against their neighbors in Russia, Poland-Lithuania, and the Ottoman domains. Today they are remembered mostly as a scourge, first as violent rebels against Poland-Lithuania who put Jewish towns to the torch, and later as the long arm of the Russian Empire. In their own minds, however, the Cossacks were defenders of the faith. They fought on behalf of Orthodox Christianity against Catholics and Muslims alike. No story better encapsulates their self-image than the Song of the Baida.

In life, the Cossack Dmytro Vyshnevetsky, a typical lord of the bor-der, was cunning, ruthless, and eternally willing to sell his allegiance to the highest bidder. For the king of Poland, he fortified an island in the Dnieper River to hold against the Tatars. For Ivan the Terrible, he raised an army in the Caucasus and used it to raid up and down the Don River. On his own account, he led his Cossacks to Crimea to capture slaves. When neither Muscovy nor Lithuania was willing to indulge his thirst for war, he threw his lot in with the despot of Moldavia in search of further opportunities for plunder.[1]

In death, Vyshnevetsky was transformed into the Baida, the legend-ary paragon of Cossack manhood, who figures as the hero of a hundred epic Cossack songs, or *dumy*. In one of the most famous, "In the Little Square in Czar-town," he appears, rather unexpectedly and all alone, in the heart of Istanbul. Drunk, he goes on a multiday spree. The Turkish sultan, dazzled by this display of manly bravado, offers the Baida his daughter's hand in marriage. But the Baida knocks it away, saying, "Your daughter is beautiful / but your faith is cursed." Furious, the sultan has the Baida captured and strung up. Hung from a hook inserted around his lowermost rib, the Baida suffers terrible torments for three days. Yet even in this mortal predicament, he somehow manages to grab hold of a bow and shoot arrow after arrow at the sultan and his jilted daughter, narrowly missing them both before finally tasting the sweet release of death. And so, intransigent and bibulous, he passes into the realm of myth.

A branch of my own family was shaped by this regime of nearly mythic borderland violence. My grandmother—my mother's mother— was born in Ukraine and grew up in Vilnius. But her surname, Terebesz, was Hungarian. Her family, which belonged to the nobility, probably came to Poland in the late sixteenth century, in the retinue of a Transylvanian prince who was elected to the Polish-Lithuanian throne. Before that, they were border fighters. Their coat of arms was a severed head, impaled on a sword, held in an armored hand. The dead man's head also figured in the family signet ring, which belonged to my grandmother's sister.

I never saw the ring as a child, but it glittered large in my imagination as my only link to an aristocratic past. It is, however, an essential clue to where this family came from. In official heraldry, the dead man's head was pictured with a forelock and a drooping mustache—a sure sign that he was meant to be a Turk. Before they were aristocrats, the Terebeszes were most likely common soldiers who were ennobled for some long-forgotten act of valor—such as taking an enemy head. This is exactly what happened to John Smith, he of later Pocahontas fame. Before coming to the New World, Smith worked as a mercenary for another Transylvanian prince. In 1602 he cut off the heads of three Turkish soldiers in single combat during a siege. As a reward, the prince bestowed upon him a coat of arms of three heads arranged in a triangle on a shield.

Taking heads was common on the frontier and was serious business.

But it could also be funny. In 1661 Evliya Çelebi, an Ottoman courtier, scholar, bon vivant, and one of the greatest travel writers of all time, joined the sultan's army on a campaign in Hungary and took part in one of its battles against the Christians. The day was a chaotic, ugly mess, but at its end, the sultan's soldiers seemed to have won. Feeling the call of nature, Evliya took the opportunity to relieve himself on the battlefield. Just as he was finished loosening his bowels, an infidel soldier burst out of the thicket above him and wrestled him to the ground. Smeared in his own shit, with his pants still around his ankles, Evliya was convinced that he was about to become a "shitty martyr."

In the nick of time, Evliya got hold of himself and managed to stab the enemy soldier in the chest. Now covered in blood too, he could only laugh, seeing as he had become the "shitty *ghazi*," or shitty frontier warrior. He then nicked the Christian's purse and cut off his head, which he took to his commander, Ismail Pasha.

> "May the enemies' misfortunate heads always roll like this one," I said, kissed his hand, and stood at attention. Those next to me moved off because of the smell.
>
> "My Evliya," said Ismail Pasha, "you smell strangely of shit."
>
> "Don't ask, my lord, what calamities have befallen me!" And I recounted my adventures blow by blow. All the officers at that victory celebration laughed uproariously. Ismail Pasha too was tremendously pleased. He awarded me fifty gold pieces and a silver turban-crest, and I cheered up considerably.[2]

On the Muslim-Christian frontier, just as savage violence could lead to sudden comedy, mutual hatred could swiftly turn into fraternal love. It depended on which emotion was more profitable and prudent in any given moment.

In the sixteenth century, the Christian *uskoks* carved out a niche as ferocious pirates on the Adriatic Sea. Based out of the port of Senj, in present-day Croatia, the *uskoks* portrayed themselves as holy warriors, but they were just as happy to prey on Venetian ships as on Ottoman ones. But sometimes even pirates needed to strike deals. In the 1580s, the Ottoman government, hoping to decrease the number of raids on their lands, banned the practice of offering ransom for captives held by the *uskoks*. On a local level, this ban served no one's interests, as it exposed the Ottoman border soldiers to danger while depriving the *uskoks* of a crucial source of revenue. So the chief of the pirates and the local Turkish administrator, the *bey*, sat down to negotiate. The two men set appropriate levels of payment for each type of captive and sealed the deal by swearing to be each other's blood brothers, a procedure that involved the consumption of a great deal of alcohol. Afterward they all retired together to sleep "in a single bed, in each other's arms."[3]

On another occasion, the *uskoks* concluded a treaty with a local Turkish *aga*, or governor. The Christian pirates promised to stop raiding the *aga's* province, as long as he granted them safe passage through his lands. They knew that the Ottoman soldiers couldn't let them pass through their lands unscathed; that would be shameful. So they agreed that the Turks could fire one or two shots at them, for the sake of their honor.

Shoot—but not too much, and not too accurately: an honorable solution to the problem of inconvenient affections. To Christians on both sides of the frontier, the *uskoks* were heroes, worthy of being celebrated in song. These ballads generally failed to note how cozy their relations could often be with their so-called enemies. A similar tension ran through the folk poetry of the entire region. Across the Balkans, the heroes of epic songs tended to be great Christian rulers and generals, men like Prince Marko, John Hunyadi, and Vuk the Fiery Dragon, who defied the Ottoman armies during the first waves of conquest in the fourteenth and fifteenth centuries. Miloš Obilić, star of *The Battle of Kosovo*, the greatest cycle of Serbian heroic ballads, is famous for assassinating an Ottoman sultan—but only after the main battle was already lost and the Serbian army destroyed.

The South Slav epics, to which *The Battle of Kosovo* belongs, are often tales of bloodshed and interreligious strife. But read closely, they reveal more nuances. Often their heroes work for the sultan as well as against him. At his behest, they fight Muslim heroes and highwaymen, who are the Christians' equals in strength and valor. When the Christian prince Marko fights the monstrous Muslim bandit Musa Kesedžija, he is able to defeat him only with the help of a *vila*, or fairy, who tells him how to cut him open to reveal the three hearts that beat in his chest. When Marko finally kills Musa, he weeps—for he realizes that he has killed the better man.

On a different occasion, Prince Marko is pitched against the greatest hero of the Bosnian Muslims, Alija Djerzelez, or Alija the Mace-Wielder. Alija rides a winged horse and has the strength of twenty men. Like Marko, he sports a gigantic mustache (a sine qua non of Balkan manhood), so big it looks as if he is holding a black lamb in his teeth. In one story, both men receive the same dream, which instructs them to go out into the world and search high and low for a man better than themselves. When they finally find each other, Marko weeps and embraces Alija, shouting, "Thank God and the day that's in it, for I've found my sworn brother."[4] Alija kisses his forehead, and the two warriors leave the field bound to each other by a sacred pact of friendship.

The Christian-Muslim borderland was a place of spectacular violence, sudden friendship, and above all, ever-shifting allegiances. Simultaneously menacing and enticing, it has done much to shape our image of Islam in Eastern Europe. But most of Islamic life was led far away from the frontier, in conditions of relative tranquility. It unfurled in bathhouses and caravanserais, in sleepy towns like Foča and Karnobat, and in great urban centers like Sarajevo and Sofia.

The Ottoman Balkans were an integral part of the Muslim world for five hundred years—longer than most of Latin America has been Catholic. However, sometimes it can be hard to discern all that was achieved in those centuries. Historiography plays a great role in this. The story of Islam in southeastern Europe is unfortunately an orphaned history. Historians from the Christian nations of the Balkans have tended to treat the era of Ottoman rule as a kind of cultural nuclear winter, during which nothing could grow and no new shoots could sprout. Nothing could be further from the truth.

The whole urban fabric of the Balkans is a creation of the Ottomans. The largest cities in Bosnia and Albania, among them Sarajevo, Mostar, and Tirana, all owe their existence to Ottoman foundations, while in Bulgaria, the cities of Plovdiv and Sofia were almost entirely rebuilt by them. Ottoman engineers built aqueducts, roads, and bridges

so beautiful, their construction has passed into myth. To journey down
the Istanbul-Belgrade highway in Ottoman times meant to hopscotch
from one expertly designed *khan*, or traveler's inn, to another. In the
cities, one could shop in *bedesten*, stone-built market halls, or *arasta*, covered shopping streets, the like of which can still be seen in Sarajevo's
old town. Sarajevo itself grew up around a great caravanserai, an inn
founded by the Muslim frontier lord Isâ Bey.[5]

While the Balkans were only part—and often a rather sleepy one—
of a wider Ottoman world, they were connected to the high thrum of
Istanbul by innumerable bonds based in politics, religion, and trade. In
1600 Istanbul's population of six hundred thousand was twice that of
Paris and three times that of London. A vast procurement organization,
staffed by Christians and Muslims alike, kept the city supplied with
meat and grain. Their work was so crucial that the imperial administration was apt to keep a close eye on them lest something go wrong. In
Sofia alone, the drovers' guild included ten goldsmiths, seven shoemakers, four tavernkeepers, two grocers, a potter, a boatman, a spinner of
goat hair, and two Christian sorbet sellers—one of whom was a spy for
the Islamic secret police.[6]

It was this long cohabitation, and not some sudden act of apostasy,
that brought about the great waves of conversion that left Bosnia and
Albania as Muslim-majority nations. Across the Balkans, Christians
succumbed to the slow, gravitational pull of opportunities and induce-
ments offered by the Islamic empire in which they lived, while at the
same time Muslim emigrants from Anatolia and points east melted into
the society that surrounded them.

· · ·

The Ottoman Empire provided many opportunities for Christians
willing to renounce their faith. The sultan's armies and navy were
full of defectors from Italy, Greece, Serbia, and Hungary. In the nineteenth century, these military renegades became so numerous that they
received their own army regiment, the *murtad-tabor*, or "traitors' unit."
But not everyone who crossed the frontier between faiths did so of
their own free will. Many ended up in Muslim lands because of violence, as prisoners of war or captives of Tatar raiders, who sold them

in one of the many slave markets of the Mediterranean. That was how the Ottoman empress Roxelana arrived in Istanbul: the daughter of an Orthodox priest from Ukraine, she rose out of the harem to become Suleiman the Magnificent's favorite wife and the mother to his heirs. But Roxelana's fate was exceptional. A more typical story would have been that of Theodora Tedea, an Albanian woman born circa 1580. When she was twenty-one, Theodora was captured by a Turkish slaving galley and married off to a Muslim man in the Ottoman Empire. A few years later a Greek Christian took her away and sold her to an Italian man in Naples, where she eventually told her story to the Inquisition and won back her freedom.[7]

The archives of the Inquisition in Italy are awash in stories like Theodora's. Muslims in the Ottoman Empire relied on slaves from Christian lands, and many Christians had slaves taken from Muslim ones. Life on the borders was treacherous: for both men and women, a moment's inattention could mean decades spent immured in a seraglio or rowing a galley. Indeed, this nearly happened to John Smith, who, after his adventure with the three Turks, was captured and sold to a Turkish nobleman but managed to escape back to England via Poland-Lithuania.

Captivity was a desperate fate. But for some Christian women, a voluntary move to the Ottoman Empire could open doors that otherwise would have been closed to them on account of their sex. Salomea Pilsztyn, born in 1718 to a Catholic family in what is now Belarus, married a Lutheran doctor who practiced medicine in the Ottoman Empire. Salomea learned medicine and began working as an ophthalmologist. When her husband abandoned her, she opened a practice of her own, first in Edirne and then in Sofia. There she entered an even more lucrative trade: the ransoming business. She bought captured Habsburg officers from Ottoman slavers and collected payments from their families for their return. She kept one of these ransomed officers, a German from Slovenia named Pichelstein (Pilsztyn in Polish), for herself and married him. They traveled to St. Petersburg, where she cured ladies at the court of the Empress Anna. After a few more years of travel, she divorced Pichelstein, whom she accused of adultery, extortion, and attempted poisoning. He was a rake, and not the last one she would get involved with. That said, Salomea was prone to making wild accusations—for instance, she thought a Jewish competitor in Istanbul was using black magic to steal her patients. Alone, Salomea settled down as imperial ophthalmologist at the harem of Sultan Mustafa III, then made her way to Crimea, where she went to work in the harem of the *khan*.

Salomea ventured from north to south and south to north voluntarily, but others weren't so lucky. Countless uprooted prisoners of war spent their lives pining for a lost homeland. For such unfortunates, the best hope for return came in the form of divine intercession. One folktale from Sarajevo tells of a young woman from that city, taken captive by the Austrians during the terror raid led by Prince Eugene in 1697. Taken to Vienna, she was forced to clean the prince's chambers—all but one, which she was forbidden to enter.

One day when the prince was away, she opened the door to his palace and met a kindly old man in a skullcap. He asked about her life and how she had wound up in this strange city among the infidels. She told him about her former life in Sarajevo, and the sack of her city, and how Prince Eugene had taken her north in his entourage. Then the old man asked if she was familiar with the Maghrebi Mosque on the west side of Sarajevo and if she wished she could be there now. The woman nodded. The old man said, "Stand on my robe and close your eyes!" She closed her eyes and stood on his robe. When she opened them again, she was back in Sarajevo.[8]

.   .   .

Wonder-working saints, like the anonymous Sufi who helped the woman from Sarajevo, were among the great unifiers of Eastern Europe. Their tombs attracted worshippers of all faiths. They dispensed mercy to all comers. Saint Nicholas and the Virgin Mary had Muslim followers, while Christians would often visit the tombs of Muslim holy men. Christians and Muslims likewise celebrated many of the same holidays. At Christmas, Muslims in Albania would assist Catholics in cutting the Yule log, and Catholics would take part in celebrating Bajram. On saints' days, all came together in open-air shrines to give praise and receive blessings.

This type of syncretism found an echo in popular beliefs. Christians and Muslims relied on the same folk medicines and raided each other's traditions for cures. Muslims kissed Christian icons and had their children receive Christian baptisms; Christians on their sickbeds invited Muslim dervishes, or members of Muslim spiritual brotherhoods, to read the Koran over them. In Poland and Lithuania, Muslim Tatars were thought to be the best at curing epilepsy and diseases of the mind. Before World War II, urban Christians and Jews customarily sent their mentally ill family members to live with Muslim families in the countryside.

Nowhere were Muslim and Christian beliefs more elaborately intertwined than in Albania. A single highland clan could have three branches—one Muslim, one Catholic, and a third that was also Catholic—but avoided eating pork. (The oldest brother in the clan's ancestral family had converted, the second one didn't, and the youngest kept halal out of deference to the eldest.) In 1638 an Italian friar visiting an Albanian village in Kosovo was welcomed into a Muslim house with the words, "Come in, Father: in our house we have Catholicism, Islam, and Orthodoxy." Shocked, he reported that the Albanians "seemed to glory in this diversity of religions."[9] Imagine how upset he would have been to hear the preaching of the Bektashi Sufis, who told Christians that "Mohammad and Christ are brothers."

.   .   .

Among the Islamic saints of Eastern Europe, no one assumed as many identities, or attracted followers of as many faiths, as the chameleonic Sarı Saltık. He is the preeminent folk hero of Balkan Islam: a shapeshifter, trickster, warrior, and master of that preeminent religious spectator sport, the learned dispute. Remarkably, Saltık seems to have been a real figure—a religious leader who, sometime in the thirteenth century, helped convert the nomads of the Golden Horde (a splinter-state of the Mongol Empire that ruled over southern Russia and the neighboring steppes) to Islam. Like other historical figures who became famous for their miracles, such as the Baal Shem Tov and Joan of Arc, Sarı Saltık had a legend that was quickly overgrown in myth.

Sarı Saltık rode on a magical horse and carried an impenetrable shield. With his wooden sword (which had once belonged to the Prophet Muhammad), he cleaved open rocks. With his cypress staff, he called forth holy springs. He fought Christian knights but also djinns and witches. Like Saint George, with whom he was equated, he killed dragons. He offered them the option of becoming Muslim and killed them only when they refused.

But Sarı Saltık didn't just fight; he also preached. He spoke twelve languages and had a golden tongue in each one. He often pretended to be a rabbi or a priest. He knew the Gospels and the Torah so well, he moved congregations to tears during his sermons. In Gdańsk, the legend goes, he killed Saint Nicholas, the town patriarch, then dressed in his robes. In this disguise, he made many converts to Islam.

Sarı Saltık continued to proselytize even after his death. Before he died, he ordered that his disciples should prepare to bury him in multiple places, telling them, "Bury me here, but dig other graves there. You will find me in each one of them!"[10] Saltık knew his tomb would become a place of pilgrimage and a magnet for converts, so by having many tombs, he would increase his reach. Four of the coffins were to be placed in Christian lands, and three in Muslim ones. In other versions of the story, he had twelve tombs, or even forty. Those in Christendom have never been found, but his tombs in Muslim lands are genuinely numerous—so much so that a site claiming to be the burial place of Sarı Saltık is roughly the Ottoman equivalent of American inns claiming "George Washington slept here."

To trace Sarı Saltık's tombs across the Balkans is to enter the dream life of European Islam. On this voyage, it quickly becomes apparent that he chose some of the most numinous spots in the whole peninsula for them. At Cape Kaliakra in Bulgaria, his grave sits on a rocky, needle-shaped promontory extending some two kilometers into the coral-filled waters of the Black Sea. In the Krujë district in Albania, a tomb is situated in a cave atop a mountain, from where one can survey the Adriatic Coast from Dürres to Shkodër. In the village of Blagaj in Bosnia-Herzegovina, Saltık's tomb lies beneath a sixteenth-century Sufi lodge, or *tekija*. The lodge is located at the mouth of the Buna River, at the very spot where it pours out of a cave cut into a vertical wall of hard Herzegovinian limestone. On the day I visited, the river was in spate. The lodge, surrounded by yellow pomegranate bushes and persimmon trees, seemed to tremble over the bright-green flood waters. I watched them tumble by from one of the lodge's carpet-covered rooms while the muezzin called the afternoon prayer from the balcony. Above my head, intricate ceiling ornaments in the shapes of the moon, stars, and other celestial phenomena, carved in wood centuries ago, inspired contemplation of the cosmos.

The Blagaj lodge, which today is still home to a working Sufi order, has been associated with Islamic mysticism since the time of Suleiman the Magnificent in the sixteenth century. But Sarı Saltık's most beautiful tomb happens to be located in a church. The Monastery of Saint Naum is an ancient foundation, begun in 905 by the saint himself on the shores of Lake Ohrid. Naum chose an enchanting place for his monastery. Lake Ohrid, a pane of still turquoise water shimmering in the mountain air, looks like a droplet of the Aegean plopped in the middle of the Jablanica Mountains. The monastery stands at a point on the shore—now the boundary between North Macedonia and Albania—where a series of springs emerge from the base of Mount Galičica. They are ice cold and immensely clear. The point where they emerge from the ground is surrounded by a grove of tall, ivy-covered oaks, in the midst of which stands a single spreading fig tree.

No record links the monastery of Saint Naum to Sarı Saltık, but to believers, the evidence is easy to see. In a fresco above Saint Naum's tomb in the monastery church, they recognize a member of the Bektashi order—disguised as an Orthodox monk but wearing the distinctive hat of a Sufi holy man, or dervish, which gives the game away. Next to him on the wall, another dervish sits in a chariot drawn by a deer and a lion.[11] Never mind if this meant to depict the Prophet Elijah: like the tomb of the saint, it has been infiltrated, or we might say supplemented, by Saltık's presence. Every July his followers arrive at the monastery to celebrate *their* saint. Mostly Muslim Roma from Macedonia and its neighbors, they spend the holiday camped on the beach beside the monastery, lighting candles and sacrificing live animals.

This kind of ritual animal sacrifice, called a *kurban*, is practiced all over the Balkans, by people from every social class. My cousin's father-in-law Tomasz is an anthropologist who studies traditional forms of architecture and devotion in the Balkans. While living with a family in a Macedonian village, the family head asked him to sacrifice a lamb. Tomasz was nervous: a sacrifice is risky, and done incorrectly, it can spoil a whole year's crops. He was being asked to do it, however, not for the sake of the family but for his own benefit. As an adult who had never sacrificed an animal, he was in grave danger of misfortune and ill health. This practice is not merely a rural phenomenon. Recently when Tomasz was suffering from eye trouble, his university colleagues in Sofia sacrificed a rooster to help him heal.

Of all the tombs associated with Sarı Saltık, the one in Babadag in eastern Romania seems to be the oldest and, perhaps, the most authentic. As early as the fourteenth century, the great traveler Ibn Battuta visited his tomb there, and in subsequent centuries, Ottoman sultans traveled there, as did the indefatigable Evliya Çelebi. The name Babadag is Turkish for "father-mountain," referring to a pair of small hills just outside town. Though they are no more than a few hundred feet tall, they seem enormous, for they rest on one of the flattest places in Europe, the plains of Dobruja, just south of where the Danube divides into its delta.

In the 1600s, when Evliya Çelebi visited Saltık's *türbe*, the shrine was already ancient. In the centuries after the Ottomans left this part of the world, it suffered from much neglect. By the 1960s it was near collapse. Recently the Turkish government has restored it. The disarmingly small, almost squat building, a little cube of whitewashed masonry, huddles under an inconspicuous red dome. Sarı Saltık's well-hewn wooden coffin—the last in a series, one presumes—is the only thing inside, besides a bucket and a mop. In front, a few ancient gravestones carved with Arabic script stand in a field amid orange tiger lilies.

No one in Babadag seems to pay Saltık's shrine much attention. It is tidy, well kept, and abandoned. People do pay attention to another shrine, however, that is hidden away from town at the very top of the father-mountain. I learned about it from a map once when I went to pay my respects. It is the tomb of Koyun Baba, another dervish saint who is even more enigmatic than Sarı Saltık. He was a shepherd who lived in deepest Anatolia sometime in the Middle Ages. His main claim to fame is that he never spoke. He never seems to have left Anatolia, and precisely how his grave found its way to this Romanian town is a mystery. Perhaps, like Sarı Saltık, he arrived astride a thundercloud.[12]

Intrigued, I set out in search of his shrine, heading toward the top of the father-mountain. Rain clouds approached from the west as I made my way through a forest of dwarf oak trees that covers its summit. A few hundred feet up, I could see thunderheads skipping over the plains all the way from Brăila. By the time I got to the top, they broke. An incredible din rose from the town below. Every rooster, chicken, cow, sheep, goat, and dog in Babadag mooed in delight or barked in displeasure.

I found the grave there. It sat next to a clearing dotted with wild mint and purple wildflowers. The grave itself was simple, and modern. The headstone was cobbled together out of stray bits of marble, and the body was outlined in broken pieces of concrete. Koyun Baba's name was traced in black paint next to a gold five-pointed star. The black soil in the middle of the tomb was strewn with tulips and penny candles. Above, every tree had pieces of colored cloth tied to its branches. Garlands of them hung above my head, dripping from the rain, some red, some yellow, some parti-colored, and some in blue and white stripes like a Greek flag.

By the time I came down from the mountain, the rain had stopped. The many potholes in Babadag's dirt roads were full of rainwater. A pair of Roma children jumped in and out of a large puddle, while their mother swept the water from their tile porch with a broom. Her wide hoop earrings and golden chains sparkled in the newly awoken sun.

Shrines of saints like Sarı Saltık acted as meeting places where members of different faiths could meet around a shared fountain of grace. Giving freely to all who visited, these tombs taught urgent lessons in spiritual generosity. But if holy men could be teachers, then so could adversaries, for conflict, like prayer, was a form of intimacy; sustained over generations, it too could provide an education in the gentle arts of coexistence.

Poland-Lithuania spent much of the early modern period either at loggerheads with the Ottoman Empire or actively at war with it. Both countries won great victories and suffered terrible defeats at each other's hands. Nonetheless, over time, prolonged contact between the two states gave rise to a certain familiarity. Sometimes it was visible in small acts: in the eighteenth century the commanders of frontier posts on opposite sides of the River Dniester used to send each other little presents. A century and a half later, the great-grandson of one of those border guardians still kept one of these gifts as a treasured heirloom: it was a pouch of red silk, full of yellowed pages covered in compliments written in the minuscule, feathery script of that refined age.

At other times, this closeness manifested in grander gestures. After Poland lost its independence in 1795, having been gobbled up by Russia, Prussia, and Austria, the Ottoman Empire refused to recognize its dissolution. They let the last Polish ambassador keep his post in Istanbul. For the next thirty years, they paid his salary and allowed him to sit in on meetings of the *divan* with representatives of other European powers. He was also provided with a Turkish guard, or *kavas*. According to legend, whenever he passed by the guards of the other European ambassadors, they would shake their heads and sigh with pity, "Here is the shadow of a *kavas*, of a dragoman, of a state that was wiped away from the world map!"[13]

Until Poland regained its independence in 1918, Ottoman officials would make a point of noting, at the start of every audience with Western powers, that the "deputy from Lehistan [Poland] has not yet arrived." This splendid piece of chivalry might have been inspired, or at least presaged, by something that had happened many centuries earlier. In 1622 a savage war between the Ottoman Empire and the Polish-Lithuanian Commonwealth came to an end, and it was time to sign the peace treaty.

To negotiate the deal, the Polish senate dispatched Prince Zbaraski, one of the commonwealth's richest men and a former pupil of Galileo. Zbaraski arrived in Istanbul with a splendid retinue, dispensing gifts with an open hand. Still, the sultan's bodyguards, the janissaries, were mistrustful. They showed Zbaraski the embalmed head of the vizier they had just deposed, as well as those of his many predecessors. It was a warning. The Polish envoy understood. He told them, "May my head rest there also, if I do not serve you faithfully."

The next day Zbaraski met with the sultan. He had saved his best present for this occasion. He pulled an old parchment out of a gold chest: the last treaty between Poland and Turkey, signed almost a century earlier between Suleiman the Magnificent and Zygmunt the Old. The Turkish dignitaries crowded around to touch the document that the great lawgiver himself had handled. Before the assembled court,

Zbaraski then read the closing words of the pact, addressed from the sultan to the king of Poland:

> I am seventy and you are old too, the threads of our lives are running out. We shall soon meet in happier lands, where we shall sit, sated with fame and glory, next to the Highest, I on his right hand and you on his left, talking about our friendship. Your envoy, Opaliński, will tell you in what happiness he saw your sister and my wife. I commend him warmly to Your Majesty. Fare well.[14]

At this, the chronicler tells us, everyone present wept dense streams of tears. For a moment, they were privy to a vision of comity and respect almost too sweet to bear.

Muslim tombstone. Glamoč, Bosnia.

4

Heretics

Bogomil tombstone. Lukomir, Bosnia-Herzegovina.

etween 1951 and 1953, a group of Bulgarian ethnographers traveled to Deliorman, a region in the northeast of the country, to
conduct field research among the area's Muslim communities.
The name Deliorman comes from the Turkish words for "crazy forest."
A place of dense woods and vanishing streams just south of the Danube, for centuries it served as a hiding place for bandits and a sanctuary
for refugees. Among the groups that settled there in Ottoman times
were Alevis, Turkish-speaking Shi'ites whose beliefs put them at odds
with the Sunni orthodoxy that prevailed across the empire.

The Bulgarian ethnographers could not ask the Alevis about the par-
ticulars of their religious practices. Stalinism's official atheism was the
order of the day, and discussions of faith were taboo. To avoid accidentally crossing any ideological red lines, the ethnographers restricted
their conversations with the villagers to more neutral topics such as

family structure, farming practices, and handicrafts.[1] Still, religion had a way of cropping up on its own. The villagers showed the visiting scholars their musical instruments (every home had at least one, and someone who could play it) and performed some of their songs. Many were "wise songs of *Tariqat*," religious teachings set to music, sung by both men and women.

But these were not the teachings one would hear in a mosque. They told a secret history, about the four holy books and four sacred elements and the gifts God gave to the primordial Adam. These tales, whose wisdom "burned like fire," were not written down in any book, and the villagers of the Deliorman did not own written scriptures. As one of the village elders explained to the visiting ethnographers, the wise songs of *Tariqat* were "their Koran."[2]

Eastern Europe traditionally contained many enclaves like this, places where nearly everyone was illiterate, and holy writ existed as little more than a rumor or a song. In such places, scripture was rewritten and reinterpreted as myth, to a degree which often bordered on the heretical. The story of Genesis is a case in point. The Bible, the Torah, and the Koran all tell a version of the story of how God created the universe out of void and darkness. But across Eastern Europe, very different versions of this story circulated.

From Estonia to Macedonia, people knew the story of the earth-diver—sometimes a man, sometimes a bird, and sometimes the Devil himself—who at the start of creation dove down into the primordial sea to bring up a speck of dirt from which to conjure the earth as a whole. But at the beginning of time, in some parts of Bulgaria, it was said, there was no sea and no dirt. The earth was like a ball of dough. God kneaded it and formed it into the shape of the land and the heavens the way an old woman stretches puff pastry to make *banitsa*, a stuffed yogurt and cheese pie.[3] The Hutsuls of the Carpathian Mountains in Ukraine expanded on this dairy theme, claiming that at the beginning of time the world was made not of water or dough or waste but of rich, thick sour cream.[4] God spent eons hovering over his creamy white world until one day the Devil, sick with jealousy, splashed it with tar and spoiled it. God then separated out the good cream and used it to fashion the sun and the sky, then used the polluted cream to make the earth and the mountains.

But this is only one version of the Hutsul Genesis. In another, God and the Devil aren't adversaries but collaborators. They work together on building the universe and populating it with useful things. They don't always get along, but while God has the upper hand, the Devil comes up with all the good ideas. It's the Devil who creates the sheep and goats on which the Hutsuls staked their livelihood on the high pastures of the Carpathians, and it's the Devil who invents the fiddle and flute to entertain them. He builds the first house, designs the first wheel, and lights the first fire. Clumsy and unimaginative, God can only appropriate these treasures for himself. The Devil then lashes out and spoils his own creations, by spitting, farting, or otherwise defiling them. That's the reason fire smokes, and why mankind is beautiful on the outside but disgusting within.[5]

It's a silly tale, perhaps, but it points to a deep truth about the spiritual life of Eastern Europe. Over the centuries, every kind of religious nonconformism, from folk superstition to learned magic, has flourished in the region. Where Christianity, Judaism, and Islam met, none of the three faiths could easily enforce uniformity of belief. Means of ideological enforcement common to Western Europe, such as the Catholic Inquisition, and Protestant schools and police regulations, were slow to arrive here. In their absence, heresy thrived. Ambitious rulers turned their kingdoms into sanctuaries for the persecuted. Others turned to the dark arts to soothe their anxieties about this world and the next. And although these alternative beliefs rarely found a permanent home in Eastern Europe, little islands of heterodoxy did as much to shape the region's imagination and self-image as any teaching coming from Rome or Constantinople.

Sustained in memory and folk belief, heresies could live on long after their public defeat at the hands of "official" religion. Both the topsy-turvy mythology of the Hutsuls and the sacred songs of the Bulgarian Alevis have deep roots in forbidden religious experimentation. The Alevis can trace their beliefs back to messianic preachers of the fifteenth century who taught that there was little difference between Christianity and Islam and that all property should be held in common.[6] These prophets practiced what they preached, inciting rebellions against Ottoman rule for which they were executed along with their followers, while the remaining believers fled underground.

Similarly, much of the ribald cosmology of the Hutsuls had origins in the teachings of a now-extinct Gnostic sect called the Bogomils. The Bogomils were dualists: they believed the universe was split into two competing spheres, one good and one evil. The world of good was wholly immaterial and intangible. It was a world of the spirit, created and ruled over by a benevolent God, awaiting blessed souls after death. The world of matter, by contrast, was the domain of evil. It was created by God's rival, a demiurge called Satanael, as a trap. He designed everything we see, touch, taste, and smell as a way of keeping us imprisoned in his universe of filth, death, and darkness, and as far as possible from the other world of light, grace, and eternity.[7]

In keeping with this sharply bifurcated view of the cosmos, the Bogomils' spiritual practice consisted of working to distance themselves from the material world and move as much as possible toward the spiritual one. They avoided meat, marriage, and wine. Through temperance and prayer, their leaders learned to rise out of the foul swamp of this world. Their followers trusted that they could pull them up with them.

Where did these strange beliefs come from? They seem to have arrived in Eastern Europe in the tenth century, brought there by Armenian heretics who had been expelled from their homeland by the emperor of Byzantium and exiled to that empire's far northern frontier. In today's Bulgaria and Macedonia, their teachings inspired a Slavic preacher named Bogomil, or "Beloved of God," whose name eventually was used to refer to the movement as a whole.

From the start, Bogomils were at odds with the established church. They abjured the sacraments and hated the cross, which they took to be an instrument of torture. Their teachings embraced an element of social revolution as well. According to one Byzantine churchman who knew them well, the Bogomils taught their people to "revile the wealthy" and "hate the tsar."[8] Predictably, this stance did not endear them to the powerful. Persecuted in Bulgaria, the Bogomils found refuge in Constantinople. Burned for heresy there, they fanned out across the Balkans. One place they seem to have found a more permanent home is in Bosnia. But like everything to do with the Bogomils, the truth is shrouded in mystery.

The Bogomils did not leave behind any writings—all were destroyed by their persecutors. So virtually everything we know about them and their beliefs comes from the mouths of their enemies. One rare exception comes from the medieval Russian city of Novgorod, where in the year 2000 archaeologists found a wooden tablet inscribed with fragments of a Bogomil text. This shows that Bogomil missionaries were at work, far from their Bulgarian homeland, by the year 1000. Sadly, the tablet preserves little of the actual content of their teachings.[9]

If we know little about the lives of the Bogomils, we know hardly more about the Kingdom of Bosnia, one of the least-documented states in medieval Europe. Still, we can say with some certainty that between the thirteenth and fifteenth centuries, the Bosnian church was in a state of intermittent schism with Rome. Unlike the Bulgarians, who took spiritual orders from Byzantium, the Bosnians were nominally Catholic, but at odds with the church hierarchy. Many believe the reason was that the Bosnian church was largely in the hands of Bogomils. Some think this is why more Christians converted to Islam in Bosnia than in almost any other part of the Balkans—their allegiance to the church was already nominal.

While the degree of the Bosnian Church's deviation from orthodoxy remains up for debate, the idea of a Bogomil past has become an integral part of what it means to be Bosnian. It finds its most powerful expression in a type of monumental gravestone called a *stećak*. The high karst landscape of Bosnia, and especially Herzegovina, is littered with thousands of these enigmatic monuments. Made of white limestone as pale as moonlight, they were carved with a variety of ornaments, including animals, dancers, spirals, solar disks, and stars, whose meaning remains unclear. They are part of the vanished heritage of the Bogomils, speaking to us over the centuries in a language we can no longer understand.

The Bogomils have been a powerful source of identity for Bosnians precisely because of how *different* they were from the rest of Europe. The same can be said for the Hussites in the Czech lands. Like the Bogomils, the Hussites took their name from their founder, Jan Hus. A priest born around 1370 to a poor family in Bohemia, Hus rose quickly through the clerical ranks to become rector of the University of Prague. There he preached against the greed of the bishops and the mad power-hunger of the popes. He wanted an end to the church's financial corruption. He also wanted to make it more democratic, by letting lay people take communion in bread and wine, and by encouraging people to read the Bible in the vernacular.

A century before Luther, Hus called for thoroughgoing reform of the church. If, like Luther, he had lived in the era of the printing press, he might have succeeded. Instead, he was eliminated. In 1415 Hus was lured to a church council under a promise of safe conduct, then condemned as a heretic and burned at the stake while wearing the paper crown reserved for heresiarchs. To prevent relic hunters, Hus's ashes were flung into the Rhine. But this was not the end of his movement. A few years after his execution, his followers revolted against their overlord, the Holy Roman emperor Sigismund, and fended off no less than five Crusades sent by the pope to suppress them. Although the Hussites were eventually forced into a doctrinal compromise, a hundred years later they still dominated the Czech church.

Over time the Hussites' religious rebellion was reinterpreted as a story of ethnic strife between Czechs and Germans. This conflict, as well as Hus's insistent promotion and reform of the Czech language (it was he who invented the *háček*, or inverted circumflex, thus freeing Czech from the tyrannous illogic of Polish orthography), made the Hussites the idols of later generations of nationalists. Today whole districts of Prague are named for Hussite warlords. But outside the Czech lands, a later episode in the city's history made a far greater impact on popular memory, sparking the legend of "Magic Prague."

Around the year 1600, Prague became the center of the occult world. What London was to aspiring playwrights and what Rome was to churchmen, Prague was to every chemist, conjurer, and aspiring wizard on the continent. The reason was largely the will and eccentric habits of a single man, the Habsburg Holy Roman emperor and king of Bohemia Rudolf II.

Rudolf was a seeker. He hungered after secret knowledge and was fascinated by hermeticism, astrology, and kabbalah. He is known to have met with Rabbi Judah Loew, the legendary creator of the Prague Golem, for a lengthy (and secret) discussion. Rudolf's greatest passion, however, was for alchemy, which he loved not so much for its promise of untold wealth as for the possibility it offered of joining a small fraternity of the spiritually elect.

Many have wondered what motivated Rudolf's inclination toward the arcane. Some have speculated that it emerged out of his sense of helplessness. In theory at least, Rudolf was all-powerful, but this was largely an illusion. His office granted him great dignity but little real influence. He was hemmed in on all sides by webs of customary law, privilege, and precedent. Every action or reform he contemplated undertaking got inevitably bogged down under objections from the empire's countless estates and councils.

Rudolf's inability to take action was made worse by his character. Chestnut-haired, cherub-cheeked, and lantern-jawed in portraits, he looks every bit the cheerful Olympian he had his court artists make him up to be. But if Rudolf looked the part of an Ares or a Vertumnus, his mind was ruled by Saturn. Melancholy governed his life. Rudolf was depressive, perhaps manically so. He raged at his servants and loudly proclaimed that he wished to be dead. Alarmed, his advisers wrote diplomatically that he might be "somewhat" possessed by demons.[10] The pope recommended apprehending whatever witches were responsible. None were found.

Instead, as he aged, Rudolf became increasingly paranoid, convinced that he was surrounded by enemies. He was sure that his brothers were

Rudolf II as Vertumnus. Painting by
Giuseppe Arcimboldo, 1591.

plotting against him (which they were). His subjects didn't seem much better disposed toward him. It didn't help that Rudolf was haughty and thin-skinned. In 1583, fed up with the Viennese, who had offended him by rioting and splashing his royal bodyguards with milk, he moved the imperial capital to Prague. Safely ensconced in his massive palace on Castle Hill, he became increasingly agoraphobic. Years went by in which he didn't show his face to the outside world even once.

Afraid to venture out of his palace, Rudolf brought the world inside. He was an insatiable collector. The more exotic or bizarre an item, the more he wanted it. He acquired objects from all parts of the globe: Japanese lacquer screens, Aztec headdresses, giant sea coconuts from the Indies, and precious cups made of rhinoceros horn. His collection ranged from purportedly historical items, such as King Přemysl's peasant cap and nails from Noah's Ark, to purely magical ones, such as phoenix feathers, salamander claws, and a gold bell for summoning the dead.[11] He had a mandrake root shaped like Jesus Christ and a unicorn's horn (really a narwhal's tusk). Rudolf even owned a demon. It sat in a glass case next to what he thought was the Holy Grail.

Rudolf liked live animals too. He had agents stationed abroad whose job it was to send him any wondrous creature that arrived in the ports of Spain or Flanders.[12] Among other things, they sent Rudolf a dodo and a cassowary, both of which he had painted by his favorite artists.[13] Afterward they went to live in his private menagerie, which also contained aurochs, bison, and boars. Of all these creatures, Rudolf's favorite was a lion named Mohammad, a gift from the Ottoman sultan. He had his court astrologer Tycho Brahe calculate both of their horoscopes. Brahe told Rudolf that when Mohammad died, he would die as well.

Brahe won Rudolf's favor because of his skills as an astrologer. In time, the great Danish astronomer became one of the emperor's most trusted counselors. Brahe treated the emperor's ailments with alchemical tinctures and told him who to appoint to various positions, and how to conduct his war against the Turks. In making these calculations, Brahe had help from his collaborator Johannes Kepler. At that moment arguably the greatest mathematical mind in Europe, Kepler used Brahe's

astronomical observations to discover the principles behind the ellipti-
cal motion of the planets—one of the great leaps forward in the history
of astronomy.

Kepler and Brahe were only two members of a wider community
of scholars and freethinkers who gathered around Rudolf's court in
Prague. Some were scientist-mages, like the Polish metallurgist Michael
Sendivogius, who may have been the first to discover oxygen (although
he hid his finding under so much alchemical jargon it's hard to know
for sure), and the Englishman John Dee, a great mathematician and
expert on navigation who was also convinced that he could speak to
angels with the help of a magic mirror made of Aztec obsidian. Others were radical theologians who operated on the furthest fringes of
acceptable religious inquiry—men like Giordano Bruno, who dreamed
of infinitude of worlds, and Francesco Pucci, who wanted to start a correspondence society of learned men acting on behalf of universal truth,
without regard to denomination or creed.

This eccentric fellowship also included a number of outright frauds,
men who traveled Europe pretending to have a recipe for making gold
or building a perpetual motion machine. The prince of these charlatans
was Edward Kelley, a cutpurse whose ears had been chopped off in England for the crime of forgery; he then found sudden fame and fortune
in Rudolf's service. The emperor was thrilled by his claims to possess
the formula for the philosopher's stone. To obtain it, Rudolf made Kelley a knight and, later, a baron. But when he didn't receive the secret in
return, Rudolf had Kelley thrown into one of his castle prisons, where
he died after breaking his legs in a botched escape.

Ranging from tricksters to geniuses, the figures who met in Rudolf's
Prague make a mockery of our modern-day divisions between science,
humanism, and magic. Not that those distinctions mattered at the time:
in an age before the discovery of gravity or the electron, the universe
itself seemed to be held together by a concatenation of mystic chords.
Patterns of resemblance, metaphors, and visual rhymes mattered as
much as, or more than, mathematical laws. In this world, the shape of
a snowflake had as much relevance to the inner workings of the cosmos
as the appearance of an unknown star.

Prague's own star as the center of European learning flickered all too
briefly. In 1611 Rudolf's brothers wrested the crown from him. Nine

months later he died, three days after Mohammad the lion, thus, almost, proving Brahe's prediction. Rudolf's successors were less encumbered than he was by physical and mental maladies. Unfortunately, while they were sound of mind, they were also religious zealots who helped set off the Thirty Years' War, the most destructive conflict in European history until the Second World War three centuries later. Lasting from 1618 to 1648, the war all but obliterated the achievements of the short-lived Rudolfine Renaissance.

The legacy of "Magic Prague" lived on, however, in a host of smaller incarnations. Before its lands were fully absorbed by neighboring empires in the eighteenth and nineteenth centuries, Eastern Europe was an administrative patchwork of overlapping principalities and ducal estates. In this mosaic of microstates, local rulers and powerful noblemen had broad powers to pursue their own religious policies and politics of patronage. Just as infatuated with alchemy and the occult as Rudolf, they created a constellation of miniature Pragues, scattered in an arc from Bohemia to Transylvania.

In Třeboň, in the Czech lands, the spectacularly rich Rožmberk clan maintained their own alchemical court in parallel to Rudolf's, playing host to many of the same wandering alchemists. One of these visitors, the Polish nobleman Olbracht Łaski, was an adept who conversed with Queen Elizabeth I in Latin and brought John Dee and Edward Kelley back with him to Poland. In addition to being a seeker of forbidden wisdom, Łaski was an intriguer and a rogue whose attempt to seize the throne of Moldova got the Cossack leader Dmytro Vyshnevetsky, the renowned *baida* of song, killed. Łaski funded his adventures in part by stealing his wife's dowry. Visitors to his castle in the charming Slovakian town of Kežmarok, set at the very foot of the snow-capped Tatra Mountains, can see both the place where he conducted his alchemical experiments and the tower in which he imprisoned his wife.

A little to the east of Kežmarok, the powerful Rákóczi family—no less bloodthirsty in their time than Łaski—created an island of tranquility and learning around their possessions in northern Hungary. During some of the most turbulent years of the seventeenth century, the city of Sárospatak became a safe haven for humanists and religious exiles of various stripes. In 1650 the great Czech philosopher and "encyclopedic reformer of the mind," John Amos Comenius, took over

the Sárospatak Protestant college.[14] He had his students stage plays in
Latin in the courtyard of the Rákóczi castle, a splendid Renaissance
pile framed, stunningly, between the conical, vineyard-shrouded hills of
the Tokaj on one side, and the muddy waters of the Bodrog River on
the other.

At the same time that Comenius was hatching plans for a perfected
system of education, Lithuania was becoming a sanctuary for proponents of equally radical ideas. In spite of being wedged between Catholic Poles on one side and Orthodox Belarusians on the other side,
the powerful Radziwiłł family—among the richest and most powerful
landowners in all of Poland-Lithuania—embraced some of the most
extreme strands of the Protestant Reformation. In the early seventeenth
century, their private city of Kėdainiai became home to Calvinists,
Christian Hebraists, and members of lesser-known sects like the Arians
and Socinians.

The Socinians were among the first to argue in favor of the rights of
conscientious objectors and to propose an all-encompassing freedom
of religion. Driven out of Western Europe for their beliefs, the Socinians found a safe harbor on its periphery in Lithuania and Transylvania. For a time, these distant territories rivaled cosmopolitan cities
like London and Amsterdam for their wealth of ideas and competing
intellectual currents.

This moment of invigorating plurality was not to last, however. War
and plague took their inevitable toll, as did the relentless forward march
of the Catholic Counter-Reformation. By the start of the eighteenth
century, the Radziwiłłs had all converted to Catholicism, and their intellectual adventurousness declined as their commitment to orthodoxy
increased. Still, the dream of Magic Prague wasn't completely dead.
Hieronim Florian Radziwiłł, who took over the family castle at Biała
Podlaska in eastern Poland in the 1740s, emulated Rudolf in at least one
respect—he had a fine cabinet of wonders that contained, among other
curios, an Egyptian mummy, several birds of paradise (both favorites of
Rudolf's), and a mandrake root shaped like Saint Onuphrius. He also
owned a dead basilisk and forty living bears.[15]

Rumored to be the bastard son of Peter the Great, on portraits
Hieronim looks rather like a cocker spaniel which has stuck its head

through the cushion of a Louis XV *chaise*. Perhaps I'm nursing a grudge—he turned down one of my ancestors for a plum job as the estate manager of the castle at Biržai. Although his collections were capacious, Hieronim did not otherwise measure up to the enlightened example of his own ancestors. Remembered chiefly as a sadist and a dullard, his main preoccupations were with hunting and staging bloody mock battles with his private army of six thousand men. He was also a great lover of ballet.

Hieronim's cousin, Marcin Mikołaj Radziwiłł, had more expansive tastes. At his private laboratories on his estate in Belarus, Marcin continued the Habsburg quest for the philosopher's stone. He also liked to surround himself with learned Jews and adopted some of their customs, including observing the Sabbath, and keeping kosher.[16] For a moment, Marcin may have seemed about to inaugurate a new moment of inter-religious harmony. Sadly, he was completely insane—a criminal maniac who abducted dozens of underage women and enjoyed robbing coaches for fun. When his subjects complained to Hieronim, his cousin had him arrested and declared mentally incompetent. Marcin spent the last three decades of his life rotting in his cousin's specially built dungeon in Slutsk, for the only law the Radziwiłłs respected was that which they wrote themselves.

The example of the Radziwiłłs points to the limits of a culture founded on noble patronage. Their maladies were typical of their class. Trapped on enormous estates surrounded by vast tracts of forests and cut off from wider European currents, unconstrained by duty or passion, they listened to harpsichord music, played at being soldiers, and gradually went mad. But if the old Rudolfine program for universal reform ran aground on the shoals of changing politics and shifting baronial whims, alchemy proved to be remarkably durable. Gold was always in demand, and alchemy—now no longer a spiritual quest but the search for a way to manufacture gold through transmutation—promised a quick way of getting it.

Throughout the seventeenth and eighteenth centuries, royal patrons, hoping for a quick fix for their chronically depleted finances, showered favor on shady characters like "Dr. Fortonio" and the aptly named Baron von Chaos, who was put in charge of a Habsburg royal mint and promptly embezzled from it.[17] But alchemy enjoyed a much broader social base as well. In 1785 Warsaw was home to no fewer than two thousand alchemists, and those were only the permanent residents.[18]

In the final decades of the eighteenth century—the last years of Poland's independence—all the most famous magicians in Europe passed through Warsaw. Count Cagliostro, rumored to be immortal, dazzled the Polish king with his technique for fabricating silver out of mercury. Casanova, the Venetian adventurer famous as his century's greatest lover, stopped by Warsaw as well and showed off his method for the "amelioration of gems" and other alchemical skills.

These men were part of what the historian Paweł Maciejko has called an "informal pan-European guild of itinerant charlatans."[19] They were present in every royal court in Europe, cadging checks, swapping mistresses, and cheating at cards. They presented themselves as exotic princelings, ageless wonders, or initiates of some mystic sect. They boasted about their friendships with the richest duchesses in France and the most beautiful opera singers in Italy. Each of them had a secret method for never losing at cards. But only one ever claimed to be the messiah.

Jacob Frank, who is remembered as one of the greatest heretics and blasphemers in Jewish history, was born in 1726 in the village of Koro-livka, in what is now southwestern Ukraine but was then a distant prov-ince of the Polish-Lithuanian Commonwealth, close to the border with the Ottoman Empire. Frank's father traveled there frequently to trade in gemstones and cloth, so Frank grew up on both sides of the Ottoman-Christian frontier, continually on the move between its great cities of Smyrna, Bucharest, Sofia, and Constantinople.

At some point in his travels to the south, Frank's father became a Sab-batean, or a follower of Sabbatai Zevi, the Turkish Jew whose claims of being the messiah roiled the entire Jewish world in the mid-seventeenth century. Zevi's brief spell as the *mashiach* ended with his conversion to Islam in 1666.[20] Long afterward, however, many in Zevi's inner circle and beyond continued to believe that he was God's chosen. In the Ottoman lands, these followers pretended to be Muslim outwardly but continued to venerate their leader and practice Jewish customs in secret. They came to be known as the Dönmeh, from the Turkish word for "apostate" or "turncoat."

The greatest number of Dönmeh lived in the Greek city of Salonika. At some point in his youth, Jacob Frank traveled there and made contact with the surviving cell of Sabbatai's closest followers and married the daughter of one of their leaders. Soon he claimed to be the reincarnation of one of Zevi's leading prophets. He began teaching kabbalah and revived some of Sabbatai Zevi's most controversial teachings, specifically his antinomianism, or the idea that redemption lay not in following religious law, but in breaking it.

Sin! Sin so that God may forgive you! Frank brought this vividly transgressive message back to Poland, where scattered pockets of Sabbatai's followers still practiced in secret. Frank put himself forward as their leader. His confidence and charm emboldened the heretics. After ninety years of hiding, they emerged out of the shadows. In 1756, in the small Polish town of Lanckoronie, they arranged a dance, men and women celebrating together, some without clothes. Of course, they did so at night, behind closed doors, but even so they were discovered. The local rabbi denounced them to the Christian mayor, and the entire group of Frank's followers was arrested. Under questioning, they revealed that they had come from Lviv and were on their way to Salonika to pay their respects at the grave of their master Sabbatai Zevi.

Confronted with these transgressions, the local rabbinic court pronounced a ban of excommunication against Frank and all his adherents. No Jew could have any dealings with them; their wives were to be regarded as harlots, and their children as bastards. Not content with this, the rabbis went even further: they informed the local Catholic bishop, a notorious anti-Semite named Dembowski, that heretics had come into his diocese and were in need of correction.

This last move proved to be a terrible mistake. Sensing a fissure in the Jewish community, Bishop Dembowski chose to exploit it. Isolated and aggrieved, Frank and his followers played perfectly into his hands. They informed him that they were not heretics; they believed earnestly in the Bible and the Zohar; they simply doubted the Talmud and its lies. Delighted, the bishop arranged for a series of disputations between the Frankists and the Talmudists. Insulted and abused by the Orthodox rabbinate, Frank and his followers responded by engaging in every conceivable calumny. They told their listeners that the Talmud was full of fables and lies and that it blasphemed against Christianity. Worst of all, they asserted that Christian blood was necessary to make Passover matzah, thus implying that ritual murder was a part of Jewish teaching.

This was a lie of almost unthinkable magnitude—an elemental betrayal, as it gave credence to the blood libel, the most pernicious myth told about Jews in Christian lands. Once Frank permitted it, there could be no way back to Judaism for him or his followers. In 1759, cornered and under pressure from the Polish Catholic hierarchy, all the Frankists converted to Christianity in a special ceremony held in the Lviv cathedral.

A heretic since birth and a convert to Islam during his Turkish days, Frank was now the leader of a Christian congregation made up entirely of renegade Jews. Christian Poles saw him as a herald of the coming redemption of the Jews. The Catholic establishment showered him with honors. Frank and his leading followers were granted patents of nobility and fêted by all the greatest magnates in Poland. They shaved their beards and sidelocks and began wearing sabers. Frank himself moved to Warsaw, dined off of gold and silver plates, dressed like a king, threw gold coins to beggars, went to the theater, and traveled in a chariot pulled by six horses. He also dabbled in alchemy. He distilled ethanol and ether, which, he thought, drunk in combination, would ensure his immortality. He also produced a tincture that he called "Drops of Gold" that was supposed to cure every disease.

Frank and his sect owed their fame and fortune to their conversion to Christianity, but in actuality, they existed in a religious no-man's-land. Publicly Catholic, in secret they still held to some tenets of Judaism, although interpreted in a wildly heterodox manner. They believed in a messiah, Sabbatai, who had converted to Islam, and in a prophet, Frank, who openly espoused Catholicism. Privately, however, Frank continued to pursue a particularly *Jewish* type of heresy, fusing kabbalistic ideas of the divine presence, or *Shekhinah*, with the Catholic devotion to Mary.

Frank revealed this new teaching to his followers, some of whom denounced him to the Polish Catholic authorities, who promptly had him arrested. Frank spent the next thirteen years in a monastery prison in Częstochowa. In 1772, after the first partition of Poland, the Russian army freed him, in part because he promised to convert the Jews of

Poland to Russian Orthodoxy. Instead, Frank made his way to Vienna, where he somehow managed to secure a meeting with Empress Maria Theresa. He persuaded her that he was neither an apostate nor a false messiah but a Jewish religious reformer, acting in the spirit of the Enlightenment.

Having thus secured permission to settle in the Habsburg lands, Frank began a new life, first in Moravia and then in the German town of Offenbach am Main. He returned to his alchemical pursuits, conducted séances, and let it be known that his daughter Eve was the illegitimate daughter of the czarina of Russia. With eight hundred of his followers, Frank took over a local castle and posed as a baron. He dressed in Turkish clothes and spent his days reclining on a divan, smoking a hookah. He surrounded himself with armed guards in Polish and Hungarian costumes and with children wearing red and white turbans.

Frank committed himself entirely to his new identity as a mock–Middle Eastern wizard-king. Every day at four o'clock, he would leave his castle in a carriage and go to the forest, where he performed esoteric rituals, dressed as a high priest of the ancient Jewish temple. His daughter Eve, who would inherit the sect after Frank's death, rode behind him in a second carriage with a boy dressed as a cupid. A group of "Amazons," young women wearing uniforms emblazoned with the sun, rode beside them, silver bells tinkling from their horses' necks. Meanwhile the rest of Frank's followers thronged around his castle, playing flutes and guitars and dressed in improbable costumes of red and yellow, green and gold.

People from across Germany and Austria came to Offenbach to observe these strange, colorful outcasts. It was a marvelous show, a perpetual masquerade. But it was also a betrayal. In the two centuries since Rudolf met with the rabbi of Prague, Eastern Europe's heretics, freethinkers, magicians, and mystical seekers had achieved something fragile but real: a mutual acknowledgment that there was truth in every religious tradition. This moment of intervisibility took place at the very top and bottom of society, in the Masonic lodges and alchemical laboratories of the nobility, and—largely unacknowledged—in the swirling, boundlessly inventive folklore of the peasantry.

However base or treacherous he might have been as an individual, Frank had once taken an earnest part in this movement of union and reconciliation. Now in exile, he and his followers were reduced to a tourist attraction, embodying exotic "Jewish" or "Oriental" wisdom for people who knew nothing about either Jews or the Orient. Prisoners in a spiritual menagerie, they were the human equivalent of Emperor Rudolf's cassowaries and dodos, or Count Radziwiłł's basilisk and bears.

Part II

Empires and Peoples

5

Empires

Ottoman janissary. Drawing by
Gentile Bellini, c. 1479–81.

E astern Europe is a land in between. To be Eastern European was to have had the experience of being governed from far away. It meant living under the shadow of the yoke, the knout, and the hangman's noose. It also meant harboring a grudge. In short, it was a region defined by being part—but never at the center—of empires.

Empire, as a concept, is generally foreign to Eastern Europe. Empires entered it from outside. In the Middle Ages, Eastern Europe was a region of kingdoms. They were local in provenance, moderate in size, and occasionally ambitious but never all-powerful. They fought among each other and built splendid capitals. They did not attempt to unify Christendom or conquer the world.

In the north, these kingdoms' heyday ran from the mid-fourteenth to the early sixteenth century. Beginning in around 1350, under the rule of the Luxembourg dynasty, Bohemia became a center of Gothic art and architecture. An ambitious rebuilding campaign overseen by Charles IV made Prague one of the most beautiful cities in Europe. Following their union in 1386, the combined double kingdom of Poland-Lithuania became one of the largest countries on the continent. After it defeated the Teutonic Order in 1410 at the Battle of Grunwald, Poland-Lithuania was also one of the continent's major military powers.

Hungary was one of the few countries that could match it. Much larger then than it is today, Hungary boasted one of the mightiest armies in Europe, its soldiers hardened by long combat against the Turks. Matthias Corvinus, its sovereign in the later fifteenth century, was an enlightened despot in the full Renaissance mold. He possessed a superb library of illuminated manuscripts, now sadly dispersed, while his soldiers inspired rage in Istanbul and deathly fear among a family of middling Austrian dukes called the Habsburgs.

Farther south, in the Balkan Peninsula, local kingdoms flourished somewhat earlier, between roughly 1100 and 1375. This was the era of the Second Bulgarian Empire and the short-lived Serbian Empire of Dušan the Mighty. (The Kingdom of Bosnia also came into being at the very end of this period, only to be subsumed by the Ottomans some eighty-five years later.) Though they called themselves empires, both the Bulgarian and Serbian states were really no more than regional states who organized themselves in imitation of the Byzantine Empire to the south.

Throughout this period, the Byzantine Empire remained the most prestigious realm in all of Eastern Christendom. Rulers in the "Second Rome" still set the template for what rulers should be and how they should behave. If the Byzantines had a Caesar, then their Serbian and Bulgarian neighbors wanted one too. For them, imitation really was the sincerest form of flattery. The Byzantines responded with contempt. One exiled churchman referred to the Bulgarians as "barbarians" and "bumpkins," while an envoy to the court of the Serbian king was shocked to see his wife at work at the spinning-wheel. He wrote home that "the Great King, as he is called, lives a simple life in a way that would be a disgrace for a middling official in Constantinople."[1]

Diminished in actual power and territory, the Byzantine Empire in its last years maintained its cultural superiority by dint of sheer snobbery. It could do so because it possessed a pedigree to which none of its rivals could aspire. The emperors of Byzantium were heirs to an unbroken tradition stretching back to the time of Augustus in the first century B.C. But really it went beyond that, for since Constantinople was the New Rome, its roots stretched all the way back to the founding of the original Rome by Romulus and Remus seven hundred years before the birth of Christ. The conquering Slavs were thus confronted with more than two thousand years of accumulated history. The best the Bulgarians could hope for was to be considered the emperor's sons, and for this they considered themselves lucky, for the Serbs received no such honor.[2]

Religion gave Byzantium another source of prestige. As the stewards of Orthodox Christianity, Byzantines believed that theirs was an "empire founded by God to last forever."[3] It thus possessed one of the key attributes of empire: ambition. For empire is above all an idea, a claim to universal power. An emperor is no mere lord among lords—he is a king among kings. However, Byzantium lacked the other key attribute of a successful empire, which is the ability to expand. An empire is, by nature, big. It rules over varied peoples, separated by great distances. Shrunk by centuries of military defeat, the Byzantium of the later Middle Ages was a husk of its former self. Especially after the sack of Constantinople during the Fourth Crusade in 1204, it was never more than a second-rate power, confined to western Anatolia and parts of Greece.

By the fifteenth century, Byzantium was not even a local power anymore—it was a city-state, ruled from an increasingly empty city, home to little more than the ghost of former glories. Still, the question of who ruled from New Rome mattered, above all to the Ottomans, the new world-conquerors who were poised to inherit the City of the Caesars.

Ottomans

In 1453, after a fifty-five-day siege, Byzantium fell to the armies of Mehmed II. Intoxicated by his victory, Mehmed adopted a new title. Henceforth he would be known as the "Sovereign of Two Lands and

Two Seas," indicating his lordship over both Anatolia *and* the Balkans, the Mediterranean *and* the Black Sea.[4] In succeeding years, his list of titles would only grow. In 1517 Ottoman armies conquered Egypt, and in 1534 they took Baghdad. The Ottoman emperors now possessed the ancient heart of the Muslim world in addition to the last seat of the Roman emperors. In 1538, when Suleiman the Magnificent, the greatest and longest-reigning (1520–66) Ottoman sultan, conquered the fortress of Bender in what is now Moldova, he affixed the following inscription above the door: "In Baghdad I am the shah, in Byzantine realms the caesar, and in Egypt the sultan."[5]

How did the Ottomans do it? Religion helped. Their empire began in the early fourteenth century as a tiny principality on the Muslim-Christian frontier in Anatolia. There, on the edge of Byzantine territory, a tribal chieftain named Osman gathered a group of holy warriors, or *ghazis,* around himself. Together they sacked castles and pillaged wagon trains for the greater glory of Islam. These jihadi border-raiders had found a way to make violence both pious and lucrative—a winning combination in most times and places. They made terrifyingly swift progress. In 1354 Ottoman forces made their first fateful foray into the Balkans. By 1371 they had seized most of Macedonia and Thrace. In 1389 they shattered the power of the Serbian Empire at the Battle of Kosovo. A few years after that the Ottomans finished their conquest of Bulgaria. In the decades that followed, Greece, Bosnia, and Herzegovina came under their control, as did Albania, despite heroic resistance on the part of the Albanians led by their national hero, Skanderbeg. Romania managed to elude being conquered outright, but was forced into the status of a vassal.

The Ottomans' success in the Balkans was largely a question of numbers: they were simply able to field larger armies than any of the kingdoms that stood in their way. At the Battle of Kosovo, when the Serbs faced the Ottoman armies, a Serbian poet wrote that Ottoman soldiers were so numerous that if all the Serbs were turned into grains of salt, they still wouldn't be enough to season the Turks' "wretched dinners."[6]

The Ottoman numerical superiority was partially a product of geography. Anatolia provided them with a huge reservoir of manpower in the form of nomadic Turkish tribes, whose members were always willing to try their luck in Europe as soldiers or as settlers. But it was also the result of a deliberate strategy. The Ottomans were remarkably flexible when it came to recruiting allies. Over the course of their light-ing progress across southeastern Europe, they attracted followers the way a snowball rolling downhill gathers snow. Turkic tribal leaders, Byzantine rebels, Serbian despots, Bulgarian lords, and Greek sailors all swore allegiance to their new masters. As the leading edge of the empire pushed deeper into the heart of Europe, they were joined by captured or defecting Westerners—Italians, Hungarians, Germans, and even the occasional Pole. As long as they converted to Islam, they could find profitable employment in the sultan's army and bureaucracy. Soon, though, they were joined by another, less voluntary kind of recruit, the fruits of *devşirme*, or child-levy.

The *devşirme* was a form of blood tax by which the Christian peoples of the empire gave away a percentage of their sons to be raised in the image of their conquerors. It was first instituted to counteract the influ-ence of the native Turkish nobility. As effective as it was despised, the *devşirme* created a corps of soldiers and administrators completely loyal to their sultan. Formally these janissaries were all his slaves, but in real-ity, they were more like an extended household, held together by an artifice of kinship.

The boys were taken from their families when they were between fourteen and eighteen years old. They were expected to be perfect, in body and face. Country boys, used to hard work, were considered the best recruits. Among ethnic groups, Bosnians were especially prized, though Serbs and Albanians also thrived in the imperial service. Once the young recruits entered the capital, they were completely cut off from their families and birthplace. Converted and circumcised, they were subjected to a rigorous training regime to make them proficient in both religious teaching and the art of war. Usually, the training began with a term of service on an Anatolian farm, where the young men learned Turkish and developed their physiques. Back in the palace, they contin-ued their education with courses in Islamic law, archery, horsemanship, wrestling, conversation, and calligraphy.

The creation of the janissaries, this exquisitely trained caste of soldier-administrators, transformed the Ottoman state. If the early Ottoman armies succeeded by overwhelming their opponents, the army that took Constantinople for Mehmed II was equipped with the best of everything: the biggest cannons, the strongest siege engines, and most efficient sappers. Most of all, it was a *professional* army. Venetian envoys spoke of its "marvelous order."[7] Ottoman soldiers were experts in all the arts of war: they could fight with a bow, a sword, or a lance. But where they really excelled was in the little details that ensured the success of a campaign. They had the finest tents and pitched the best camps. They knew the best way to dig a trench or a latrine. Most of all, they knew how to operate in unison. A French traveler of the fifteenth century who witnessed the Ottoman army in action was most impressed by the way they moved. During their night marches, they covered three times the distance that a Christian army could during daytime. But what was really terrifying was that they did so silently: ten thousand soldiers made less noise than a hundred Christians.[8]

The Ottoman army was as well fed as it was disciplined. Where Russian soldiers were expected to live on whatever food they brought with them—usually a thin buckwheat gruel—Ottoman soldiers feasted on meals of rice, bulgur, barley, clarified butter, coffee, honey, flour, and meat.[9] Supplying an army on the march in this way was an immense undertaking, as it devoured a million pounds of food per day.

Fortunately, the Ottomans were unrivaled masters of supply-chain logistics. No other state in Europe devoted as much energy or care to the repair of its roads. From very early on, the Ottomans became justly famous as builders of beautiful stone bridges, whose delicate arches appeared to be as delicate as eggshells but proved as durable as iron. Supplies of food, cloth, gunpowder, and steel flowed continuously over this system of roadways. Camels, able to carry twice as much as any European beast of burden, made their transport easier. Every year thirty thousand of these essential animals arrived from the Maghreb and Syria, in time for the campaigning season.[10] But the real heart of the Ottoman procurement system was its bakeries. In Istanbul alone, 105 gigantic ovens worked around the clock, baking hardtack for the army and navy stores.[11] Many more operated across the provinces.

In the seventeenth and especially the eighteenth century, the Ottoman army gradually lost its technological edge over its European counterparts. But as long as the bakeries functioned, it still had a fighting chance against its Russian and Habsburg opponents. In 1711, when the Ottomans humbled the army of Peter the Great in Moldova, the famished Russians had to purchase food from the army that had beaten them. Sixty years later, when the Ottoman army went to fight Catherine the Great, its advantage had disappeared. Thanks in large part to corruption, the procurement system collapsed, and the Ottoman soldiers were forced to eat bread made from the dust of forty-year-old biscuits, which was mixed with powdered mud and lime.[12] Many who ate this bread died on the spot. The rest were slaughtered by Catherine's guns.

What did the Ottoman Empire look like to its Christian subjects? To them, the empire was a gigantic burden, 20 million mouths to feed, and hundreds of thousands of soldiers and bureaucrats to support on top of that. Regardless of the fact that Ottoman taxes tended to be relatively light compared to the rest of Europe: from the depths of the countryside, the empire seemed little more than a hostile world of tax assessors, census-takers, and customs officials, all looking to take their cut of an honest peasant's labor.

An old Macedonian folktale conveys what the weight of empire felt like to ordinary Christians.[13] In the story, an old man hears that in Istanbul people are buying eggs for a silver penny apiece. The old man promptly loads his donkey with a thousand eggs and sets off for the capital. As he makes his way south, he encounters a series of tax officials, each of whom helps himself to a basket of eggs, without paying, of course. By the time the old man arrives in Istanbul, he has no eggs left. Having nothing left to sell, he takes a page from his oppressors' notebook and appoints himself the guardian of an Istanbul graveyard. Armed with a fake document of authorization, he begins charging the noblemen and -women of Istanbul for the privilege of being buried. The tale thus makes life in the Ottoman Empire seem a perfect circle of corruption, following its subjects from the cradle all the way to the grave.

But Istanbul was not merely a hungry maw, thirsty for bribes; in Ottoman times, it was also a center of opportunity, pulling in young people from across the Balkans and the Middle East. Some came to feed the city. By 1600, just keeping Istanbul's population of over seven hundred thousand provisioned required a titanic effort. Every day barges plying the Black Sea brought wheat from Bulgaria and Romania, while Moldovan cowboys drove great herds of cattle from the headwaters of the Dniester. In fact, we owe these cattle drovers a great civilizational debt, for they were the inventors of pastrami, whose Yiddish name ultimately derives, by way of the Romanian *pastramă*, from the Turkish *bastırma*, or "pressed meat."[14]

Others migrated to Istanbul in search of work in its many urban factories, which included everything from saltworks to cannon found-ries. Many of these jobs were taken by Albanians. Mountainous and infertile, Albania in the Ottoman period was a constant exporter of manpower. Albanians took some of the city's toughest jobs, such as burning lime or working in the great bakeries that supplied the army. They also found a niche for themselves in a much more comfortable profession—that of *tellâk*, or bathhouse attendant.

In Istanbul, bathhouses, or *hammams*, were an industry unto them-selves. Nearly two hundred of them operated in the old city alone.[15] Islamic law required full-body ablution, but bathing was also deeply pleasurable. At a *hammam*, one could bathe, soak, steam, drink a coffee, and get a massage or a shave. The bath attendants were responsible for keeping the fires lit, the waters warm, and the patrons well scrubbed. They also offered services of a more intimate nature, which placed bathhouses at the center of the city's homoerotic imaginary.

Hammams were places to converse and indulge. They were also good places in which to plot and scheme. Like the coffeehouses of London, they were often filled with political talk. Ottoman authorities knew this and kept them well-stocked with spies. At times the surveillance was lacking, and seditious talk spilled out onto the streets. In 1730 the Patrona Halil rebellion, begun by an Albanian janissary and bath atten-dant, even managed to depose a sultan. By then, the title "janissary" was largely empty; far more janissaries worked as shopkeepers than as soldiers. Together these rootless young men from the provinces formed an urban mob very much like the Parisian sans-culottes who helped foment the French Revolution. More proactive than the French mon-archy, the Ottomans tried to stem the tide of urban migration, intro-ducing special passports and registrations. Mostly these efforts failed. Grasping at straws, the government reached for the last instrument in its arsenal: banishment to the frontier.

Hundreds of miles to the north of Istanbul, the Ottoman Empire pro-tected itself from its Russian neighbor by building a series of forts on the northern shore of the Black Sea. These fortresses were manned by Albanians, Bosnians, and Kurds drawn from the slums of Istanbul. In this way, the empire acted like a great human pump, pulling in people from the provinces, then spitting them back out to the frontier. The soldiers who found themselves exiled to the north consoled themselves by smoking opium, drinking Ukrainian vodka, and writing poems full of homesick longing.[16] Most Ottomans considered their surroundings terrible. "I will destroy you in the Black Sea Steppe" was a curse common enough to become a proverb. Later, ironically, Soviet citizens would view these same territories as among the balmiest and most fertile in the entire USSR.

It took as long as four months to travel from Istanbul to the "hellishly cold" Black Sea fortresses. Moving people and matériel over such a vast distance required a mastery of paperwork as well as logistics. Before an army could march, before its soldiers could be fed, all the necessary taxes and people had to be assembled. This required detailed knowledge of all the empire's villages and households and free-roaming tribes.

In 1672, after the armies of Mehmed IV conquered Podolia (a chunk of present-day Ukraine) from Poland-Lithuania, a group of tax officials called *defterdars* immediately set about surveying all the provinces' arable land and counting all its employable men. The tax register they compiled lists nine hundred different geographical locations. No map of this territory made before the start of the twentieth century was more detailed.[17] The Ottoman official Halil Efendi supervised the effort, accompanied by an interpreter, David, most likely a Jew or an Armenian. Armenian elders assisted in compiling the lists of Armenians. Rabbis prepared lists of Jews. In the villages, Ukrainian headmen compiled lists of their neighbors. Every hamlet had at least one literate man. These lists were then transcribed from Cyrillic into Arabic script by specialized translators, probably Bulgarians, after which they were sent to an archive in Istanbul, where they have remained to this day.[18] This is what it means to see like an empire.

When the Turks took Podolia from Poland, they were celebrated as liberators. The Jewish community of Kamianets-Podilskyi, the province's main town, greeted them by saying that they knew how happy life was "in the shade of the people of Islam."[19] The town's Armenians were equally pleased, as were the Ukrainian peasants in the countryside, glad to be rid of their Polish landlords at last. Only the Polish noblemen, many of whom were forced to abandon their lands and flee back to the commonwealth, took the conquest poorly. Some Poles did find favor with the new regime, however, primarily by giving the Ottomans access to precious tax registers and census rolls.

This moment of intercultural harmony did not last long; Poland reclaimed its lost territories in 1699. Fearing reprisals for cooperating with the Turks, rich Jews and Armenians fled south. The Armenians started a trading colony in Plovdiv, Bulgaria. Settling outside Istanbul, the Podolian Jews became famous producers of kosher butter and cheese. Compared to the chaos that was then overtaking Poland-Lithuania, the Ottoman Empire appeared to be an oasis of calm. But this harmony would prove to be short-lived. In the following century, the grip of the empire on the Balkans began to disintegrate, succumbing first to the influence of Muslim warlords in the eighteenth century, and then to Christian nationalists in the nineteenth. Once this last group took over, the peaceful "shade of Islam" in which the Jews of Kamianets found refuge would be no more than a memory.

Russians

Poland-Lithuania itself was an "almost empire." It was a big state, incorporating, at its height, most of present-day Poland, Lithuania, Latvia, and Belarus and the western half of Ukraine. It was also diverse. The Grand Duchy of Lithuania had a majority population of Ukrainians and Belarusians, respectively, ruled over by a Polish-speaking noble class of mostly Lithuanian origin, augmented by numerous settlements of Jews, Tatars, Armenians, and Germans.

Poland-Lithuania failed to become an empire, however, because it never centralized. After 1572, when its last Jagiellonian king, Zygmunt II August, expired the dual state became an electoral monarchy. Nobles chose their monarch, giving them immense sway over the government, a control that they also exercised through the chaotic and veto-ridden parliament, the Sejm. Because of this fractious arrangement, Polish kings had great difficulty collecting taxes or raising an army. They built few bridges or roads. Their realm made a correspondingly chaotic impression on visitors. Ahmed Resmî Efendi, an Ottoman statesmen who traveled through Poland-Lithuania in the mid-eighteenth century, said that it "was a republic in which every region and every city had a different administration, and they neither paid attention to one another, nor obeyed the kings."[20]

For Poles, there were only two empires in Europe: "the Muslim Empire" of the Ottomans, and the "Christian Empire" of the Habsburgs.[21] Their greatest enemy, however, was a different state altogether: the Grand Duchy of Moscow, or Muscovy. This was the state that surrounded the city of Moscow in the Middle Ages and that developed by stages into Muscovite Rus, Russia, and the Russian Empire.

If Muscovy was not an empire—its rulers were not emperors, but merely princes, until Ivan the Terrible crowned himself czar in 1547—it was certainly a country apart. Its institutions were shaped by its Eastern Orthodox faith and its long contact with the Golden Horde, which ruled over the Russian steppes following the Mongol conquests of the thirteenth century. Part of this inheritance was a tradition of unitary rule. The princes of Moscow did not have to contend with the various intermediary institutions that most Western rulers had to deal with, such as parliaments and an independent clergy. They did not have to *consult*. They ordered. And as they ordered, their principality grew.

In 1480 Muscovy defeated the last remnants of the Golden Horde. In 1552 it annexed the Khanate of Kazan, a Turkic-Muslim polity to its east. Four years later it annexed the Khanate of Astrakhan, by the Caspian Sea, taking Muscovy to the very edge of Asia. Seen from the West, Russia was thus an enormous, almost continent-crossing domain. Its main rivals became Poland-Lithuania and Sweden, the two states cutting off its access to the Baltic Sea. But despite Russia's immense size, throughout the sixteenth and seventeenth centuries, both nations largely held their own against their eastern neighbor. A series of conflicts between Russia and Poland-Lithuania ended largely in a draw.

Members of my own family took part in these seldom-remembered wars. The first of my relations to appear in the historical record was Jakub Terebesz. Probably of Hungarian (or Transylvanian) origin, he served as master of horse to the hetman, or military commander, of Lithuania. In 1658 Russian forces captured both Terebesz and the hetman outside Vilnius, after which they were imprisoned together in the Kremlin. At some point in the next four years, my ancestor was freed and sent back to Warsaw to arrange an exchange of hostages for the hetman's freedom.[22]

This little episode marked the start of the Terebesz family's career in government. For the next 130 years, its members served in a variety of offices, most commonly as royal bailiffs or county administrators in western Lithuania. These good times came to an end in 1795, when the Russian Empire completed the third of its three partitions of Poland-Lithuania, thereby erasing it from the map of European states. The Poles put up some resistance, but they had little hope of challenging Russia, which by this time was a behemoth, compared to which all other states of Eastern Europe were mere minnows.

Muscovy grew enormous by swallowing the vast and sparsely inhabited territories that lay to its east. The conquests of Kazan and Astrakhan opened Russia's way to Siberia, where its fur-trappers and soldiers made incredibly swift progress. In 1580 they crossed the Urals. By 1639 they were on the Sea of Okhotsk, a distance of over three thousand miles. This means that Russian soldiers reached the Pacific Ocean 150 years before they entered Minsk.

From a European perspective, the Russian Empire grew from back to front. It expanded to the east much faster than to the west, where, unlike in Siberia, it faced formidable organized opponents, armed with the latest in European military technology. Still, between the mid-seventeenth century and the end of the eighteenth, Russia defeated them one by one. The first to fall was Ukraine.

Everything to do with Ukraine is complicated, beginning with its location. For much of its early history, it was a frontier zone, sandwiched between Russia to the east, the Crimean Khanate—the last remnant of the Golden Horde and a vassal of the Ottoman Empire—to the south, and Poland-Lithuania to the west. Through the mid-seventeenth century, most of western Ukraine formally belonged to Poland-Lithuania, but it was really more of a no-man's-land, where the only law was that of the gun. There was little effective government. People who settled in central Ukraine were subject to terrifying Tatar slave raids. But lawlessness also had its attractions. For many, it meant freedom—from serfdom and from states.

The people of the Ukrainian steppe were in charge of their own defense. In the sixteenth century, they built forts and organized themselves into armies or "hosts." These were the first Cossacks. Their society was intensely militaristic—every man was expected to be a soldier. It was also democratic—soldiers elected their officers and commanders, the hetmans. Finally, it was very male. Their most famous central encampment was the Zaporozhian Sich, located on an island in the Dnieper River. The members of the Sich kept all their property in common, and they were forbidden to associate with women while in camp. Nikolai Gogol, writing with only a bit of fantasy, compared the Cossacks' lifestyle to an "uninterrupted feast that began noisily and had no end."[23] The Sich fortress, meanwhile, was like a boarding school, "where students [were] given full board" but spent all their time hunting, fishing, and partying instead of studying. The Cossacks did not bother with military training, for in their opinion warriors were formed only in the blaze of battle.

Cossacks made excellent mercenaries, but they were hard to control. In 1648 the rebellion of Bohdan Khmelnytsky, the hetman of the Zaporozhian Cossacks, caused a nightmare of destruction for the Jews of Poland-Lithuania. It was also a political disaster for the Polish-Lithuanian Commonwealth and the beginning of a short-lived, but hugely significant, moment of independence for Ukraine. The Cossacks, having won their freedom from Polish control, soon found it hard to maintain. To keep out the Polish-Lithuanian invaders, they needed allies. They turned to the Tatars and the Swedes but ultimately settled on an alliance with Russia.[24] This choice had a clear logic: Russia was similar to Ukraine in language and identical in religion. Russia also offered the Cossacks a wide measure of autonomy, which they treasured. It was not to last.

For a time, the Zaporozhian Sich continued to exist alongside Russia, albeit in reduced circumstances. Originally a wild brotherhood of sworn warriors devoted to daring acts of plunder, it now served as a defensive force, guarding the Russian Empire's southern borders from Turkish incursions. After Catherine the Great defeated the Ottoman Empire in the Russo-Turkish War of 1768–74, this usefulness came to an end. In 1775 she had the Sich fortress razed and exiled the last Zaporozhian hetman to the Solovetsky Islands, in Russia's far north. Already an old man at the time of his arrest, the hetman spent the next quarter-century imprisoned in a tiny cell, knee deep in his own filth, from which he emerged with a matted beard and enormous fingernails, looking more like an animal than a man.[25]

Catherine the Great destroyed the Zaporozhian Sich because it was a remnant of a past she despised. Inspired by the Enlightenment, the empress was determined to reform and rationalize the Russian Empire. This did not mean granting Russians more freedom. Instead, it meant streamlining and solidifying her own power, so that she could rule without impediment. The various inherited privileges enjoyed by the Cossacks were just a hindrance to her. During Catherine's long reign, which lasted until 1796, the Cossacks lost nearly all their old institutions. The most powerful and wealthiest Cossacks were made into Russian noblemen, with all the privileges the title guaranteed them. The rest gradually were reduced to little more than common peasants, with only the memory of their former status to sustain them.

The example of the Ukrainian Cossacks is a lesson in how Russia assembled its empire. As it expanded, its strategy was almost always to identify and co-opt a local elite. To rule, it relied on a rigid class system, whose differences it accentuated and enhanced. The Baltic countries are another excellent example. When Peter the Great conquered Latvia and Estonia from Sweden in 1710, he confirmed the local nobility in all its past privileges. They got to keep their lands, their serfs, and their parliament. They even got to keep their Lutheran church and their language, which in the case of the nobility was almost exclusively German. Their serfs, however, spoke Latvian or Estonian, depending on where they lived. This arrangement was very ancient and very fixed, so much so that in Estonian the very word *saks*, or "Saxon," came to mean not just a German but any member of the upper classes. Serfdom—particularly harsh along the Baltic—further solidified this distinction. While German landowners grew extremely rich off their captive labor force, their serfs remained desperately poor.

The Russians' conquest did nothing to change this. The czars looked on the German-Baltic nobles as a tremendous resource. They were wealthy, well connected, and willing to work directly for the throne, without the hang-ups about rights and privileges that Russian aristocrats sometimes brought to the job. As Czar Nicholas I (reigned 1825–55) once put it, the "Russian gentry serve the state, the German ones serve us."[26] This was a relationship that benefited both parties. Baltic

Germans staffed many of the highest positions in the imperial government and military. In return, they were given free rein to administer their home territories as they saw fit. The local Estonians and Latvians, meanwhile, were excluded both from imperial service and from local government. Their only way of seeking redress for their suffering was to rebel against their landlords—a prime reason why ethnic Latvians became some of the most ardent Bolsheviks after 1917.

Until the October Revolution, Latvia and Estonia proved relatively easy for the Russian Empire to govern. By contrast, the lands it took over from the Polish-Lithuanian Commonwealth were a headache from the beginning. The Polish lands were the largest and richest prize in Russia's western expansion. They were also the most difficult to manage.

Russia acquired its Polish territories at the end of the eighteenth century, by which point the Polish-Lithuanian Commonwealth was in its death throes. Weakened by corruption and self-dealing on the part of the Polish aristocracy, the electoral monarchy was no match for the rising powers that surrounded it. Between 1772 and 1795, the commonwealth's neighbors, Russia, Prussia, and the Habsburg empire, carved the country up between themselves over the course of three so-called "partitions." After the third partition, in 1795, nothing whatsoever was left of independent Poland-Lithuania.

Soon after the first partition of Poland, the philosopher Jean-Jacques Rousseau predicted that the country would be easier for Russia to swallow than to digest.[27] He was right. For the next 123 years, Russian-ruled Poland was home to innumerable conspiracies and revolutions aimed at restoring Polish independence. One of the first of these uprisings was led by Tadeusz Kościuszko, of American Revolutionary War fame, in 1794. After it failed, thousands of Poles emigrated to France to continue the struggle from there, while many of those who remained were stripped of their lands and possessions.

In spite of this defeat, the Polish rebellions kept coming. An armed revolt led by military cadets in 1830 (the November Uprising) ended in fiasco, as did another revolt (the January Uprising), which began in 1863 and lasted until 1864. My father's great-grandfather, a Polish Catholic from near Gniezno, fought in this one. In 1863 Jan Haremza, a free farmer, crossed the border from Prussia to Russian Poland to fight in the January Uprising. The campaign, doomed from the start, cost him his arm. When he came home to his farm, he was no longer able to hold a plow, and the family slowly starved, finally fleeing the countryside for the nearest town. My great-great-grandfather Haremza was lucky he wasn't sent to Siberia. Thousands of other Polish combatants were less fortunate. Over the decades of Russian rule, Siberia became the grave-yard of Polish national aspirations.

Poles began to be sent to Siberia even before the first partition of 1772. Over the next century and a half, tens of thousands of Poles would be exiled to the frozen, mosquito-filled immensity of the "sleeping land." Most arrived there through the *katorga*, a system by which convicts and rebels were brought to perform forced labor in remote locations from which there was no escape, at least in theory. The punishment began with the journey itself.

Prisoners usually walked to Siberia, bound by iron shackles. During the journey these chains never came off, not even in the *banya*. Groups of prisoners walking down Siberian roads made an unholy racket, with a hundred men or more rattling and tripping over their chains.[28] Along the way they stayed in cramped, smoke-filled shacks, teeming with bed-bugs. After such a voyage, work in a mine or lumberyard came as a relief. Indeed, for most *sybiraks*, boredom and homesickness proved harder to bear than forced labor.

Over time, however, the *katorga* strictures loosened. By the second half of the nineteenth century, rail and ship transport gradually replaced the long voyage on foot. Shackles were still used, but largely for show. Once prisoners were on board a train, car, or boat, they typically came off.[29] As labor demands from the state decreased, many exiles had time to devote to reading and other intellectual pursuits.

In fact, exile sometimes proved to have unexpected benefits. Thanks to the *katorga*, exiled Poles cultivated a centuries-long relationship with Siberia, doing much to develop it economically and scientifically. The first potatoes planted in Yakutia were brought there by a veteran of the 1863 rising. Other Polish *sybiraks* became leading students of native Siberian ways of life. Most of the early ethnographic and linguistic research on the Yakut or Sakha people was conducted by Poles. The same was true for the Ainu of Sakhalin.

Some Poles went to Siberia willingly. The Russian Empire was vast—it spanned fourteen time zones at its height—and offered its subjects multifarious opportunities. In the boom years of the 1880s and '90s, thousands of Balts, Poles, and Germans found careers across the rapidly industrializing Russian Empire. The modernist painter Kazimir Malevich's Polish parents settled in southern Ukraine to run a factory on a sugar beet plantation. Czesław Miłosz's father, from a down-on-their-luck noble family from Lithuania, found work building railways across the Russian Empire. He brought his wife and son with him everywhere from Riga to Semipalatinsk.

Still, not everyone from the former Polish lands was equally free to move around the empire. Jews in particular were severely restricted in regard to where they could settle and work. In most cases, their experience of the Russian Empire began with the partitions of Poland-Lithuania. Before the end of the eighteenth century, Russia had been home to very few Jews, and even anti-Jewish prejudices were rare. But in the territories it acquired from Poland and Lithuania, Jews represented a sizable minority of the population—upward of 20 percent in many places. Moreover, Jews dominated the commercial and social life of the many small towns and market villages, especially in the eastern part of the former commonwealth. As a group, they were enterprising, active, and hungry for commercial opportunities. They thus posed an obvious threat to Russia's urban merchants and craftsmen, whose positions were often hereditary and kept free from competition by guild and state law.

The Russian Empire's solution to this predicament was to keep the Jews in place. Jews were forbidden to settle outside the provinces that had formerly belonged to the Polish-Lithuanian Commonwealth.[30] This was the famous Pale of Settlement. When Catherine the Great established it in 1791, it simply confirmed the status quo: Jews were to remain where they were, and nothing more. Over time, however, the Pale became a pressure cooker. It was like a giant reservation: poor, overcrowded, and far from the centers of either commerce or culture. It was a place from which people wanted to flee—to America, to Palestine, or to Moscow. It was also the incubator of every major current of Jewish political and social radicalism.

For Jews, the Pale of Settlement came to be felt as a cage impeding their aspirations. It also created problems for the Russian Empire itself. One of the most basic was how to identify and track Jews in the first place—they rarely had last names and tended to be understandably wary of government officials like census-takers and tax officials. Like the Ottoman Empire before it, Russia had to teach itself to see like an empire. Confronted with its newly acquired Jews, it counted, classified, and named them, often from scratch. Indeed, a great proportion of contemporary Jewish last names—including my own—come from this great moment of stock-taking in the early nineteenth century.

Census-taking is an ambiguous enterprise. For most people, it was an imposition. Being counted meant being incorporated into a vast system of surveillance, regulation, and taxation. But over time, the meaning of those great imperial registers has changed. Today censuses are often the only extant trace of people who lived in Eastern Europe's three great empires. Over the years, I have come to love these punishingly dry documents, compiled without thought for the character or individuality of the people whose lives they marked down. I first became acquainted with them while trying to trace my own family's genealogy back into the nineteenth century. But when I began to work as a genealogical consultant for other people, I learned incomparably more.

Over the years, I've traced the fates of Czech cowherds, Belarusian cobblers, Dalmatian sailors, Lithuanian shopkeepers, Romanian doctors, and Hungarian winemakers. The documents they leave behind are prosaic, but fascinating. For me, even their physical textures are transporting. I've learned to enjoy perusing entries of the Austro-Hungarian census, arranged in twenty-four fastidious columns, recording their subjects' age, profession, religion, and significant possessions, down to every last rooster and calf. I've also taken patient delight in perusing the long, repetitive pronouncements of Russian notaries, written in eyeball-straining Cyrillic cursive, in which Jewish householders present their newborn children and make various excuses for not declaring them sooner.

From family lore, I know that the notaries could be fooled: my great-uncle Turnowski's grandparents bought their last name from the family of a dead Pole; they were really the descendants of a Drohobycz rabbi named Rudniewicz. Switching last names was a common means of avoiding the draft in Imperial Russia. A Russian soldier, once drafted, was required to serve for twenty-five years. In effect, this meant conscription for life. For Jews in the czar's service, it was very nearly a death sentence. Young men were willing to do almost anything to avoid this fate. As an old Yiddish song had it, "Better to study Torah with Rashi / Than to eat the army's kasha."[31]

Even more than the sudden, spectacular violence of pogroms, the waves of anti-Jewish rioting that swept through the Russian Empire at the turn of the nineteenth and twentieth centuries, the constant dread evoked by the draft propelled Jews to leave Russia for America. But they weren't alone in trying to dodge it. Other than Cossacks, who considered army service a hereditary duty, most of the peoples beholden to the czar saw the draft as a dreadful punishment and were willing to do almost anything to avoid it. Young Jewish men frequently starved, poisoned or even blinded themselves in one eye[32] in the hopes of gaining a deferral. In 1823 a group of five young men from Estonia had all their teeth pulled out so they could be ruled unfit for military service. Their deception was revealed, however, and each received twenty lashes on his back. Worst of all, they still had to join the army.[33]

Young Estonians and Jews were equally eager to avoid spending twenty-five long years serving the czar. This equality of suffering could even lead to a certain rough solidarity among the empire's peoples. In 1905, when Jacob Marateck, a Polish Jew from Warsaw, was sent to Manchuria to fight the Japanese, he found that the majority of his regiment consisted not of Russians but of "Poles, Jews, Ukrainians, Balts and even Germans, all of whom loved the Czar (as well as their Russian comrades) about as warmly as a chicken loves the fox."[34]

Jews, of course, suffered in an additional way, not shared by the rest of the conscripts. Life in the army made it impossible for them to follow their religious law. The army made no provision for keeping kosher or observing the Sabbath. The effect may have been even harder on their relatives. One young Jewish woman who grew up in Belarus wrote that just *seeing* her cousin drill on a Sabbath made her feel "unholy," as if she had sinned herself.[35]

Paradoxically, this was because the Russian army was one of the very few institutions in the empire predicated on a certain level of equal treatment. In almost every other respect, the Russian Empire presumed a virtually universal *inequality*. It treated everyone differently. Members of different social classes paid different taxes and were tried in different courts. Depending on one's ethnicity and faith, one could be subject to different privileges and penalties. In this patchwork system, discrimination was universal.

Although it may seem odd to us, such comprehensive discrimination had its advantages. One of the biggest was that it allowed for an unprecedented degree of religious toleration. In the Russian Empire, Christians, Muslims, Jews, Buddhists, and pagan animists all coexisted in a single state. They were free to follow their native faiths and, for the most part, didn't have to worry about missionaries. In this respect, Russia was more like the Ottoman Empire than any Western European state. Both realms were home to vast, multiethnic, and multireligious populations, and both relied on accentuating differences of class and estate to strengthen their rule.

These empires maintained their power by violence, but there was a certain wisdom to the way they were constructed. They possessed a flexibility, and an openness to diversity, that was lost to the nation-states that succeeded them. Here I must admit to stumbling sometimes. There is a parallax effect at work in observing empires. From a distance, the Ottoman Empire appears to have been a multifarious, fascinating place. But if I had lived in one of its subject lands, I might be writing about the "Turkish Yoke" and its "centuries of darkness." In the same way, from afar, the Russian Empire might seem to have been capacious and accommodating. But to me, it is a blinded eye, a toothless mouth, and a severed arm.

Habsburgs

In the history of Eastern European empires, the Habsburgs are a phenomenon unto themselves. Most dynasties rise to take control of a state and are then molded by it; the Habsburgs first declared themselves a dynasty and only afterward went looking for a state. How this family of German robber barons, despised in their native Switzerland, came not only to believe that they possessed a world-historical destiny, but actually to fulfill it, is one of history's greatest testimonies to the power of tenacious self-belief.

The Habsburgs made their start around the year 1000, as lords of an obscure county by the headwaters of the Rhine. Gradually, they came to possess ever more land in the neglected frontier region of the Holy Roman Empire that we now refer to as Austria. In the later Middle Ages, they used this not-very-important-or-prosperous home territory as a launching pad for ever more ambitious ventures. In 1440 a Habsburg, Frederick III, was elected Holy Roman emperor. A major selling point guiding his selection was that he appeared to be a harmless nonentity. A notably lazy and sluggish individual (his nickname was Erzschlafmütze, "Arch-Sleepyhead"), Frederick nonetheless declared that the Habsburg family motto should be *Austriae est imperare orbi universo,* or "Austria will inherit the whole world," and took the first steps to bring this about.

Frederick secured the election of his son Maximilian to the imperial throne; Maximilian then proceeded to marry his many children to some of the most eligible young monarchs in Europe. A series of lucky births and fortunately timed deaths subsequently placed Habsburgs on the thrones of Burgundy and Spain, which by then ruled parts of the New World and the Philippines. The Habsburgs were thus inaugurated as a genuine world power. A further lucky break came in 1526, when the king of Hungary died fighting the Ottomans at the Battle of Mohács. Only twenty at the time of his death, Louis II, who was also the elected king of Bohemia, left behind no legitimate heir. His Habsburg brother-in-law, Archduke Ferdinand, stepped in to fill both roles.

The Habsburgs would continue to rule over Hungary and Bohemia for the next four hundred years. They were more than mere carrion birds; they possessed a guiding idea of their family's predestination for greatness, even if the specifics of the mission they set for themselves changed several times over the course of their rule. First the Habsburgs fought the Ottoman Empire over Hungary, guarding Christendom from the Turks. Then they fought Protestantism on behalf of the Catholic Counter-Reformation. Finally the Thirty Years' War (1618–48) and the Czech revolt that sparked it gave them a reason to strip their wealthiest nobles of their land, laying the foundation for their future as absolute rulers.

But Habsburg absolutism was always more a theory of governance than an actual practice. Writing about it as it appeared in the seventeenth century, the historian R. J. W. Evans denied that the Habsburg realm was an empire at all, describing it rather as "a mildly centripetal agglutination of bewilderingly heterogeneous elements."[36] The Habsburg realms were simply too varied to accommodate a uniform system of rule.

Today, when the empire has long since ceased to exist, historians may best glimpse it in the *Kronprinzenwerk*, a twenty-four-volume encyclopedia of the monarchy compiled by 432 imperial employees, working under the direction of Crown Prince Rudolf prior to his death in 1889. In college, I used to descend to the library basement stacks to leaf through its dusty pages, letting myself be transported to another time by aquatints of Tyrolean villages and Carpathian weddings. This is the world captured retroactively by Joseph Roth in his 1938 novella *The Emperor's Tomb*, written during his long interwar exile in the hotels and drinking dens of Germany and France, where he recalled the empire's astonishing plenitude of human types:

> The gypsies of the Puszta, the Huzulen of Subcarpathia, the Jewish coachmen of Galicia . . . the Swabian tobacco growers from the Bacska, the horse breeders of the Steppes, the Osman Sibersna, the people of Bosnia and Herzegovina, the horse traders from the Hanakei in Moravia, the weavers from the Erzgebirge, the millers and coral dealers of Podolia: all these were the open-handed providers of Austria; and the poorer they were, the more generous.[37]

Seen from a speeding train, all this variety began to blur, and a certain underlying uniformity started to emerge. According to Roth, it could be spotted in the feathered hats and ocher helmets of policemen, the green sword knots on tax inspectors' sabers, "the red trousers of cavalrymen," the "blue uniform tunic and black saloon pants" of the infantry, and the "coffee-colored jackets of the artillery."[38] Across the empire, on every town square stood the same chestnut roasters, invariably Slovenian, and the same peddlers, typically Bosnian or Moravian, and when the church clock towers in those squares struck nine, they all played the same melody.

The Habsburg colors were black and gold, which is why the doors of all the imperial-and-royal tobacco stores were always painted in black and gold stripes, while the walls of all the empire's police stations, postal offices, and provincial train stations were painted the same yolky "imperial" yellow. Today, at the rail station in Przemyśl, an old cathedral town in Poland by the Ukrainian border, one can still see the remains of this infrastructural pomp. The old railway café, entirely done up in pink and pale gold, looks as if it were still ready to greet visitors waiting for the 12:04 train from Vienna. A painted panorama of the city, elegantly spread out on a hillside by the River San, hangs on the wall opposite the bar. It only takes a blink of the eyes to imagine its dining room full of Viennese coffees served alongside *Cremeschnittes,* Esterházy tortes, Pischinger cakes, and all the other confectionery delicacies pioneered in the long nineteenth century and whose continued presence in Eastern European pastry shops marks the true borders of the vanished realm known as Mitteleuropa.

Trains and tortes, however, were not enough to hold together a state that by 1914, shortly before its collapse, numbered over 50 million people. The empire needed laws as well. It gained them quite rapidly, first in the great burst of Enlightenment reform under Joseph II in the eighteenth century, and then again in the long, bright twilight under its last great emperor, Franz Joseph I. By the time of his death in 1916, Austria-Hungary enjoyed a working (though incredibly complex) constitution, universal male suffrage, and a meticulous code of civil law. Small crimes received small penalties. The punishment for stealing an onion was four hours in jail. Large crimes received great ones, but they were scrupulously applied. When he fired the shot that started the First World War, Gavrilo Princip was still a minor, by twenty-seven days. He therefore received the maximum allowable sentence of twenty years in prison. It was thanks to these laws that, of the three Eastern European empires, Austria-Hungary seemed the least "imperial," and the most humane.

It is also the empire most indissolubly associated with failure. Unlike Russia or the Ottomans, Austria-Hungary had no direct heirs to take up its legacy after Franz Joseph I passed. Except for the palaces and collections directly amassed by the Habsburgs themselves, all the cultural achievements of its peoples now seem to belong to someone else. The image of the empire that exists now in memory is a mixture of Kafka's bureaucratic nightmares and Robert Musil's fantastical *Kakania,* or "Shit-land." Opinions on this may be shifting, as they often do. Not long ago a historian of the Habsburgs told me that Austro-Hungarian scholars had recently done an about-face: they decided that the empire, despite not existing anymore, wasn't a failure—it was actually a success. They just couldn't prove it yet. The historian estimated it would take another ten years before they would know for sure.

Even in its heyday the Habsburg realm seemed less a nation than an elaborate legal fiction. In the absence of a shared language, religion, or history, it had little to bind its subject-citizens together other than the ruling family itself.

Franz Joseph I took over the empire in a moment of crisis, during the revolutionary fever of 1848, which threatened to end the monarchy for good. He was eighteen and ruled continuously until his death sixty-eight years later. Because of this, the empire became coterminous—especially in memory—with this one man. Generations grew old with him. They swam in the sea of his life. His family tragedies—which were numerous and sordid—became their own tragedies. Every citizen in the empire knew the story of his son Rudolf, his doomed romance with the seventeen-year-old parvenu Baroness Marie von Vetsera, and their mutual death by pistol shot in the cursed hunting lodge at Mayerling.

Rudolf seems to have convinced Vetsera to enter into a murder-suicide pact, for reasons that remain murky even today. Rudolf's death devastated Empress Elisabeth, Franz Joseph's wife, who met her own tragic end a few years later, stabbed through the heart by an Italian anarchist while strolling on a Swiss promenade. But many in the empire assumed that the fault for Rudolf's tragedy lay with his father, who wouldn't allow him to wed his true love, although the fact that Rudolf tried to entice *another* of his mistresses into the same pact rather negates this theory.

In popular memory, however, Rudolf began to seem like a romantic hero. To many Hungarians—never among Franz Joseph's greatest fans—Rudolf was the ideal prince, honor and justice personified. Some suspected that Franz Joseph had him killed because he loved Hungary *too* much.[39] Others were convinced that Rudolf was still alive, wandering in exile in America, waiting for his father to summon him home. Indeed, among the Ukrainians of Galicia, it was common knowledge that Rudolf was alive. He was either in Brazil[40] or roaming the Carpathian Mountains disguised as a Hutsul shepherd, visiting the poorest huts, giving out gifts, and scolding corrupt tax collectors.[41]

Crown Prince Rudolf inspired a cult, but Franz Joseph remained the center of a religion. To the writer Bruno Schulz, who came of age in the sleepy Galician town of Drohobycz in the last days of the empire, Franz Joseph seemed the guarantor of the world, a distant god who "squared the world like paper," setting down the proper attire for postmen and the correct color of a sunset.[42] Jaroslav Hašek, far more dubious of Habsburg power, treated the emperor with a good deal more skepticism. The Czech soldiers in *The Good Soldier Švejk,* his comic epic of the First World War, all assume that Franz Joseph had gone insane long before the war started, and that for this reason he could not be let out of the Schönbrunn Palace.

Franz Joseph was not an imaginative man, nor even a clever one, but neither was he the utter imbecile imagined by Hašek. He was, instead, a creature of habit. Every evening he dined alone on boiled beef, and every night he slept on an officer's iron bed. In summer he awoke at four a.m., and in winter at five. He worked all morning and all afternoon, pausing only to eat lunch and take a midday stroll. Lunch consisted of sausages with horseradish and a glass of brown ale. His stroll took exactly thirty minutes. He conducted it in his garden, which was reserved exclusively for him.[43]

In many ways, Franz Joseph's mind remained forever fixed at the moment of his coronation, past which point he seems not to have developed much. He liked to ride trains, since those existed in his youth, but he absolutely refused to engage with such innovations as the telephone, the elevator, or the motorcar. He thought automobiles "stank," and that bicycling was "an epidemic." A general since childhood, he adored the army—the slightest imperfection in an officer's uniform could send him into a rage—but he refused even to inspect his navy, since, as he put it, "he knew nothing about it." "In his world," wrote one historian, "there was no room for a conversation between equals, and nothing could be more dangerous than sarcasm, or more likely to undermine one's authority."[44]

Franz Joseph was an excellent rider, a bad lover, a god in the provinces, and a bourgeois at home. He loved soldiers and uniforms but had no mind for strategy. He believed in power but not in politics. He was polite, hardworking, reliable, dull, and vastly tolerant. Unlike his heirs, or his rivals, he resisted the urge to become German. He remained, until his dying day, an emperor for all his peoples, even those who disliked him: "it made no difference to him," observed István Deák, "whether his subject was German, Hungarian or Slav, so long as the subject did his duty."[45] He accepted the blessings of Catholic priests, Galician rabbis, and Bosnian imams with equal grace. Somehow this was enough to hold his empire together through the high winds of late-nineteenth-century nationalism—though in the end, the price of keeping it all together may have been a world war.

Toward the end of Franz Joseph's life, his every cough and sniffle was front-page news. By then, he was both a god and a laughingstock. Never one to trust in popularity, throughout his life he did not attempt to charm or entertain. He believed wholeheartedly in the innate greatness of the throne. His task, as he saw it, was to occupy it devotedly, unflinchingly, untiringly.

Service had a way of erasing national boundaries. Over generations, Austrian officers came to constitute a caste above—or beyond—nationality. No matter where they came from originally, the army became their truest homeland. In his 1935 novel *Salt of the Earth*, Józef Wittlin presented a portrait of one such imperial servant, Regimental Sergeant-Major Rudolf Bachmatiuk, chief instructor of a regiment of Galician infantry. His job was to take raw, unlettered recruits—a mob of Ruthenian cowherds and Jewish rag-pickers—and mold them into efficient, honorable soldiers. Christened by his Ukrainian parents after Franz Joseph's only son, Bachmatiuk had long since ceased identifying with anything outside the dynasty. A Ukrainian by birth, "in the course of many years of military service his nationality had dissolved and merged into the black-yellow breed. He had become entirely Austrian."[46]

Officers of the Habsburg army lived in two worlds at once. One was the modern world of duty, consisting of drills, watches, and artillery emplacements. The other was the universe of honor, where they lived like medieval knights, expected to draw their sword at the slightest insult that could besmirch their honor or, by extension, that of the army as a whole. These two realms could impinge on each other at the most inopportune times. Insults that merited a duel—in fact, that *required* one—could be trifling indeed. They included calling someone a liar; failing to greet a lady in the company of a gentleman; pushing someone on board a tram; staring at someone while playing with a dog whip; or just looking at someone arrogantly. An insult to a lady had to be corrected immediately by one of her male friends or relatives, but insults *between* ladies held no such gravity—only men could challenge each other's honor. When an officer's honor was under attack, he was required to render immediate correction, preferably with a sword. Therefore an officer had to carry his sword on his person at all times. Furthermore, because only an officer in uniform was entitled to defend his honor, students of dueling argued, officers should never appear in a public place in civilian clothes—least of all in cafés, where hostile civilians were known to gather and where insults were especially common.

It was not just the pressures of dueling that separated officers from the average run of life. Officers could not get married without regimental approval. Even then, they had to put an enormous amount of money into obtaining a bond called a *Kaution*. Those without capital—which was incredibly hard to amass on an officer's salary—were doomed to remain single. So most officers remained unmarried and found solace in bordellos or in affairs with the daughters of town burghers and the wives of their fellow officers. They could also expect to be posted to the farthest-flung regions of the empire. Hungary was generally thought to be uncivilized and dirty, but its women were said to be beautiful, and its people knew how to throw a party. Croatia and Transylvania were like Hungary, only worse. Bosnia was barbaric but exotic. Bukovina was desirable on account of its rich cultural life. Galicia—filled with mud, lice, and conceited Poles—was reputed to be the worst posting of all.

In these remote outposts, boredom was a constant worry, as was the money it took to relieve it. Many officers found themselves sinking into debt from their efforts to escape the tedium of provincial life. Of course, a more desirable posting to the capital carried temptations of its own. Meanwhile the need to equip and dress themselves properly weighed heavily on many officers of modest means. The army provided neither uniforms nor horses to its officers free of charge. Serving in the cavalry was ruinously expensive, but serving even in the infantry and artillery could be a strain.

Latter-day knights, the officers of the Austro-Hungarian Empire were creatures apart. Purposefully so; they were meant to have as little to do as possible with local identity or civilian morality. They had neither ethnicity nor family. To mark officers' difference from their surroundings, the emperor and his generals made sure it was signaled in their costumes. Officers were birds of bizarre and splendid plumage. The price could be exorbitant.

The uniforms of its officers were the pride of the Austro-Hungarian army. Their sheer, stark white fabric, when properly maintained through assiduous brushing, gave off a delicate, light-blue shimmer. They were very beautiful—and very costly. Officers routinely went deep into debt to afford them. To pay off their debt, they ate only bread and went without firewood in winter. The uniforms had to be kept spotless; the slightest wear or spot would bring a reprimand, and the need to buy a new one, at crippling expense.

One day in the 1850s, one of the emperor's generals, a certain Count Gyulai (who, according to one historian, a fellow Hungarian, was "a martinet of the worst sort" and "indisputably stupid"),[47] required every officer in his army to sport a black mustache. Blonder officers could achieve this transformation only with copious amounts of black shoe polish. That day the officers assembled with their troops on the parade ground. As they stood at attention with their soldiers, waiting for inspection, it began to rain. The black shoe polish ran down from their mustaches onto their white uniforms. The uniforms were ruined, as were the officers.

What expense! What useless waste! But maybe it wasn't so useless after all. Franz Joseph's seemingly mad obsession with uniforms and parade punctilio hid a deeper wisdom: the knowledge that his empire was little more than a very fancy, very expensive, and only occasionally bloody charade. It was a kind of play, in which costumes were just about the most important part. The emperor knew from bitter first-hand experience that, especially when force of arms failed, one had to rely on élan alone to keep the performance going.

In 1867, during a war with Prussia, the empire suffered a terrible, crippling defeat. Its military was humiliated. Afterward its provinces grew restless. Some threatened to rebel, and there was no army left to stop them. Papering over the crisis required establishing a new constitution, one that granted many regions wide autonomy. Hungary was transformed from a province into a separate kingdom, whose king just happened to be the Austrian emperor. This was the origin of the so-called Dual Monarchy, or Austria-Hungary. To make the arrangement official, Franz Joseph had to go to Budapest to be crowned, this time as king rather than as emperor.

Ancient Hungarian custom, suddenly revived for this occasion, required kings to appear before the assembled people, in the open air, and salute the four cardinal directions with their sword of office. In 1867 this performance was to be done atop a mound of soil collected from all the provinces of Hungary. To the alarm of everyone present, the emperor decided to ride up the steep slope of this artificial hill at full gallop, golden sword of Saint Stephen in hand. His horse, a gray charger, became spooked by the cheering crowd and the blasts of celebratory cannon-shot and reared up four times. Spectators thought the steed, foaming and terrified, was about to vault over the balustrades and into the square below. But Franz Joseph, a superb horseman, managed to keep it in check with a single, masterful gesture.

Forty-nine years later, after Franz Joseph finally succumbed to death, it was time for his grand-nephew Karl to receive the Hungarian crown. Even though it was the middle of the First World War, he too had to go to Budapest and salute the four directions from atop a steed with his sword. A much worse rider than his granduncle, poor Karl was unable to mount a horse without the help of a footstool. Miklós Bánffy, a Transylvanian aristocrat, politician, and brilliant novelist who was then serving as head of the Budapest theaters, was asked to coordinate the coronation. Bánffy knew that a stool would make a ludicrous impression on a Hungarian audience, so he resorted to a bit of stagecraft: a tiny staircase concealed behind a wall next to the grandstand. By this means, the diminutive emperor-king could be conveyed to the summit of a horse's hindquarters without suffering undue embarrassment.[48]

Postcard with Emperor Franz Joseph I, 1908.

Two years later, when the war ended with Austria-Hungary's defeat, no footstool remained for poor Karl. Rioting soldiers, returned from the front, filled the streets of Vienna. People were calling for a republic or the dissolution of the empire into its constituent parts. There was talk of storming the Schönbrunn Palace. Karl seemed ready to acquiesce to the protesters' demands, but he also wanted to hang on to the throne. But in this wish he was alone. The great aristocrats, the high priests of the clergy, and the chieftains among the bureaucracy had all abandoned him. Inside the palace, only a group of teenage cadets, press-ganged from a nearby military academy, were left to defend Karl from the mob.[49] His royal bodyguard, the magnificently costumed Arcièren, Trabanten, and Hungarian Noble Guards, drawn from the highest nobility and sworn to defend their emperor to the death, were nowhere to be found.[50] Karl was forced to flee. The empire was over, and all its beautiful birds had flown home.

6

Peoples

Two women from Shkodër, Albania, 1921.
Two Hungarian men, 1900.

Eastern Europe is a very complicated place. In 1937 Eleanor
Perényi discovered this very abruptly when she suddenly
became the mistress of a crumbling Baroque castle in the
shadow of the Carpathian Mountains. Eleanor was an American (née
Stone), born and raised in Washington, D.C. Her mother was a novelist
and her father served in the navy. One night in Budapest, while traveling through Europe with her parents, she met a handsome and charming Hungarian nobleman who spoke near-perfect English. A few weeks
later they were married.

Thus, at only nineteen, Eleanor landed in what was then Czechoslovakia. Her home there was surrounded by countless acres of beautiful forest and some of Central Europe's northernmost vineyards. Zsiga, her husband, was its baron. As the new baroness, Eleanor was expected to manage the harvest, tend the gardens, furnish her apartments, stock the kitchen, and do countless other jobs that go into the managing of a great—and cash-strapped—estate. This, in turn, meant navigating a human landscape of remarkable complexity.

The corner of land where Eleanor found herself had originally belonged to Hungary. After the First World War, it was briefly occupied by Romania, then fell under Czechoslovak control. (It is now in Ukraine.) Czech power in the district was represented by a single morose Moravian grocer and a local official named Hlaváček, who seems to have been a spy. Official business was conducted not in Czech but in German. Aside from a few Romanians, most of the farmworkers on Eleanor's estates were Ruthenian, as were most of the peasants in the district. They were Orthodox Christians who spoke a language similar to Ukrainian.

To Eleanor, the Ruthenians appeared to be an "undependable, dreamily fatalistic" people who "believed in werewolves and Draculas" and were overly fond of denatured alcohol.[1] Some of her antipathy to the Ruthenians may have been related to a mishap. While she and Zsiga were driving in the mountains, their car accidentally hit a cow. A group of angry Ruthenian men surrounded their car, yelling insults. At this point, a tiny old Jewish man with a white beard bobbed up at her side and said, in perfect Brooklynese, "Listen lady, ya bedda get outta here. Dese guys is awful tough."[2]

The Jews of Vinohradiv did more than remind Eleanor of New York. They had their place in the local social fabric too. When Eleanor needed basic provisions, she went to the Moravian grocer, but for anything out of the ordinary, she had to appeal to Fried, the Perényi family's house Jew. For centuries, all noble clans in Hungary kept one of these useful individuals on hand. Officially Fried was an upholsterer, but really he was a jack-of-all-trades who could accomplish anything from arranging a business deal to finding a rare rug for the parlor. He knew Hungarian but thought it was déclassé and preferred to speak to Eleanor in German, even though she hardly spoke it herself.

As the title of his office implies, Fried made house calls, but there were some jobs that even he couldn't handle. When Eleanor decided to build a brick wall for her garden, she discovered, to her great surprise, that only the Roma could do it. In other parts of Eastern Europe, Roma worked, among other things, as specialist coppersmiths, horse traders, and fortune tellers, but in this corner of the Carpathians, their three main occupations were playing the violin, digging privies, and baking bricks.[3] Why? Because it had always been so.

This kaleidoscopic patterning of languages, professions, and castes structured life in Eastern Europe. Where empires tried, and failed, to impose some kind of uniformity, at least at the level of administration, tradition conspired to create a society of almost infinite heterogeneity. The resulting mixture of peoples and faiths was often puzzling for outsiders, but it could pose challenges to locals as well. Merely to be born a Pole in the valley of the Dniester River was a source of end-less confusion and complication, as the great essayist Jerzy Stempowski reminds us. Born in 1894, Stempowski grew up in what is now central Ukraine, surrounded by a landscape of rapturous diversity. Decades later, exiled to Switzerland, he tried to recapture some of this profusion from memory and, in the process, found a template for an entirely dif-ferent Europe from the one he was living in:

> The whole immense part of Europe lying between the Baltic Sea, the Black Sea and the Adriatic was a single giant chess-board of peoples, full of islands, enclaves and the most pecu-liar combinations of ethnic mixtures. In many places, every village, every social group, every profession almost spoke a separate language. In the middle Dniester valley of my youth, landowners spoke Polish, peasants, Ukrainian, and bureaucrats, Russian, but with an Odessa accent. Merchants spoke Yiddish, while carpenters and cabinetmakers, as Filip-pians and members of the Old Believer sect, spoke Russian, but with a Novgorod accent, while the *kabannicy* swineherds spoke a vernacular of their own. Besides these, in this region there were still villages of petty nobility speaking Polish, villages of the same nobility speaking Ukrainian, Moldo-van villages speaking Romanian, Gypsies speaking Gypsy, and Turks, who, although absent, still left their mark in the

minarets standing in Kamianets-Podilskyi and at Khotyn on the other side of the Dniester. Ferrymen on the Dniester still called the Podolian side of the river Lech-land and the Bessarabian side Turk-land, even though there both Poland and Turkey belonged to the rather distant past.[4]

How to account for this wondrous and mystifying mélange? Stempowski's answer had to do with nations and states. In the West, he wrote, the equation between ethnic and linguistic belonging and political allegiance began very early. Western rulers worked hard to homogenize their states. Beginning in the Middle Ages, priests and prelates imposed their particular strands of Christianity on the populations, executing heretics and unbelievers. Meanwhile kings expelled their Jews and confiscated their property. If a realm contained Muslims, they were likewise forced to convert or were banished. By the nineteenth century, national belonging replaced religion as the dominant template to be imposed on society. Little armies of bureaucrats and educators fanned out into the countryside, making sure that all the people there spoke the same language. Across the territory conquered by the French kings, peasants were *made* into French people, and if the Scots didn't concurrently become English, they certainly adopted the English language. Virtually everywhere, the machinery of the state worked like a giant steamroller, ironing out differences wherever they could be found.

In all these regards, Eastern Europe was different. There empires tended to *accentuate* difference rather than suppress it. In the Balkans, the Ottoman Empire offered many Christians and Jews a wide measure of autonomy, allowing them to manage their own affairs. The Russian Empire, Stempowski's birthplace, afforded religious minorities an even greater degree of freedom. The Habsburg empire did its best to impose Catholicism on its various peoples, especially the rebellious Czechs, but even so, it remained home to numerous Orthodox Christians and Jews. More importantly, the Habsburgs made hardly any effort to turn their various constituent peoples (around 1900 the empire was home to eleven official nationalities) into Germans. These empires took a laissez-faire approach to governing. They taxed and counted their subjects, but they did not intervene too deeply in the inner structure of their communities. In this respect, the rival empires were like battleships fighting in the Pacific: they clashed with one another on the water's surface. Meanwhile, far below, coral reefs of psychedelic complexity grew undisturbed.

This relatively hands-off style of rule practiced by the Eastern European empires was born of pragmatism. Social divisions were not a flaw to be overcome but a tool to be used. In these realms, universal citizenship did not exist. People lived not as individuals but as parts of wider social estates, each of which came with its own set of privileges and prohibitions. Everyone was discriminated against to some extent, except for the sultan or czar. Everyone also had a function. To most people, before the arrival of modernity, the idea of equality before the law was unthinkable. What mattered most in life was to be allowed to fulfill their role undisturbed. Meanwhile what mattered most to rulers was that the sum total of these various roles added up to them staying in power. For this, outsiders could be just as useful as locals and often showed themselves to be more dependable.

The process of inviting helpful strangers into Eastern Europe began very early. Eastern European monarchs began looking abroad for talent in the Middle Ages. Compared to Western Europe, the East was underpopulated, lacking cities and the specialized craftsmen and traders who inhabited them. Eastern rulers also sat uneasily on the intersection of multiple frontiers: between pagan and Christian, Christian and Muslim, and Catholic and Orthodox. Because of this, they needed all the help they could get cultivating, defending, and administering their realms. In the eleventh century, a Hungarian king lectured his son about the usefulness of immigrants:

> As guests come from various areas and lands, so they bring with them various languages and customs, various examples and forms of armament, which adorn and glorify the royal court. . . . For a kingdom of one language and one custom is weak and fragile. Therefore, my son, I order that you should feed them with goodwill and honor them so that they will prefer to live with you rather than inhabit any other place.[5]

The young prince took his father's advice to heart. By the thirteenth century, the kingdom of Hungary harbored, within its fragile borders, groups of Jews, Muslims, Armenians, Slavs, Italians, Franks, Spaniards, and Germans. Jews and Muslims all worked together in the royal mints. Muslims also provided a bodyguard of skilled lancers. Germans supplied the royal army with heavy cavalry. Perhaps most exotically, whole tribes of Turkic-speaking Cumans manned the kingdom's eastern frontiers. The Cumans had arrived in Hungary from the steppes, as refugees from the Mongol onslaught of the 1240s. Pagans, they practiced shamanism, buried their warriors along with their horses, and swore oaths over the bodies of dismembered dogs. They were strange bedfellows for a Christian king, and the pope wrote several strongly worded letters of protest, but such was life in the borderlands—sometimes you had to fight nomads with nomads.

Like the Cumans, the Lipka Tatars, another steppe people, arrived in Poland-Lithuania as refugees. After their khan, Tokhtamysh, picked an ill-advised fight with Tamerlane, which he lost, in 1395, his entire horde appeared in Lithuania, seeking protection. Grand Duke Vytautas welcomed them and allowed them to keep their Muslim faith. In return, the Tatars pledged to support him in his wars. For centuries, the Tatars were renowned as some of the Polish-Lithuanian Commonwealth's best cavalry fighters. Most lived on small rural farms; it is still possible to see their wooden mosques, painted in lovely shades of yellow and green, in out-of-the-way villages scattered across the territory where Poland, Lithuania, and Belarus meet.

On a visit to the cemetery of the Tatar settlement of Kruszyniany, on the Polish side of the border, I walked past gravestones engraved in a mix of Latin, Cyrillic, and Arabic script. Some of the oldest headstones, dating back to the eighteenth century and sheltered by the tallest pines, were still topped with the silver crescent of Islam. Across the street, a massive new hotel and restaurant complex catered to tour buses of Polish tourists looking for a taste of what has sadly become little more than an exotic memory.

Tatars weren't only a rural minority, however. In the sixteenth century, they also settled in towns, above all in the Lithuanian capital of Vilnius, where they worked as tanners and butchers and fishermen. The Tatar district was purposefully kept outside the city walls, in a suburb called Łukiszki. Unlike Muslims in virtually every other part of the world, the Vilnius Tatars had no muezzin; instead, in imitation of local

Jewish custom, they relied on a town crier, who wandered the streets summoning the faithful to prayer.[6]

This crier would have had to raise his voice very high in order to be heard over the din of the city, for in those days Vilnius was a true Tower of Babel. In addition to Tatars, it was home to Poles, Lithuanians, Germans, Ruthenians, and Jews. Each of these groups spoke a different language and worshipped in a different temple. In the seventeenth century, in addition to a mosque and a synagogue, the city was home to churches belonging to five different denominations—an extraordinary total for a town of only twenty thousand people, all the more so in an age of religious war.

The situation in Vilnius was mirrored by that in Poland-Lithuania as a whole. Generations of kings and dukes had followed Vytautas's lead in welcoming useful foreigners to the commonwealth. One early invitation backfired spectacularly. In 1226 Duke Konrad of Mazovia invited the Teutonic Knights to help him fend off the Baltic pagans. They agreed, stayed, and eventually conquered most of the northern Baltic Coast—and thus became Poland's mortal enemies in the process. As a result of this policy of openness however, Poland-Lithuania became one of the most diverse countries in Europe.

But the true source of Poland's diversity was neither a royal plan nor a grand design. Rather, it was the product of a kind of benign neglect. In the sixteenth and seventeenth centuries, while the rest of Europe was convulsed by the wars brought about by the Reformation, Poland stayed largely above the fray. Before it was swallowed up by its neighbors at the end of the eighteenth century, the commonwealth became a haven for dissidents and dissenters of every stripe—New England on the Vistula. In fact, this was not the only way in which Poland-Lithuania resembled the Americas. In the seventeenth century, unlike most of Western Europe, the commonwealth was still home to vast tracts of forest, still waiting to be cut down and farmed. For this reason, aurochs and European bison survived longer in Poland than anywhere else on the continent.

In the eighteenth and nineteenth centuries, Eastern Europe stood sharply apart from Western Europe in having multiple areas that were still in the process of being settled. Usually these territories were "open," so to speak, on account of having been depopulated by war. Imperial frontiers were home to endemic conflicts. The worst of these clashes occurred on the fringes of Islamic territory—especially the northern edges of the Ottoman Empire and the Crimean Khanate, itself an Ottoman vassal nestled on the northern shores of the Black Sea.

As both of these powers began to decline, their Christian rivals seized many of their territories. In 1716 Austria took the Banat, a region covering parts of today's northern Serbia and western Romania, from the Ottomans. In 1774 it added Bukovina, presently split between Romania and Ukraine. At the time of their acquisition, both territories were ravaged by war and plague and terribly depopulated. In the eyes of its new masters, the Banat was home to no more than a thin smattering of Serbian shepherds. Bukovina, memorably, if unfairly, described by the British historian A.J.P. Taylor as a "meaningless fragment of territory for which there could be no rational explanation," seemed similarly barren. When Bukovina was first annexed, a Czech journalist in Lviv wondered aloud what the emperor was going to do with the "animals in human form" he had thereby inherited.[7]

A century later this question would have been unthinkable. By then, both Bukovina and the Banat were as much a part of Austria-Hungary as Moravia or the Tyrol. Their capitals, Czernowitz (now Chernivtsi in Ukraine, but Cernăuți when it was part of Romania between the world wars), and Temesvár, were among the empire's most cosmopolitan cities. Though far from the imperial/national centers of Vienna and Budapest, both were home to modern, metropolitan pleasures. Temesvár was the first city in Europe to be illuminated by electric lights, and Czernowitz boasted of one of the empire's finest universities. At the Kaiser Café, Czernowitzers drank real Bohemian pilsner and read German-language newspapers from Lviv, Prague, and Vienna, only a day or two out of date. As in Vienna, Czernowitz's cafés were populated by a multitude of writers, many of them Jewish, who helped to make the city a great incubator of German- and Yiddish-language literature.

Like Odessa, Galați, and other cities that mushroomed in the less-populated borderlands of Eastern Europe in the nineteenth century, Czernowitz and Temesvár were largely built on immigration. Bukovina's abundant land attracted neighboring Ukrainians and Romanians, as well as migrants of German, Hungarian, Polish, Slovak, and Jewish origin. By 1900 Bukovina was one of the most diverse places in all of Europe, one of the few where no single language or religious tradition could claim a majority of the population. Because of this, it was said that in Czernowitz, hotel concierges had to be fluent in five languages just to keep up with the local clientele.

As for the Banat, over the course of the eighteenth century, it was settled by hardy German Catholic farmers from Swabia, sent there as part of a colonization effort sponsored by Empress Maria Theresa of Austria. They were soon joined by Christian refugees from the Ottoman Empire, among them Romanians, Bulgarians, and Serbs, as well as peasant settlers of Hungarian, Czech, Slovak, and Ruthenian extraction from the Habsburg empire itself. For a moment in the eighteenth century, the Banat was even home to a colony of dyspeptic Catalan insurrectionaries. By the end of the nineteenth century, population maps of the region looked like a painting by Joan Miró: that is to say, a classic Eastern European jumble.

Temesvár, renamed Timişoara when it became part of independent Romania after World War I, was where that mess found its form. According to Victor Neumann, the city's leading historian, Timişoara was a genuine melting pot, a place of countless mixed marriages, where conversations constantly shifted between different languages, sometimes within the span of a single sentence. The feeling of intercultural harmony that suffused the waning days of the Habsburg empire lasted right up until World War II. It could be seen in Timişoara's cosmopolitan orchestra, its many trilingual newspapers, and above all in its incomparable soccer team, the triumphant Ripensia FC.

In the 1930s Ripensia was the greatest soccer club in Romania. It repeatedly won the national championships and became a star on the European stage. It was also a symbol. At a time when soccer clubs tended to be segregated by religion and nationality, Ripensia's roster included players of German, Romanian, Hungarian, Jewish, and Serbian ancestry. During matches, they worked together seamlessly, as a fluid dynamic whole. According to Neumann, a great booster for the club, even seventy years on, Ripensia's success sent a message to the rest of Romania about the spirit of the city, its "spirit of cooperation," and the "inherited pacifist values" that lay beneath it all.

—

It is easy to fall into nostalgia when discussing the diversity of Eastern Europe before the world wars, and to romanticize its multiplicity of languages, faiths, and cultures as a lost Eden. But "melting pots" like Timişoara were rare. Much more common was the situation that prevailed in Czernowitz, where, though people might have lived side by side, sports teams remained segregated along strictly ethnic lines: Germans, Ukrainians, Romanians, and Poles all had their own teams. The Jews had two—one Zionist (Maccabi), and one not (Hakoah).

The supporters of the main German club, Jahn, were notably anti-Semitic, but none of these clubs particularly liked one other.[8] Indeed, according to one chronicler of Czernowitz's sporting history, by the 1920s all the teams were engaged in an "intricate feud" that would last the rest of the decade.[9] Occasionally, the tensions erupted into outright violence. In 1926 fans of the Jahn Athletic Club caused a near-riot when Hakoah seemed about to beat them in a league cup semifinals match. They invaded the pitch, causing the referees to suspend play. When the players returned after an interval, they found that the field had been turned into a moonscape of craters and pickax holes. A subsequent police investigation discovered that an engineer in a nearby factory had sent four of his workers to destroy the pitch to keep the Jews from going to the finals.

Intricate feuds, like those that bedeviled the activities of the Czernowitz Athletic Association, were a frequent occurrence in Eastern Europe.[10] In most places, segmentation, rather than integration, tended to be the rule. During times of peace, such divisions could manifest in a spirit of healthy rivalry. In the small towns of Slovakia's German-dominated Spiš region, Germans, Jews, Slovaks, and Hungarians all had their own soccer, tennis, and hockey clubs. Target shooting, however—perhaps because it was an individual sport—tended to be integrated. In Sarajevo, the spirit of competition was channeled above all into musical performance. By 1905 all the city's major ethnic groups had their own choral societies. The Serbian Sloga, the Croatian Trebević, and the Ladino-speaking (and -singing) Sephardic Jewish La Lira choirs all tried to outdo one another in putting on the city's best concerts. The Bosnian Muslim El-Kamer club, primarily a bicycling and gymnastic association, doubled as a vocal group and organized recitals as well as races.

Such partitioning according to ethnicity extended far beyond voluntary associations and clubs. Across Eastern Europe, cities themselves were often segmented, divided into separate quarters according to language and religion. In Ottoman Monastir, Muslims lived in the garden-strewn north of the city, Christians lived in the more overbuilt south, while Jews occupied a warren of narrow streets across the river from all the rest. In Elbasan, Albania, the population lived in three concentric circles, with Christian Albanians in the center, surrounded by an inner ring of Muslim Albanians and an outer ring of Christian Vlachs.

Dvinsk (now Daugavpils), a river port in eastern Latvia, was similarly divided into an inner town and its suburbs. The center city belonged to Germans, Russians, and Poles. The outskirts were home to Old Believers—Russians who had broken with the official Orthodox Church—Jews, and Roma, some of whom worked together as *borisniks,* or brokers in the sale of stolen horses. Latvians—that is, Latvian-speaking peasants—lived exclusively in the countryside and came into town only to sell food in the marketplace.[11]

This diversity had a fractal quality, as patterns of division that structured entire provinces reappeared at the level of cities and towns. Around 1900 the little town of Hvizdets (Polish Gwoździec), famous for its splendidly painted wooden synagogue (now lost, though a reconstruction is now in the Polin Museum in Warsaw), was home to about 2,400 people. They were divided into four quite separate neighborhoods, one each for Ukrainians, Poles, Germans, and Jews.[12]

Time and again a traveler in Eastern Europe would find that people lived together but apart. Barriers of class—usually reinforced by differences in faith and language—worked together to create patterns of inclusion and exclusion that reached down to the smallest village. Around 1900 Verbivtsi, a tiny hamlet not far from Hvizdets in southwestern Ukraine, was home to about 150 families. Four of them were Jewish; the rest were Ukrainian. The Ukrainians were all peasant farmers and lived in roughly built huts covered in thatch. The Jews ran Verbivtsi's only shops—really just a couple of market stalls—as well as a little tavern, leased from the nobleman who owned the village. This nobleman was a Pole and a Catholic. He lived a little outside Verbivtsi itself, in a manor house on top of one of the two hills next to the village. An Orthodox church, patronized by his Ukrainian tenants, stood atop the other one.

Verbivtsi was a very small place, but the distance between the thatch-covered huts on the plain and the manor house on the hill was very great indeed. In the words of Alexander Granach, who grew up in Verbivtsi before leaving to make a career as an actor on the Berlin stage, the Pole's house, with its whitewashed walls and flower beds, was part of another world. No one from the landlord's manor mixed with the people of Verbivtsi, not even his servants. As Poles, they spoke a different language and worshipped at a different church. They also dressed differently, in rubber boots and gloves, and ate different foods such as white bread, which was otherwise unknown in the village. The gulf had another dimension too: on the rare occasions when the landowner's children drove by Verbivtsi in their carriage, they "looked down at us crossly and haughtily . . . just as their father looked down on the village."[13]

In Verbivtsi, as in all of Eastern Europe, the separation across cultures and across class, between peasants and their landlords, was reinforced by habit, custom, and myth. Crossing these borders could have terrible results. An eighteenth-century Baltic German pastor observed that local German landowners would "feel humiliated if they had to sit down at the same table" with one of their Latvian or Estonian serfs.

Serfdom in the Baltic countries was exceptionally harsh. The German law of *Hausrecht* permitted estate owners to beat their serfs with any of twenty selected implements. On the manor, the owner's word was law. Almost every Latvian and Estonian peasant family "had a story of drudgery, flogging, and hand-kissing" to tell. Those memories died hard. The Baltic Germans at least shared a faith—Lutheranism—with their tenants, but even there, the gulf made itself known. Peasants and nobles attended separate church services, segregated by language and estate.

In much of Eastern Europe, landlords and tenants differed either in language or in religion. In the Czech lands, German-speaking Catholics had Slavic-speaking tenants, while in Hungary, Slovaks worked for Magyar-speakers. In Bosnia, Slavic-speaking Muslim noblemen employed squads of equally Slavic-speaking Orthodox Christian serfs. Sometimes groups differed in religion as well as language. In what was once eastern Poland, Catholic Poles ruled over Orthodox Ukrainians and Belarusians. Likewise in Transylvania, Catholic and Calvinist Hungarians owned lands farmed by Orthodox Romanians.

Separated by class, language, and creed, landlords and peasants seldom mingled. Often they barely seemed to share the same world—or afterlife. When Romanian peasants in Transylvania painted the Judgment of Heaven and Hell on the walls of their lovely wooden churches, they pictured themselves in the role of the saved. And they made all the sinners look like their Hungarian landlords.[14] Similarly, many Latvian and Estonian folksongs locate their German masters in Hell, tossed into vats of boiling pitch as a punishment for making their servants "dance on the end of a cane."[15]

Often the differences between owners and owned appeared so great that mythology was called upon to explain it. Polish noblemen in the seventeenth century believed they were descended from Noah's blessed son Japheth, while their serfs came from his cursed son Cham, whose name still means "boor" in Polish. But the Poles' Ukrainian and Belarusian tenants had a different explanation for what separated them. According to an old Ukrainian legend, God fashioned the various types of human beings (Muscovite, French, etc.) out of clay, but when it came time to make Poles, He ran out of dirt and had to use bread dough instead. God's dog immediately ate the first Pole, so God had to remake Poles from its vomit. According to an equivalent Belarusian tale, God's dog shat the dough out, so the work of making Polish landlords had to begin there.[16]

Peasants worked, while nobles profited—that was the rule throughout the Europe of the ancien régime. This type of feudalism generated tensions anywhere it was practiced, but in Eastern Europe, they were sharpened by the fact that the gulf between castes was made to appear as a gap between cultures. This is why later nationalist conflicts were so bitter and hard to resolve, for when one people owned the land, and another worked it—who deserved to inherit the state? But for all the animosity the system generated, it was predicated on a certain symbiosis, however unequal.

In the mid-eighteenth century, the Ottoman traveler and statesman Ahmed Resmî Efendi described how this system worked in Poland-Lithuania. The Polish nobles held two groups under their sway:

Ukrainians and Jews. Each contributed something different to the kingdom: the Ukrainians "were responsible for heavy work like agriculture,
while the Jews were in charge of buying and selling, and of customs
duties and taxes." The Poles, meanwhile, profited from the work of
both and "busied themselves with the pleasures of life."[17]

It was an ancient arrangement, one that far outlasted the commonwealth itself: a tripartite division of society into those who owned, those
who farmed, and those who sold. This third group—the merchants—
were a necessity, for peasants and landlords could not exist in a vacuum.
They needed someone to bring goods from the wider world outside the
village and to market the peasants' surplus abroad. Often these intermediaries belonged to a group of outsiders, differing from both peasants
and landlords in their religion and language. The Ashkenazi Jews of
Poland, Slovakia, Hungary, Moldova, and the Pale of Settlement are
the paradigmatic example of such an outgroup. In Bulgaria, Macedonia,
southern Romania, and Bosnia, Sephardic Jews played a similar role.

But it wasn't only Jews who bought and traded. In sections of the
Balkans, it was Greeks and Činčars (or Aromanians) who dominated
commerce, while Germans did the same in much of Croatia, Slovenia,
and Bohemia. For a time, in Poland, Scots were prominent as merchants
and peddlers, to the point that Scotophobia became a definite, if tem-
porary, social ill.[18]

These commercial intermediaries occupied an ambiguous position
in their respective societies. They were neither at the top nor at the bottom of the social hierarchy. Their presence was an economic necessity,
yet they were often feared, mistrusted, and resented. They could serve
as mediators and intercessors; their advice was equally welcome at village assemblies and noble courts. Yet they were resented and despised as
traders, an inherently dishonest profession. To peasants, merchants represented one of life's eternal but unavoidable burdens, like hailstorms or
the plague. Alone in their shops, doing God knew what all day, merchants often seemed at once lazy, mysterious, and sly. Jews, Germans,
and even certain itinerant craftsmen, such as potters and tailors, were all
suspected of practicing black magic and consorting with the Devil.[19]

Meanwhile, at the top of the social ladder, snobbery prevented commercial minorities from mixing with the aristocracy. The Jewish factor

Transylvanian shepherd, c. 1900–40.   Belarusian woman, 1911.

Fried had been allowed into the Perényis' manor house to show off some carpet samples, but he would not have been invited to stay for dinner. Similarly, in the Transylvania of Miklós Bánffy's novels, young noblemen might call on their wealthy Armenian or Jewish neighbors when they lost too much money gambling and needed a loan. They might even conduct an illicit affair with the daughter of their banker or estate manager. But they would never marry—the social gulf was simply too great.

Today, more than eighty years after Bánffy completed his *Transylvanian Trilogy,* traces of the world he sketched are still visible. In Transylvania, a day's walk can still take you through a fortified German town, a Hungarian castle, a Romanian village, or an Armenian cathedral. Although some of these structures are now abandoned or have new owners, they testify to the past existence of a social landscape of unrivaled intricacy. Part of the reason is that, for centuries, Transylvania acted like a miniature, concentrated version of Eastern Europe as a whole.

The traditional societies of Eastern Europe, arranged in a hierarchical order of occupations, and separated by language as well as faith, resemble layer cakes, in which every level has a different flavor and texture. Transylvania embodies this tendency at its most baroque.

Transylvania was originally a province of the medieval kingdom of Hungary. Following the Hungarian defeat at the Battle of Mohács in

1526, it became an independent kingdom, perched uneasily between the
Ottoman Empire and the Habsburgs. Like Poland-Lithuania, it was an
electoral monarchy and a haven for religious dissidents. Unlike Poland,
however, where political life was in the hands of a fairly uniform Polish-
speaking nobility or *szlachta*, Transylvania was dominated by three distinct privileged castes: Hungarians, Szeklers, and Saxons.

The Hungarians and the Szeklers, both of whom spoke Magyar,
or Hungarian, were the kingdom's soldiers and aristocrats. Most were
Catholic, though many of the most important landowners were Calvinist. The Saxons, by contrast, were German-speaking Lutherans. Most
were farmers and merchants, and they dominated Transylvania's urban
life. Indeed, their seven great gated towns gave Transylvania its German
name of Siebenbürgen, or "Seven Fortresses."

Although the Hungarians, Szeklers, and Saxons were the most powerful groups in Transylvania, most of the kingdom's population was
composed of Eastern Orthodox Romanian serfs. Transylvania, therefore, was split into four groups, whose members belonged to four different churches and spoke three different languages. Characteristically,
the Romanian peasants, the largest of these groups, had the least say
over their own affairs. But even this did not exhaust the kingdom's
diversity: many of its merchants were either Greeks or Armenians.

Armenians had settled in Eastern Europe for centuries. Their communities, which stretched in a vast arc from Moldavia to Polish Galicia,
were part of a vast commercial diaspora that reached from the Balkans
to India. Although the Germans of Transylvania did their best to keep
them out (they didn't want the competition), by the seventeenth century
the Armenians had established themselves as some of the kingdom's
wealthiest merchants. They even had their own city, Armenopolis (now
Gherla), and built a series of Armenian Catholic cathedrals, scattered
like jewels across the kingdom.

I once stumbled upon one of these Armenian enclaves, in the village
of Dumbrăveni, while driving through the Transylvanian highlands on
my way to the famous fortified German church at Biertan. Dumbrăveni
was once an important place, the seat of Prince Michael I Apafi, one
of the last independent rulers of Transylvania. Today, sitting a few
miles off the main road between Sighişoara and Mediaş, it receives few
visitors.

Most of the traffic heading into or out of Dumbrăveni today consists of horse carts, some piloted by Roma children accompanied by large canary-yellow sheepdogs. When I drove through town, one of these dogs, sensing a threat, broke off in pursuit of our car, narrowly missing getting itself killed. The children in the cart yelled their approval at its boldness. Meanwhile, in Dumbrăveni's main square, their parents were busy selling firewood and potted geraniums. St. Elizabeth's Church, once the seat of an Armenian Catholic bishop, stood closed. One of its towers is missing its steeple, and time has worn the sandstone steps leading to the front door down to flaking nubs. Climbing them felt like walking on the pages of a burnt book.

Three centuries ago Armenian monks of the Mekhitarist order came all the way from their island haven in Venice to care for the souls of the merchants here. Today a sign hung over the door says, in Armenian, that services have been suspended. Nearby the Apafi Palace stands apart in magnificent desolation. No placard marks it. Most of the second floor is full of discarded office furniture. Every windowpane is broken. The back garden has been converted into a vegetable patch and a garage. But for an ancient Latin inscription, chiseled in stone above a magnificent, verdigris-covered door, one would never know that this edifice was erected by the "lawfully elected king of Hungary" in 1563.

Kept visible by their churches and graveyards, the Armenians' centuries-long presence in Transylvania is now largely a question of memory. They are not alone, however; Eastern Europe abounds in such odd pockets of people—isolates, breakaways, and geographic exceptions—whose continued existence seems forever on the verge of ending.

Only some 250 people identify as Livonians, speakers of a Finno-Ugric language similar to Estonian but native to Latvia. The last native speaker of Livonian, Grizelda Kristiņa, died in 2013, leaving the language purely in the hands of revivalists. Things do not look much better for the Afro-Albanians of Ulcinj. Their ancestors were African slaves brought to the shores of the Adriatic by Ottoman traders in the nineteenth century, who intermarried with and adopted the language of the local Albanians. They became some of the most prominent sailors and sea captains of this Montenegrin port. As of this writing, none still live there.[20]

The Karaites of Poland-Lithuania, barely a handful of whom still live in Eastern Europe, form another one of these fragile ethnic islands. Their story is among the strangest of them all, proof of just how mutable an identity can be when pushed to extremes. Reputed to be the smallest minority in all of interwar Poland, the Karaites' roots were ancient, stretching back to eighth-century Babylonia. Like many splinter groups, they began as heretics. Unlike most other Jews, Karaites obeyed the Torah alone, rejecting the Talmud and all the rabbinic literature that followed it. Breaking off from the mainstream of Jewish religious practice, the Karaites found a new home for themselves in Constantinople and in the Crimean Peninsula, where they had their own city, Chufut-Kale, whose name means "Fortress of the Jews" in Tatar. There the Karaites adopted a new language, a dialect of the Kipchak Turkic spoken by members of the Golden Horde.

Around the fourteenth century, some Karaites began arriving in the Kingdom of Lithuania. In the medieval cities of Halicz, Łuck, and Trokai, they far outnumbered their rabbinic brethren.[21] In the twentieth century, Trokai emerged as the Karaites' spiritual and intellectual capital. In the 1930s this tiny community of no more than eight hundred people was producing at least five separate journals, published in three different languages and scripts. In nearby Vilnius, though, the Karaites were best known for their unusually large and sweet cucumbers, which were said to have come straight from the Orient and were famous as far away as Warsaw.[22]

Today Trokai is a village a day's walk from Vilnius. There one can still see the remains of a Karaite *kenesa*, or synagogue. Hardly anyone worships there. Karaites were never numerous to begin with, but only a handful are left in Lithuania. Most of those who survived World War II have emigrated to Israel. Those who didn't have assimilated into their surroundings.

But even before the war, the Karaites weren't sure whether they fully qualified as Jews. The belief that their origins were actually Turkic rather than Jewish flourished in the early twentieth century thanks mainly to the work of one man, Hajji Seraya Khan Shapshal. In 1928 the Karaites of Poland appointed Shapshal as their *hakham*, or community leader. By that time he had already been hard at work, crafting this unusual history for these exceptional people.

Shapshal's own background was extraordinary too. He grew up in the Karaite heartland of the Crimea and studied oriental philology at the University of St. Petersburg. Upon graduation, he became a Russian tutor to a young heir to the Persian throne. During his stay in Teheran, he seems to have spied for the czar and helped organize an antidemocratic coup. When the Bolsheviks took control of Russia, Shapshal organized a Karaite library in Chufut-Kale in the Crimean Mountains. Targeted by one of the counterrevolutionary armies in the Russian Civil War, he escaped south, disguised as a woman.[23] In Istanbul, where he had also worked as a spy, he became an avid pan-Turkist.

All this time Shapshal never stopped working as a scholar. The idea directing all his work was his conviction about the Turkic origins of the Karaites. He believed that, ethnically speaking, they weren't Jews at all but were descendants of the mighty Khazar Empire, whose khans converted to Judaism in the eighth century. In article after article, he tried to prove the Altaic-Turkic origin of his people. He showed that they were more soldiers than scholars and that their original religion was paganism. Like the ancient Turks, they honored the sky-god Tengri, and like the pagan Lithuanians, they once worshipped trees.

I went looking for traces of Shapshal in the place where the Karaites first settled in Lithuania, the ancient pagan capital of Trakai. Today Trakai is a bustling tourist destination, famous for its redbrick castle, perched on an island in the bend of a horseshoe-shaped lake. The remains of the old town, now interspersed with Soviet-era health resorts, sit on an isthmus in between the two sides of the lake. Its main street, covered in cobblestones, is named after the Karaites. Their presence, now almost purely confined to memory, is one of Trakai's main attractions. A Karaite restaurant serves supposedly Karaite dishes such as *kibinai*, pasties stuffed with a variety of fillings, including—rather unkosherly—pork. A standing cardboard cutout allows passersby to be photographed in Karaite costume. The Karaite *kenesa*, or prayer house, a stout, autumnal-yellow cube resting under a pyramidal roof of patterned tin, is closed to visitors.

The Karaite Ethnographic Museum next door, however, was open. Named after Shapshal and dedicated to his memory, it receives few visitors. There are photographs of Karaite gatherings, Karaite magazines from the 1930s in half a dozen languages, souvenirs from Paris and

Evpatoria, Polish legal documents, old calendars, and beautiful old tea sets and cups for drinking Karaite brandy. Mannequins sport Karaite costumes, both those worn in Poland-Lithuania and those remembered from the Crimea.

One room across the way held assorted objects from Shapshal's private collection: an elephant-hide shield from Sudan, a bow and arrow from Kenya, Persian swords, and a full set of samurai armor. I brushed past them quickly. After all, as the kind docent told me, they had nothing to do with Karaites. Only later did I realize that these objects were the key to Shapshal. To this man of many identities and faces, the former royalist, tutor, and spy, the story of the Karaites' pagan-Turkic origin was just the last in a series of disguises. Like the Japanese breastplates and chainmail shirts he collected, it was intended as a suit of armor, and it very nearly worked—until it didn't. When the Nazis arrived in Vilnius in 1941, they accepted his thesis about the racial distinctiveness of the Karaites. They agreed to spare as many as they could. However, so that no other Jews could claim this identity for protection, they demanded that Shapshal give them a list of all the Karaites in the country. Then, in time, they killed most of the Karaites anyway—ethnicity be damned.[24]

Shapshal himself survived until the arrival of the Soviets. He found work on a collective farm specializing in the cultivation of cucumbers—the particularly sweet cucumbers of the Karaites that had been brought to Lithuania hundreds of years before, directly from the Crimea, along with sacks of precious, nurturing soil, gathered from beneath the spreading oaks of the Valley of Jehoshaphat, beside Chufut-Kale, the Fortress of the Jews.

7

Wanderers

Caravan of Zlatari Roma. Romania, c. 1880.

Motion is the enduring principle of Eastern Europe. Motion of people, motion of faiths, motion of ideas. This is the reason why population maps of Eastern Europe, especially old ones, look so disorderly, like slabs of marbled beef or a cup of coffee before the cream has settled. The migrations leading to the creation of Western European nations happened in the very distant past. In Eastern Europe, they never stopped. Long after the Visigoths and Franks, Saxons and Jutes of the West were a distant memory, nomadic Cumans and Pechenegs were still arriving from the steppe. Tatars were still conducting great slave raids in the territory around Lviv in Mozart's day and only ceased when Catherine the Great finally put a stop to them.

Warfare on the fringes of empires created a constant churn of captives and refugees fleeing across the frontiers. In territories left abandoned by war, agricultural settlers quickly arrived to try their luck on fallow ground. Members of commercial diasporas soon joined them. Some practiced specialized trades, like the Saxon miners of Transylvania or the Scottish gunsmiths and surgeons of Poland-Lithuania.[1]

Eventually, members of all these groups settled down. But some groups of people in Eastern Europe never stopped their wandering, as their identities were inextricably linked with being mobile. For some, such as the Hutsul and Vlach shepherds of the Carpathian and Balkan ranges, wandering was a way of life; for others, such as Jewish and Christian pilgrims and wandering Sufis, travel was a source of religious inspiration; and for still others, such as peddlers, itinerant craftsmen, minstrels, and bards, travel was a profession. But the greatest wanderers of all were the Gypsies, as they have been traditionally called by others, or Roma, as they call themselves, who have been an integral feature of Eastern European life since their arrival in the Balkans a millennium ago.

In spite of their importance, all these wanderers are hardly spoken about. Moving between states, they have largely avoided inscription in official history. And yet they are vital. Taken together, they are the great cross-pollinators and hybridizers of Eastern European culture. For centuries, they have carried melodies, traditions, vernaculars, and stories across borders.

The most ancient form of nomadism in Eastern Europe stemmed from human relationships with animals. Grazers like cows, sheep, and goats live in constant search of new pasture. The people who raised them learned to follow their movements in a pattern of mobility called transhumance. Most commonly, transhumance involved a negotiation of altitude: a journey up into the mountains each spring when the grass turned green and luscious, and down into the valleys each fall when the air grew sharp and cold.

In the Carpathian and Balkan mountains, ancient customs dictated the movement of herds and peoples between the highlands in summer and the lowlands in winter. Among the Hutsuls of Ukraine, managing the summer pastures was a sacred occupation. Only men could take part in it, and the entire season was watched over by a holy fire that was never allowed to go out. In the hilly borderlands between eastern Herzegovina and Montenegro, whole families spent summers with their cattle and sheep and goats in the *katun*, or pastoral mountain community, on the slopes of Mount Zelengora.[2] The trip to the mountains began in mid-June and lasted until the end of August. It took many days of sweaty travel to reach the high pastures.

Led by the *domaćin*, the elected head of the mountaineers, this procession of bleating cattle, women, and children preferred to "follow neglected sections of an ancient Roman road," instead of a modern one, so as to avoid gendarmes and customs officers.[3] Once they were on high, life became more relaxed. They spent mornings milking animals and evenings making cheese. This left plenty of time during the day to whittle, wander, and dream.

Shepherds could traverse places few others dared to go. In the mountainous country that prevails in coastal Croatia, Montenegro, and Albania, they were natural merchants. From the Middle Ages to the twentieth century, most of the caravan trade in this part of the Balkans was in the hands of the Vlachs.

The Vlachs, also known as Aromanians, are a diasporic people, widely scattered over the Balkans. Most Vlachs are Orthodox Christians, and they exerted a profound cultural influence on all the territories they settled. Originally speakers of a Romance language closely related to Romanian, they often adopted the language of their neighbors as well, whether it was Greek, Bulgarian, Serbian, or Albanian. Traditionally Vlachs worked as shepherds and roamed the highlands of Eastern Europe, from the Polish-Czech border to the uplands of Macedonia. They also made a living from trade. Masters of moving cargo through mountain passes, they connected the remote interior of the Balkan Peninsula to the ports of the Adriatic Sea. In the process, they grew rich. Before the twentieth century, many of the wealthiest merchant families across the Balkans were Vlach.

Mechanized transport and the end of empires took away much of the Vlachs' economic advantage, while the rise of nationalism forced many to assimilate to a dominant culture that was not their own. But in some places, the cultural legacy of the Vlach diaspora can still be felt. Perhaps the most significant is the little village of Voskopojë in Albania. It sits at over a thousand meters in elevation. One reaches it by climbing a narrow road through a forbidding canyon above the town of Korçë. Voskopojë itself rests in the bowl of a beautiful valley, surrounded by tall mountains covered in pine and fir trees. Close your eyes, and it could be Colorado.

Today Voskopojë is home to no more than a few hundred people, some goats, and many brightly painted beehives. Three hundred years ago, however, it was a city known as Moschopolis. Famous as the "City of the Shepherds" during its eighteenth-century heyday, Moschopolis was one of the greatest trading emporia in the Balkan Peninsula. Its merchants traveled as far as Salonika, Dubrovnik, Venice, and Leipzig. Back home, twenty-four churches and several monasteries looked after the inhabitants' souls. An orphanage took care of abandoned children.

Many of the churches are still there, but most are padlocked for want of parishioners. They contain gorgeous frescoes in late Byzantine style, the fruits of a tremendous intellectual and artistic flowering that took hold in these mountains around 1750. In those years, Moschopolis was a great center of learning as well as a magnet for wealth. A Greek school, the New Academy, taught the children of the merchant elite. A printing press—one of very few in this part of the world—provided books to read.

In 1788 a devastating raid by Muslim Albanian soldiers in the service of Ali Pasha of Ioannina, a brigand leader and sometime Ottoman official known in his time as the "Muslim Bonaparte," put an end to Moschopolis's greatness.[4] When I visited Voskopojë, in the summer of 2019, all that was left of the press and the academy was a few stones heaped up behind a chicken coop. At St. Nicholas Church, one of the town's most beautiful, I met a few other visitors, a pair of older couples, one German and one French. To enter the basilica, we called the local Orthodox priest on his cellphone. When he first arrived, no one could understand anyone else, until suddenly it became clear that the German couple, from Reutlingen, were actually Saxons from Braşov in Transylvania. When they spoke to the priest in Romanian, he answered in fluent Aromanian, which to their ears sounded like an antique dialect of Romanian. The priest said he had a son in Mainz and a daughter in Trier. Few young people, he told us, stayed put in the mountains anymore.

—

If the roads of the highlands belonged to shepherds and their flocks, the roads of the lowlands belonged to beggars. To live on the road without a herd or an animal of one's own meant to live at the mercy of others. Beggars deserved respect, though, for one never knew who they might be. Prophets, such as the Jewish Elijah and Khidr, the immortal "Green One" of Islamic mythology, were both thought to roam the earth in disguise, bestowing miracles and aiding the poor.[5] One wouldn't want to accidentally miss out on their blessings.

Towns had licensed paupers of their own, enrolled in the beggars' guild, but some preferred to find their fortune wandering from place to place. In Lithuania, at the turn of the previous century, most of these peripatetic paupers belonged to a single extended family, the Bezruch-kas, whose name means "missing a hand" in Russian. Their founding patriarch had many children, all of whom were married off to other beggars. The original Bezruchka used to drive this brood in a wagon from town to town in search of sustenance. When he grew too old to continue, he divided Lithuania among his sons and sons-in-law, giving each a territory in which to beg.[6]

Poverty might be fate, but it could also be a calling. The most inspired beggars of Eastern Europe were the Sufi dervishes of the Balkans. In becoming Sufis, they gave up everything they owned in order to pursue a life outside the regular bounds of society.

The wandering Sufis were God's unruly friends, whose calling mixed equal parts renunciation and excess. Like the mendicant monks of Western Europe, they lived entirely from alms. The very word *dervish* meant "poor" or "indigent" in Persian. Sufi dervishes carried all their earthly belongings with them, which typically consisted of a begging bowl, pouch, spoon, belt, bell, needle, flint, razor, candle, hatchet, and club.[7] They also generally carried at least one musical instrument, usually a tambourine or drum. More often than not you could hear a band of dervishes long before you saw them.

All dervishes were men. Their dress varied from group to group. Most were barefoot. Some wore loincloths or dressed in rough woolen cloaks, the traditional garb of village outcasts. Others went about naked. The Abdals of Rum, members of the dervish group most common in the Balkans, dressed exclusively in animal hides in order to signal their distance from society. The dervishes' hats ranged from tall, conical caps to wide-brimmed, tasseled *tarbooshes*, likewise sending the message that they stood outside the prescribed orders of settled life. However, the most shocking element of the dervishes' appearance was the way they styled their hair.[8] Most of them shaved off their hair, beard, mustache, and eyebrows in a fashion called the "four blows." This was a deeply transgressive act; the Prophet Muhammad himself had mandated the wearing of beards and mustaches. Going without facial hair meant losing all honor and status. But that was how the dervishes preferred it.

Various groups of dervishes could be met on the roads of Muslim Europe, each with its characteristic accessories. The Haydaris liked to wear iron rings around their limbs and tied a long iron chain around their chest. More startlingly, according to some observers, they sometimes kept their penis caged in an iron ring or sheath lest it misbehave. Less chaste but perhaps more intimidating, the Abdals of Rum went everywhere carrying long-handled hatchets. They burned spots onto their temples and tattooed their chests with the sword of Ali, and their arms with pictures of coiled snakes.

Every Abdal carried two leather pouches: one for flint, and the other for hashish. Hashish played a great role in dervish life. If dervishes' nudity and baldness were a way of sloughing off the weight of the world, then hashish, especially when paired with music, was their gateway to ecstasy. Abdals believed its use helped them embrace the true, hidden nature of reality and thereby recover some of the lost radiance of life in Paradise. After a long session of dancing, smoking, and eating, they lay on the cold ground to sleep. When they awakened to the sound of a horn, it was as though the archangel Israfil had summoned them from death.[9] Thus every morning was a resurrection, just as every night meant a descent into the grave.

The Abdals emerged in Central Asia sometime around the thirteenth century. The Sufi master Otman Baba brought them to Europe in the mid-fifteenth century. According to a biography written by one of his followers, Otman Baba came from Khorasan in Persia, near the border with Afghanistan. He arrived in Anatolia following Tamerlane's armies, after which he wandered the high plateaus of Asia Minor and the Balkans with a few hundred of his closest followers. He lived over a hundred years and spent most of that time nude. His tomb rests in southern Bulgaria, on the road between Haskovo and Kardzali. Built around a green spring, it is a place of profound calm. One has to close one's eyes and strain one's ears to sense any trace of the departed dervishes, the rattling of their chains, the scream of their horns.

· · · ·

Musicians always had to travel, as few communities could support a band full time. A village would struggle to employ even a single musician. In Ukraine, two main types of minstrels dominated the scene. These were the *kobzary,* who sang to the accompaniment of a lute called a *kobza,* and the *lirnyki,* who sang to the accompaniment of a *lira,* or hurdy-gurdy. The repertory of both groups was similar. They sang religious songs and begging songs, songs of justice and injustice, and satirical songs. They sang epics about the Cossack wars of the seventeenth century and shorter songs about prisoners in Turkish jails and women widowed by war. They sang the great song of the Baida, the Cossack warlord who was hung from a meathook in Istanbul but still managed to thumb his nose at the sultan.

In Ukraine as in much of the Balkans, performing music was a form of licensed begging. Like dervishes, minstrels lived from their begging bowls. Unlike the dervishes, though, musicians begged in a highly structured way. Both the *kobzary* and the *lirnyki* were organized into guilds governed by elaborate rules. They allotted separate territories to musicians, governed the training of new apprentices, and regulated the transmission of the secret knowledge that was at the heart of the minstrels' craft. Among these secrets was a coded language, called the *lebiiska mova,* known only to members of the itinerant minstrels' guild. The *mova* was based on a core vocabulary of transposed Ukrainian, supplemented with words borrowed from Greek, Romanian, Hungarian, Turkish, Hebrew, Russian, and even Swedish, to create a true cryptolect, comprehensible only to the initiated.

Revealing the meanings of this secret speech was a violation of guild law. However, in the minstrels' code, one cardinal rule stood above all others: all *kobzary* and *lirnyki* had to be blind. Blindness was an absolute precondition for performance. Although they had set territories in which to beg, the minstrels also traveled to town and city fairs, journeys that took them deep into Galicia, Belarus, and Russia. No matter how far they traveled, the power of the guild held sway. The guild adjudicated the most important matters concerning all the blind beggars of Ukraine. It had its own officers and subofficers, patterned on the Russian military, as well as its own treasury. This supraguild met every year in spring in a forest south of Kiev, where its leadership gathered in secret courts to settle disputes and make rulings on the finer points of guild law.[10]

Blind minstrels needed sighted guides to lead them on their journeys. Serving as a guide though carried temptations that could put one at odds with the various guild rules. One such guide, Oleksander Dimnych, was an orphan who loved music and the wandering minstrel life. He desperately wanted to be a *lirnyk*, but unfortunately he could see, which made him ineligible. Nonetheless, he managed to teach himself some songs. Worse still, he taught some of these songs to another child. This was a grave crime. Anyone who taught the minstrel science, or *nauka*, to a sighted person was liable to be banned from begging entirely. For the blind minstrels, this was a terrible punishment, amounting to a virtual death sentence. Being sighted, Oleksander wasn't exposed to the same danger. Nonetheless, a group of minstrels caught him and beat him terribly. Oleksander managed to escape, however, and evade his pursuers as they chased him through the countryside.[11] Dimnych didn't let the beating deter him though. He spent years performing for free and later married a blind woman and took on a blind guide, so the public would accept him as a true *lirnyk*.

Minstrels served a necessary function in a world without recorded music or mass entertainment. Technology later posed a threat to this order. However, the end of the minstrel guilds didn't come from modernization—it was decreed from on high. According to a widespread story, Stalin liquidated the minstrels by luring them to a conference in Kharkiv, where they were all shot.[12] This tale appears to be apocryphal, as the proposed dates for the fatal conference range from 1933 to 1940, and no eyewitnesses survived to describe any such meeting. But while no single document has been unearthed to prove that a massacre was ordered from the top, it is certainly true that, by 1940, there were virtually no living minstrels left in Ukraine. They had all either died of starvation in the Great Famine (or Holodomor) of 1932–33 or been executed for promoting Ukrainian nationalism during the Great Purge that swept through the Soviet Union in 1937–38.

. . .

The Roma are Eastern Europe's quintessential wanderers. The life of no other people—perhaps in the whole world—is so tied up with the road. But where did they come from, and how did they find themselves in Europe? In the eighteenth century, philologists determined on the basis of their language that they must have come from somewhere on the Indian subcontinent—possibly Rajasthan, in the desert north. The date of their departure seems to have been sometime between the eighth and tenth centuries. What prompted their exodus is unknown. Some have speculated that it may have been connected to the Muslim invasion of Sindh or the Byzantine seizure of Antioch a century later, but this is sheer guesswork. Like the Slavs before them, the Roma's progress from their point of origin took place in conditions of complete obscurity.

The first mentions of Roma in written sources date to the eleventh century. In 1054 a group called the Atsingani appeared in Constantinople.[13] They had no fixed home but were skilled in the arts of magic and clairvoyance. The Byzantine emperor hired them to rid his private gardens of wild beasts, a task that they accomplished with the aid of poison. The Atsingani appear sporadically in Byzantine sources over the next century, usually carrying snakes and somehow involved in the business of fortune telling.

Whether these were genuinely Roma remains open to debate, but by the early fourteenth century, they can at last be spotted with a degree of certainty, living in various parts of island Greece. A few decades later they begin to appear regularly in the rest of the Balkans. By the 1390s, the princes of Moldavia and Wallachia (the two principalities which unified in 1859 to form the core of modern-day Romania) were regularly donating hundreds of Roma slaves to Romanian monasteries. Whether they were prisoners of war or had been previously enslaved by the Tatars or Turks is uncertain. Their numbers seem to have been increasing, though, for in 1445 Prince Vlad II Dracul of Wallachia, father of the

Prince Dracula of legend, brought back a few thousand slaves who looked "like Egyptians" after a successful raid into Ottoman-controlled Bulgaria.[14]

So much for written history. The true history of the Roma is contained in their language. The core of its vocabulary and grammar originates in India. Many of its words have roots that reach back to the Sanskrit of the Vedas. The Romani word for "church," *khangeri*, descends from the Sanskrit for "tower"; the word for "cross" comes from the Sanskrit for "trident"; and the word for priest, *rashai*, comes from *rishi*, Sanskrit for "bard." Thus, etymologically speaking, when Roma people hear mass in a church, they are listening to a bard perform in a tower before one of the ancient symbols of Lord Shiva.[15] Such inheritances could be identified indefinitely. The truly remarkable thing about Romani, however, is that it has acted as a sponge for words from other languages. Its many borrowings, scattered across two dozen dialects, are a palimpsest tracing centuries of migration and change. A Romani dictionary is thus not a mere list of words, but an atlas.

The deepest layer of these borrowings comes from Persian, which gave Romani its words for "star," "honey," "forest," and "luck." Armenian added the words for "oven," "heart," and "horse." Greek left an especially heavy imprint, testimony to the years the Roma spent in the bosom of the Byzantine Empire. It contributed the names for countless basic items, such as "sky," "soup," "grandfather," and "road." Contact with the Slavic languages of the Balkans began early and lasted long; their bequest included the words for "bed," "barn," and the color green.

Turkish left a comparatively small trace on Romani, but it did add one term of particular importance—a clue to when and why the Roma might have left India in the first place. In the dialects of Romani that are spoken in the Balkans, the word for "Turk" or "Muslim" is *Koraxaj*.[16] This word descends from Karakhanid, the name of a dynasty that ruled over Central Asia between the ninth and thirteenth centuries, before being snuffed out by Genghis Khan. Most likely, the Karakhanids were the first Muslims the Roma encountered on leaving the Indian subcontinent. Perhaps they served in their armies or played music in their camps.

Whatever the Roma's true origins, groups of them began to appear in Europe outside of the Balkans in the fifteenth century. At first, people weren't sure quite what to make of them. They arrived in groups of between fifty and a few hundred, riding fine horses and trailed by heavily laden wagons. These dark-skinned strangers dressed in brightly colored clothes, wore earrings, and were skilled at palm reading. When asked where they came from, they said that they were converts from Islam, sent on a pilgrimage (lasting seventy years!) by the pope as penance for the time they had spent worshipping the false god of the Saracens.

This story, tailor-made to play on the heartstrings of medieval Christians, came with apparent proof. Most Roma bands in medieval Europe carried impressive-looking documents, festooned with seals from popes, kings, and emperors, testifying to the truth of the tale. For over a century this imposture worked like a charm. Cities from Augsburg to Seville welcomed the newcomers with food and shelter. Gradually, though, the ruse wore thin, and the countries of Western Europe began to expel these strangers.

Eastern Europe was slower to catch on. The Kingdom of Poland was one of the last to welcome a group of pilgrims from "little Egypt." They arrived in 1542, led by Peter Rotemberg, who said he was a knight and a count. He carried a letter from the Archbishop of Lyon, describing a penance imposed by the pope and stating that all those who helped Peter and his fellow "Philistines" would receive absolution for their sins.[17]

Thanks to the chance preservation of a sheaf of documents related to Peter and his group, we can track their movement across Poland and Lithuania over the next twenty years, as they moved in a great circle around the borders of the commonwealth, taking their wagon train all the way from Kraków to Estonia and back. During these travels, city fathers, bishops, and powerful noblemen received them with open arms. Gradually, though, Peter's grip over his people began to weaken. The "Philistines" grew increasingly destitute. More and more ran away. Some slipped out at midnight to start wagon trains of their own. Others absconded with Peter's silver plate and horses.[18] On yellowed parchment scrolls, we can glimpse Peter as he appeared to those around him: ever more alone, begging the courts for help in chasing down his fugitive friends, no longer a count or knight or even a pilgrim but merely a Gypsy like all the others.

In subsequent centuries, many Roma settled in the commonwealth, especially in its eastern, Lithuanian half. There they met with general acceptance, especially early on. The kingdom was a mosaic of faiths, languages, and religions, in which the Roma didn't stick out very much. Most stopped being nomadic and settled down in villages, making their living as craftspeople and servants.[19] A number went to work for the Radziwiłłs, an immensely rich Lithuanian magnate family with a bottomless appetite for power and pleasure.

Not content to be among the greatest landowners in all of Europe, the Radziwiłłs longed to be kings. Their fellow aristocrats envied their wealth and influence and never allowed them to ascend the Polish-Lithuanian throne. Frustrated in politics, the family excelled in other areas, such as the training of dancing bears. Throughout the eighteenth century, the best-trained dancing bears in Europe came from a single source: the Bear Academy in Smarhoń, in today's Belarus. Smarhoń was one of dozens of towns owned by the Radziwiłłs. Really, it was less a town than a collection of settlements scattered across the forest, inhabited variously by Belarusians, Poles, Jews, Tatars, and Gypsies. The academy itself was located on Street of the Skoromokhs, or jesters. Dozens of baby bears were sent to the academy every year from the vast Radziwiłł forests—the Gypsies of the academy trained these bears as well as ursine pupils brought by private clients, who had to pay their charges' room and board for the duration of their stay. The bears were taught not just to dance but to play the role of servants—bringing water to the table, playing waiter at dinner, and performing many other tricks besides.

One of the most famous feats performed by the bears of the Smarhoń Academy took place at the end of the eighteenth century. In those years, the school and the town belonged to Prince Karol Radziwiłł, who was known universally as Panie Kochanku, or "Lord Lovey." He was preposterously rich, possessing sixteen cities, 683 villages, and twenty-five forests, as well as a mansion in Paris. Prince Karol was openhanded, adventurous, and prone to violence. He was also an inveterate reveler, a drunk, a womanizer with a scandalous fondness for Jewish women, and a teller of tall tales. He is remembered as a kind of Lithuanian Baron Munchausen—except that in his case, at least some of the stories told about him were real.

In Karol's day, the Gypsy community at Smarhoń, and across most of Lithuania, was headed by the "king" Jan Marcinkiewicz. A later memoirist describes him as a tall, powerfully built man with fiery eyes. As a sign of his station, he wore a hat like a crown with a peacock feather in place of the cross, as well as a necklace of white beads ending in a pendant portraying a monkey and a bear.[20] One day Marcinkiewicz decided to play a bit of a trick on Lord Lovey. He had his Gypsies teach a group of bears how to pull a horse carriage. He then put six of them in harnesses and rode off to the prince's castle at Nesvizh. Radziwiłł was so delighted that he received Marcinkiewicz like a real king, treating him to a feast lasting many days. When they were finished, they all rode off together to his summer palace, trailed by crowds of bears, Gypsies, burghers, and noblemen.

The Roma who worked for the Radziwiłłs did so as free men. But in the Balkans and especially in the Romanian principalities of Wallachia and Moldavia, most Roma were enslaved. Slavery's roots in the region stretched back to the early Middle Ages, and it lasted deep into the nineteenth century. However, little documentation survives about either its origins or its development. Today Roma slavery remains one of the most understudied subjects in all European history. From the records that have survived, we can piece together a picture of an institution that strongly resembled its counterpart in the New World in some regards and was starkly different in others.

Enslaved Roma in Wallachia and Moldavia had no civil rights. They could be leased out for their labor or sold outright. They could not testify in trials. Slaves could not marry freemen, and the children of any such union retained the status of slaves. Their spouses would also be enslaved. This was quite unlike the custom in nearby Ottoman lands (Wallachia and Moldavia were only vassals of the Ottomans), where slavery was almost never hereditary. Romanian slave owners also had a free hand in applying punishments, which could be terrifyingly cruel. Harm committed against slaves was treated as a crime against property, not people. According to the law, the murder of a Roma by a free person was punishable by death. In practice, however, it was usually settled with a fine.

In Moldavia and Wallachia, few people were wholly free: slavery and serfdom operated in tandem, as two sides of a single coin. Serfs, who made up the bulk of the population, were likewise bonded laborers who had no way of escaping their servitude. However, serfs did enjoy some basic civil rights, such as the ability to testify in court. Conversely, Roma slaves, though not legal persons, sometimes benefited from less direct demands on their labor. Roma slaves paid less tax than the peasants, and they were free—and sometimes even obliged—to wander.[21] They could earn cash wages and sell their own products in the market, though some of that money had to be turned over to their owners.

Princely slaves stayed on their owners' estate in winter, when it was difficult to travel. Otherwise they would stop by only twice, on St. George's Day in April and St. Michael's Day in November, to pay the tax they owed their masters.[22] The rest of the year they spent on the road, practicing their trades. Different Roma clans specialized in different activities: the Ursari led dancing bears around the countryside; the Lingurari carved spoons and other wooden objects; the Lăieşi were mainly blacksmith, but also worked as masons and comb makers; the Auraris, or Zlatari, panned for gold in the swift-flowing rivers of the high Carpathians.[23]

These traditional arrangements allowed certain groups of Roma freedom of movement. Nevertheless, they remained on the bottom of the social pyramid, which remained dominated by a narrow stratum of princes, boyars (magnates), and priests. These social barriers were not completely insurmountable, however. Some masters freed their slaves, and some Roma worked as free farmers and craftspeople.[24]

The most spectacular case of a Roma overcoming the circumstances of their birth comes from the late sixteenth century. Ştefan Răzvan was the son of an enslaved Roma owned by the prince of Wallachia. As a child, he belonged to the metropolitan of Iaşi, the most important church official in Moldavia, who gave him a good education and later freed him. He went on to serve as an ambassador, conducting missions to Istanbul and to the Cossacks of Ukraine. From there, Ştefan became a colonel in the Polish army, a Romanian nobleman, and finally the commander of a Cossack horde, which he used to conduct a number of successful raids on the Ottoman Empire.

Backed by these mounted soldiers, and by some Polish allies, Ştefan overthrew the reigning prince of Moldavia and named himself hospodar in his place, thus becoming the first, and possibly the only, Roma head of state in history. His reign did not last long. After five months on the throne, his Polish backers betrayed him in favor of a more pliant puppet candidate. In his short life, Răzvan was a slave, soldier, *boyar,* Gypsy, Cossack, and king. Beaten in battle by the combined forces of his usurper and the Poles, he met his end impaled on the tip of a stake.

In the mid-nineteenth century, Roma slavery shifted to a much more commercial footing. Trade in slaves was practiced on a mass scale, and the old, unwritten rules preventing the breakup of families fell by the wayside. Auctions involving hundreds of people became commonplace. One particularly large auction, held in Bucharest in 1855, scandalized public opinion.[25] At almost the same time, Harriet Beecher Stowe's *Uncle Tom's Cabin* was translated into Romanian and became an immediate best seller, read by "boyars, soldiers, priests, ladies," and even emancipated Roma.[26]

In both Wallachia and Moldavia pressure for abolition mounted, but little was done until foreign powers intervened. One of the provisions of the Treaty of Paris, which ended the Crimean War, required both principalities to abandon slavery. In 1856 the Romanian principalities passed laws requiring the state to buy slaves from their owners and then free them en masse.

Initially, they faced some difficulty, in part because many Roma hesitated to have their status changed, preferring to retain the tax advantages and freedom of movement afforded by slavery.[27] After a time, though, the floodgates opened, and the old nomadic clans, used to wandering within the Romanian principalities, streamed out into the wider world. Among the most numerous—and enterprising—of these clans were the Lovari, traditionally horse dealers, and the Kalderash, who worked mainly as coppersmiths.

The Roma who left the Romanian principalities wandered first to the neighboring Balkan kingdoms of Bulgaria and Serbia. Before long, they spread across the rest of Europe. In 1863 groups of Kalderash began arriving in Poland. One band appeared in Warsaw, across the Vistula from the Old Town.[28] Their appearance was startling and magnificent. The women wore golden earrings and necklaces made out of Austrian silver thalers, paired always—for this was the Kalderash signature—with something red: red kerchiefs, red dresses, red coral necklaces, and red ribbons woven into their braids. The men—tall and hale, with piercing eyes—were just as splendid. Most wore special jackets ornamented with buttons of hammered silver, each the size of an egg.

Enterprising, footloose, and entrepreneurial, the Kalderash were within a decade the wealthiest and most visible Roma groups in Poland, Lithuania, Russia, and Bessarabia. The "kings" who ruled over Poland's Roma (or at least acted as if they did) always came from this most numerous and aristocratic clan.

After their emigration from the Romanian principalities, the Kalderash found themselves traversing a much larger world than the one they were used to. They adapted quickly. Within a generation of their arrival in Europe beyond the Balkans, their members could be found in every European country, as well as North and South America and Australia. The other great Roma collectives likewise experienced a sudden broadening of their cultural horizons. Emancipation brought about a cultural renaissance in dress, music, and crafts. In literature too—although since theirs was an almost exclusively oral culture, we know little about the details of this transformation.

One singular exception is Gina Ranjičić. We know about her life and work as the result of a lucky accident—the meeting, in 1890, of an out-of-work teacher and an old woman living out her final days under the open skies of eastern Croatia. The teacher was Heinrich von Wlislocki. The son of a Polish noble father and a Transylvanian Saxon mother, from an early age, he had a passion for linguistics. He wrote his dissertation on Old Norse philology and translated the Icelandic *Edda* into Hungarian. Wlislocki was fascinated by the Roma, learning their language and spending summers traveling with some of the nomadic clans. This was not such a rare preoccupation at the time. Emperor Franz Joseph I's cousin, Archduke Joseph Karl, likewise studied the Romani language, compiled a Romani dictionary, and hosted Roma wagon trains on the grounds of his Hungarian estate.

Over time Wlislocki became one of his generation's greatest experts on Gypsy ethnography and mythology. He was introduced to Gina Ranjičić in the last year of her life, alerted to her presence by the Serbian consul in Sombor, who had heard that she had a volume of poems he wished to purchase. They found her caravan outside Osijek. At first they could hardly believe that the tiny wizened figure before them, wrapped in rags, had ever been a great beauty, much less a poet, but this changed as soon as she began to speak. As Wlislocki wrote, "The thin, self-absorbed figure stood up proudly; with her dark, great eyes, still shining with an eerie fire, she sought, as it were, to penetrate into the innermost depths of the heart."[29] Soon Ranjičić unspooled for these strangers the events of her extraordinary life.

Gina's first memories were of the failed Hungarian revolution against the Habsburgs in 1848. At that time, she was living in Croatia with a group of nomadic Roma who called themselves the Nevelja. When Croatian troops tried to press them into fighting against Lajos Kossuth's Hungarians, the group fled south to Serbia. At age twelve, Gina joined the household of a wealthy Armenian merchant in Belgrade. Caught stealing from Turkish troops, the Nevelja were forced to flee back across the Sava River to Hungary. Gina stayed behind with her Armenian merchant. Soon he adopted her as his daughter and took her to his home in Constantinople, where she went to school and learned how to read and write.

In time, the Armenian's brother Gabriel fell in love with her, and they became lovers. Thus began one of the best periods in her life. Gina wrote her first poems, in Armenian, Turkish, and Romani. According to her, she began composing because of "how happy she was with her old man." One day, however, a handsome young Albanian named Grigor stepped into their house. He told Gina that the sultan was about to slaughter all the Armenians in the city and that she should run away with him if she wished to live. Grigor took her to Adrianople, in Turkish Thrace, and told her that she could not return home because the Armenian brothers had been killed and that she was a suspect in their deaths.

Grigor began traveling, working as an armed guard for caravans heading to and from the Hungarian frontier. On one of these trips, he hijacked a caravan. Together, he and Gina ran off to hide their booty in the Albanian mountains. But Gina wished to return to Constantinople, which Grigor forbade. They quarreled, and Grigor beat her savagely. To make it up to her, he promised to track down her remaining relatives in Serbia. While he was away, she went to live with a Hungarian in Adrianople. There she began her most passionate affair, with a Serb whose name she kept secret, only ever referring to him as "the white man." The Serb robbed Gina and left her starving and in rags, begging in the streets of Adrianople. She was now twenty-three, and her adventures were only beginning.

Gina's later life was just as eventful as her youth, with episodes in Vienna, Naples, Paris, and Bucharest. She gained and lost fortunes. She was charged with murder and rescued from a shipwreck. When illness finally robbed her of her beauty, she returned to her people, the Nevelja, and spent the last twenty-five years of her life, in terrible poverty, with the caravan.

Wlislocki wrote that if Gina Ranjičić had been born to a different time and to different circumstances, she would have been remembered as "one of the greatest poets of all time." Her poems are almost always about love—the ecstasy of its first growth and the horror of its betrayal. She burned brightly and could barely keep still. In one of her verses, she wrote, "When I am in the hills, I want to be in the valleys, and when I sleep in the fields, I want to be on the sea."[30]

Gina Ranjičić is barely remembered today, to the point that some have even questioned whether she was a real person or a product of Wlislocki's imagination. Similar things were said about the pioneering Polish opthamologist Salomea Pilsztyn, until a historian found her name in the secret dispatches of the Russian ambassador to the Crimean Khanate. No such doubts surround Bronisława Wajs, the greatest and arguably most tragic Roma poet of the twentieth century.

She was born in 1908, and though her given name was Bronisława, she went by Papusza, which means "doll" in Romani, a nickname given to her on account of her beauty. Papusza's mother belonged to a clan of Galician Roma. Her father, whom she barely knew, died in Siberia, where he was exiled for theft. Her stepfather gambled and drank. He took the family to Grodno, which is now in Belarus, but was then in Poland, where they stayed for five years.

Grodno became Papusza's favorite city. She learned to read there. She never went to school, but a Jewish woman, a shopkeeper with a store off the main square, agreed to teach her the alphabet. There was a price, though; Papusza had to steal a fat hen every Friday for the shopkeeper's Sabbath dinner. She stole, and she learned. After a few weeks, she could read a newspaper. Later she read books borrowed from the municipal library—Polish classics by Adam Mickiewicz and Henryk Sienkiewicz.[31] Reading helped her tell fortunes, which she had started to do when she was just four years old. Sometimes her clients lent her their books. She especially liked stories about knights and about great love affairs.

When Papusza was eighteen, an older man paid her mother to marry her. Dionizy Wajs was a bandleader, whose orchestra included a violin, bass, drums, dulcimer, accordion, and three harps. Even though the harps were huge—taller than a man and almost as heavy—Dionizy and his bandmates held on to them throughout World War II, even when they were hiding in swamps, even when winter came and they had nothing to eat. Once the harps saved their lives.

The band was traveling down a country road in their wagons, when a German patrol appeared in the distance. One of the wagons hit a pothole, and a harp fell out onto the road. The Germans hesitated, thinking that the harp might be an artillery piece. Suddenly, in Papusza's words, "the wind blew along the ground, hit the harp strings, and they played more beautifully than it ever had before. The Germans stood still and listened, and we crept up and took the harp and ran away."[32]

For one brief night, the group enjoyed a respite. Long years of terror remained. The region of Volhynia, in western Ukraine, was an especially terrible crucible of war. While the Germans were executing Jews and Roma, the local Poles and Ukrainians fought a murderous war against each other. To avoid getting caught up in either conflict, Papusza's band had to remain constantly on the move. Dionizy and Papusza never knew where they would sleep on any given night. Often they had to hide deep in the woods, sometimes even in ponds, up to their necks in water. They slept in holes they dug in the earth. They suffered from starvation, cold, and typhus.

Once the war was over, Grodno became part of the Soviet Union. Papusza's band relocated to western Poland, to the lands that had recently been "reclaimed," or annexed, from Germany. One day in 1949 a stranger walked into their camp. Jerzy Ficowski, a Pole, had fought in the Warsaw Uprising and spent time in the infamous Pawiak prison. From adolescence, he had a passion for everything beautiful and strange, especially in literature. He loved Bolesław Leśmian's poetry and Bruno Schulz's prose. In 1942 he sent Schulz a letter, hoping to meet with him, not realizing that he was already dead. Ficowski later collected Schulz's surviving correspondence, and much of what we know about Schulz's life comes from his efforts. After the war, as a former Home Army partisan, Ficowski faced harassment from the secret police. They interrogated him persistently, trying to force him to become an informer on his former brothers-in-arms.

Ficowski refused to collaborate. Finally he decided to escape. His friend Edward Czarnecki, a musician who had traveled and played with Roma from all over Poland, suggested a place. He knew Dionizy's band—he had fixed his harps, and they had often played banjo together. Czarnecki thought this wagon train, or *tabor,* might make for a good place for Ficowski to lie low when the secret police came calling for him again.

Once Ficowski arrived, he was introduced to Papusza. Someone told him that she was a poet and that she composed songs and sang them on the spot.[33] Ficowski gave her a pen and paper and asked her to write one for him the next time inspiration struck. She titled her first poem "A Gypsy Song Papusza's Mind Arranged." In Ficowski's words, it expresses all her longing "for wandering, for the forest, and for her youth."[34] It begins: "I grew up in the forest like a golden bush / in a Gypsy tent shaped like a mushroom. / Like my own heart I loved fire.

Roma caravan. Pruszków,
Poland, 1957.

Winds great and small / rocked the little Gypsy girl in her cradle / and set her wandering the wide world."

When Papusza's poems first appeared in print, translated into Polish by Ficowski, they provoked wonder from the Polish literary establishment. Papusza's fellow Roma were less pleased. They accused her of overstepping the bounds of what was proper for a Romani woman and of revealing secrets to the *gadje*, the non-Roma. This impression was strengthened after the appearance of Ficowski's *Polish Gypsies* in 1953, a book that relied heavily on what he had learned during his time in Dionizy's camp. After its publication, Papusza found herself increasingly persecuted and shunned. Meanwhile Communist authorities launched a massive campaign called the Great Halt, which aimed to put an end to Roma wandering by forcing Poland's Roma into state housing. Isolated and alone, Papusza settled down in the western city of Gorzów Wielkopolski.

Far from the woods of her childhood, Papusza sought to re-create them in her poems. There the forest is a constant companion, teacher, haven, and home. It is a living presence: it stands still like someone wise; it answers questions with its echo. Bears walk through it at night, looking like great silver moons, while overhead, the stars of the Hen and Chicks (which we call the Pleiades) point the way to the future. Even during the war, the forest comes to Papusza's aid. In her epic poem *Bloody Tears*, she describes how her extended family hid in the unmeasured woods, how the forest fed them, and how the woodland streams carried the sound of their suffering off to faraway lands.[35]

8

Nations

Sokol mass gymnastics display. Czechoslovakia, 1921.

One would like to ignore the complex conflicts of Eastern Europe's peoples, but sadly this is impossible. They are too important and too destructive to ignore, for ultimately the fate of the world depends on their petty hatreds and putrid ambitions. Eastern Europe is a powder keg, a nest of assassins, a tangle of murderous animosities.

If, at any time in the past two centuries, you were to poll Western Europeans as to their opinion of their Eastern neighbors, you might get some version of the above. It's a prejudiced view, of course, but one founded on a grain of truth. For those two hundred years, Eastern Europe really was a constant headache for diplomacy, and the main culprit was nationalism.

During the nineteenth century, the Poles couldn't stop revolting against Russia. They even gave Austria and Prussia trouble. Nationalism likewise spurred the Christian subjects and vassals of the Ottoman

Empire to stage rebellions. The Serbs went first, revolting in 1804 against their janissary overlords, who were themselves in revolt against the empire. The first Serbian uprising was therefore technically in the name of the sultan, not that this made him particularly well disposed toward it. Although this first rising was put down, the Serbs continued fighting, finally winning their autonomy in 1830. At nearly the same time, Greece won its independence, with Western help, and the Romanian principalities of Moldavia and Wallachia gained a measure of sovereignty under Russian protection. Their cumulative example proved magnetic. In 1875–6 Bosnians and Bulgarians both rose against the Ottomans, with the final result that Bulgaria became (virtually) independent and Bosnia became a de facto part of the Habsburg empire—and an enduring pressure point for international relations.

By the end of the nineteenth century, the Ottoman Empire in Europe was crumbling like a mouthful of rotten teeth. In the Habsburg realms, the one great bid for independence was made by the Hungarians, in 1848. Their revolution was crushed, but only nineteen years later, Hungary won its autonomy as a result of a crisis brought on by Austria's defeat in its war with Prussia. The absolutist Austrian Empire now became a dual monarchy, with a kingdom of Hungary inside a shared Austro-Hungarian Empire. The two states shared a monarch (Franz Joseph) but had separate parliaments and prime ministers. The only parts of administration they shared were those related to foreign policy and defense.

This arrangement was unique, and on the face of it, impractical. One historian has compared it to an "egg with two yolks."[1] Some see it as the Habsburgs' most fateful error, for it meant in practice that two groups—Germans in Austria, and Hungarians in Hungary—gained a level of control over all the other peoples in the empire. Hungarians ruled over large minorities of Croatians, Romanians, Slovaks, Ruthenians, and Serbs. All chafed against the rule of their new masters.

In the Austrian half of the monarchy, things were similarly complex. Czechs clashed with Germans over control of Bohemia. Poles in Galicia tried to preserve their autonomy, which meant oppressing the local Ukrainians. Slovenes in Carniola and Croats in Dalmatia both made appeals for self-rule, but the Austrians had scant interest in expanding autonomy for their subject peoples. Neither did the Hungarians. As one Hungarian prime minister put it to his Austrian equivalent, "You look after your Slavs, and we'll look after ours."[2]

In keeping with the dual nature of everything in the Habsburg monarchy, Bosnia, incorporated into the empire in 1878, was ruled by a joint commission of Austrians and Hungarians. Little did they know that this little province would prove to be the bomb that would destroy their whole state. It was a Bosnian Serb who pulled the trigger on Franz Ferdinand in 1914. The archduke's death was meant to spark a revolution that would end in the liberation of all the South Slavs in the empire and their unification in a new nation called Yugoslavia.

All these conflicts were driven by variations on a single notion, that peoples should rule themselves. But what was a people? And what qualified them to be a nation? The answer, most commonly, was language. Those who spoke a given language were those who belonged to a given nation. This equation of language and nation was a rather peculiar idea and a very Eastern European one. Its earliest proponents were priests and polyglot intellectuals. Its legislators were poets. Out of their dusty journals and sweaty verses came the birth of states and the ruin of empires.

.   .   .

When Moldovans sing their national anthem, "Limba noastră" (Our Tongue), they do not mention any great historical triumphs, legendary leaders, or calls to battle. Instead, they sing in praise of their language. "Our language is a treasure," begins the song; it is a "burning flame," a "tongue of bread," and "a necklace of precious gemstones scattered over the land."

More than in any other part of the world, Eastern European nationalists worshipped language. To them, it was the very soul of a nation. Yet ironically, in this fractured and prolifically polyglot place, the relationship between spoken language and identity was rarely straightforward. Indeed, it could be staggeringly complex. By way of example, the poet who wrote "Limba noastră" was thinking not of the Moldovan language, which he would have considered a dialect, but of Romanian.

Nationalists in Eastern Europe didn't just celebrate languages. They refurbished, revived, and rejuvenated them. Again, in the words of the

Moldovan national anthem: "Resurrect now this our language / rusted through the years that have passed / Wipe off filth and mold that gathered / when forgotten through our land." They had to put in this effort, because the languages on which they pinned their hopes rarely had much in the way of currency or cachet. They were not the languages of the imperial elites. They weren't even the preferred tongues of the educated classes. By the early nineteenth century, Czech was a tongue of village clerks. Croatian was spoken by peasants and petty traders. Slovak was succumbing to Hungarian influence, and Ukrainian to that of Russian, while hearing speakers of Estonian, Latvian, Lithuanian, Belarusian, or Slovenian required making a trip deep into the countryside.

For the political entrepreneurs of the Romantic Age, these untutored tongues were dry kindling, needing only a breath to burst into flame. Because the fate of nations was thought to be so tied to that of their languages, in Eastern Europe the political quest for independence was begun most often not by politicians and revolutionaries but by scholars, linguists, and poets. The Czechs were among the pioneers on this front.

In the kingdom of Bohemia in the days of Emperor Rudolf, in the early seventeenth century, Czech and German were on roughly even footing. Both languages were widely spoken and used in government. After the defeat of the Bohemian revolt at the Battle of White Mountain in 1620, the Czech language went into a long period of eclipse. As part of their reconquest of the rebellious province, Habsburg rulers banished it from state administration, journalism, literature, and the schools.[3]

By the late eighteenth century, German was edging out Czech in virtually all walks of life, as generations of Bohemians had received almost their entire education in some combination of Latin and German. This was not so upsetting as long as German possessed only practical advantages. Educated Bohemians were, at a minimum, bilingual. Few were kept out of jobs for lacking German. Only when German began to press claims of spiritual superiority did its status became worrying.

Following the lead set by the French Enlightenment *philosophes*, German intellectuals of the early nineteenth century began to proclaim not just the equality but the *supremacy* of the German language as a vehicle for culture and thought. The threat implicit in this maneuver was felt most strongly in Bohemia, because the Czechs there were already so similar to their German neighbors. They went to the same (mostly German) universities and read the same books. But it was precisely where people were the *least* disadvantaged by linguistic changes that new ideas of language's connection to identity first took root.

Nationalism thrived on what Freud called the narcissism of minor differences. In the Czech lands, language was very nearly the only thing that set Czechs and Germans apart. Language thus became the primary focus of Czech nationalism in its early decades. The Czech nation, quite literally, had to be spoken into existence.

This took some effort, for at the start of the nineteenth century, the very idea of "Czech culture" seemed like a contradiction in terms. The Czech language was thought to be spoken by stable boys and serving girls. A village priest might use it to converse with his flock. An aristocrat might drop a few phrases of his "native" language during a session of parliament to show his contempt for some visiting Viennese grandees, but he would never use it at home with his wife. Czech literature was thought to be similarly limited. It was possible to use Czech for comedies and low farces, but it was hard to conceive of a novel written in Czech. Anything pertaining to the upper classes was off limits, since as one nineteenth-century book reviewer pointed out, "every facet" of their lives took place in German. Writing as if they spoke Czech would simply sound false.[4]

Confronted by this general attitude of contempt, the Czech revivalists went to work resurrecting their language. They compiled dictionaries and grammars. They revived old words from the Middle Ages and coined countless new ones. They translated works of physics, chemistry, mathematics, aesthetics, and philosophy. In the process, they devised entire new vocabularies of scientific and technical terms. That no one could read these tomes, larded as they were with wholly unfamiliar words, was almost beside the point—any Bohemian who wanted to read about algebra or Kant could already do so in German. The revivalist translations were not products for consumption; they were statements of intent. They announced the arrival of a cultured reading public and an autonomous Czech intellectual sphere, even if no such communities yet existed. Educated Czechs would arrive in time, and when they did, these texts would be waiting for them.

In the meantime, at the dawn of the "national awakening" of the 1810s and '20s, small cells of existing Czech patriots struggled to make themselves understood by a wider public. One Czech novelist wrote that Czech patriots were "fellows who wish to help out the poor, old mother tongue, but at the same time speak or write in such a manner that not a living soul can make sense of it."[5]

Such disregard did not matter hugely to the early nationalists, since their movements were more like cults, or eccentric crusades, than the political parties they would later become. Like many sectarians, Czech revivalists underwent intense periods of conversion. As self-professed "awakeners" of the nation, they first had to wake up to their own Czechness. The great Czech historian František Palacký discovered this reality one night in a Slovak inn, when the master of the house asked him for help reading a Czech newspaper. Although Palacký came from Moravia, he didn't know the language, and his shame at that moment propelled the whole of his later career. Others came to this realization more gradually, through personal contacts or by reading one of the great—though, sadly, fake—works of medieval Czech poetry.

However one's conversion came about, its final arrival had to be marked with a ritual of some kind. Typically, awakened Czechs announced their new status by changing their names to ones that sounded more Slavic: Barbaras became Boženas and Benedikts became Blahoslavs. Thus rechristened into Slavdom, they were ready to fight for the nation, one journal article and ode at a time.

For the Eastern European language revivalists, the forms of writing mattered as much as the content. Throughout the region, almost every nation-in-utero devised new scripts and new ways of spelling to differentiate themselves from their oppressors. It was often hard to get everyone to agree over what the new "national" script should be.

In 1825 the learned priest Franc Metelko introduced a phonetic alphabet for Slovene. It looked like a blend of Latin and Cyrillic scripts, with a dash of Cherokee. Its one great advantage as an alphabet was that it was entirely phonetic. Its main disadvantage was that it was only suited to writing the Lower Carniolan dialect, when most Slovenian writers used the Upper Carniolan dialect. (Slovene, while spoken by relatively few people, nonetheless possesses some forty-eight dialects, grouped into seven main clusters.) These writers went to battle against Metelko, setting off a literary conflict that came to be remembered as the Slovenian Alphabet War.

Alphabet wars were a recurring phenomenon among the nationalist activists of nineteenth-century Europe. The Ruthenian Alphabet War of 1834 pitted proponents of the Cyrillic alphabet against champions of Latin. The intellectual who suggested switching to Latin, and therefore Polish, orthography argued that this change would put the whole of European learning at young Ruthenians' fingertips. His opponents countered that abandoning the Cyrillic of their Ukrainian-speaking forefathers would amount to treason against tradition.[6] Tradition carried the day.

To language revivalists, the script one wrote in could mean the difference between slavery and freedom. Spelling was just as important. Every hook, *haček*, and circumflex could potentially determine the future of a nation. Great emotions attached to these tiny symbols. One of Metelko's main supporters in the Slovenian Alphabet War, Jernej Kopitar, sided with him because his alphabet lacked diacritical marks. Kopitar thought diacritics were unforgivably ugly and looked entirely too Czech. To Kopitar, written Czech's swarms of inverse circumflexes, umlauts, and *accents aigus* looked like "specks of fly shit" dotting the page.[7] He hated them.

Lithuanians saw the same Czech letters—*č, š, ž*—that Kopitar thundered against as agents of emancipation. In 1877 the Lithuanian priest Kazimieras Jaunius declared that he would create a Lithuanian script to replace the Polish Latin and Russian Cyrillic alphabets. He began by vowing to never use *sz* or *ż* ever again, for as he wrote, "these two letters are Polish, and in our orthography there should not be even the smallest trace of Polish."[8] Replacing *w* and *ż* with the functionally identical *v* and *ž* did not noticeably improve the readability of written Lithuanian. It did, however, strike a blow against centuries of cultural domination by Poles.[9]

In the taxonomy of nineteenth-century language reformers, the Lithuanians were splitters, who tried to make their language and orthography seem ever more distinct from that of their neighbors. At the other end of the spectrum were the joiners, who attempted to gather a collection of dialects under the umbrella of a single language. The Illyrianists, who tried to devise a single language for all the South Slavs, made up one such movement. Their ideas—but not their language—later found political expression in Yugoslavism, and—ultimately—in the country of Yugoslavia itself.

Sometimes a single language could shuttle between these two camps. In the process of devising a standard literary language for the Slovaks, the poet and language reformer Ľudovit Štúr boldly abolished the letter *y*, which had been inherited from Czech. This made Slovak more distinct from its linguistic neighbor—a win for the splitters. A generation later, the tide among Slovak intellectuals swung toward proponents of Czecho-Slovakism, who thought Czech and Slovak should be made as similar as possible. They had the Slovak *y* brought back. Score one for the joiners.

In Estonia, the letter *y* was also the subject of bitter polemics. After Estonia declared independence from Russia in 1918, many felt that the country needed a new writing system to reflect its new position in the world. In 1920 the linguist Johannes Aavik gave voice to some of these thoughts in the perfectly titled pamphlet "Ü or Y? Y!"[10] His proposal was simple: replace the letter *ü* with *y*. Aavik gave eight reasons why this should be done, two of which were that it would bring Estonian closer to its sister language Finnish, and move it further away from German, whose influence Estonia was still trying to escape. Some people liked Aavik's change, but outside nationalist-artistic circles, it never quite caught on. Between 1918 and 1939, this didn't seem so important, as Estonia's independence—cultural as well as political—seemed assured.

After World War II, when Estonia was annexed by the Soviet Union, questions of orthography and politics once again loomed large. Soviet authorities closely regulated Estonian spelling. The use of the Aavik *y* was strictly forbidden. Its use now began to blossom in the cultural underground, appearing in *samizdat* journals and in the manuscripts of dissident poets. Originally introduced to bring Estonian closer to Europe, *y* now signified a rejection of everything Russian and thus, ironically, made it a stronger signifier of Estonian-ness.

In Estonia, as in most Eastern European nations, language and script were inextricably linked to religion and identity. To be Estonian or Lithuanian, and not Russian, meant being Lutheran or Catholic, and not Eastern Orthodox. This in turn meant using the Latin alphabet instead of the Cyrillic. Alphabets represented faiths, which made the choice of script all the more difficult and fraught for peoples who practiced more than one religion. Nowhere was this more true than in Albania, where people were divided among the Catholic, Eastern Orthodox, and Muslim faiths. Before the twentieth century, Albanian wasn't much used as a literary language. Indeed, it was seldom written at all, but when it was, it might be set down in the Arabic, Latin, Greek, or Cyrillic alphabet.

In central Albania, where the three faiths overlapped most completely, selecting any one of these scripts as a standard must have seemed hopeless. In the eighteenth century, local savants, sensing a need, began devising their own alphabets. With fewer readers than any European country besides Montenegro, Albania nonetheless became a veritable laboratory of orthographic invention. The city of Elbasan alone had at least two different alphabets. One was devised by an Orthodox cleric, the other by a learned silversmith.[11] Both men studied in Moschopolis, the Vlach merchant capital and great lost center of Balkan learning. They seem to have arrived at their scripts independently and to have used them largely for the conduct of local church business.

There have been at least ten Albanian scripts, and some seem to have been mostly private affairs. Only one of these varied alphabets was created with a genuinely national purpose in mind. It was the work of Naum Veqilharxhi, a lawyer and scholar whose family came from the town of Vithkuq, near Korçë. He ultimately settled in Romania, then the center of the Albanian émigré community, where he worked as a lawyer. In his spare time, he devoted himself to devising and promoting a script that could unify Albanians of all faiths.

The alphabet that Veqilharxhi came up with was utterly unique. He based it neither on Latin nor on Cyrillic, so as not to prejudice Muslims or members of either Christian denomination against it. He hoped that his script might become truly national, and encourage Albanians to cultivate their own language and stop its replacement by foreign tongues. To this end, he prepared spelling books and primers for children and had them distributed over southern Albania. A few pupils seem to have learned the new alphabet and remembered it into old age, but Veqilharxhi did not live to see his limited success. A year after a revised version of his spelling book appeared in 1845, he was dead. Rumor had it that he was poisoned in Istanbul by assassins sent by the Greek Orthodox patriarch of Constantinople. Nationalism wasn't a threat only to empires. Any national movement among Ottoman Christians had the potential to weaken the church's hold on the faithful. Religions, too, felt their grip loosening in the face of this powerful new source of group identity.

Nationalism created nations. An ideology of belonging, it drew people toward itself. It appealed especially to those who felt themselves powerless or adrift and sought a way to make themselves count on some larger "world" scale. In the words of one historian, it was a means by which "small men, heading small communities, could yet partake of wholeness."[12]

In this pursuit of recognition, culture mattered at least as much as politics. Like language, it was a scene of battle.

In the eighteenth century, Enlightenment philosophers had regarded culture as part of a universal pursuit of reason (which was to be conducted, naturally enough, in French), but by the nineteenth century, culture seemed like an international contest over which people possessed the greatest spirit. The Germans kept insisting it was Germany—who else could boast of a Goethe, a Kant, a Beethoven? And which of their eastern neighbors could claim a language of equal antiquity and elegance? Where were the ancient songs of the Slavs?

In the early nineteenth century, Eastern European nationalists thirsted for a way to answer this challenge. They needed masterpieces that they could claim as their own, as well as a heroic history to boast about. Ideally, an epic work from the distant past that might satisfy both cravings. Where none could be found, one would have to be invented.

The age of nationalism was a golden age of forgery. Again, the Czechs led the way. Beginning in 1817, a series of miraculous discoveries shook the budding Czech intellectual scene. First a medieval manuscript was found in the basement of a church in the small town of Dvůr Králové, on the Elbe River. It dated back to the thirteenth century and contained a number of epic poems and ballads, including some about a Slavic-led revolt against Charlemagne, that—wonder of wonders!—were written in Czech. Germans had been crowing for decades about *their* rediscovered national epic, the *Nibelungenlied*. Some literary critics had even begun calling it the "German *Iliad*." Now, miraculously, Czechs had an *Iliad* of their own, full of medieval combat and chivalry, that was just as ancient and poetic.

The second discovery was even more sensational. In 1818 another forgotten manuscript surfaced, seemingly out of nowhere, in the hands of Václav Hanka, a brilliant young scholar and active "awakener" with a passion for everything related to Slavic antiquity. According to Hanka, the manuscript arrived in an anonymous letter sent by a Bohemian aristocrat who was sympathetic to the Czech cause. The sender claimed that he had found the text, which was written in green ink on an ancient piece of parchment, while visiting the castle of Zelená Hora, or Green Mountain. He was afraid that the castle's owner, a German who hated all things Czech, might destroy the fragment if it came into his possession. Therefore he was entrusting it to what he hoped would be Hanka's more discerning hands.

The main part of this mysterious text, known as the Green Mountain Manuscript, was a poem that was later dubbed the "Judgment of Libuše." It seemed to date to the eighth or ninth century—that is, to the very dawn of Slavic prehistory. It told of Libuše, the pagan priestess who ruled over the Czechs before they accepted Christianity. The description of Libuše in the poem departed sharply from previous versions of the story. Medieval chroniclers, generally hostile to a strong pagan queen, portrayed Libuše as a somewhat debauched sorceress who sprawled about with her sisters in a nest of pillows and possessed a rather unnatural degree of power over her male subjects. By contrast, in "Judgment of Libuše," she is a stateswoman, seated upon a golden throne before the assembled nobles of the Czech state.

As the poem starts, Libuše has been called upon to settle an inheritance dispute between two brothers. One brother wants to follow ancient Czech custom and manage their father's property jointly. The other wants to follow the German way and split it up.[13]

Libuše makes her decision on the basis of written laws, as civilized people should. A blazing fire of truth testifies to the soundness of her conclusion. Everyone present opposes following the foreign custom. As one excited prince shouts forth, "It is wrong to go for the truth to Germany; we have our own truth and holy laws." Libuše agrees. To the Czech awakeners, her message, transmitted over a millennium, was clear: Czechs deserve Czech laws, administered by a Czech state.[14]

This very of-the-moment message was perfectly tailored to the needs of Bohemia's rather timid nationalists, who sought little more than limited autonomy within the tight bounds set by Habsburg absolutism. Its very topicality inspired instant suspicion: were these really the words of a medieval pagan priestess?

From the moment of their discovery, prominent philologists and Slavicists questioned whether the "Judgment of Libuše" and other rediscovered manuscripts were real. But by the time the manuscripts were published, it was too late for skepticism: they had already become the focus of a patriotic cult. Czechophile teachers slipped copies of the "medieval" poems to their favorite pupils. Schoolboys cut class just to read them, their hearts ablaze with "inexpressible joy" at the sudden knowledge that they too were Czech.[15] Decades later, when Bohemia received its first Czech-language university, its students were taught that the manuscripts' songs were finer than the works of Homer.[16] When a Czech-language National Theater finally opened in Prague, its first performance was an operatic retelling of Libuše's story written by the composer Bedřich Smetana.

Still, questions of authenticity kept swirling around the manuscripts. German scholars insisted they were fake. Czechs patriotically insisted they were real. By then, belief in the manuscripts had become part of the national credo: to doubt Libuše was to doubt the rightness of the Czech cause itself. It was all the more surprising, then, that in 1886 it was a Czech scholar, Tomáš Masaryk, who finally proved that the manuscripts were fraudulent. He would go on to become the first president of an independent Czechoslovakia. But not even his brilliant analysis could put an end to the controversy.

Later, during the period of High Stalinism in the early 1950s, the question of the manuscripts' authenticity was a forbidden topic for researchers. It resurfaced during the ideological thaw of the late 1960s. Shortly before the onset of Prague Spring in 1968, the manuscripts were taken out of their archive and moved to the Criminological Institute of the secret police, where they were subjected to a battery of new tests. Secret police experts determined that the manuscripts were indeed a forgery, though one skillfully concocted out of genuine materials. Suspicion fell most heavily on their discoverer, Václav Hanka, a skilled philologist who had had all the scholarly tools needed to create the brilliant fake. But by the time the analysis was complete, the topic of the forgeries was once again forbidden, and the results of the investigation were guarded as a state secret.

Not every people in Eastern Europe had to resort to forgery to reconstruct an epic past. Among the Serbs, for instance, songs about past heroes had circulated for centuries. They told, among many other things, of the wars fought long ago against the Ottomans: the defeat at the Battle of Kosovo, the sacrifice of Prince Lazar, and the assassination of Sultan Murad—in short, the whole, heroic demise of the Kingdom of Serbia in the fourteenth century. Wandering bards would retell these stories to the accompaniment of a stringed instrument called a *gusle*. Sometimes they would compose new versions of their own.

In the early nineteenth century, the Serbian philologist and anthropologist Vuk Karadžić collected many of these tales and published them abroad, to wide international acclaim. Karadžić couldn't publish them in Serbia itself, however, because its ruler, Prince Miloš Obrenović, thought they were too incendiary. Serbia was then still nominally a vassal of the Ottoman Empire, and Obrenović worried that publication of Karadžić's epic songs might inspire Serbs to stage a fresh revolt, thus imperiling his rule.

In publishing his *Serbian Folk Songs* outside Serbia, Karadžić tapped into a living bardic tradition, whose improvisatory techniques would later be studied by American scholars to understand the composition of ancient masterworks like the *Iliad* and the *Odyssey*. The peoples of the Baltic countries, also suffering from the epic fever of the nineteenth century, had no equivalent of those heroic tale-cycles to draw on. But neither did they imitate the Czechs and resort to forging stories out of whole cloth. Rather, they relied on a sort of poetic bricolage, fabricating their national epics out of a jumble of history, fantasy, and myth.

Inspired by the Finnish *Kalevala*, first published in 1835, Friedrich Reinhold Kreutzwald cobbled together the Estonian national poem, the *Kalevipoeg*, out of local legends and a Finnish ballad about a wayward giant. Andrejs Pumpurs likewise created the Latvian national epic, *Lāčplēsis*, or *The Bear-Slayer*, out of folktales explaining the origin of various place names, which he strung together around a tale set during the medieval wars between the pagan Latvians and Christian Crusaders.

Although both works aimed to convey a sense of the primeval, they were very much a product of their time. The Latvian *Bear-Slayer* includes explicit advocacy on behalf of liberal democracy. In the opening acts of the epic, the titular hero kills a bear with his bare hands and fends off various other threats to the community, ranging, in order of increasing menace, from ogres to Germans. Afterward the hero's father patiently explains to him that all his fancy deeds in no way entitle him to leadership of the tribe. Unlike some other, unnamed peoples, Latvians elect their rulers, who serve for strictly limited terms. Readers could hardly miss that this was not the case in the Russian Empire to which Latvia then belonged.

The Estonian *Kalevipoeg* preached a similarly progressive creed. It was particularly vehement in its insistence on nonviolence, a core principle of the Estonian national struggle against czarist Russia. However, this was a somewhat odd value to express in a poem purportedly written in the chaos of the barbarian age. The poem's main plot concerns a bloodthirsty giant who wanders the Baltic coast ravaging maidens and challenging other giants to duels. It is the hero's own sword that delivers the message of tolerance and the need for just laws to circumscribe mankind's more irrational impulses. Then, because of a misunderstanding—and a blacksmith's curse—the sword cuts off the giant's feet.

Belonging to a nation meant speaking a single language and dreaming a single dream. Epics—whether bogus or not—satisfied both cravings. Some nationalists thought that was enough. In 1839 a Baltic German journalist advised his Estonian readers that if they wanted a nation, all they had to do was to create "an epic and a history," and all would be won. But the truth was that nations also needed heroes.

In the Eastern Europe of the nineteenth century, national heroes were rarely statesmen. Most often they were living (or preferably, recently deceased) writers, whom audiences elevated to the status of bards, champions of language. Bards created works of genius and raised their peoples' speech to heretofore unknown heights. They suffered profoundly—for their art, but also for their devotion to their homeland.

Bards were more than poets. They were martyrs and saints, on whose shoulders rested all the aspirations of the tribe. They were also quintessential products of the Romantic mind. At the beginning of the nineteenth century Percy Bysshe Shelley wrote that the poet "is a lawgiver for humanity." Much of Eastern Europe took this ideal literally.[17] Bards were expected to be activists as well as symbols, giving voice to the nation not just in their works but in their deeds. Their lives often mattered at least as much as, or more than, their words.

So did their style, for which Lord Byron, as both a poet and a man of action, served as the main inspiration. Of all the national poets, none imitated him more closely than Poland's Adam Mickiewicz. Usually dressed in fashionably striped trousers and wide-collared shirts accented with colored scarfs, the poet had a penchant for sitting atop mountain crags while gazing pensively at the horizon. In photographs, he likewise preferred to be shown staring into the middle distance, as if on the cusp of receiving some fresh prophecy.[18]

Matchboxes with pictures of
Adam Mickiewicz. Warsaw, 1899.

Montenegro's Petar II Petrović-Njegoš achieved the same Byronic effect as Mickiewicz, but he came by it much more naturally. As prince-bishop, he was simultaneously his country's secular ruler and its highest religious dignitary. Tall, thin, and regal, sporting a magnificent black mustache and beard—and dying of tuberculosis to boot—Njegoš looked every inch the Romantic hero. Whenever he traveled abroad, he traded his bishop's cloak for the shirt and trousers of a Montenegrin warrior. Njegoš was also the author of long verse epics that described Montenegro's bloody history of wars with the Ottomans, as well as the workings of the universe. Sadly, he was one of the very few literate people in his country. Virtually the whole of Montenegrin literature up until that point had been penned by previous prince-bishops, who wrote down the events of their respective reigns. Nonetheless, Njegoš's works entered into oral tradition and became so popular that even recently it was not uncommon to meet people in Montenegro who, though otherwise illiterate, could recite long stretches of Njegoš's *Mountain Wreath* from memory.[19]

Not all bards were cut from such heroic cloth. Karel Mácha and France Prešeren, the poets responsible for the national poems of the Czechs and Slovenes respectively, were made of rather more bourgeois stuff. A pair of small-town lawyers, both men were devoted to beer drinking and extramarital sex and struggled with stunted careers. Somewhat plump and quite plain, their longish hair was the only signifier of an incipient bohemianism.

By contrast, Romania's Mihai Eminescu looked the part of a true nonconformist. Shabbily dressed, stocky, hairy, coffee-swilling, and chain-smoking, he resembled a crumpled beat reporter more than the Romantic idol he would one day become. He made up for his appearance through sheer misery. Ignored throughout his life and intensely manic-depressive, he died, unnoticed and unmourned, after years of terrible suffering in an insane asylum. In time, his fellow Romanians' neglect became an integral part of his legend.

Overfed, sex-crazed, disheveled, preening, and reckless, the national bards were flawed vessels for great ideas. It was their fate, as well as their fortune, to suffer in the name of the nation. Suffering mattered a great deal. As a Slovenian critic once wrote about their national poet France Prešeren, becoming a Slovenian culture hero required a certain "degree of unhappiness."[20] Like the martyrs of old, they were expected to shed blood to prove the justice of their cause.

Bad luck was virtually a prerequisite to national sainthood. A tragic death was also a must; ideally, it would come in the course of securing the nation's lost statehood. Hungary's Sándor Petőfi was killed in battle with the Russians during the failed Hungarian Revolution of 1848–9. True, he participated in the battle only as an observer, and he died as he was fleeing the enemy. But those details hardly mattered: Petőfi's legend as Hungary's tragic prophet was secure from that moment on. In the words of one critic, he was the "only poet who personally led a popular revolution."[21] And this reputation was at least partially earned. Petőfi's recitation of his own poems from the steps of Budapest's National Museum really did help to spark the revolt.

In terms of quantity of verse, at least, Bulgaria's Hristo Botev was not much of a poet—in the course of his brief life, he wrote no more than twenty verses. But he was a superbly tragic rebel. The revolution against the Ottomans he planned in 1876 with a few dozen of his émigré friends came to nothing; it ended in his death and the capture or execution of nearly everyone involved. Later enshrined as the quintessential national martyr (and more dubiously, as an ardent Communist), Botev was commemorated in the names of a mountain, a city, countless streets, an asteroid, and an Antarctic cape.

Taras Shevchenko, Ukraine's national poet, never got a chance to prove his courage on the battlefield. Born into serfdom, he showed an early talent for art, which persuaded some painters to buy his freedom. For the crime of insulting the wife of Czar Nicholas I in one of his satiric poems, Shevchenko was imprisoned in St. Petersburg and then sent into exile. In his poetry, he railed against Peter and Catherine the Great as the twin destroyers of Ukrainian liberty.[22] In keeping with the internationalist bent of mid-nineteenth-century nationalism, he also praised the rebellion of the Czech heretic Jan Hus and extolled the valor of Islamic insurgents fighting the Russian Empire.

But even poets whose deaths had nothing to do with the work of national liberation found themselves canonized. The Czechs' Karel Mácha died from a cold he caught after helping some neighbors put out a house fire. Romantic legend recast it as a case of poetic exhaustion: having poured all his strength into his work, Mácha died spent, at the peak of his creative powers. This story persisted long after Mácha's unpublished diaries revealed him to have been a compulsive womanizer and masturbator—not quite the delicate flower described by his disciples. Still, over time, Mácha's legend became enormous. The process by which this happened allows us to glimpse the way nationalism transformed from an essentially literary movement into the stuff of mass politics.

Mácha died in 1836. In 1859 a ball was held in his honor in Prague. At the time, this was one of the very few forms of gathering permitted by

Austrian authorities, who otherwise banned all forms of mass protest or association. At the high point of the evening, the guests gathered to read a poem about Mácha. They had to do so silently, because public speeches and declamations were also forbidden.[23] One thing the celebrants could do was sing, so the night ended with a performance of Czech national songs. Two years later the funeral of Václav Hanka, the discoverer (or really forger) of the "Judgment of Libuše," was capped by a stirring performance of Czech songs sung by a 120-member all-male choir. The choir, named Hlahol after the sound of bells and the ancient Glagolitic alphabet, was an instant success. It quickly grew to enormous size and led to the creation of a Czech-wide network of copycat "national" choirs.

Similar developments took place in other Eastern European countries. Choral societies blossomed in fin-de-siècle Sarajevo. In Estonia and Latvia, choirs, and especially song festivals, played a genuinely pivotal role in their respective national revivals.[24] In the Czech lands, however, the proliferation of singing societies was merely one symptom in a broader move to nationalize every aspect of life. Competition with the large and economically successful German minority spurred this process into overdrive. Any cultural institution or association dominated by Germans had to have a separate Czech equivalent. Beginning in the 1860s, Czechs founded their own artistic societies, theaters, and schools.

This process of nationalization reached well beyond the confines of high culture. Starting in 1862, to counter the German-supported gymnastic clubs called Turnvereine, Czech patriots began patronizing their own clubs, called Sokols, or "Falcons," which sought to hone Czech bodies for the glory of the nation. From 1882, they held huge jamborees in Prague, during which thousands of muscular Czech men (and eventually women) exercised in unison, creating a vast visual spectacle of Czech strength.

At the same time, Czech buyers rebelled against the supremacy of German beer. In towns throughout Bohemia, Czechs founded their own breweries, while Czech customers began buying exclusively Czech beers. The terms of this rivalry even wove themselves into Prague's urban fabric. One reason the city has so many fine art nouveau and Secession-era buildings is that Czech and German developers tried to outdo one another in the wealth of ornament and ingenuity of decoration incorporated into their properties. Hence the profusion of wonderful facades dating to the turn of the century. One of the prettiest was the headquarters of the Hlahol Choirs. The association's motto, "From the Song to the Heart, From the Heart to the Homeland," spelled out in gold letters above a mosaic of a rainbow-winged phoenix, conveys the heady atmosphere of that music-drunk age.

However, by the time that phoenix was completed in 1905, most Czechs were no longer content to just sing about their grievances. In the last decades of the nineteenth century, the politics of nationalism in the Austro-Hungarian Empire steadily hardened, as the invisible walls between communities rose higher and higher. At the same time, the empire as a whole had liberalized itself, dropping many previous restrictions on free speech and creating venues for actual voting and mass movements. Czechs no longer had to read encomia to their lost bards in silence. They could celebrate them in the streets, as could the Slovenes, Poles, Croats, and all the other nationalities of the empire. Paradoxically, this had the effect of making many tensions worse. Once-minor disagreements over the details of language policy and educational regulation now felt like battles for survival.

By the year 1900, parliamentary politics in the Austro-Hungarian Empire revolved almost entirely around minutiae of national precedence. In 1897 the introduction of a law that would have required bureaucrats in Bohemia to learn Czech sparked rioting across Austria, especially among university students furious at this insult to the supremacy of German. When the law was withdrawn, a second wave of riots spread out from Prague across the Czech-speaking lands. In a subsequent campaign, Czech nationalists tried to get their army recruits to answer roll call with the Czech *zde* instead of the German *hier*. This seemed so threatening to Emperor Franz Joseph that he threatened the Czechs with martial law.[25] In 1906 the Hungarian Diet ground to a halt over the equally trivial question of the colors of the tassels on Hungarian army officers' sabers: should they be in the imperial black and yellow, or the Hungarian red and green?[26]

Regarded in isolation, each of these controversies appeared small, but their cumulative effect was genuinely ominous. A spiderweb of fractures was appearing on the once-placid surface of the old monarchy. Under the impetus of defeat in the First World War, these cleavages would prove fatal, but they were also impossible to avoid. If Eastern European nationalists approached issues of language with a vehemence that seemed unusual, or even irrational, to their coequals in the West, it was because they were haunted by the threat of cultural extinction.

These fears of disappearance would be hard for anyone from France or England to understand, but to many Eastern Europeans they appeared as a terrifyingly real possibility. At the close of the nineteenth century, Polish- and Ukrainian-language education was largely prohibited within the Russian Empire. In Hungary, Slovak and Romanian were steadily losing ground to Hungarian, while across the Austrian half of the monarchy, the force of German economic might and influence beckoned inexorably.

The historical precedents were equally ominous. As the Czech and Slovak "Awakeners" of the early nineteenth century knew well, much of eastern Germany had once been a Slavic heartland, populated by tribes of obdurately pagan tree-worshippers. But who today remembers the Polabians, Obotrites, or Wagrians that once lived there? Centuries of Teutonic expansion had driven most of them to assimilate. The only traces they left behind were a few scattered place names and the last surviving speakers of Wendish, whose numbers had shrunk to a handful by the late eighteenth century.

The Baltic languages, too, had suffered terrible losses since the Middle Ages. Curonian, Sudovian, Skalvian, and Semigallian all vanished from the shores of the Baltic, their speakers killed, Christianized, and ultimately transformed into German-speakers by the long onslaught of the Teutonic Knights in the thirteenth and fourteenth centuries. Old Prussian (a Baltic, not a German language—the name "Prussia" is another thing the Crusaders nicked from the pagans) survived a bit longer: its last speakers died of the bubonic plague sometime around 1710. But it lasted long enough to acquire a small print literature, almost entirely religious in nature. The secular content of Old Prussian writing, by contrast, appears to be restricted to a single rhyming couplet. Scribbled on the margins of a Latin philosophical treatise held by the University of Basel, it was discovered in 1974 by an American graduate student. The couplet reads: "Cheers Sir! A fine friend you must be / if you want to drink but refuse to pay the fee." It seems to have been written by a Prussian student in Prague around 1369 who was upset with the stinginess of his drinking buddies.[27]

National revivalists lived in dread that their languages might join Old Prussian in the linguistic graveyard. Hence the urgency of their task. But once the work of awakening had begun, where should it end? Oppression was usually just a matter of scale. If empires were the jailers of nations, then nation-states were themselves prison houses of smaller peoples. Each of these lay in wait for a champion of their own to guarantee their place in the sun.

.   .   .

Óndra Łysohorsky was one of Eastern Europe's last national awakeners. His quest was also among the most quixotic. He was born Ervin Goj in 1905 in Moravian Silesia, a border region near the place where today the Czech Republic, Poland, and Slovakia converge. Łysohorsky was a pseudonym—Goj took it from the names of a seventeenth-century Silesian bandit and the mountain that served as his base. His birthplace, the town of Frýdek, was well known as a local pilgrimage site. People there spoke a multitude of languages: German, Slovak, Polish, Moravian, and Czech. They also spoke a language all their own, incorporating vocabulary and features from them all. Łysohorsky named this tongue, which wasn't written down or taught in schools, "Lachian." He resolved to become its poet laureate.

Beginning in the 1930s, by which time Frýdek was already part of an independent Czechoslovakia, Łysohorsky developed a writing system for Lachian, one that borrowed features from both Polish and Czech. This infuriated Czechs, who accused him of trying to subvert national unity. Poles, meanwhile, hardly noticed. Nonetheless, Łysohorsky persisted, publishing poetry and prose in a language no one had ever read before. A few disciples responded to his summons and formed a literary society, but the outbreak of World War II put an end to their experimentation.

Łysohorsky spent most of the war years in the Soviet Union. There he continued writing in Lachian, even though the Czechoslovak Communists in exile demanded that he stop, for like the capitalist Czechs, they were afraid Lachian would drive a wedge through unified Czecho-slovakia. In 1944, driven to despair by their interference, Łysohorsky wrote to Stalin to complain about his troubles. The move backfired, and he soon found it even more difficult to publish his work. In subsequent years, W. H. Auden championed his poems, and Marina Tsvetaeva and Boris Pasternak translated them into Russian. Still, Łysohorsky had few opportunities to communicate in his chosen tongue at home.

By then, these disappointments could not have come as a great sur-prise. Łysohorsky was always out of step with his times. He started his work of awakening too late, long after the vogue for linguistic revivals had passed. Not many people in his native Silesia read or cared about his writing in Lachian. Few could even read it fluently, for although Łysohorsky liked to claim that as many as 2 million people across Poland and Czechoslovakia spoke Lachian, the specific language he wrote in corresponded to the speech of only a tiny area, delimited by the valley of the Ostravice River.

Before his death in 1989, some of Łysohorsky's Czech critics begged him to soften his stance and admit that Lachian was just a dialect of Czech. Barring that, they told him that even small concessions, like substituting a Czech *v* for the Polish *w,* could win him more readers. But Łysohorsky remained steadfast. When pressed, he would recall his childhood and the little alleyway by the Church of St. Mary in Frýdek where he grew up. He could still recall all his neighbors: there was Mrs. Lehner, a German; Staš and Gladyš, the Poles; and Skotnica, Hesek, Farnik, and Zawadsky, all Lachs.[28] To the end of his life, Łysohorsky kept faith with them. He didn't concern himself with armies or govern-ments; his nationalism was the nationalism of a single street in a single town.

Part III

The Twentieth Century

9

Moderns

Three sisters on a motorbike. Poland, 1910.

No part of Europe is more remote, or farther removed from civilization, than the Pripyat Marshes. Located in Polesia, along today's border between Belarus and Ukraine, the marshes were a land of impassable bogs, meandering streams, and sucking muds, with nary a bridge or a road in sight. The area was fabled for its backwardness and inaccessibility, two facts that gave rise to the legend—as persistent as it is spurious—that it was the primordial homeland of the Slavs. In short, the marshes were not a place where one would go to appreciate the latest fashions or styles. And yet by 1900, the gifts of modernity had arrived even here.

Janina Puttkamerowa was eleven years old in 1900. She grew up among the Polish gentry of the Vilnius Governorate of the Russian Empire, but she spent her summers and holidays at Dereszewicze, her grandmother's manor in Polesia. It was a grand house, built on a bluff just above the Pripyat River. In her memoirs, Janina writes that the view of endless flooded fields across the river from the manor terrace put her in mind of America, just before the pilgrims came to spoil it.[1]

Once a day a steamboat would pass below the manor. Often it brought guests. Cheerful Aunt Wiwa, who arrived waving an ostrich feather boa, in a dress covered in so many silk flounces and lace ribbons that she looked like a ship at full sail. Or moody Aunt Isia, who wore modest but expertly tailored dresses, freshly purchased from the finest Vienna couturiers. Isia's favorite gown was made of rose-colored moiré silk, lined with iridescent taffeta. It made a gentle rustling noise when she walked, perfect for discreetly announcing her presence when gentlemen callers dropped by.

The routine at Dereszewicze was pleasant but unvarying. The adults, back from seasons on the Riviera or in the Swiss Alps, played cards in the parlor and read French journals while the children played croquet and took drawing lessons from an English governess. Every evening the whole household gathered for a stroll in the gardens. Together they walked in the shade of ornamental poplar trees and through avenues lined with flowers. They admired the smell of the blossoms: the sharpness of verbena, the sweetness of phlox, the muskiness of carnations.

The highlight of every summer came on August 4, when the family held a great picnic in honor of Janina's grandmother's birthday. Everyone in the house took rowboats downriver to a certain meadow, where the servants, all dressed as sailors, laid out baskets of fruit, cakes, and ice cream. At dusk the company gathered back at the manor for a night of amateur theatricals. Garlands of blue, pink, and yellow lanterns hung above the patio. Under their colorful glow, the ladies of the house presented a series of living tableaux, drawn from the works of Shakespeare, Mickiewicz, and Titian. One year Aunt Isia, always the most dramatic Puttkamerowa sister, threw a fit when the fireworks didn't go off in time to illuminate her nymph costume.

Isia was also the most modern of the siblings. She kept abreast of all the newest trends in art, and she introduced all of Dereszewicze to the works of the decadent Young Poland movement—the scandalously abstract poetry of Włodzimierz Tetmajer and the alarming Stanisław Przybyszewski, whose plays were considered so intoxicating that in St. Petersburg it was said only cocaine and ether could offer comparable stimulation. Not everyone at the house shared her enthusiasm for these authors. To the older generation, they seemed utterly perverse, signs of a culture in the midst of a stroke.

Beautiful and gifted, Isia was prone to violent changes of mood. For many years, she carried on an affair with the Russian governor of Minsk, Count Musin-Pushkin. Every day at noon his black carriage appeared in front of her husband's manor—that is, until he was dismissed for combating protesters too gently during the aborted revolution of 1905.

With her lover back in Petersburg, Isia succumbed to a lengthy and mysterious illness. In 1906 she walked into the river running through her Minsk estate. Her husband, who had maintained a discreet silence during her affair, planted a Manchurian apricot tree on the spot where she drowned and proceeded to lose everything he had to speculators and con artists. The rest of Isia's family remembered her with the help of three painted portraits, two in Warsaw and one in the country. But as her niece Janina wrote, in a country like Poland, where "everything is lost from wars and invasions," none of these survived the disasters of 1939.[2]

During her brief life, Isia was convinced she was ahead of her time. In this, she was perfectly *of* her time. A new spirit had taken hold of Eastern Europe by 1900. It might be most easily characterized as a violent disjuncture between the heart and the head. Materially, things had never been better. Europe was nearing the end of almost a half-century of (barely) interrupted peace. Most adults had never heard a shot fired in anger. That same half-century witnessed an unprecedented burst of economic growth and technical innovation. When steamships were dropping passengers off at Dereszewicze, citizens of Budapest were already riding the city's first underground metro line, which had opened in 1896. Cities, for the first time, were illuminated at night, something Eastern Europe took an unexpected lead in: Lviv was the first city to use modern kerosene lamps, and Timişoara, in present-day Romania, was the first city in Europe to be lit by electricity.

Railways now crisscrossed the continent, reaching even Janina's home in the forgotten Lithuanian hamlet of Bieniakonie. Grain from Ukraine flooded the American market, while wood from the remotest forests of Lithuania could be shipped all the way to Liverpool and beyond. Buoyed by these new connections, landowners grew suddenly and unexpectedly rich. Janina's family, rich in timber, spent their holidays alternately in Provence, Florence, and St. Moritz.

But however prosperous things might have seemed, spiritually there was a feeling of mounting crisis. Everywhere people put their trust in progress and scientific discovery, to the detriment of older faiths. In politics, nationalism still held sway—indeed, its influence had never been greater—but in the arts, its primacy had begun to wane. The great national bards were still being celebrated, but more as icons of struggle than as writers to be read. Young people especially craved something new. Many were in open Oedipal revolt against their parents. Freud's work was not yet widely known, but it soon would be; *The Interpretation of Dreams* appeared in 1900.

Drunk on Nietzsche, and in awe of what was happening concurrently in Vienna and Paris, the writers of Eastern Europe's fin-de-siècle blasphemed Christ and consumed masses of opium. As a group, they died of alcoholism, syphilis, morphine, and suicide, usually in combination. The Czech writer Ladislav Klíma, who wrote eyebrow-singeing novellas about incest and necrophilia, starved himself and ate dead mice in the name of something he called "absolute will." Urmuz, the great hidden genius of the Romanian literary avant-garde, shot himself because of "the paralysis that makes one's life impossible." He was found in the bushes behind a fashionable Bucharest restaurant.[3] Géza Csáth, the Hungarian author of gorgeous, gemlike stories about magic, opium, and ennui, might have had the worst end of all: a botched murder-suicide, during which he killed his wife in a drug-induced haze, forgot about it, then poisoned himself after discovering what he had done.

. . .

The writers of 1900 thought of themselves as rebels, even though it is often hard to pinpoint exactly what they were rebelling against. They wrote with a sense that the complacent certainties of European civilization lay over everything vital and real in life like a suffocating blanket of snow. Their younger siblings, writing with the benefit of hindsight, looked back on the same years as a lost paradise. To them, the turn of the century was Europe's Indian summer, its last great, tragic flowering before war and revolution wiped away all the gains of peace and industry. When they returned to it after a gulf of decades, it was to a world of sensual delights. They remembered the feel of the pearl-colored leather gloves worn by gentlemen when they went courting, the smell of fresh butter wrapped in coltsfoot leaves, and the taste of real Chinese tea, brought by caravan across the steppe, still smelling of campfires and open skies. Above all, they thought of meals, especially those extraordinarily elaborate meals that required an army of servants to prepare, and that were as much a casualty of the First World War and the Great Depression as the gold standard and House of Habsburg.

Eugenie Fraser was brought up before the revolution in a well-to-do Scottish-Russian merchant family in distant Arkhangelsk, by the White Sea. She recalled the Easter feasts of her youth, featuring dishes of tender veal, pink ham, black and orange caviar, and pastries—pashkas, kuliches, and rumbabas, all arranged in a precise order around a great pyramid of eggs, colored crimson, blue, gold, and green.[4] The novelist Miklós Bánffy, the lord of Bonțida Castle and so a member of the highest aristocracy of Eastern Europe, remembered even grander occasions: *chaud-froid de bécasses panaché à la norvégienne* in a duchess's Budapest palazzo, and hunting feasts in the country, attended by archdukes, which were always capped with that "pièce de résistance at all Transylvanian banquets": cold Richelieu turkey with truffles.[5]

Most of the writers at work during this epoch of abundance were too absorbed in their neuroses and experiments to pay it much attention. The one great exception—who managed to bridge the generation that took the Belle Époque for granted, and the one who looked back on it as a distant dream—was the Hungarian novelist, journalist, and short story writer Gyula Krúdy. His work, abounding in sheer enjoyment of the finer things in life, may be the most *useful* body of literature ever compiled. Read, in combination, his writings will teach you everything worth knowing: how to die gracefully in a duel; how to behave after winning a tremendous amount at cards; how to manage hauntings, both romantic and sinister; what to order at taverns in every district of Buda, Pest, and even far-off Nyíregyháza; the right way to pickle cabbage, drink a beer, and pay a madam without causing insult; the best thing to have with a cold mug of beer (hot, fresh cracklings, cool green peppers, and a slice of brown bread); and the correct color of gravy to serve with a platter of roast duck (a deep golden yellow, like a glass of fine Tokaj).

Krúdy was not from Budapest; he grew up in the Hungarian provinces, far to the east. When he came to the city in 1896, he was only
seventeen, a disinherited, spendthrift youth and would-be poet. Krúdy
was also a wunderkind, already established as a writer for the back pages
of many newspapers, and a soon-to-be author of literary best sellers. He
fell upon the capital with an unrivaled appetite for pleasure. The city
answered him.

By then, Budapest was the largest city between St. Petersburg and
Vienna, a modern metropolis home to electric tramcars, first-rate
hotels, an excellent racetrack, and some of Europe's finest bordellos.
This was Krúdy's world. He became the great poet of taverns and ball-
rooms, casinos and racetracks, and the people who inhabited them:
manic newspaper editors, deadbeat journalists, Slovak barmaids, day-
dreaming waiters, and bloodthirsty officers with secretly tender hearts.
Krúdy lived amid them all, losing fortunes on horses and roulette and
drinking huge amounts of country wine, yet somehow managing to
write sixteen pages every day regardless, each one a testimony to the
sustained indulgence that only the Belle Époque, that most relaxed and
indulgent of all eras, could accommodate.

·   ·   ·

The long idyll came to an end quite abruptly, on July 28, 1914, in the
middle of a long and exceptionally beautiful summer. Most Eastern
Europeans who survived what followed remembered exactly where they
were and what they were doing on that fateful day.

The Hungarian artist Béla Zombory-Moldován was out for a swim.
He was staying at a resort near Abbazia on the Croatian coast—then
still a part of Hungary, and only a few hours by train from Budapest.
That morning he went out to a favorite spot on the coast, a sandbar by
the town of Novi. When he returned, a bathing attendant told him the
news: a month after the assassination of the heir to the throne, Archduke Franz Ferdinand, in Sarajevo, the monarchy had declared war on
Serbia. Conscription notices were already being posted at all the resorts
along the shore. In the time it had taken Béla to swim to the sandbar
and back, the world that he had known his entire life up to that moment
disappeared. Back in Budapest, he reflected in his diary that only one

thing was certain about the future: "the twentieth century would be the century of the Jews, and of revolutions."[6]

In Austria-Hungary as in Western Europe, news of the assassination and the declaration of war spread like lightning. In Russia, the news traveled much more slowly and was received with less immediate comprehension. In his old age, Mikhail Dmitrievich Bonch-Bruevich, then a general in the Russian army, remembered how the war arrived in Chernihiv, in northern Ukraine:

> Summer was at its peak. Tables somehow knocked together at the town fair were bursting under the weight of rosy apples, silver pears, flaming tomatoes, lilac-colored sweet onions, five-inch-thick pieces of salt pork that would melt in your mouth, fat-dripping, home-made sausages, all the things in which the flourishing Ukraine is so rich. A cloudless, blindingly blue sky hung over the dreaming town. Nothing, it seemed, could disturb the measured flow of peaceful provincial life.... Suddenly, at five in the afternoon on the 29th of July, the adjutant brought me a secret dispatch from Kiev . . . for the immediate putting of all units of the garrison on a premobilization footing.... Three days later came an order for general mobilization.... But with whom were we to fight? No one knew.[7]

Unbeknownst to all its participants, the war, which seemed at first as if it might be over by winter, would last four long, demoralizing, and ultimately disastrous years. For all of Eastern Europe's empires, regardless of which side they fought on, the war proved a death blow. In 1917 Czar Nicholas II abdicated, and the Russian Empire, as constituted since the conquests of Ivan the Terrible in the sixteenth century, came to an end. Austria-Hungary followed a year later. The Ottoman Empire, at least on paper, staggered along until 1922, at which time it transformed into the secular nation-state of Turkey we know today.

By then, the map of Eastern Europe was completely transformed, dotted with states that were either brand new to history, like Yugoslavia, Latvia, Estonia, and Czechoslovakia, or had lain dormant for centuries, like Poland, Hungary, and Lithuania. Over the course of the previous century, independence had become the dream of a great number of Eastern Europeans. Few expected the war to bring it about, or foresaw how much it would ultimately cost.

In the first days of the war, the dominant emotion was exhilaration, the kind that comes from an expectation of certain victory. This overconfidence led to moments of misplaced chivalry. On the day when Austria-Hungary declared war on Serbia, the chief of the Serbian general staff, General Radomir Putnik, happened to find himself stranded in Budapest, deep in enemy territory. Putnik was a ferocious commander, a hero of the recent Balkan Wars against the Ottomans and Bulgarians. The Habsburg high command demanded his immediate arrest. Franz Joseph considered this unsportsmanlike and ordered that he be let go. A special train was summoned for the general, which whisked him off to Belgrade, where he immediately proceeded to whip the invading Austrians.[8]

The elation felt at the start of the war was followed swiftly by confusion, chaos, and defeat. Russia joined on the Serbian side, as did England and France. Germany and the Ottomans sided with Austria. The Austrian strategy called for a swift thrust into Russia from Galicia. Elite cavalry regiments, staffed by the cream of the Polish and Hungarian aristocracy, prepared themselves for daring reconnaissance raids into Russian territory. Resplendent in their beautiful navy blue jackets, decorated with yards of red and gold braid, the cavalrymen streamed over the border, only to be mercilessly cut down by machine-gun fire.

The infantry fared little better. During the August mobilization, hundreds of thousands of men, drawn from the whole of the empire, were rounded up on trains and flung haphazardly at the enemy. Jaroslav Hašek's epic novel *The Good Soldier Švejk*, the comic *War and Peace* of the Eastern Front, is set almost entirely in these first chaotic weeks of the war. By September 1914, over a third of the nine hundred thousand men who had attacked Russia just a month earlier were either dead, wounded, or captured.[9] The officer corps was hit especially hard. Some regiments lost as many as 92 percent of their officers. By the end of 1914, the army as a whole had lost about half its officers. This was a deep disaster, for despite the parade of idiocy and incompetence depicted by Hašek, the officer corps was the backbone of the army.

The officers were especially crucial since the Austro-Hungarian army's very diversity represented a staggeringly complex problem of coordination and control. Only a superbly trained officer corps could hope to handle it. In theory at least, German was the language of command in the Austrian army. Recruits—no matter their native language—were supposed to memorize a list of eighty German instructions. Officers, meanwhile, were expected to become proficient in the language, or languages, of their troops.

On both sides, reality fell short of this ideal. Ill-trained soldiers struggled with their lists of memorized commands, while most of the better-educated officers were killed in the first months of the war. Some regiments resorted to a kind of improvised sign language to get their meaning across. Others found different means: a mixed Hungarian-Slovak-German regiment used English to communicate. The officers knew it from their time in fancy Austrian boarding schools, while the enlisted men had learned it abroad, while working in American steel mills.[10]

While the clash between the German, French, and British armies in France and Belgium quickly settled into a deadly slog of trench warfare, the battle lines to the east remained far more fluid for the duration of the war. Towns in Galicia changed hands many times. Stryj, my grandmother's birthplace, fell under the Russian army's control in the first few weeks of fighting. Along with the Russians came detachments of Cossacks, sitting astride tiny horses and sporting woolly Astrakhan caps. They made a great impression on the young Polish-Jewish writer Julian Stryjkowski, whose older brother risked going out into the streets to sell them cigarettes. The Cossacks didn't care about price and simply threw whatever silver rubles they had in their pockets into the mud. This made for good profits, but the Cossacks remained frightening customers. A few months later, when the Germans retook Stryj, the relieved townspeople greeted them with cigarettes and candies.[11] Later, when Russians reoccupied the town yet again, they renamed all the major thoroughfares in town after great Russian authors. For a few months, inhabitants of this Galician shtetl found themselves walking down streets named for Pushkin, Lermontov, and Gogol.

German soldiers generally behaved much better than Russian ones, even on Russian soil. They paid for food in cash, didn't loot, and treated civilians—including Jews—respectfully. The German army left a very good impression, so much so that when World War II started, one of my grandfather's cousins in Warsaw refused his pleas to leave the city and flee to the Soviet Union, saying that she knew the Germans and trusted that they were good people.

As an arena of war, the Eastern Front was unique for the fact that it had no winners. All the belligerent empires in the East ultimately lost. Russia hit the skids first. In February 1917 shortages of food triggered massive protests and strikes in the capital of St. Petersburg. Soon the city garrison joined in. In just a matter of days, Czar Nicholas II was forced to step down, to be replaced by a Provisional Government drawn from the fledgling Russian parliament.

For eight disastrous months, the Provisional Government kept Russia in the war against the Central Powers. During this time, the army suffered defeat after defeat on the battlefield, while in the streets, power reverted increasingly to street-level committees of soldiers and peasants called soviets. In October 1917 the Bolsheviks—who claimed to speak on behalf of the soviets—toppled the Provisional Government in a well-organized coup. One of their first acts was to signal their readiness to end the war and come to an agreement with Germany and Austria-Hungary.

For a moment, the Central Powers seemed to be ascendant. The German army swept through the Baltics, while Austrian troops pressed deep into Ukraine, setting up puppet governments wherever they went. However, away from the front lines, Berliners and Viennese were starving. In the summer of 1918, as a fresh wave of North American recruits arrived in France, German resistance crumbled in the West, while Austria failed to hold off the Italians. Even though foreign troops had yet to set foot on German or Austrian soil, the clock was already running out.

In Austria, the catastrophe began in the summer of 1918 with the disastrous campaign against Italy. By fall, as it seemed increasingly clear that Germany was about to lose, the Habsburgs' subject peoples began to set up their own national states. The Czechoslovaks went first, proclaiming their independence on October 28. In the following days, the Poles and Croats announced their intention to do the same. At the same time, Hungary tried to distance itself from the rest of the Habsburg monarchy, in the ultimately futile hope of securing a peace agreement on more favorable terms.

By November 3, the Austro-Hungarian Empire was no more. Scattered across the battlefields of the Balkans and the Italian Alps, soldiers of various ethnic groups marched off to their homelands, now reorganized as independent nation-states. This was fine for enlisted men, but Habsburg officers faced a more difficult quandary. At a stroke, thousands of men who regarded "the Monarchy as their extended family and their regiment as their immediate one"[12] awoke to find themselves with neither a purpose nor a home. These men belonged to a caste rather than a country. Now all of a sudden, their place of legal residence— once a nearly meaningless entry in their personnel file—determined whether they were to be citizens of Austria, Hungary, Czechoslovakia, Poland, Yugoslavia, or Romania.

Some of these newly formed states welcomed these now stateless men; others barred their doors against them. Many former Austrian officers fled to their spiritual home in Vienna, where they worked to secure pensions that immediately dissolved thanks to runaway inflation. There they were joined by tens of thousands of fellow officers, newly arrived from Russian captivity. Regular soldiers could count on spending their years of internment in Russia doing hard labor and dying of cholera. Officers were kept apart. If nothing else, prerevolutionary Russia respected rank. While interned, officers were exempt from all work and free to indulge their passions for music, language, or whittling.

Some undertook more unusual pursuits. At her manor in Vinohradiv, the American-born baroness Eleanor Perényi learned Hungarian from her tutor, Györffy. He had spent the war as an Austrian prisoner of war interned near Tomsk, where he learned fluent Russian and became a traveling salesman of children's games. Eventually, he tried to flee home to Hungary but he was stopped at the border on suspicion of being a spy. He had to spend the next two years in Siberia, where he was jailed by the Communists.[13]

Györffy was one of tens of thousands of Austro-Hungarian prisoners of war who got a chance to witness the Russian Revolution firsthand. Some became dangerously attracted to its ideals. Jaroslav Hašek, for instance, left a POW camp, joined the Bolsheviks, and briefly became a commissar and deputy military commander of the Bugulma District in Soviet Tatarstan. Hašek gave up politics on his return to the newly independent Czechoslovakia, but many other former prisoners remained radicalized by what they had seen. One of them even managed to stage a successful revolution of his own. Before the war, Béla Kun was a muckraking journalist from Transylvania. Captured in 1916 and interned in the Urals, a passing acquaintance with Lenin vaulted Kun into the revolution and the leadership of the fledging Hungarian Communist Party.

Kun arrived back in Budapest a week after the war's end. The Hungarian People's Republic was only a few days old, and already it was melting away, carved apart by soldiers advancing from the neighboring countries of Czechoslovakia, Romania, and Yugoslavia. When these losses, which amounted to 72 percent of the country's territory, were ratified into law by the Paris Peace Treaty, the government's position became untenable. The liberal prime minister abdicated. Kun, then in prison, did not even have to seize power; he won it by default.

The Hungarian Soviet Republic lasted exactly 133 days, from March to August 1919. During this brief reign, the writer Gyula Krúdy was summoned, along with a group of other "bourgeois journalists," for an audience with the people's commissar. The meeting took place in a villa confiscated from a count. Ragged soldiers armed with hand grenades filed through the streets. At first, Krúdy thought Kun was going to have them all executed. Soon, it became apparent that Kun merely wanted the support of as many writers as he could sway to the side of the revolution. For the next few hours, Kun harangued the assembled journalists about the soviet republic's plans for the collectivization of literature. During this speech, Krúdy looked in vain for the "charismatic note" that was supposed to have made Kun irresistible to proletarian crowds, but all he could see was "an insignificant looking man . . . normal enough to pass for the bridegroom at a village wedding."[14]

A few weeks later the revolution was over, and the Red Terror inflicted by Kun's "Lenin Boys" against their political opponents was replaced with a White Terror against the Communists, led by Admiral Miklós Horthy, formerly of the Austro-Hungarian navy, and soon to be regent of the unoccupied Hungarian throne. Kun himself was forced to flee, under rather dramatic circumstances. According to the novelist Dezső Kosztolányi, Kun began his escape at five in the afternoon, when he rose from the roof of the Soviet headquarters in the Hotel Hungaria in a twin-engine airplane. Kun flew the airplane himself, staying so close to the ground that his face could be clearly seen by those walking below:

> He was pale and unshaven as usual. He grinned at those below and gave an occasional shabby and sardonic wave of farewell. His pockets were stuffed with sweet pastry. He carried jewels, relics of the church and precious stones that had once belonged to well-disposed and generous aristocratic women. There were other valuables too. Great gold chains hung from his arms.[15]

As the airplane rose over the city, one of these gold chains fell down in the middle of a Buda park, where an elderly clerk from the Krisztina district picked it up. The plane finally disappeared from sight, and with it, Béla Kun vanished forever into the land of the soviets.

By the standards of the moment, the four months of the Hungarian Soviet Republic were practically an eternity. As empires crumbled in the wake of the war, new, provisional forms of social organization winked in and out of existence. Seen from above, the political map of Eastern Europe in the years immediately following the end of the First World War resembled a sky full of shifting clouds.

Beginning in 1916, a short-lived French-backed Albanian Republic ruled over a rump territory from the town of Korçë above Lake Ohrid; its one lasting accomplishment was teaching French to the future dictator Enver Hoxha. In 1918 two different clusters of Ruthenian villages, both nestled in the Carpathian Mountains, proclaimed their independence as the Komancza and Lemko republics, before being merged against their will into newly independent Poland. Meanwhile, on the border between Poland and Lithuania, the tiny republic of Perloja thrived under the rule of its revolutionary committee until 1923, when it was partitioned by its two neighbors.

To different degrees, each of these ephemeral states attempted to preserve a degree of local autonomy apart from the terrifying uniformity of the nation-state. Nowhere was this desire felt more keenly than in the Banat, one of Eastern Europe's most dazzlingly diverse regions and the home of the cosmopolitan city of Timişoara. In November 1918, as the Austro-Hungarian Empire was coming undone, the

German-Jewish lawyer Otto Roth proclaimed an autonomous Banat Republic, which he hoped would bring together the national aspirations of all the area's Hungarians, Germans, Romanians, and Serbs. German and Hungarian workers backed his vision; Romanian and Serbian farmers opposed it.

The Serbs organized a national council; the Romanians summoned a militia. Meanwhile most of the countryside belonged to peasant revolutionaries, known as the Greens, while two Serbian villages simultaneously declared themselves to be independent soviets, answerable to no one but themselves. By February 1919, the whole thing had fallen apart. The Banat Republic fell. Yugoslavia, Romania, and Hungary divided up its territory. Otto Roth fled but continued to dream of an independent Banat, perhaps, perversely, under the protection of the French overseas empire.

If the situation in the Banat was complicated, conditions in Ukraine bordered on total anarchy. In March 1918 Lenin, desperate for a peace agreement with the Central Powers, signed the Treaty of Brest-Litovsk, which effectively ceded Ukraine to German and Austrian control. For a few months, the Germans propped up a conservative government run by a new, pseudo-Cossack "hetman." By November, Germany had lost the war, and the hetman's days were numbered.

Over the course of the following year, Ukraine descended into chaos. In 1919 alone, six different armies operated on Ukrainian territory, and Kiev changed hands five times in less than a year.[16] Much of the territory in the country came under the control of local warlords, each of whom professed different aims and ideologies. Some were monarchists. Others allied with the Bolsheviks. Still others dreamed genuinely utopian dreams. In southern Ukraine, anarchists led by the revolutionary Nestor Makhno established the so-called Free Territory, a vast, self-organizing swath of agricultural communes spanning an area bigger than Belgium.

Defended by an army of horse-drawn machine-gun carts called *tachankas*, the Free Territory survived from 1918 until its defeat by the Soviet Red Army in 1921. In this respect, it shared the fate of all those who dreamed either of creating an independent Ukraine or of restoring the czar. What doomed all the Ukrainian national movements ultimately was a failure of vision. If they had embraced social revolution and given the peasants the land they longed for for centuries, they might have won their allegiance. As it was, they had to look to foreign allies to shore up their crumbling armies. Disunity furthered their disorganization, for where the various factions of Ukrainian social conservatives, royalists, and nationalists had many different ideas about how to return to the past, the Bolsheviks had one big idea about how to step into the future.

. . .

This idea was infectious and not just for Russians. Its essence was contained in the *soviets*, the self-administering and self-organizing councils that had ushered in the revolution against czarism and were only later co-opted by the Bolshevik Party. Each of these councils was a revolution in miniature, a claim that regular working people had as much right to administer their own affairs as aristocratic officers or crowned heads of state. My own great-grandfather, Salomon Mikanowski, joined one such soviet, organized by Red Army soldiers in the city of Vitebsk, where he was stationed as a soldier in what had been, until recently, the Russian Imperial Army. Salomon served as a judge in one of the soviet's improvised courts—the kind of tribunal that sentenced royalist officers to death for treason.

Vitebsk was not a particularly prepossessing place. A small, sleepy city in what's now eastern Belarus, it was described in a 1910 encyclopedia as "an old town, with decaying mansions of the nobility, and dirty Jewish quarters."[17] Five years of war, revolution, and civil strife could not have done much to improve things. And yet during the months my great-grandfather spent there, Vitebsk had a legitimate claim of being the center of the world. Three revolutions converged there simultaneously: one in politics, one in technology, and a third in the arts.

The last of these revolutions was launched from a former banker's house on Resurrection Street, now renamed after Lenin's close collaborator Nikolai Bukharin.[18] This was to be the site of the Vitebsk People's Art School, or UNOVIS, an all-ages, tuition-free institution whose aim was the artistic development of the proletariat and the dissemination of useful knowledge to the masses.

The school's first director was Marc Chagall, who in 1919 was not yet a purveyor of shtetl kitsch but a painter of strident revolutionary convictions, whose canvases bore such titles as *Peace to the Huts, War on the Stately Homes*. Searching for fellow instructors, Chagall invited the painter Kazimir Malevich to join him at the Vitebsk School. Tall and pockmarked but armed with the eyes of a hypnotist and a voice like a rapier, Malevich was by that point already an accomplished modernist. He was the leader of an artistic movement called suprematism, which called for rendering emotions through vector, shape, and color, without any reference to the "objective" world. Together with his acolytes, Malevich forced the more delicate Chagall out and took control of the school. Vitebsk now became the world center of not just suprematism but of the global avant-garde.

Malevich grew up on farms in the black earth country of central Ukraine. His father was a Polish engineer who managed sugar beet plantations and who had moved to Kiev after the failure of the 1863 uprising against Russian rule. As a child, Malevich came to know the smell of dirt and the sight of wide horizons. Now he sat in the UNOVIS offices writing—never painting—for twelve hours a day, plotting the construction of a new world. Outside his windows, he could see the Red Cavalry—Semyon Budyonny's Cossack squadron—passing by underneath on its way to fight the capitalist Poles—along with the Red Army's precious few airplanes, which were being transported to the front by rail.

Those airplanes were part of their own revolution. In 1909 Franz Kafka and his friend Max Brod traveled from Prague to Italy to see an air show at Brescia. The bravest French and Italian pilots stayed aloft for entire minutes at a time and managed to reach the unthinkable height of 650 feet.[19] Only a few years later, some of the same planes were being used to rain death down on civilian populations on the Eastern Front. There, airplanes appeared as terrifying apparitions. When the Austrians first used biplanes for reconnaissance over Galicia, their own troops tried to shoot them down.[20]

Planes also attracted rumors. Many of them centered on Jews, who were suspected of signaling enemy bombers in all sorts of ingenious and implausible ways, such as by standing on a porch with a mirror or simply by sneezing. In the Ukrainian town of Volodymyr-Volynskyi, it was said that after an enemy plane was shot down, it was found to contain, in addition to the pilots, a Jewish cobbler from Kovel who had told the

Germans where to drop their bombs.[21] This was pure fantasy, but it led to real violence. In retaliation for the supposed espionage, Cossacks burned down Volodymyr's entire Jewish district.

Two years after the end of the First World War, fighter planes were being used by both sides of the Polish-Soviet War. Isaac Babel, famous for his short stories depicting Jewish life in early-twentieth-century Odessa, embedded as a journalist with Budyonny's Cossacks during the 1920 campaign against Poland, saw some of them in action. In his *Red Army* stories, he writes movingly about one of his commanders, the naïve but courageous Pashka Trunov, who was machine-gunned from the air during an engagement in the town of Sokal.

The planes that killed Pashka fought on the side of Poland, but they were piloted by American and Canadian volunteers who stayed in Europe after the end of World War I to fight the specter of Communism. Their commander, Cedric Fauntleroy, was an ace pilot from Mississippi. His best friend, Merian Cooper, who recruited him into the squadron, went on to produce and direct *King Kong* in Hollywood. Babel met him after he was shot down over Belyov. The two men conversed in French. They discussed Paris, New York, detective novels, and the true nature of Bolshevism. In his diary, Babel wrote that the imprisoned American pilot, "barefoot but elegant, neck like a pillar, dazzlingly white teeth, clothes covered with oil and dirt," made a "sad and delicious impression" on him.[22]

Cossacks and King Kong, beet fields and biplanes: the collision of old and new was enough to make your head spin. Malevich got drunk on it. Writing in his unheated Vitebsk schoolroom, with the war raging around him, he prophesied a techno-mechanical future in which men would take the place of gods, molding nature itself to fit their needs. Malevich chose a black square as his emblem. For him it symbolized eternity and infinity. Like the Dadaists in Zurich at the same moment, half of whom were Romanian Jews and came from towns in Moldavia every bit as forlorn as Vitebsk, Malevich wrote nonsense poetry in which language shook off the shackles of rhyme or sense. *Onon Kori Ri Kossambi Moyena Lezh.* He envisioned artists as airmen, breaking the chains of gravity and flying into pure white infinity, beyond meaning or time: "after me, comrade aviators, sail into the chasm," he intoned.[23] This was the true, hidden meaning of revolution. It was not a mere change of government: it was a type of levitation. Modernity in the East was not going to be achieved by slow, patient progress, as in the West, but all at once, in a single gigantic leap, from the mud to the stars.

.   .   .

Writing in 1949, from her home in exile in the United Kingdom, Janina Puttkamerowa struggled to recapture the world of her childhood in distant Belarus:

> It is hard now, after two world wars and bloody revolutions, to convey the feeling of safety that prevailed in our empty and lonesome Polesia. The windows of our house had no shutters, and none of the doors leading from the manor to the outside were ever locked. I don't remember bad dogs or any mention of a night watchman. You went for a walk at dusk, in the snow, over a deserted road or in an empty park. Peace and quiet rested in the vast expanses of meadows, oaks, frozen fields and forests.[24]

Those who did not share Malevich's faith in the revolution, and who had lived through close to a decade of bloodshed, famine, and unrest, found it hard to look upon the time before the First World War as anything but a lost paradise. To Stefan Zweig, these years were the "Golden Age of Security" when everything had been predictable, and every item "had its norm, its correct measurement and weight."[25] Danilo Kiš, the Yugoslavian writer, thought of them as "those ancient, mythical times when men still wore derbies."[26] For Bruno Schulz, it had simply been the "age of genius."

When Schulz reached back in his memory to recover the lost world of his childhood, two figures loomed larger than any others. One was the Habsburg emperor Franz Joseph I, and the other was Anna Csillag, a woman whose image seemed to appear in every newspaper in Eastern Europe before World War I. Advertisements, drawn in the coarse lines of folk woodcuts, showed her dressed in a flowery peasant frock, holding three lilies aloft in one hand. The most striking thing about her, though, was her hair: almost two meters long, it cascaded down her back like a woolly Niagara.

An accompanying text explained this remarkable growth. Translated into whatever language the newspaper was printed in, it always began the same way: "I, Anna Csillag, possess an immense, 185-centimeter growth of Lorelei-like locks thanks to fourteen months spent using my specially-formulated pomade." Sometimes, when culturally appropriate, she compared her locks to those of a *rusalka*, a Slavic river-nymph, instead of the more Germanic siren. Schulz remembered Anna's story as an almost "Job-like" tale, in which the young woman, cursed with a meager growth of thin and unappealing hair, lived in dread of ever finding a mate and was pitied by her entire village for her affliction.

One day, however, salvation arrived. While working with chemicals and herbs, Anna stumbled upon a truly miraculous medicine that not only cured her baldness but worked as a sort of hair-growing wonder drug. After using the mixture a few times, her hair grew in an uncontrollable torrent from her own scalp. Soon all the men in her family likewise boasted astounding pelts of lustrous black hair—fanlike beards stretching past their waists, and ropelike mustachios coiled around their trunks and midsections like so many boa constrictors. It was a blessing, one that Anna shared with the world through a stream of paid print advertisements that appeared unceasingly in the daily newspapers of Budapest, Kraków, Łódź, Vienna, Helsinki, Riga, and all points in between.

So ubiquitous were Anna Csillag's ads that they became part of the background hum of life in the Eastern Europe of the Belle Époque. Many writers besides Schulz thought of Anna when they recalled that vanished golden age. Czesław Miłosz, Gyula Krúdy, Karl Krauss, and Kálmán Mikszáth all discussed her, while Józef Wittlin, the great chronicler of prewar Lviv, devoted a whole poem to Anna, in which she becomes the symbol of every sweet and foolish thing that had vanished from the world. For me, though, Schulz's version of the story remains the most memorable. It blends seamlessly into his vision of Drohobycz as a place of unnatural, excess growth and proliferation, where the work of Creation was never completed and even dead things possess a spectral life of their own. So much so that for years I assumed that Schulz had invented the figure of Anna Csillag himself, out of thin air. In fact, she was a real person, even if much of the story she told in her advertisements was fake.

Anna Csillag's real name was Anna Stern—both Stern and Csillag are the German and Hungarian words for "star." She was born in 1852, not in "Karlowitz in Moravia," as her advertisements claimed, but in the town of Zalaegerszeg in Hungary. Anna opened her business sometime around 1876 and operated it alternately from Vienna and Budapest. Sometimes she worked in partnership with her brother, and sometimes alone. They sold her wonder-working pomade as well as a line of secondary products, including the "best soap in the world" and special hairbrushes and combs meant to enhance the effects of her elixirs.

The Austro-Hungarian bureaucracy, divine in its thoroughness, inspected each product. It found the "best soap in the world" to be a very hard, red-brown toilet soap of the "worst quality," and her special "tea for washing the hair" to be just chamomile. Most disappointingly, the pomade was nothing more than a mixture of fat and bergamot oil. It was white-gray in color, had the consistency of lard, and appeared grainy when spread out in a thin layer.[27]

With the benefit of hindsight, however, we can say with confidence that the imperial inspectors missed their mark. They evaluated a physical product, when the real miracle sold by Anna Csillag was her message. Repeated over and over in advertising, it acquitted the force of a cryptic gospel or a prayer. At least one observer realized this right away. While still a penniless art student living in a men's dormitory in Vienna, Adolf Hitler was simultaneously transfixed and enraged by the hirsute "Moravian" damsel who greeted him in the paper every day.

According to one of his few friends from this time of obscurity, Hitler would spend hours poring over Csillag's promotional materials. He was particularly fascinated by the letters of gratitude sent to the firm. Through careful investigation, he learned that these had been faked, and that the supposed senders were all dead. He thought he had discovered the key to a great mystery—the secret of propaganda. He liked to rant about its power. "Propaganda, good propaganda, turns doubters into believers," he told his friend, continuing, "Propaganda! We only need propaganda. Of stupid people there are always enough."[28]

According to another friend from this period, Hitler was so taken with Csillag's success that he wanted to turn his men's dormitory into a kind of "advertising institute." All the residents would dedicate themselves to selling some product—perhaps a glass-strengthening paste—and promote it regardless of whether it worked. To succeed, all they needed to do was repeat their message as frequently as possible. That, combined with a talent for oratory, would win them all the customers they could want.

Hitler's friend replied that while that might be, they still needed something worthwhile to sell. After all, oratory on its own was useless.

Anna Csillag
advertisement, c. 1900–10.

10

Prophets

Faith healer with portrait of Lenin,
Polish-Lithuanian border.

O ne evening in 1908 or 1909, Jerzy Stempowski and his father
were walking through the streets of Berdychiv, in northern
Ukraine, when they heard something that stopped them in
their tracks. It was a voice, intoning as if in prayer.[1] This in itself was
not surprising. At this time, most of Berdychiv's population was Jewish and Hasidic; Hebrew prayers rang out continually from Berdychiv's
seventy-four synagogues. But what the Stempowskis heard that evening
was not the music of the psalms: it was lines from the first volume of
Karl Marx's *Das Kapital*, read aloud.

Jerzy's father tapped on the window of the house to find out what
was going on. They were led inside, and father and son spent the rest
of the evening listening to Marx with members of a local tailors' guild.
The owner of the single copy of *Kapital* read in a singsong voice, pausing

after every sentence to answer questions. As the night wore on, the text—difficult to begin with—became even less clear, but that did not deter the tailors. According to Stempowski, they read "in the manner of true believers," listening to the recitation as if it were the encapsulation of a revealed truth. At the time, Stempowski thought there was something unnatural about this unthinking acceptance of a secular doctrine. Raised among positivists and freethinkers in the Russian Empire, in the old Polish-Ottoman borderlands, he did not yet know that a similar yearning for prophetic guidance would soon spread over much of his world.

The two decades that followed the end of the First World War were a time of profound crisis in Eastern Europe. The war that President Woodrow Wilson said would make the world "safe for democracy" had done no such thing. Although the peace treaties that followed it led to the creation of a number of new nation-states, few became the thriving liberal democracies that Wilson had imagined and hoped for. By 1938, only Czechoslovakia remained a multiparty state, and even it was in the process of being cannibalized by Hitler's Germany.

The postwar settlement left other scars as well. In a single swoop, the ancient empires of the Habsburgs, Ottomans, and Romanovs vanished from the face of Europe. But there were other losers as well. The 1920 Treaty of Trianon confirmed Hungary's full independence but stripped it of 72 percent of the territory that it had possessed in its half of the Dual Monarchy. This titanic blow would embitter Hungarian politics for generations, driving it into the hands of any power that could promise to recoup its losses.

Bulgaria, another loser of the war, was forced to surrender far less territory by the Treaty of Neuilly in 1919. So poisonous was this agreement, however, that Aleksandar Stamboliyski, the prime minister who agreed to it under duress, faced a military revolt by 1923, which ended with his capture and assassination. The unfortunate man's head was sent back to Sofia in a biscuit box. For good measure, the executioners also chopped off the hand that signed the treacherous treaty, though they don't seem to have mailed it anywhere.[2]

A wave of repression followed Stamboliyski's execution, mostly targeted at Bulgaria's peasant movement. In 1923 Moscow ordered Bulgaria's Communists to counter it by staging a revolution. It failed, leading to another burst of government-sanctioned killings. The Communists got their revenge in 1925, bombing a church in Sofia during the funeral of a general, whom they had also assassinated. The cathedral roof caved in, killing 150 people, which triggered yet another round of terror in the countryside.

This sequence of atrocities is emblematic of the fanaticism that entered political life after the war. People no longer quarreled about sword tassels and military salutes. They fought pitched battles in the streets over what felt to them like the fate of the world. The whetstone sharpening all these conflicts was the threat of revolution. Depending on where one stood on the political spectrum, any measure was worth taking to either prevent it or to bring it about.

Throughout the interwar years, the example of the newly formed Soviet Union appeared to many as either a promise of Heaven or the threat of Hell. The Russian Civil War that had led to its establishment had an immediate impact on its neighbors. In the Baltics, a furious civil war pitted Latvian and Estonian nationalists against both local Bolsheviks and the Red Army. Latvia's right-wing government called on reinforcements from demobilized German troops, organized in mercenary battalions—the dreaded *Freikorps*—turning this conflict into a training ground for a future generation of fascists.

Fascism itself was a born out of these early battles between the forces of revolution and counterrevolution. Its ideas—a hazy mix of street-thuggery, *dirigisme*, and the leader principle—made sense only when animated by the fear of apocalyptic class revolt. But while Eastern Europe was an early proving ground for fascism (many *Freikorps* members went on to have brilliant careers in the Nazi Party), it was not the scene of its greatest political successes. Eastern European fascist parties of the interwar years tended to be shoved aside or used as tools by other, less radical authoritarians, who deployed their capacity for violence at strategic moments. This pattern can be seen in the case of Hungary, whose immediate postwar trajectory closely mimicked that of Latvia and Bulgaria.

In 1919 Béla Kun's short-lived soviet republic was brought to an end by anti-Communist Hungarian soldiers, organized as a "National Army" under the leadership of Miklós Horthy, the last commander of the Austro-Hungarian navy. Beginning in August 1919, Horthy, riding a white horse and surrounded by a bodyguard of barons, swept through the country. By November, he was in Budapest. A wave of killings followed his assumption of power, aimed at punishing all those who had supported Kun and his regime.

Some three thousand Hungarians died in this "White Terror." Seventy thousand more ended up in prison, and one hundred thousand more fled the country.[3] About half of those killed were Jews, who were already bearing the bulk of the blame for, in Winston Churchill's words, "creating Bolshevism."

·   ·   ·   ·

The equation of Jews with Bolshevism was another deadly legacy of the war. The Russian Revolution really did have a special attraction for a number of the empire's Jews. For some, it appeared, at first, as the fulfillment of a long-held dream: all of a sudden a world of equality appeared in Russia, and all the old barriers erected by faith and poverty no longer applied. Many got swept away in their enthusiasm, plunging headfirst into the Red Army and the nascent Soviet bureaucracy.

For Jews outside Russia, however, the consequences of this involvement were often dire. Although only a relatively small proportion of Eastern European Jews took part in the Russian Revolution, in much of Europe they became inextricably identified with the specter of Bolshevism. This made them a target for political violence of a type and ferocity that had hardly existed in Eastern Europe before the First World War.

But this wave of postwar reprisals was only the beginning of a broader pattern. In the following two decades, states across Eastern Europe passed a raft of anti-Semitic legislation that kept Jews out of government and the army, limited their participation in higher education, and curtailed their role in the economy. This naturally drove many of them toward Communism, the one political movement that promised equality and seemed capable of delivering on its word.

Of course, this was only one option among many. In the first decades of the twentieth century, Eastern European Jews found themselves forced to choose among a labyrinth of forking destinies, each with its own politics, homeland, and native tongue. They could set sail for

America, learn English, and begin the long process of assimilation; they could opt for Palestine, Zionism, and studying Hebrew; or they could choose the Soviet Union, Communism, and Russian. Finally, they could stay home, join the Jewish Labor Bund or some other Diaspora-based Jewish party, and continue living and arguing in Yiddish. However, by the interwar years, even the decision to continue speaking Yiddish, the traditional language of the shtetl, could be a fraught one, as many more progressive-minded Jews abandoned it for the local vernacular and replaced their devotion to religious tradition with an attachment to secular culture. Hungarian Jews thus found themselves entranced by the poetry of Sándor Petőfi and Endre Ady, while Polish Jews began to sigh after that of Słowacki and Mickiewicz.

My own grandfathers—on both sides of the family—opted for Communism. For them, it was a family affair, as were its discontents. My grandfather Jakub began working for the Polish branch of the party as a teenager. First, he had to go through a trial period. Later, he distributed illegal pamphlets while working as a porter in a chemical factory. His sisters, Jadwiga and Edwarda, joined the Communist youth movement and the influential seamstresses' union. They were great readers; one sister was loyal to Proust, and the other to Dostoevsky; both oscillated between tradition and modernity, established religion and atheism.

My other grandfather, Czesław Berman, came from a more traditional environment. Born with the name Bezalel into an Orthodox Jewish home, he joined the Communist Party at a time when it was illegal in Poland. For this transgression, he was kicked out of high school and sent back to live with his grandparents in the family's shtetl, Zambrów. His brother Zygmunt, also a party member, was similarly forced to emigrate to France. The brothers didn't know at the time how lucky they were to have been in Poland and not the Soviet Union. During the Great Purge of 1937–38, the USSR executed nearly every member of the Polish Communist Party on trumped-up espionage charges. The cadres that took over the Polish party after World War II had mostly survived this massacre in the safer confines of a Polish prison.

For the Berman brothers, though, Communism was a path to a wider world. It opened up new horizons, as Zionism did for their cousins, and as emigrating to America did for many others. It was a way of joining a worldwide struggle against a ferocious opponent. It was also a way of becoming cosmopolitan—of reaching beyond the shtetl and the Jewish slums of Muranów where they lived—but without leaving home. It also probably saved their lives. When Poland's war with Germany began, a Ukrainian friend from the Communist underground helped my grandfather Czesław cross the Bug River into the Soviet-occupied zone and safety. Later, he would find himself in an NKVD prison camp in Uzbekistan, half-mad from typhus fever, and later still, in 1945, he would serve with the Red Army during the siege of Berlin.

To members of my grandparents' generation, the international nature of Communism, the sense of participating in a fight beyond boundaries of religion or nation, was a major part of its appeal. But Communism wasn't the only political movement with a global reach. Fascism, too, knew how to draw supporters from across the continent. Even before Hitler and Mussolini came to power, their examples inspired a whole constellation of imitators all over Eastern Europe. One of them was the Hungarian poet and sometime journalist Zoltán Böszörmény. The son of a bankrupt landowner, he worked at times as an apprentice, a messenger, and a day-laborer.[4] The counterrevolution of 1919 gave him a taste for combat. A short stint at the University of Budapest put Böszörmény in contact with the violently patriotic subculture of student fraternities, but it was a fateful meeting with Hitler which revealed his life's purpose: creating a Magyar equivalent to the Nazi Party. For the symbol of his *Hungarian* National Socialist Worker's Party, he chose two scythes laid atop each other—a kind of rural swastika. Soon his party came to be known as the Scythe Cross.

In his own mind, Böszörmény was a poet, a sage, and a warrior ready to fight to the death for Mother Hungary. The Budapest press treated him like a joke, but in the *puszta*, the arid grasslands of central Hungary, where peasants still toiled in conditions akin to medieval serfdom, his message was electrifying. The only problem was that no one could fully explain what this message was. When a journalist questioned two members of the Scythe Cross about their beliefs, all they could manage to say was that their cause involved hating the "Communists and the Gentlemen."[5]

This vagueness posed no hindrance to recruitment. In fact, it was probably an advantage. Only a year after Böszörmény started the Scythe Cross, the group had over twenty thousand members, as well as its own storm troopers. He urged his followers to commit acts of violence against Jews, Habsburgs, and other opponents of the Hungarian race. Few heeded his call. In 1936 he decided that his only path to power was to stage a full-scale revolution.

Böszörmény prophesied that on May 1 of that year, he would gather an army of 3 million peasants, march them to Budapest, and burn that sinful city to the ground. When the day came, a few thousand followers actually did show up, but most were easily apprehended by the local gendarmes. Some seven hundred peasants were arrested, of whom 113 stood trial together. In their courtroom appearance, the accused party members presented a sad spectacle. According to a witness, they wore "torn trousers, miserable overcoats or old sheepskin vests." None had on a decent shirt. Their poverty was more than skin deep; 98 percent of Böszörmény's followers didn't own a house or any land. When the judge presiding over their case asked the group what they were fighting for, they declared themselves ready to die for the "Idea," but when pressed, they couldn't explain what it was.

Despite its failure, the Scythe Cross was a kind of distillation of fascism: a movement of desperate people in search of a transcendent cause, who gave no thought to what that cause should be. But not all of Eastern Europe's fascists were quite so hapless. In Romania, the Legion of the Archangel Michael, or Iron Guard, grew from an organization of college students into a political party that briefly held the nation's fate in its hands. The key to their success was a charismatic leader and an approach to politics that owed as much to religious proselytizing as to street warfare.

As in Germany, fascism in Romania first crystallized around fears of a spreading Bolshevik contagion. Corneliu Codreanu, the founder of the Iron Guard, was born in 1899. Too young to take part in World War I, he gained his experience of combat at home, in military school, and in street battles with striking workers. For Codreanu, beating up trade unionists was a way of staving off a revolution. However, he soon came to the conclusion that the workers—the Romanian ones, at least—were blameless; the real fault lay with their Jewish-Communist puppet masters. Codreanu now focused his energies on keeping Jews out of the university. He and his gang drove them out of student clubs and dormitories, broke up Jewish theatrical performances, and beat up leftists wherever he could find them.⁶ In 1923 Codreanu coordinated a student strike that kept Romania's universities closed for a whole semester. He capped off this triumph by starting a political party, the National-Christian Defense League, whose sole aim was the introduction of quotas limiting the number of Jews admitted to high schools, universities, and the liberal professions.

Codreanu's party, which, prompted by a divine vision instructing him to become Romania's savior, he later reconstituted as the League of the Archangel Michael, swiftly grew in influence, in large part because of its excellent ground game. Codreanu's legionnaires fanned out across the Romanian countryside, reaching forgotten villages in the hinterlands of Transylvania and Moldavia that until then had never been visited by politicians of any party. Villagers received the activists with lit candles and singing, after which the young legionnaires set to work on community service projects, digging drainage ditches and fixing roads.⁷

Sometimes, in the course of these expeditions, Codreanu and his men traveled incognito. Someone would be sent ahead to a village to build anticipation for his arrival, whispering conspiratorially about "the One who had to come." When Codreanu finally appeared, he moved through the landscape like an apparition. He rode atop a white horse, surrounded by a few of his most trusted lieutenants. In every village square, he would dismount and kiss the earth, then ride off without speaking to anyone. People asked, "Was this the Saint?" wondering whether they had just witnessed the passage of a holy man or a messiah.⁸ Codreanu's followers were on hand to assure them that he was both.

Unlike fascists in Germany or Italy, who tended to view organized religion as a rival, the Iron Guard was fluent in the language of faith. The legionnaires carried bags of holy soil around their necks, celebrated giant outdoor masses, and patronized various small-town mystics who saw God or spoke to the Virgin Mary.⁹

Like most demagogues, Codreanu preached a doctrine that was at once vague and contradictory. He was against democracy but in favor of the people. Universal suffrage was detestable because it allowed Jews to vote. But Jews weren't Codreanu's only enemy—he hated Greeks, Turks, Bulgarians, and Hungarians as well. He saw the Romanian nation in religious terms, taught his disciples special prayers, and spoke in parables akin to fairy tales. He told his legionnaires that they had to pass through various sufferings on their way to becoming the "New Man." These trials included the *mountain of pain*, the *forest of wild beasts*, and the *swamps of despair*.[10]

It was childish stuff, but it worked like magic on some of Romania's most sophisticated intellectuals. One prominent Romanian thinker who was taken in was Mircea Eliade, the great historian of religion and one of the world's leading scholars of mysticism. Eliade believed that the Iron Guard was fighting in an elemental war, a struggle that pitted the "world of the stomach"—the old world of political parties and market economics—against a new world that "dared to believe in the Spirit." Similarly, the prominent philosopher of pessimism Emil Cioran wrote in praise of Codreanu's young storm troopers, seeing in their beatings and spontaneous murders "an explosion of energy" that hid the "seed of an idea, the passion of spiritual individualization."[11] When Codreanu was killed in 1938, on orders from the king of Romania, Cioran lamented the passing of a man who had accomplished more in his life than anyone besides Jesus Christ.

As a Jew, Mihail Sebastian, a close friend to Eliade and Cioran and the best Romanian novelist of his generation, could only stand by and listen. In his diaries, Sebastian wrote of close friends like Eliade who called for government ministers to be shot and strung up by the tongue, then switched in a single breath to relaying the latest literary gossip.[12] Even more grotesquely, these friends sometimes complained that they hadn't been given a share of stolen Jewish property, without paying heed to the fact that Sebastian might be put in that position himself.[13]

Sebastian saw a whole generation of his country's most brilliant writers and intellectuals fall under the thrall of a subliterate mystical fascism. The playwright Eugène Ionesco, another member of the prewar Romanian intelligentsia, likened it to waking up to discover that one's friends, once human beings, had all suddenly become part of a monstrous herd—a process he called rhinocerization. Yet despite their strident anti-Semitism, those same intellectual rhinos never stopped being Sebastian's friends.

In part, this continued closeness can be explained by the fact that the intelligentsias of Eastern Europe were extraordinarily small spheres, in which everyone knew everyone else. The combination of great passions and tiny stakes created an air of unreality around political conflicts. In

Romania, this had been true for a long time. Already in 1886 one prominent politician-playwright (a very Eastern European combination) described the Romanian regime as "a stupid comedy played by stupid actors before a naïve public."[14] Democracy existed in theory but not in practice. In the provinces, crooked officials delivered votes to local party bosses, while wealthy magnates did the same with their many serfs.

This type of corruption removed much of the sting from ideological conflict; as long as everybody was on the take, it didn't seem out of place to share a coffee with an opponent, even if you might fight a duel with them the following day. Political life in interwar Hungary and Poland was likewise characterized by this same combination of official animosity and personal intimacy. In Poland, under the rule of the national liberator-cum-military-dictator Józef Piłsudski, Communists and anarchists faced the constant threat of censorship and arrest. Nonetheless radical artists often remained close to members of the regime.

Exploiters and revolutionaries could be hard to tell apart. Aleksander Wat, one of Poland's leading Futurist writers, dressed in fine suits and always wore a pocket square or carnation in his buttonhole. With his short combed mustache and deep-set undertaker's eyes, he resembled a more earthbound Charlie Chaplin. (My mother's aunts, who worked as salesgirls in Wat's sisters' Warsaw hat store, thought he was quite handsome.) Wat, who later traded avant-garde literature for radical politics, recalled that left-wing writers visiting Warsaw from the West were shocked to see him and his fellow Marxists sharing Viennese coffees with members of the ruling right-wing military junta.[15] These contacts could be extremely useful, however. In 1932 Wat and the entire editorial staff of his literary journal ended up in prison—whereupon one of his friends, a colonel in the government, sent them all a giant care package of vodka and caviar from Hirschfeld's Delicatessen.[16]

In Budapest, a similar informality reigned for much of the interwar era. Clashes between right and left were certainly real, but after the twin horrors of Béla Kun and the White Terror, things settled back to the easy sociability of Franz Joseph's time. Here, as the historian István Deák wrote of the city, "even the wildest anti-Semite had his Jewish friends, and the most persecuted revolutionary seemed to have useful connections." Budapest society was "permeated by a certain lightheartedness and by a sense of humor" that often made the great ideological clashes of the age feel more like a "musical comedy" than a struggle between good and evil.[17]

Sometimes this music hall quality to politics could be disturbingly literal. One militia leader who supported Miklós Horthy during his march on Budapest in 1919 was Anton Lehár, whose brother was the composer Franz Lehár, best known for penning the operetta *The Merry Widow*. Two years after his troops helped to sweep Horthy into power, Anton took part in a farcical coup attempt to give Hungary's technically still vacant, and therefore available, throne to the Habsburg emperor Karl, Franz-Joseph's great-nephew who couldn't mount a horse. After this debacle, Anton was forced into exile in Berlin, where he gave up life as a right-wing warlord for a job publishing light music. But lest Lehár's career seem like the stuff of a musical comedy, he was also a leader in the White Terror, and one of his fellow militia leaders liked to collect the severed ears of his Jewish victims as lucky charms.

Interwar Eastern Europe was a strange place, where atrocities coexisted with the little comforts of city life. To a whole generation of writers and intellectuals, civilization seemed on the precipice of collapse, which in itself was exciting. One major school of Polish poetry named itself the Catastrophists, whose members wrote poems prophesying the end of everything.

At the other end of the avant-garde spectrum, the Futurists declared that the world was being born anew. Everything—down to language itself—seemed ripe for reinvention. In Wat's words, the Futurists began by making "antipoetry and antiliterature."[18] Gradually, though, politics replaced avant-gardism as their driving passion, and they embarked on another quest: to create work that would seduce the masses and lead them to a promised utopia.

Ten years later this optimism had vanished. Wat felt as if he and his fellow Polish writers were trapped in a vise, caught between "two enormously powerful, dynamic monsters,"[19] Stalin's Soviet Union and Hitler's Nazi Germany. Amid jackboots and concentration camps, language games lost their savor. Antifascism appeared to many writers as the only moral choice. The international Communist organization, the Comintern, was supposed to spearhead that movement, but tragically it led its members down a dark path. By the end of the 1930s, it was wholly

under the sway of Stalin and the USSR and proved much more dangerous to Communism's friends than to its supposed enemies.

Decades later Wat would describe his youthful attraction to Communism as a philosophical malady, a form of "demonism" or "moral
insanity." As a political commitment, it dominated his life for over a
decade, but he did not learn the full price of adherence to Moscow until
after the Soviet invasion of Poland in 1939. Arrested in Soviet-occupied
Lviv, Wat spent over a year in Moscow's Lubyanka Prison, then nearly
died during his subsequent exile to Kazakhstan.

Bruno Jasieński, Wat's close friend and fellow Futurist, shared his
infatuation with Communism but never got a chance to repent his allegiance. Jasieński was born Wiktor Zysman in 1901, in the part of Poland
under Russian rule. His mother was a Catholic aristocrat and his father
was a Jewish doctor who converted to Protestantism. When the First
World War began, his family evacuated to the Russian interior. In Moscow, young Jasieński got to see the Russian Revolution firsthand. He
was enraptured, but more by its aesthetics than by its politics. By the
time he came back to Poland at eighteen, Jasieński—now Bruno—was a
full-fledged apostle of the liberated word. In thrall to the Soviet Futurist poet Vladimir Mayakovsky and the Dadaists, he nonetheless styled
himself more as a dandy than a proletarian. Dressed in a top hat, mono-
cle, and wide red cravat, Jasieński took to reciting blasphemous verses in
Kraków cellars. He would later recall this epoch in his life as "a strange
and beautiful time . . . when poetry was cooked up like dynamite, and
every word was a primer cap."[20]

Translating Lenin into Polish converted Jasieński from Futurism to
Marxism. In 1925 he left Poland with his wife for Paris. While there
he came across a novel called *Je brûle Moscou* (I Burn Moscow) in the
window of a bookstore. The title infuriated Jasieński, whose knowledge
of French wasn't strong enough to realize that it was slang for speeding
through Moscow rather than torching it. It was better he didn't know.
The book he wrote in response, *I Burn Paris,* a pulp thriller about a
proletarian commune in the heart of Europe, was the best work of his
career. In it, Paris is ravaged by plague, and its residents break up into
warring camps of proletarians and royalists, White Russians, Bolsheviks,
African dock workers, Chinese Marxists, and even some Americans. All

fight to defend their neighborhoods and secure dwindling supplies. In time, the battle proves futile. The plague kills everyone, except for the inhabitants of the central prison, who are kept alive by their accidental quarantine.

Left alone in an abandoned and ruined city, the prisoners create an ideal working commune. To protect themselves from the outside world, they broadcast a radio signal warning the rest of Europe of continued infection. Left to their own devices, utopia blossoms. Fields of grain ripen in what was once the Place de la Concorde, while cabbages and cauliflowers fill the Luxembourg Gardens. The Tuileries become a single, enormous communal nursery, in which thousands of workers' children play in identical red caps.[21] When the rest of the world learns of the Parisians' ruse, Western capitalists declare war on the commune, only to have their own workers revolt against them. In the last sentences of the book, the masses, "shuddering like titanic ships," have all taken up the banner of revolutionary Paris.

I Burn Paris, published in 1928, marked the end of the Parisian phase of Jasieński's career. Expelled from France for exuding a "blind and stupid hatred for Western European culture," he fled to Leningrad, where he was greeted as a hero.[22] The first Russian edition of *I Burn Paris* became an instant best seller, and Jasieński embraced his status as a prominent Soviet writer. He threw himself into the Sovietization of Tajikistan, agitated for increased cotton production, and wrote a novel about a secret policeman supervising the building of a canal in Central Asia. He acquired a fine Moscow flat and a new Russian wife. At some point, he even had a mountain in the Pamirs named after himself.

The good times didn't last. In the winter of 1934, a fellow Polish writer touring the Soviet Union visited Jasieński and was shocked to be received in a squalid, freezing apartment. The tables were piled high with beluga caviar and imperial crystal, but the friend had the impression that the fine food and drink were for display, a show of Soviet luxury for a visiting Westerner, and that the moment he left, someone would arrive to sweep it all away. Jasieński himself seemed frightened: "his eyes flew around in all directions, his hand shook when he poured the drinks."[23] His apartment had become a Potemkin display, a message for Polish writers of the rewards they could expect to gain if they joined the side of revolution.

Jasieński was right to be afraid; the noose was tightening around his neck. On July 31, 1937, at the height of the Great Purge, he was accused of being a Trotskyite and a Polish spy. Police interrogators kicked his teeth in and pulled out his fingernails. Eventually, Jasieński signed his confession, which he soon recanted. He wrote a series of letters addressed to Stalin, protesting his innocence and asking to be set free. Then he begged to be shot rather than endure any more torture. He got his wish on September 17, 1938, in the basement of Butyrka Prison in Moscow. A few months later his Russian wife shared the same fate. Their son was taken to an orphanage; supposedly, he grew up to become a major figure in the Soviet-era mafia.

Unlike the more middle-class Wat and Jasieński, the Romanian novelist Panait Istrati came to revolutionary politics from the very depths of the proletariat. His mother was a Romanian laundress; his father, whom he never met, was a Greek smuggler. Like Mihail Sebastian, he grew up in the river port of Brăila on the Danube. In those years, Brăila was like a miniature Odessa and home to a motley collection of Jews, Turks, Greeks, Bulgarians, Syrians, Tatars, and Russians, working variously as stevedores, grain traders, sponge divers, and salep sellers. These people became the subject of Istrati's first novels. But before he could write them, he had to become a writer, a journey that itself took some twists and turns.

At twelve, Istrati ran away from home and took to the road. Hiding aboard cargo ships, he crisscrossed the Mediterranean from Beirut to Bari, working as everything from a pastry cook to a pig farmer. A friend of his from this era described him as "a tall, slim young man, with a greedy mouth but gentle, obedient eyes." By turns depressive and ebullient, Istrati had passionate affairs with men and women that lasted through several marriages. Moved by suffering and enraged by his own penury, he joined various revolutionary movements. He wrote his first published stories for the socialist press. Suffering from tuberculosis, he taught himself French by reading François Fénelon's *The Adventures of Telemachus* while staying in a Swiss sanatorium.

In 1921, back in France, penniless and desperate, he attempted to take his own life by slitting his throat. He did not succeed and was taken to a hospital in Nice to recuperate. The night before his suicide attempt, he had written a letter to the French novelist Romain Rolland, who was then at the height of his fame as the "conscience of Europe." Someone found the letter in his clothes and sent it to Rolland while Istrati was in the hospital. The letter was a cry of despair, as well as the story of his life. It was also funny, passionate, and enthralling.

Rolland wrote to Istrati, begging him to commit more of his stories to writing.[24] The result was Istrati's first cycle of novels, *Adrien Zograffi's Accounts*. Enormously entertaining, it begins as a homosexual fantasia on oriental themes—harems, slave boys, etc.—and ends as a patriotic apologia for the Moldavian-Wallachian Union of 1859. Its third and best volume, *The Hajduks,* begins in a cave, with a group confession by a series of bandits. Starting in 1924, the cycle was published in France by Henri Barbusse, the left-wing press baron who also serialized Jasieński's *I Burn Paris.*

Once Istrati became a well-known author and a public figure, he became a passionate advocate for the Soviet Union. He was not a member of the Communist Party and knew nothing concrete about Marxism, but he sympathized with the poor, the downtrodden, and the insurgent. In 1927 he spent months traveling the breadth of European Russia, sailing down the Volga and calling on new friends in Nizhny Novgorod and Baku. The Moldavian Socialist Republic in particular fascinated him. It seemed to him a miniature Romania, where socialism was already being built. He spent a long time talking to Dr. Ecaterina Arbore, once a militant Romanian socialist and now Moldova's minister of health. The things she told him in confidence about the reality of life in the Soviet Union shocked Istrati.

In 1929 Istrati returned to Paris, ill, disoriented, and disillusioned.[25] The way Stalin had dealt with the Trotskyists, by torturing, impris-oning, and executing them, shook his conscience. He felt that he had to break with the Bolshevik left but worried about the consequences. On a visit back home to cover a workers' strike, the Romanian secret police followed him and searched his mail; Istrati was widely consid-ered an agent of Moscow. At the same moment, in the Soviet Union, his dalliance with Trotskyism had been noted, and he was regarded as a dangerous provocateur. Istrati's fears proved to be justified when the Soviet-allied press caught wind of his planned defection from their camp and called him a paid stooge of the secret police, a mercenary, and a Soviet sheep transformed into a fascist wolf. His publisher, Henri

Barbusse, coordinated the press campaign against him from Paris, while in Moscow Bruno Jasieński attacked him in the *Journal of Foreign Literature.*[26]

Even Mihail Sebastian, who maintained an independent line between right and left, piled on, calling Istrati's politics "hilarious, pretentious, mediocre and—let us say it clearly—stupid." In a final blow, Istrati's great mentor Romain Rolland severed ties with him, calling him the "blind and unhinged instrument of the worst politicians."[27] In failing health and politically homeless, Istrati flailed about in search of safe harbor. For a time, he fell in with a left-leaning offshoot of the Iron Guard called the Crusade of Romanianism. Istrati, like many other intellectuals of his generation, no longer saw any middle ground between fascism and Communism; to reject one meant to embrace the other. Not long after Istrati joined the Crusade, its leader was killed in an exceptionally brutal assassination carried out by his former colleagues in the Iron Guard. Istrati was now truly alone.

In 1935 Istrati died in a Bucharest sanatorium. Two years later the 1937 edition of the *Great Soviet Encyclopedia* heaped a last bit of scorn on his name, describing his novels as "colored by facile romanticism" and marred by the "mediocre ideology" of "petty-bourgeois revolt." Just as these words were being published, the Great Purge, an orgy of killing that would claim the lives of Isaac Babel, Bruno Jasieński, and nearly a million other innocent Soviet citizens, was moving into its deadliest phase.

The purge marked the death knell of all the utopian dreams unleashed by the Russian Revolution. In their different ways, Jasieński, Istrati, and Wat had all been inspired by it; all of them had hoped to find a way to bring about the future through art. When this failed, they attached themselves to political movements, which ultimately betrayed them in turn. The same could be said of Cioran and Eliade on the right, though for them it was less history that let them down than their own co-conspirators.

Meanwhile, through it all, poor Mihail Sebastian stayed faithful to an older version of civilization, a world of pure expression exemplified by his artistic idols, Beethoven and Molière. His devotion to this ideal left him as politically homeless as Istrati. At the same time, Sebastian's religion made him unemployable. With the introduction of racial laws at the end of the 1930s, as a Jew he was banned from publishing his novels or staging his plays. He survived the war, living on a pittance earned from teaching at a Jewish college, only to be killed a week after it was over, in May 1945, hit in the street by a truck. It's unlikely that Sebastian would have felt more at home had he lived.

The writers of the interwar years seized on political commitment as a way to navigate a path through the wilderness of their moment. For them, ideology was a form of divination. Communism and fascism didn't just address present concerns; they foretold the coming of a new world. For a moment, it seemed as if artists were going to be its heralds. By the 1930s, it was clear they would merely be its servants.

Still, some people remained who believed in older forms of prophecy. Religion was still a potent force in Eastern Europe. The Orthodox monasteries of Bukovina and Volhynia thrummed with prayer, while in Albania and Bosnia Sufi masters preached in close proximity to nationalist revolutionaries. In the Poland of my grandparents' generation, Hasidism was still every bit as much a force as Communism or Zionism. And in some places, the Russian Revolution itself seemed like the fulfillment of the greatest prophecy of all.

.   .   .

In the mid-1930s a prophet appeared in the woods of eastern Poland. He attracted disciples from his village, some of whom became his apostles, and others, his wives. His followers included peasants and farmers, as well as mountebanks, charlatans, and would-be czars. Together, they built a church for their new faith. Then they began work on a new city called Wierszalin. At first it was just a collection of farms, but they believed it would soon become the capital of the whole world. Then the war came and swept it all away, leaving just a few scattered believers to keep the legend of the holy city alive.

The story of Wierszalin began a few years before the First World War with the peasant Eliasz (or Elijah) Klimowicz. He lived in the village of Stara Grzybowszczyzna, "the Old Mushroom Grounds," a backwater located near what is now the Polish-Belarusian border. Klimowicz came to prominence thanks to an expedient act of piety. When a bandit was preying on the farms around his home, Klimowicz traveled to see the holy man John of Kronstadt to pray for help. While he was away, someone killed the bandit. Credit went not to the killer but to Klimowicz, for having the foresight to seek divine intervention.

Now something of a local hero, Klimowicz became obsessed with building his own church. To raise money, he sold all his land—a shocking act for a peasant in that time and place—and then set out in search of donations. He worked miracles, curing the sick and casting out demons. Gradually, his fame grew. Then he began to preach. He foretold the redemption of the world, and the people he met began to believe that he was a prophet—the Prophet Elijah, returned to earth. And then, finally, the rumor spread that he was Christ reborn, come to establish his kingdom in the Grzybowszczyzna woods.

From across the region, people flocked to be near Elijah's court, which he kept in an isolated farmstead a few kilometers from Grzy-bowszczyzna in a place called Wierszalin. Men left their wives, and women left their husbands. Widows and virgins proved especially keen to join his flock. Regular people found themselves thrust into bibli-cal roles. The lumberjack Aleksander Daniluk became Elijah's Apostle Simon. The cloth-dealer Pawel Bielski became his Apostle Paul, writing down Klimowicz's deeds and praising him in hymns.

These men and women belonged to the last generation of Polish-Belarusians to be born into the undisturbed rhythms of nineteenth-century peasant life. Those rhythms were shattered by the outbreak of the First World War. Most of the people from Grzybowszczyzna and other points near the empire's western border were evacuated deep into the interior of Russia as part of the czar's scorched-earth strategy for dealing with the advancing German troops. There they encountered new languages, new customs, and new ways of being. My great-grandmother was one of these evacuees, or *bieżancy*. The Russian military made her and her family, illiterate peasants from a village near the Polish town of Kutno, leave their homes and go east, where she met her husband, a penniless Polish nobleman from southeastern Lithuania.

In 1917 the October Revolution arrived with the force of a thunder-bolt. Many saw it up close. Some even served in the Red Army or its fleet. When the fighting was over, and the evacuees returned to now-independent Poland, they were left to wonder about its development from afar.

Aleksander Daniluk, the prophet's chief propagandist and court theologian, explained the true, religious significance of the Russian Revolution to his followers. The red star of the Soviet Union was the same star as the one that had appeared in the skies to presage the birth of Christ. As they were then, millennial changes were now in the air; all Elijah needed to do, Daniluk said, was "tell people the truth, so that they understand, that their lives are not just simple, ordinary run-of-the-mill lives, but the fulfillment of the greatest prophecies and biggest events in the history of the world."[28]

In the holy city of Wierszalin, great things were afoot. The apocalypse was near, and Lenin was going to work with the archangels to bring it about. Time, normally confined in narrow channels, began to run wildly in every direction. In the village of Cieluszki, Olga D. ran through the streets naked smashing windows and yelling "Repent!" to all who could hear. Jana D. toppled crosses at the cemetery, broke fences, and smashed windows with her bare hands, shouting, "An end to everything old!"

It was the kind of thing a Dadaist might have said on stage in a Zurich café, but it turned out to be the truth. Wierszalin's time was up. On a hot summer day in 1936, at harvest time, a procession of peasants made its way down sandy tracks to Elijah's home. A man at the head of the parade carried a wooden cross. Another held a whip, and a third, a crown of thorns made from a length of barbed wire torn from a fence. A fourth carried a hammer and nails—the thick, square kind they used during Calvary processions at Easter.

Opinion remains divided as to whether the pilgrims intended to give the cross to Elijah as an offering or if they intended to crucify him and thereby bring about the end of days. Elijah himself seems to have assumed the latter. He was terrified by the procession and the instruments of crucifixion. Before the procession's chosen Judas had a chance to kiss him, Elijah fled and hid in one of his farm's root cellars, covering himself in straw. Three days later he emerged, as if from the dead. This was not the resurrection his followers had hoped for, though, and many began to drift away.

Elijah's fall began in farce but ended in tragedy. In 1939 war came again to Wierszalin. When the Soviets arrived to occupy eastern Poland, it is said that Elijah was denounced by one of his own apostles.

The Russians laughed at him, calling him the "Polish God." According to one report, they killed Klimowicz on the spot. According to others, they deported him to Siberia, where some believe he preached for many more years. Others claim he died soon thereafter, in a nursing home somewhere east of Krasnoyarsk. Records might exist somewhere that explain the truth, but they have not yet been found.

After Elijah's death or disappearance, most of his followers abandoned belief in the prophet. A handful of his followers kept their faith, however. Every year they would return to Wierszalin and visit the holy hill of Grabarka, which would have been Elijah's Golgotha, had everything gone according to plan. Afterward they would meet in Wierszalin's sole remaining house to recite prayers and sing songs lamenting their lost paradise.

Włodzimierz Pawluczuk, a Polish journalist and sociologist, spoke to most of the remaining believers in the early 1970s and described their fates. The Apostle Simon sold pears in a nearby town square. Paweł Toloszyn, who helped Elijah build the Wierszalin church, lived on his farm and became an inventor of ingenious labor-saving devices. Miron, once the archangel Gabriel in the Holy Court, became a beekeeper. Pałaszka, who was once one of Elijah's mothers-of-god and one of his fiercest defenders, became a noted weaver. In 1970 she wove a splendid rug in honor of Lenin's one-hundredth birthday, whose beauty was much remarked upon in the local press. It even found its way into the Grodno town museum.

The onetime "capital of the world" was never close to the centers of worldly power, and reaching it today requires driving for miles on dirt roads through the great Kniszyn Woods in easternmost Poland. The villages where Klimowicz once preached are almost gone, replaced by forest. Every so often, around a bend in the sandy road, two or three wooden houses will appear, some leaning severely, all outfitted with hand-carved eaves, whose filigree woodwork, weathered by a hundred winters, has faded to the color of old newsprint. Wierszalin, Klimowicz's earthly Jerusalem, still exists, but it is uncommemorated, unornamented, and mostly forgotten. It sits amid deep woods, tall pines interspersed with thin little birches. For the most part, it looks like a remote, neglected farmyard.

Forty years before my visit, a handful of the prophet's mothers-of-god still lived here. Twenty years before, Elijah's house still retained some of its original decorations, such as the window shutters painted, Belarusian style, in blue and white. Now moss grows on the wooden shingles of his roof, and the yard is covered in frost. The church Klimowicz built with his own hands—his first miracle—stands a few kilometers away, just outside the village of Stara Grzybowszczyzna. It belongs to the Orthodox Church now.

An old wooden cross stands in the garden outside Elijah's church. Farther out, in the woods proper, lies the local cemetery. All the gravestones belong to Belarusians. A few have inscriptions in Cyrillic. Certain years—1943, 1945, 1949, 1950—crop up again and again for entire families.

Later that day Marta, a heroic historian-bookseller in the nearby town of Krynki, will point out to me that many of the gravestones bear an explanatory note: "shot by Polish bandits." The bandits they're referring to were part of the Polish Home Army, or AK. Today they are considered patriotic heroes, honored everywhere by the government. People in this corner of Poland remember them quite differently, for here the partisans were involved in a hidden war waged by Poles against Belarusians. This was only one of the many internecine conflicts conducted below the surface of the Second World War in Poland, Yugoslavia, and elsewhere, wars waged by neighbor against neighbor, whose psychic poison remains heavy on the land.

The prophet's cabin. Wierszalin, present day.

11

War

Dieter Keller. Farmhouse on fire. Ukraine, c. 1941–42.

It only takes two hours or so to complete an inventory of Bruno Schulz's life, work, and death. All took place in the small Galician town of Drohobycz, about seventy-five kilometers south of what is now Lviv, Ukraine. During World War II, the local Jews were beaten, starved, confined to a ghetto, shot in the streets, deported to camps, and in the end, forced to dig their own graves. Of the ten thousand Jews who lived there at the war's start, only some four hundred were still alive by its end. The town itself, however, was largely spared—it's still possible to see what Drohobycz was like before the catastrophe. Not only that, walking its boulevards, one can travel back even further in time, to Bruno Schulz's childhood, the "age of genius" portrayed in his fiction.

Since Schulz's death in 1942, time in Drohobycz seems to have flowed at a slower pace than in the rest of the world. When I visited in the summer of 2019, much of the city seemed to be immersed in the gentle apathy of decay. The old Jewish hospital was surrounded by a wild swath of undergrowth. At the Henry Sienkiewicz Gymnasium, where Schulz's fiancée, Józefina Szelińska, taught Polish, vegetation had seized control of the roof. Giant weeds sprouted out of second-story balconies. The humble wooden home where Szelińska lived when she stayed in town leaned precipitously and seemed on the verge of sinking into the ground.

Some of the finer buildings of that era were still in good shape, however, largely thanks to the fact that most of them were appropriated by civic institutions in the Soviet days. The Villa Bianca on Taras Shevchenko Street, described by Schulz in his story "Spring," is now a museum of "local studies" that rarely opens. The old mayor's villa, which once belonged to the richest man in town, is now home to the biology department of the local teachers' college. In Soviet days, it was a house of pioneers. During the German occupation, it was an officers' casino. Schulz is said to have drawn murals for it, though these have since vanished.

Schulz's house is only a short walk away. It remains a private residence. An official plaque, carved out of black granite, identifies it. Another sign warns about the house owner's dog, a ferocious-looking German shepherd that casts evil glances at passersby from a window by the porch.

Schulz has his own street too, inaugurated in 2001. It is unmarked and leads to an abandoned brickworks. Only a few hundred meters long, it dead-ends in a cul-de-sac covered with trash. But maybe that's fitting: Schulz was, after all, the Proust of rubbish heaps. In his stories, all of which are set in his hometown, Drohobycz appears as a rainforest of the overlooked, in which all sorts of discarded matter—old newspapers, broken dolls, pipes, rubber hoses, cracked plaster walls, and curling wallpaper—grow and multiply and breathe according to their own rhythms.

In Schulz's youth, Drohobycz was a polyglot community, as could be seen in the very fabric of the cityscape. Its biggest streets were named for famous Polish poets, Ukrainian bards, and local Jewish leaders. Each of the three main resident faiths lived in its own district: Orthodox and Greek Catholic Ukrainians, mostly in the streets running from downtown to the railroad station. Jews, to the north of the main square. Catholic Poles, in the district of brownstones between the two.

All three groups mingled in the great market square. Bruno's father, Jacob, had a dry goods store there, which went belly-up after the First World War. The nearby "Street of Crocodiles" was miles—maybe continents—away in terms of psychic space. This was Drohobycz's "Little Klondike," an Americanized district of tawdry commercial establishments. In Schulz's telling, the street was bleached of color, a place where reality itself seemed half-finished, the "concession of our city to modernity and metropolitan corruption."

Today, Stryjska Street, the real-life equivalent of the "Street of Crocodiles," is home to a whole new set of tawdry businesses, though few would call them American. After the Soviet occupation of the city in 1939, Stryjska was home to the headquarters of the secret police, where Schulz was detained for a time. His offense was adding too much blue and yellow (the colors of the Ukrainian flag) to a mural honoring "the liberation of Western Ukraine"—that is, its annexation from Poland—thus making it seem overly Ukrainian and insufficiently Soviet.

A few blocks in the opposite direction, and closer to the city square, stands the building that once housed the Jewish council of Drohobycz's ghetto. On November 19, 1942, Schulz walked there from his home on Floriańska Street to pick up a loaf of bread. As he was exiting, SS officer Karl Günther shot him in the head. It wasn't a random act of butchery but the conclusion of a private vendetta between Günther and another officer, Felix Landau, who was head of the local division of Einsatzkommandos.

In his youth, Landau had worked as a cabinetmaker in a Vienna atelier, and despite his long service in the SS, he still fancied himself a patron of the arts. Early in the occupation, he became aware of Schulz as an artist. He had Schulz paint his children's bedroom with scenes from Grimms' fairy tales. One of the figures in these murals—a dwarf—seems to wear Schulz's face. It is his last known work. During a "wild action"—a killing spree prompted by an SS man's altercation with a Jewish apothecary—Landau killed Günther's "pet Jew." Günther then shot Schulz in revenge, telling Landau, "You killed my Jew—I killed yours."

The conventional image of the Holocaust is inextricably bound with the concentration camps, above all Auschwitz. This can have the effect of making the murder of Europe's Jews seem like a rather impersonal, mechanized process. In some histories, it almost becomes a question of logistics, in which German ingenuity—with a little help from local atavism—triumphs over problems of men and matériel. But in most of Eastern Europe, the Holocaust was an intimate slaughter. It was conducted up close, often face-to-face, in the presence of scores of witnesses and neighbors.

The Holocaust therefore should be thought of as a question not of populations but of individuals. No one lived the whole experience of a nation or a tribe. Instead, they experienced the catastrophe on their own terms, as the death of a pet or a family member, or the disappearance of a community. Schulz's death, and the massacre of the Jews of Drohobycz, stands as a synecdoche of the catastrophe as whole, just as any other act of violence could. And every Jewish family in Eastern Europe, including mine, had a Drohobycz of their own.

.   .   .

The week of January 20, 1942, was bitterly cold in Novi Sad in modern-day Serbia. The temperature dropped to thirty below, and the Danube, which flows through the city, froze solid, as did the nearby Tisza.[1] Novi Sad's population was made up mostly of Orthodox Serbs but also sizable numbers of Hungarians, Germans, and Jews. Formerly part of Yugoslavia, the city and surrounding region, Bačka, had come under Hungarian rule the year before. Soon thereafter Hungarian troops reported the presence of partisans in the area. To preempt any attacks, they took hostages—mostly Serbs and Jews from the city. This hostage-taking swiftly devolved into a massacre. Soldiers pulled citizens—including the writer Danilo Kiš's father, Eduard—out of their homes at gunpoint and marched them down to the Strand, a stretch of bathing huts and restaurants by the Danube. There they forced them to undress and stand in line, waiting for their turn to be shot in the neck by Hungarian gendarmes. The dead were then pushed in batches into the Danube through holes in the ice. Their bodies were discovered months later, after a thaw, by which time they had drifted to Belgrade and other points downstream.

Between 880 and 1,255 people perished over those three days in Novi

Sad. When the massacre was over, a measure of calm returned to the region. In Hungary, as in other countries allied with Nazi Germany—which by 1942 included Bulgaria and Romania as well as the Slovak and Croatian puppet-states—violence tended to come in brief, staccato bursts, coupled with sudden dramatic shifts in policy. All these countries pursued somewhat different strategies toward their Jewish citizens, navigating between their own domestic needs and German dreams of a Jew-free Europe. For instance, Bulgaria largely protected its Jews at home but was ruthless toward them in occupied Macedonia, which it seized from Yugoslavia. There Bulgarian-directed deportations erased the centuries-old Sephardic communities of Monastir, Skopje, and Štip.

Like Bulgaria, Hungary was happy to execute Jews in lands it had acquired from its neighbors, but it was much more reluctant to do the same to its own Jews. Indeed, for much of the war, Hungary was one of the safest places for Jews in all of Eastern Europe. However, in the spring of 1944, this situation came to an abrupt end. In March, Hungary's head of state, Miklós Horthy, realizing that the Allies were about to win, tried to negotiate a separate peace for Hungary. Getting wind of this, the German army immediately invaded, and presented Horthy with an ultimatum: comply with our orders, or step down. Transports to Auschwitz began the following month. By July, over 400,000 Jews had arrived at the camp. Most were killed on the spot.

This initial wave of deportations mostly affected the countryside. Until the fall, Budapest remained something of a safe haven for Jews. However, on October 15, 1944, Horthy again tried to withdraw Hungary from the war. German special forces kidnapped Horthy's son in retaliation. Using his life as leverage, they forced Horthy to install Ferenc Szálasi, head of the fascist Arrow Cross Party, as the country's prime minister. During the three months Szálasi was in power, his death squads killed some 38,000 Jews, continuing their deadly work even as the Soviet army reached the outskirts of Budapest. By February 1945, over two-thirds of Hungary's 770,000 Jews were dead.

Romania similarly pursued a mixed strategy in regard to its Jews. In territories it had annexed from its neighbors, it was utterly merciless. In Bessarabia and Bukovina, Romanians organized death camps and massacred Jews alongside their German allies.[2] In 1941, closer to home in Iaşi, Romanian secret police organized a deadly pogrom that claimed some fourteen thousand lives.[3] Iaşi, capital of the northern region of Moldavia, had been under Romanian rule for centuries. But while the Romanian government's willingness to perpetrate atrocities there seemed to signal that it would do the same nationwide, for a variety of reasons the expected catastrophe never materialized. The government never deported Jews en masse from Bucharest. Hemmed in by various Nazi-style racial laws, Jews living in the capital were subjected less to terror than to a steady drumbeat of insults and humiliations.

For Mihail Sebastian in Bucharest, these insults had to do above all with his job and his apartment. First came the news that he could no longer practice law. Next he learned that his novels could not be published and his plays could no longer be staged under his own name. Then his phone was shut off, as Jews were no longer permitted to have phones. Finally, he was kicked out of his lodgings, which were outside the quarter reserved for Jews.

As Sebastian struggled to make a living as a teacher in a Jewish school, his journal shifted from chronicling his meetings with the cream of Bucharest's intelligentsia to endless fretting about where to live. Meanwhile terrifying news of mass deportations and executions bubbled up from the Soviet frontier. Then, in January 1941, the Iron Guard beat and tortured to death over a hundred Jews in Bucharest itself, then hung their bodies from meat hooks in a butcher shop under signs that read, "Kosher Meat." That massacre shattered Sebastian's calm for good. Throughout the rest of that winter, he continued to listen to his beloved classical composers and to read Shakespeare and Molière, but he could never recover his equilibrium.[4]

While Jews in Bucharest were forbidden from having phones, in German-occupied Prague they were banned from owning pets. This was far from the worst prohibition enacted against them, but to many Jews, it was the one that stung the most. For Leo Popper, the father of the great Czech writer Ota Pavel, the worst day of the war was the one when he had to take the tram into town to give away his family's dog, Tamik. A world-champion vacuum cleaner salesman and onetime deserter from the French Foreign Legion, Leo was a great lover of animals. A fanatical fisherman and hunter, he was also adept at killing them.

Throughout the German occupation of Bohemia, which lasted from 1939 until 1945, Leo fished carp illegally out of what had once been his pond. Jews were now forbidden to fish or to own ponds. He traded these fish for flour and lard to send to his sons, who were being held in the infamous Theresienstadt (Terezín) Ghetto. Leo was married to a non-Jewish Czech woman; under the byzantine racial laws in effect in the German Protectorate, this gave him a reprieve from the camps, but it did not spare two of his three sons. Just before his son Jiří was about to be sent to Mauthausen, and from there to Auschwitz, Leo took the even riskier step of poaching a stag. If he had been caught, it would have meant a certain death sentence. It proved to be worth the risk. When Jiří came back from Auschwitz, where he survived a selection supervised by Mengele himself, he weighed only forty kilos. Precious calories from the "beautiful deer" saved his life.[5]

Leo Popper's near-contemporary, the Czech Jewish writer Jiří Weil, didn't hunt or fish, but he proved to be just as skilled at survival. A teenage convert to Communism, Weil, after finishing college in 1922, made a pilgrimage to the Soviet Union. He returned a decade later to translate Lenin's writings into Czech—and narrowly avoided getting swept up in the Great Purge. Weil has the distinction of writing the first novel about the purge and the first novel about the gulags, both of which were banned for decades. The first one caused the death of one of Weil's friends: the NKVD shot him for the crime of appearing in a foreign novel.

After the Reich annexed Czechoslovakia in 1938, Weil married his Czech lover Olga in one of the last permitted "mixed marriages" in occupied Bohemia. Since he was Jewish and Communist, this would not spare him from deportation under the new Nazi laws. To save himself from being sent to a camp, Weil faked his own death, staging a mock suicide by throwing a "body" off the Hlávka Bridge in Prague. He spent the rest of the war hiding in hospitals and illegal apartments. During this time he kept writing stories, scribbling them on scraps of paper. The most human characters in them are animals—stray cats and dogs who "hadn't learned to distinguish people by their badges and uniforms."[6]

The experiences of Kiš, Sebastian, Weil, and Popper were all in some way peripheral to the true horror of the Holocaust. They were spared the worst, either by being only half-Jewish or by living in countries that dodged the full force of the Nazi war machine. Had it been otherwise, none of them would have survived. During the early years of the war, Germany's allies and protectorates maintained a veneer of legality. Eventually they dropped the pretense, and the mechanisms of the Final Solution—the total elimination of Europe's Jews—clicked into place. While the veneer lasted, though, it gave people some room to maneuver. For most Jews of Czechoslovakia, Romania, and Hungary, however, the war years ultimately brought degradation and want, ending in eventual deportation and death.

In Poland and in the territories the Nazis seized from the Soviet Union and Yugoslavia, the racial state operated without the slightest impediment from the rule of law. It was a utopia of murder, where killing happened on a scale so vast that it wore out the killers. Much of this killing took place in broad daylight. In the east, the Holocaust of the camps was preceded by a more local slaughter: 1.5 million Jews were executed, usually by firing squad, in batches of a few hundred or a thousand, in the towns where they lived. This so-called "Holocaust by bullets" ended only when the SS ran out of ammunition and men. Executing people individually or in groups was arduous, manpower-draining work. The concentration camps solved this problem of logistics and morale. They were primarily intended not to make the killing secret but to increase its efficiency. They marked a shift from artisanal to industrial killing.

But the concentration camps were only a single component of the extermination machine erected by the Nazis. The Holocaust didn't happen inside Auschwitz alone. It took place in huge, city-spanning ghettos and in small-town squares, in remote work camps and in surrounding woods.

Moreover, the Holocaust was only part of the hell brought about by the war. Virtually everywhere they went in the territories they acquired, German forces unleashed a Pandora's box of fratricidal strife by partnering with fringe political formations. Prior to the Nazis' arrival, fascist parties in Eastern Europe had had little success, except for the short-lived rule of the Iron Guard in Romania. In many places, the Germans' arrival signaled an opportunity for extreme nationalists to fulfill long-held ambitions of achieving ethnic and religious uniformity.

In Latvia and Lithuania, the Germans' local fascist partners formed auxiliary forces that assisted in the elimination of Jews and Roma, who were likewise slated for extermination according to the dictates of Hitler's racial state. In Slovakia and Croatia, Germans did more than just recruit troops—they created entire fascist regimes, puppet governments that pursued their own active policies against Jews and other minorities.[7] The Croatian Ustaše were particularly active in this regard. Although they persecuted, imprisoned, and deported Jews on their territory, their real animus was aimed at Serbs. Over the course of the war, the Ustaše murdered some two hundred thousand Serbs at the Jasenovac concentration camp, which was also used to execute thousands of Jews and Roma.

In the Ustaše regime's effort to create a Serb-free Croatia, the government's soldiers formed just one corner in a complex quadrilateral of violence. During the years of German occupation, the territory of Yugoslavia was home to several wars at once. One pitted Germans and Italians against the Allies. Another was directed at the Yugoslav resistance. A third war was directed by Croatian extremists against their Serbian opponents. A fourth was fought within Serbia between two main groups of the Yugoslav resistance, the multiethnic Communist partisans led by Josip Broz Tito, and the Serb-dominated pro-monarchist Četniks. With no reliable allies, Bosnia's Muslims fought on nearly every side of this conflict and found themselves perpetually caught in the crossfire.

A similarly complex situation developed in the ethnically mixed region of Volhynia. There, in a territory of what had been eastern Poland and is now part of Ukraine, Ukrainian nationalists waged a war of elimination against local Poles, who retaliated in turn in areas where they were in the majority and Ukrainians in the minority. While this bloody civil war was raging, Soviet partisans continued to fight behind German lines, while divisions of the SS pursued Jews and Roma, including the poet Papusza's band, which had to dodge units of both the Wehrmacht and the Ukrainian Insurgent Army. Once they were even saved from execution by their ability to recite the Lord's Prayer in Ukrainian.[8]

The Germans did not consider Poles—unlike Croats, Slovaks, and Ukrainians—to be worthy collaborators. Their place was to serve, not to fight. But although the Germans never trusted the Poles with even limited degrees of autonomy, at a local level individual Poles did assist Germans in the elimination and execution of their Jewish neighbors.

Some of my own family members were killed in this way, denounced by fellow countrymen who should have been their allies. But this is a larger story that I can tell only in fragments. It begins where most of my family were living when the war began, and where most of them died long before it ended: in the Warsaw Ghetto. This prison-metropolis of almost a half a million people was designed with only one purpose in mind: to kill. So many people died there that reconstructing what happened requires the skills of an archaeologist. The ghetto was like a black hole, swallowing not just light but information. Its captives were aware of this, and many did all they could to leave testimonies that would outlast them. Whenever I have tried to understand what happened to my family, this is where my search begins.

The ghetto was like a burning ship, and the works written within it were like so many messages in a bottle, cast into the depths. As with every element of life in the ghetto, chance played a determining role in what survived and what didn't. A hiding place for the writings was needed, but it could rarely be counted on. Eugenia Szajn-Lewin hid hers in a secret compartment under the floor of her Warsaw apartment. She died in the Warsaw Uprising, but her manuscripts survived. Ludwik Landau hid his chronicle of the occupation in two places: buried underground and hidden under a coal heap in his house outside Warsaw. Only the half under the coal heap survived. Before the war, Władysław Szlengel was one of the stars of Warsaw's cabaret stage. An author of tangos and popular songs, during the war he turned his hand to poetry. After the war, a junkman found some of his poems hidden in the double-top of a wooden table, abandoned for scrap.

The single most important set of documents to cross out of the Warsaw Ghetto and into our world was the Ringelblum Archive, an enormous compendium gathered by workers and archivists under the direction of the historian and Yiddishist Emanuel Ringelblum, between the start of the war in September 1939 and the last large deportations to Treblinka in January 1943. Imprisoned in the ghetto himself, Ringelblum saw that every day precious documents of ghetto life were disappearing, consumed by flames or thrown into the trash. He created an organization, Oneg Shabbat, to salvage as much as they could; they sent representatives to the apartments of deported writers, but they only seldom found anything. In Ringelblum's words, "The great flood of deportation covered everything, ruined everything, and left no trace behind."[9]

This tide of destruction made preserving the archive they had amassed all the more pressing. Oneg Shabbat took meticulous care to find a safe place to keep the collection they were able to amass. They buried the first part on August 3, 1942, while German blockades were going up on the streets of the ghetto. They packed the documents into metal boxes, then carefully sealed them and buried them in the basement of a storage shed. Six months later they buried the second part at the same spot, packed in two large steel milk cans. The third and final part was buried at a separate location, just before the start of the Warsaw Ghetto Uprising on April 19, 1943.

After the war, in 1946, the first tranche of the archive was recovered. The second part, buried in milk cans, wasn't uncovered until 1950. The third part was never found. The documents that did survive became saturated with moisture from the ground. Photographs dissolved, the poor-quality wartime ink ran off pages, and papers were eaten by mold. But after years of careful conservation work, most of the documents were made readable once again.

The buried papers allowed researchers to reconstruct the archivists' final moments. Just before the last box was sealed, Nahum Grzywacz added a handwritten note to the pile of documents. It read, "It is August 3, 1942 at 1:40 p.m. I would like to live. Not only because I want to save my own life, but to warn people and the whole world!" Another archivist wrote, "The next street over is under siege. . . . We are digging the last hole. . . . I would like to live to see the day when the treasure hidden by us gets unearthed, and the world learns the whole truth."[10]

Neither of these men survived the war. I owe them both a tremendous debt, though. My mother's grandmother Sabina and her aunts Rachel and Róża; my father's grandfather, grandmother, and youngest uncle; and many more cousins and other relations all perished in the ghetto. Most were swallowed whole, without a shred of information about their passing. The only exception is my mother's aunt Róża. Róża worked as an assistant in a hat shop in Warsaw. She was twenty-six when the war broke out, and she had recently given birth to a son named Jakub. By 1941, she was starving. She ventured outside the ghetto in search of work

Róża Mikanowska and her brother
Jakub. Poland, late 1930s.

and food. While on the Aryan side, she was spotted and denounced
while riding a tramcar, supposedly by a Polish child. She was arrested
for the crime of traveling outside the ghetto while Jewish.

After her arrest, Róża was sent to the Gęsiówka women's prison at
24 Gęsia Street. She and sixteen other young women were executed on
December 15, 1941. This was before any of the deportations to Treblinka or the major ghetto *Aktions*: the death of seventeen young women
still counted as a tragedy. Adam Czerniakow, the head of the Ghetto
Authority, even made a special note about it in his journals.

Before her execution, Róża had shared a cell with Bajla Keselberg,
a woman who managed to record her story and pass it to someone
connected to Oneg Shabbat. Bajla's story covers four pages. During its
years in the earth, the cheap, brown paper turned a pinkish yellow.[11]
The handwriting is a neat if somewhat childish cursive—a girl's handwriting. The voice is that of an eyewitness. The text contains multiple
crossings-out and exclamation points. When the emotion is strongest,
the text grows darker, from the force of the pen on the page. Soon after
Bajla wrote it, she escaped Gęsiówka through the prison hospital. I
don't know what happened to her later, but it does not appear that she
survived the war.

Here is what Bajla wrote:

> During the first execution [of] eight of the condemned all
> the prisoners were taken into the darkness so that they didn't
> even hear the shots. They saw the second execution with their
> own eyes. Two of those sentenced to death, 17-year-old Sal-
> werowna and 28-year-old [Róża] Mikanowska, the mother
> of a two-year-old child, were held in one cell with Bela. Until
> the last second they didn't expect anything. In no way could
> they make themselves believe their terrible fate. They lied
> to themselves, deluded one another, that they would avoid
> death. The first execution was just to scare them, the execu-
> tioners would not dare to commit such a monstrous, shame-
> ful crime!... It was only when they were led to the place of
> execution that they understood what lay in store for them.
> Incredible shrieks and laments tore through the air. They
> screamed that they wanted to live. At the place of execution
> there were 8 posts left over from the previous execution. A
> rabbi arrived, before whom the condemned recited a final
> prayer.... The condemned were divided into two groups
> because there were only eight posts. Four Jewish policemen
> tied each of the condemned women to a post, and the Polish
> police shot at them with a machine gun.
>
> Salwerowna, the youngest of the condemned, whose
> mother was also condemned to death and died in the hos-
> pital, cast her last words at the executioners—why were they
> killing her[?]... She threw herself, and bit the hands of
> the policemen and wouldn't let herself be tied up. It was
> the worst with Mikanowska. With superhuman strength she
> kept tearing herself away from the post, yelling that they
> bring her her child, so she could feed it from her breast....
> She threatened the executioners, or begged them, to spare
> her, because she wanted to raise her child. The prisoners
> watched the execution from their windows. The women
> especially experienced a nervous shock. Were they not wit-
> nessing their own fate? The cries of the prisoners mingled
> with those of the condemned.[12]

If it wasn't for Ringelblum's milk can, I never would have known about Róża's scream. And if it wasn't for her scream, she wouldn't have left any trace at all. Today hardly any trace of the Gęsiówka prison remains. It was demolished during the war, and the surrounding neighborhood suffered so much destruction that the street grid no longer matches what it once was. But for me, Róża's scream reverberates over the whole area. I am haunted by that scream.

In the part of Poland under direct German occupation, known as the General Government, the Holocaust took place in three distinct phases. In the first phase, Jews were locked inside town and city ghettos, where they were worked to death, starved, or were shot outright for various minor infractions. The second phase, which took place largely in the fall of 1942, was that of the ghetto clearances. In successive *Aktions*, the Jews of the ghettos were driven into cattle cars and delivered by train to concentration camps, where the vast majority were immediately gassed to death. Those few who were spared were made to work in prison factories and quarries, where most wasted away from hunger and disease, before their own turn in the gas chamber arrived.

The start of the second phase, the clearances, coincided with the start of Operation Barbarossa, the Nazi invasion of the Soviet Union, which began on June 22, 1941. My grandfather Jakub and his sisters Jadwiga and Edwarda were all in Minsk, where they had fled from Warsaw after Germany invaded Poland on September 1, 1939. That day was the start of World War II as a whole, but Jadwiga remembered June 22 even more vividly. So did virtually everyone living in the Soviet Union. That was the day German planes began raining bombs down on Minsk. Jakub was recruited to drive a truck for a hospital brigade and was soon taken prisoner near the front lines. Jadwiga and Edwarda walked east toward safety and managed to arrive in the city of Mogilev ahead of the German army. Their father, Salomon, had been working at a plant nursery somewhere outside Minsk; he was never seen again.

After Hitler's betrayal of Stalin, the nature of the war changed: it was no longer a campaign of conquest but a fight to the death between rival ideologies, in which everything was permitted. Those Jews who had been living in eastern Poland, under Soviet occupation, since 1939 suddenly found themselves in a terrifying new reality.

Zambrów, my paternal grandfather Czesław's shtetl, came under

German domination on the very first day of the invasion. Not long afterward the patriarch of my grandfather's mother's family, the Golombeks, was set to work digging trenches as part of their forced labor allotment. One day a German officer came up to him and asked, "Jew, what is your occupation?" "I am a tenant farmer," he replied. The German screamed at him wildly, "You lie, Jew, you are lying!"

After asking some of the other forced laborers about him, the officer discovered the truth: my ancestor really was a farmer. Amazed, he called over other Germans to look at this rare specimen—a farmer Jew. The German took him aside, gave him a loaf of bread, and told him never to come back to the trenches but to go back to his farm. This was his first inkling something terrible was coming and that his family should hide.[13]

The massacres began a month later—only two months after Germany invaded the Soviet Union. On August 22, 1941, which came to be remembered as Black Tuesday, soldiers ordered three thousand of Zambrów's Jews to assemble in the market square. Fifteen hundred of them were chosen for what they were told would be a labor assignment. In fact, they were driven in groups of fifty to the woods, where they were shot and dumped into pits.[14] Later that year, in December, a ghetto was set up in Zambrów for some two thousand remaining Jews.

Overcrowding in the ghetto quickly led to outbreaks of typhus and other diseases. People fled into the nearby forest when they could. Some tried to join local detachments of the Home Army, or AK, the Polish anti-Nazi partisans, but most were turned away. In November 1942 some twenty thousand Jews from Zambrów and the surrounding areas were rounded up and prepared for transport to Auschwitz. The transit began in January 1943 and continued in batches of two thousand a night. By the end of the war, only a handful of Jews in Zambrów or the vicinity remained alive.

The liquidation of the Polish ghettos marked the beginning of the third and final phase of the Holocaust in Poland. From the summer of 1942 until the arrival of the Soviet Army in the fall of 1944, those Jews who had managed to avoid or flee the ghettos, or who by some miracle escaped from a transport, now had to find a place to hide in the forest or countryside. To survive, they had to rely on bribes, the kindness of strangers, and an unearthly amount of good fortune. Most had to constantly change their hiding places, with no guarantee of finding safety anywhere. They had to depend almost entirely on the mercy of Catholic Poles, who quite literally held the power of life and death over their Jewish neighbors. A great many were denounced to the Polish or German police, or tortured and killed outright.

The moment immediately after the end of the ghetto liquidations in 1942 was among the most dangerous. This was the period of the *Judenjagd*—the hunt for the Jews.[15] Its initial stages were an orgy of violence, in which wandering Jews were rounded up and shot. German troops and their auxiliaries, the Polish "Blue" Police, directed the hunt, and village watches, construction and fire brigades, and local volunteers executed it. Later, the hunt became a more refined pursuit. The victims, for the most part, were no longer lost and confused escapees but local citizens who had consciously sought shelter with people they knew and trusted. These victims had names and personalities, whole histories known to their benefactors and their persecutors alike. As a result, their deaths lodged much more powerfully in people's memory than the anonymous mass killings of the first years of the war.

Only some 6 percent of Jews who paid to be hidden survived the war, as opposed to nearly half of those who were hidden out of altruism. The sheer length of the war was a great factor. Had the war ended a year earlier, tens of thousands more Jews would have survived, and there would have been proportionally more stories of righteous gentiles defying the odds.

Hiding Jews was dangerous business. The Germans might burn one's house or kill one's family outright. But the greatest risk came from other Poles. In a time of hunger, Jewish life could be bought very cheap. The official reward for delivering a Jew to the German authorities could be as much as fifty kilograms of sugar, a case of vodka, or ten cubic meters of potatoes.[16] More often, though, it was much less, as little as ten kilograms of sugar, or even a single kilogram plus the rights to the clothes of the dead.[17] Jews were denounced for as little as a pillow, a winter coat, or a few yards of silk.

People in villages watched each other assiduously. Even the smallest village had a hundred eyes, and everyone was on the lookout for the smallest deviation from the norm—a freshly painted barn, a haystack moved, a new pair of boots. Purchasing a piece of land or wearing a new dress to church could spell death for a whole family. Secrecy was very hard to maintain.

Sometimes just making too much noise was enough to sentence one to death. While my grandfather's cousin Adela was hiding outside Warsaw with her daughters, her husband became sick. With no way to treat him or to conceal his loud coughing, their hosts simply shot him. In a village, one was equally at risk from benefactors as from neighbors. But at least in the village there was hope of food and aid; in the forest there was neither.

As Emanuel Ringelblum put it in his history of the German occupation, by the last years of the war, to many Polish villagers and townspeople, Jews had ceased to be human beings. Hunted, pursued, living in bunkers and attics, starving, covered in filth and fleas, they seemed worse off than wild beasts. It was well known by then that every Jew was destined for the gas chambers or the execution squad. In the minds of those around them, they were simply "the deceased on leave."[18] Killing them or giving them up to be killed had no more moral consequence than killing a pigeon or a stray deer. Jewish life was no longer just cheap; it was of no importance at all.

For a Jew, being banished to the woods meant to be completely on one's own. Fishel Zilberman owned fields and orchards in the village of Strzegom. It was a perfect hiding place—close to a forest and far from any German watch post. Fishel built a hiding place—a dugout, carved into the earth—for his family and their friends. The hideout lasted untouched for a year before locals raided it, demanding that the Jews turn over all their valuables in exchange for keeping its location a secret. After that they were never safe. The villagers came by again and again. Their demands for money escalated into beatings, followed by murders. Fishel's daughter, Rut, recalled walking back to her family's den through fields of ripening wheat, thinking to herself that "the world is so beautiful, and I am here hunted like an animal."[19]

Around the same time that Rut was hiding in the country, another young Jewish girl, Fajga Pfeffer, was also trying to stay alive. She had survived two liquidations of the ghetto in Peremyshliany, near Lviv, once by hiding under some straw in a shed, and the second time by concealing herself in an orchard. After that she joined a group of Jews who hid out in the woods.

One day Fajga was stopped by six policemen. They asked her where the other Jews were and told her that she should tell them if she wanted to live. Fajga replied that they shouldn't search for cursed Jewish gold, because they had enough gold already, as well as dark soil and white bread, which were better than gold. They kept questioning her, when suddenly some shots rang out. Fajga ran. Before she fled, she warned the men that "they shouldn't hunt Jews like animals, because the time will come when these souls will have to be paid for."[20] The equation of Jews with animals was by then a commonplace, but her words carried the weight of a curse.

By the end of the war, in May 1945, the weight of such curses could be felt across Eastern Europe. In Poland alone, three million Jews had been killed during the war—some 92 percent of their total numbers.[21] Every village had its missing people, its misappropriated cattle and goods, its houses and clothes taken from the dead. And when every town was a crime scene, peace brought not tranquility but fear. In many places, this fear, which combined a dread of punishment with a desperate desire to keep ill-gotten gains, led to terrible acts of violence. The worst and most famous of these was the Kielce Pogrom of 1946.

The city of Kielce is located about one hundred miles due south of Warsaw. Before the war, it was a sizable place, home to about 70,000 residents, about a third of whom were Jews. I have, or *I had*, family from there. My cousin Ania's grandfather Julian Gringras was born in Kielce. His father, Koppel Gringras, owned the biggest photography studio in town, the Studio Moderne. Koppel learned the art of photography in Zurich. When he returned to Kielce, he opened a shop on the city's main boulevard. It was a handsome establishment, with frosted windows, glass walls, and a glass roof that let in enough light for a proper photograph. The one downside to all that pretty glass was that it shattered whenever there was hail.

Koppel took most of the pictures at first, but as he grew older, his brother Artur and his older sons took over for him. For portraits, they kept a few props—curtains and columns and the like—in the studio. The photographs were made using glass plates. Sometimes Koppel's wife, Fajgla, helped to retouch them, spreading a very light, pale ink across light patches on the plate. She had to be careful, for any mistake would redound to the advantage of Studio Rembrandt, their rivals across the street.

When the war started, Koppel's family fled east—by bike, on foot, and in hired carts. Julian and his wife, Fela, crossed the River Bug on a ferry piloted by Belarusians. In Kovel, a small town in western Ukraine, they met up with Julian's parents and oldest sister, Rozalia. Rozalia's husband, Obarzanski, persuaded her and Koppel to go back across the river and return to Kielce and the German zone of occupation. Obarzanski said "that you could work things out with the Germans, you could get along."[22] Julian's family did not last long in Kielce, however. His father and mother were sent to their deaths in Birkenau. His sister was shot in a quarry. Her husband, Obarzanski, met the most horrible fate of all: dragged to death behind a car.

None of Koppel's extended family returned to Kielce after the war. But a hundred or so of the city's Jews did. On July 4, 1946, over a year after Germany's defeat and the end of the war, forty-two of them were shot or beaten to death by a mob made up of local Poles, acting alongside a Polish police detachment and a unit of the Polish army.

This pogrom began with the disappearance of a child. On July 1, nine-year-old Henryk Błaszczyk, the son of a Kielce tailor, went missing. When he reappeared on the third, he told his parents that he had been kidnapped and kept in a basement. It later emerged that he had really gone to a nearby village to pick cherries. One of the Błaszczyks' neighbors suggested that the kidnappers must have been Jews, out to get blood for their Passover matzah. Henryk's father agreed and took the matter to the police.

The investigation began the following day, at a house where most of the city's remaining Jews, many of whom had recently returned from the Soviet Union, were then living. Little Henryk singled out one of the residents, an Orthodox Jew named Kalman Singer, as the person who had lured him into the basement.[23] The police entered the house, which they soon discovered had no basement to speak of. Meanwhile a crowd gathered outside and started to throw stones, yelling, "They've killed our children." Then the mob rushed into the house and killed the Jews huddled inside.[24] Soldiers sent to keep the peace joined in the violence, which soon spread to the rest of the city. Armed gangs moved through the city streets, beating and murdering any Jews they happened to find.

After the violence was over, people tried to pin the blame for the Kielce Pogrom on outside agitators—the NKVD, the anti-Communist underground, and even Zionists. Subsequent research has shown that it was a local event, rooted in deep mistrust of the returning Jews. Coming back, seemingly from death, Jews took on a sinister aspect in the eyes of their former neighbors. Fear that they might take back the property they had lost merged with fantasies of revenge. Both anxieties fed into ancient stereotypes and myths. Here the blood libel was not a pretext—it was an urgent motive. To those raging in the Kielce streets, the legend of the Jew as bloodsucker and vampire was not a metaphor but a reality. The cries uttered by the mob tell the story: "Jews, where are our children? Enough of the Jews, kill them, they grab up Polish children and torture them."[25] And again, elsewhere: "You killed Jesus, and now you'll pay for it. You've drunk enough of our blood."

The Kielce Pogrom was not an isolated incident; nor was Poland the only country where returning Jews met with violence. Other pogroms occurred in Rzeszów and Kraków, where Jews were suspected of stealing blood for transfusions as a means of reviving their weakened bodies after the trauma of the camps. Similar events took place in Hungary and Slovakia. In the Christian folk imagination, Jews had long been the quintessential strangers, a role that combined menace and allure in equal measure.[26] Now all that ambivalence had melted away, as dead neighbors returned in the shape of living monsters.

Beyond the cities and the camps and deep in the countryside, the Holocaust effected a profound, almost metaphysical unraveling of the social fabric. Across Eastern Europe, Jews were suddenly absent from a landscape they had inhabited for centuries. They were seldom mourned. For some, their disappearance was the fulfillment of a prophecy. In the 1980s, when the Polish anthropologist Alina Cała was gathering information on peasant beliefs about the Jews, she heard frequently that the war had been sent by God as a punishment, and that the Jews themselves knew it.

For others, the end of Jewish life in Eastern Europe was little more than an occasion for plunder. Christian neighbors took over Jewish businesses, seized Jewish land, and moved into Jewish homes. People even sifted the soil underneath concentration camp crematoria, searching for gold fillings and discarded rings. Soon the signs of Jewish presence on the land became few and far between: a shattered headstone; the imprint of a mezuzah on a doorframe; apple trees growing in what had once been a Jewish orchard.

In Zambrów, hardly anything remains, just the old town square, now bisected by a major road, and a patch of grass where the Jewish cemetery used to be. In Kielce, the Studio Moderne is long gone, but some of the photographs that had been taken there remain. One is of a Jewish boy from the countryside who became a famous chess prodigy. Another is a portrait of the future Pope John Paul II's mother, taken in 1915 while she was visiting her husband, a sergeant in the Austro-Hungarian army. Still others are of ordinary people: a man with a military haircut and a seagull-wing mustache; a woman wearing a fox fur stole and a string of pearls; six children wearing their Sunday best.

In Drohobycz, the whole city serves as a tacit memorial. The synagogue, far taller than any other such building in Poland and until recently a storage place for salt, towers over its district of the city. Of the Jews who were deported from Drohobycz, there is not a whisper. Virtually all of them were sent to Bełżec, the most hidden and least remembered of the camps. This was the pyre that consumed the lives of the Jews of Lviv and most of the rest of Galicia. Before the Nazis evacuated it in the summer of 1943, they did everything they could to obliterate all evidence of the camp. They burned down and buried every building, to make it look as if the entire complex had been a farm. The mass graves were exhumed, by Jewish laborers, and the bodies burned as well, after which any surviving bone fragments were pulverized and mixed with ash so as to give nothing away.

When archaeologists dug there in the 1990s, they found signs of former trenches, which showed up as slight disturbances in the soil. For a long time, though, they could find nothing in them; then finally their drills probed deep enough to be stopped by a thick layer of carbonized bones. Beneath them was fat. Time and chemistry had turned whatever bodies remained there into a kind of human soap.

12

Stalinism

Pro-government parade with images of Lenin,
Rákosi, and Stalin. Budapest, 1950.

Warsaw, February 1945. Snow is falling on the capital. The right bank of the Vistula swarms with Red Army soldiers, refugees from the East, and returnees from displaced-persons camps. The left bank—formerly the heart of the city—is nearly empty. Six months have passed since the outbreak of the Warsaw Uprising on August 1, 1944. After two months of exceptionally brutal street fighting, the Germans declared victory, shot anyone they could find still alive, and withdrew from the city for good. In the wake of this defeat, Warsaw has become a husk of a city, a place where the dead outnumber the living. In this respect, the city as a whole has come to share the fate of the Warsaw Ghetto, which was savaged, emptied, and cauterized after *its* rebellion a year prior, in the spring of 1943.

Visitors to Warsaw in 1945 were shocked by the state of the former ghetto. In the center of the city, some individual buildings were still standing, and even rows of townhouses by which to orient oneself. In the ghetto, there was nothing. In Muranów, the prewar neighborhood at the core of what became the ghetto, not a single house was left upright. All that remained of the district was a layer of finely sifted rubble, about the height of a man. One visitor to the ghetto wrote that he spent hours searching through the snow-covered debris without finding a hint of what had been there before. Another wrote that the ruins made him think that the walls that surrounded the Jewish cemetery were pointless; both sides of the barrier now belonged to the dead.[1]

Four years later Muranów looked quite different. What had once been an urban desert now teemed with activity. For three years, brigades of young volunteers worked to clear the area of debris, which often included unclaimed pieces of human bone. Some of these volunteers came from as far away as Bulgaria and Yugoslavia, drawn by the call of a fellow socialist nation. Now it was time to build. Plans had been drawn up for a model neighborhood, a workers' paradise featuring thousands of apartments, each a modest but comfortable 450 square feet, arranged in large blocks separated by spacious boulevards full of greenery and trees. The scheme was visionary, and the process to bring it to fruition was equally utopian.

Teams of expert bricklayers, some of whom were women—this was a new kind of building site—equipped with the newest working techniques and armed with the spirit of socialist competition, worked at a breakneck pace to erect as many "speedscapers"[2] as they could in a given amount of time. One apartment building was ready in twenty-three days, another in eight, another in six.[3] Poets could only marvel. One wrote in praise of the "splendid district of new, socialist life."[4] Another poet, struck dumb by the pace of construction, asked for assistance from the "Muse of the Six-Year Plan."

It was shameless puffery, but many of those present thought what was being accomplished over those summer days in Muranów really *was* socialism. Never mind that the construction work was as shoddy as it was swift, that the pipes leaked, the plaster was loose, and the floors were uneven—it still looked like a miracle. Something had been conjured out of nothing. Sheer determination had moved mountains. The future, it seemed, belonged to the workers and to a system that put them at the heart of every decision.

In this new world, housing would be free, land would be used in common, and factories would be owned by the state. These ideals represented more than just a change in economic arrangements: they brought with them a revolution, affecting everything from the way people dressed to the way they spoke and wrote poetry. This new reality also had many sinister implications, for this revolution was imposed not from below but from above, and not from within but from without.

The process of Sovietizing Eastern Europe began in 1939 with the Soviet Union's seizure of eastern Poland, which had been negotiated beforehand with Nazi Germany as part of the Molotov-Ribbentrop Pact, a nonaggression agreement that included, among its provisions, a new partition of Poland between the two superpowers. The takeover continued in 1940, as the Soviets annexed the independent states of Lithuania, Latvia, and Estonia, as well as the regions of Bukovina and Bessarabia from Romania. All now fell under the Soviet Union's direct control, a change which meant that their previous history and traditions of statehood would have to be immediately swept aside.

In the summer of 1940, the Soviet foreign minister Vyacheslav Molotov explained the reasoning behind this sudden march westward in a conversation with Lithuania's deputy prime minister. It was only two weeks after the initial Soviet takeover, and it still seemed possible to salvage partial independence for Lithuania. However, in the midst of negotiations, Molotov suddenly let the mask slip and told the minister what was really going on:

> You must take a good look at reality and understand that in the future small nations will have to disappear. Your Lithuania along with the other Baltic nations, including Finland, will have to join the glorious family of the Soviet Union. Therefore you should begin now to initiate your people into the Soviet system which in the future shall reign everywhere, throughout all Europe, put into practice earlier in some places, as in the Baltic nations, later in others.[5]

Lithuania's initiation into the Soviet system was indeed swift and brutal. Within weeks of the arrival of the Red Army, bogus elections were held to elect a Communist-dominated parliament, while peasant lands were broken up and merged into collective farms. At the same time, Soviet authorities arrested tens of thousands of politically suspect or socially undesirable citizens, deporting most of them to Siberia and Central Asia. The roundup included the Baltic countries' heads of state. Lithuania's president Antanas Smetona managed to slip over the border to Germany, but Latvia and Estonia's leaders, Kārlis Ulmanis and Konstantin Päts, respectively, weren't as fortunate. Ulmanis died of dysentery in 1942 while in transit to prison in Turkmenistan. Päts spent most of the rest of his life imprisoned in psychiatric hospitals scattered across the Soviet Union. One symptom of his supposed madness was that he kept insisting he was the president of Estonia.[6]

The Soviet Union repeated this process of social cleansing through mass expulsions and arrests in all the annexed territories.[7] In this way, they were swiftly broken and decapitated, easing their integration into an alien political system. The transformation this introduced proved to be lasting. Although all these territories had been conquered by the advancing German army in 1941, after their reconquest by the Red Army in 1944–45 they remained part of the Soviet Union until its disintegration half a century later.

The incorporation of these western borderlands was only a preview of the empire the Soviet Union would build in Eastern Europe after the war. By 1950, all of Eastern Europe belonged to a single integrated social, political, and economic system. From Poland to Albania, every country in the region was a one-party state, dominated by a local version of the Communist Party. Each had a command economy designed on the Soviet model, and each was led by a dictator modeled after Stalin. With the important exception of Yugoslavia, which was led by its own native partisan leader Josip Broz Tito, these leaders depended on Stalin for their power and looked to him for how to rule. Stalin approved their candidacies, dictated their domestic policies, and determined their relations with the rest of the world.

For as long as Stalin was alive, these satellite countries acted like provinces of a single gigantic state. And yet this was a strange kind of empire. Unlike the Baltic countries and the Belarusian-Ukrainian borderlands, Poland, Czechoslovakia, Hungary, Romania, Bulgaria, and Albania remained independent states, and they expended a great amount of effort to make it seem as if their allegiance to the Soviet Bloc were entirely voluntary. Despite the overwhelming might of the Red Army (the poet Czesław Miłosz, who witnessed its advance in Poland, compared it to molten lava flowing across the land), the Soviet Union did not immediately impose its will on Eastern Europe. Instead, it acted through its proxies: local Communist parties, often minuscule at the outset, whose leadership usually came from the Comintern schools in Moscow.

Starting in 1945, these Communist parties expanded their memberships, competed in elections, and formed coalition governments with other (usually pro-Soviet) parties. Within these governments, Communists typically held authority over the all-important interior ministry and secret police. With these two levers of power, they could terrorize their political opponents and rig elections in their own favor. By 1948, Communist parties were firmly in charge across the region, having come to power in ways that appeared, if not exactly legal, then at least driven by local desires.

In Czechoslovakia, this appearance contained a kernel of truth. There the Communist Party did quite well in elections without resorting to fraud, winning 38 percent of the vote in 1946. The party itself grew at an astounding rate, from 28,000 members in May 1945 to over a million by March 1946.[8] However, it still came to governmental power as the result of a coup in February 1948, though one that parts of society received quite positively. Thousands of students in Prague protested the Communist seizure of power, but hundreds of thousands of factory workers attended rallies to celebrate it.[9]

These rallies may not have been *entirely* spontaneous, but they did reflect something about the changing mood in the country. Whether legally or not, the future had arrived. As the novelist Milan Kundera would later write about the period after the coup, "a new life had begun, a genuinely new and different life."[10] These were at once the "most joyous of years" and a time of absolute seriousness, when "anyone who failed to rejoice was immediately suspected of lamenting the victory of the working class."

Joyous but deadly serious; imposed by force but greeted with enthusiasm: Stalinism could support these contradictions because it was more than a political system: it was a civilization, with its own styles, stories, and heroes. It believed in progress and claimed it could bring it about almost instantaneously. It called for the immediate eradication of class differences and an equally abrupt jump into the future. As part of this leap, young people were invited to step into the drama of making new lives for themselves. Usually this project of inner transformation took place in a factory, which took on the role that cathedrals had once held in medieval Europe. These factories were not mere workshops, however: they were free-standing cities, surrounded by their own housing developments, cultural centers, and schools.

The immediate postwar era was a boom time for the construction of industrial settlements. Most were centered on massive iron works. They include Nowa Huta in Poland, Sztálinváros in Hungary, and Dimitrovgrad in Bulgaria. Often, as in Muranów, they were built from scratch, on bare earth. Young people by the thousands left their villages in the Galician countryside and the Hungarian plains to help in their construction.

Sztálinváros under construction. Hungary, 1950.

The cities they built are still standing. Nowa Huta is a distant suburb of Kraków, a sleepy, pleasant place whose gigantic alleyways—fit for huge May Day processions—are largely empty of any traffic besides the slow shuffling of pensioners on their way to pick up their daily bread. In Sztálinváros (now renamed Dunaújváros—"Danube-town" rather than "Stalin-town"), the furnaces at the Danube Ironworks are still running, filling the air with the acrid smell of the blast furnace and acid-pickling baths. The entrance to the mill, preserved as it was in the 1950s, is a titanic cement colonnade, the inside of which is decorated by a mural depicting "The Worker-Peasant Alliance." In this fresco, executed with Picasso-esque aplomb by Endre Domanovszky, gigantic peasant women deliver gargantuan loaves of bread to grateful (and equally enormous) steel workers. The ensemble as a whole is a triumphal arch for the working class, a sign that this is not a mere factory but a monument to the victory of the proletariat.

To those who felt sympathetic toward Communist rule, nothing seemed more beautiful than the sight of molten steel. The Czech writer Bohumil Hrabal thought glowing ingots at the Poldi Steelworks in Kladno looked "airy and graceful and unreal." Hrabal was there as part of a program called Putting 77,000 to Work, in which tens of thousands of people who, like him, had no background in industrial labor were suddenly plucked from their jobs and sent to factories and collective farms across Czechoslovakia.[11] These "volunteers" were people whose former functions were no longer needed by the new order—owners of nationalized businesses, professors of theology, politicians from banned parties, and writers of socially irresponsible fiction. Hrabal belonged to this last category. For years as a budding author, he had experimented with surrealism. His literary idols were Rimbaud and Éluard, as they were for many of his Prague peers. The Poldi Steelworks brought him back to the concrete.

Hrabal fell hard for Poldi. It wasn't an easy love. The plant was an inferno of heat and grime. Acid fumes stung his eyes and throat. He saw workers crushed by steel beams, torn by hanging wires, and scalded by molten metal. Some died on the plant floor; others were taken to the hospital, never to return. Hrabal worked with disgraced judges, trade unionists, petty thieves, and former prostitutes. Together they processed scrap arriving by train from all over Czechoslovakia: iron crosses pulled from village churchyards, pieces of tanks, grave markers, sewing machines, and bathtubs twisted into strange shapes by incendiary bombs.[12] These remnants of an old world were melted down and reforged into something better. The metaphors practically wrote themselves. In a short story written at this time, one of Hrabal's characters explains what it all meant:

> Don't you understand that you've been loading all that stuff, the very tools of your trade, into those furnaces, and the ingots that pour out of those furnaces are meant for a different era? A year from now, where will all those small businesses, those crappy little companies, and their machinery be? Gone! And what'll become of you? The same as all this scrap, the tools of your trade . . . you'll be ingots too.[13]

The great steelworks at Kladno, Nowa Huta, and Sztálinváros were melting down the past. They were also forging a new kind of human being—heroes for a proletarian age. In the USSR, these new people were called Stakhanovites, or heroes of labor. They were prodigies of productivity, shock workers whose feats of strength or efficiency served as living proof that sheer effort could triumph over lack of material or means. In other words, it was not technology but will that would lead the socialist East to surpass the capitalist West.

The Stakhanovite movement felt democratic because its heroes could come from anywhere. In 1949 Piotr Ożański arrived at Nowa Huta from a tiny village in southeastern Poland. Twenty-four years old, an army veteran, and a member of a Polish Youth Brigade, Piotr dreamed of performing a "new exploit of youth," or triumphant feat of labor, in construction. Trained as a bricklayer, he decided that his deed would consist of laying twenty-four thousand bricks in a single shift. On July 14, 1950, his wish came true. In eight hours, his team laid 34,727 bricks.[14] Within a few weeks, his face was on parade banners.

Worker heroes received praise in works of fiction as well. Overnight a new genre came into being: the production novel. It too was an import from the Soviet Union. Most production novels were set in factories. Their titles tell their stories: *At the Construction Site, Coal, The Offensive, Number 16 Produces, The Tractor, Tractors Will Win the Spring.* Tractors, or "peace tanks," as they were sometimes described by the poetically minded, were an especially popular topic. At once ubiquitous and revolutionary, tractors promised to sweep away the old feudal-patriarchal order in the countryside. Heralds of a new age, tractors made ideal subjects for artists of all kinds. As one Slovak painter opined in 1949, reflecting the orthodoxy of the moment, "a man on a combine harvester" was to his era what "a man in armor or in princely robes" had been for the Renaissance.[15]

Creating a new literature also meant getting rid of the old one. Poland and Hungary simply banned various prewar publications and pulled thousands of titles off the shelves of public libraries. Czechoslovakia took the task of refurbishing its national reading list more seriously. Between 1949 and 1952, a special "liquidation committee" judged the worthiness of all the literature in the country and found much of it wanting, often for aesthetic reasons rather than ideological ones. Nationwide, some 27 million books were shredded, pulped, and turned into cardboard.[16] After his stint at Poldi, Hrabal worked at one of these literary recycling plants. If he had stayed long enough, he could have watched his own novels vanish under the hydraulic presses.[17]

What would take the place of all those books destined for the incinerator? A new literature would be drawn from the lived experiences of the working class and written by the same. At least that was the hope. Communist cultural authorities in Poland were constantly on the lookout for such self-taught artists. They sponsored special contests for aspiring songwriters, sculptors, painters, and especially writers. A special "literary help desk" was even set up to shepherd budding talents from the darkness of the slush pile to the light of the printed page.

Aspiring writers responded in droves. I once found an enormous trove of letters, nearly untouched, in the National Archives in Warsaw. They were from would-be poets, frustrated novelists, and assorted graphomaniacs of every description. The majority of them were young people, members of the generation of the so-called *awans społeczny*, or "social advance." Many had recently arrived from their native villages in the city to enroll in the new workers' universities, which provided an accelerated course of instruction for proletarian youth. They wrote of wanting to travel to the Soviet Union, earn scholarships, appear in magazines, and find jobs as leaders of industry.

The poems these would-be writers submitted incorporated every cliché of socialist realism. There were poems in praise of the Red Army, the Polish Workers' Party, an obligatory ode to tractors titled, not very imaginatively, "The Music of Tractors." One sixteen-year-old girl sent in a song on the least exciting subject of all—Bolesław Bierut, the current president of Poland and chief of the Polish Workers' Party—a gray blur of a man who functioned as Stalin's eyes and ears in Warsaw.

Like the leaders of all the people's democracies, Bierut received gifts from his grateful subjects, all of which were announced in the press. For one birthday, he received ninety-nine presents from the people, among them samples of road gravel, circuit breakers, and a model of the presidential palace crafted entirely out of sugar. This largesse paled in comparison to the bounty bestowed on Stalin. For his seventieth birthday, in 1949, the Father of Nations accepted 811 presents from grateful Poles. They included the last meter of jute fabric produced according to the specifications of the three-year plan, a nine-hundred-kilogram statue of himself carved out of rock salt, and the favorite pipe of an elderly Kashubian.[18]

Gifts to the leader were often quite personal, even handmade. They could be touching and dangerous in equal measure. In Budapest in the early 1950s, one enterprising butcher placed a bust of Mátyás Rákosi in the window of his shop. Rákosi was Hungary's equivalent to Bierut, known throughout the Soviet Bloc as "Stalin's best Hungarian pupil." The butcher sculpted the bust out of raw pork fat—quite a feat, but one that swiftly backfired. Not wanting to be outdone, all the other shops on the butcher's street likewise displayed portraits of the leader. What had started out as an advertisement now became a compulsory act of obeisance. However, as winter turned to spring and temperatures started to rise, the original butcher's bust began to melt. Rákosi—already unsightly—started to look truly monstrous. Panicking, the butcher hastily took his sculpture down and sold off its remains as lard.[19]

Of all the "little Stalins" who ruled over Eastern Europe in the early 1950s, Hungary's Rákosi did the most to foster his own cult of personality. A dim apparatchik, his main claim to fame was surviving fifteen years in one of Admiral Horthy's jails. Now thrust to the summit of power, he became the symbol of the new order. Poets extolled him as a wise teacher and father of the nation. In perhaps the most truthful of these encomia, a writer praised him for giving poets a subject for their poems.

But the main vehicle of Rákosi's cult was visual. Photographs of his egglike bald head, framed by heavy coal-black eyebrows, hung from the wall of nearly every office, schoolroom, shop, coffeehouse, and waiting room in the country. The most popular picture showed Rákosi standing in a field of grain, thoughtfully inspecting a stalk of wheat. Reproduced over fifty thousand times, this image was the apotheosis of everything Rákosi wanted Hungary to see in him: his tenderness, his agronomic expertise, and his solicitude toward grain. In the words of one of his court poets, who later defected to the West, it conveyed "all the benevolence that radiated from Mátyás Rákosi toward the people, whether the people desired his benevolence or not."[20]

The leaders of the other Communist Bloc nations were accustomed to similar flattery, but the greatest honor waiting for them—immortality—arrived only once they were dead. Again, the template came from the Soviet Union. After Lenin died in 1924, his body had been embalmed and placed on permanent display, in a specially built mausoleum on Moscow's Red Square. The rulers of the people's democracies, if they were truly his heirs, could be granted no less.

The moment Georgi Dimitrov, the head of the Bulgarian Communist Party, died in 1949, a team of embalmers from the Lenin Mausoleum began taking tender care of his body. Dimitrov's mausoleum, a vaguely neoclassical cube executed in off-white Bulgarian marble, was built in just six days. Teams of shock workers toiled around the clock to finish it before the end of the week. The embalming process used on Dimitrov was similarly swift and exacting. As was done with the mummies of ancient Egypt, his innards were first carefully removed and replaced with antiseptic gauze. The country's best air-conditioning system was installed inside the tomb, to maintain just the right balance of temperature and humidity. Specialists from the Moscow Art Theater designed a lighting system to cast just the right amount of dramatic shadow on Dimitrov's rather haggard face, without simultaneously warming his body up in a way that might speed its decomposition.

One problem stymied the embalmers. What exactly should Dimitrov look like in his new, eternal guise? The chemical baths and injections used to keep his face and hands lifelike bleached his skin white. A layer of makeup had to be added to restore his original color. To decide what shade this should be, the embalmers studied the pigmentation of

150 Bulgarian students and arrived at an average, "ideal" Bulgarian skin tone, which they then applied to the mummy. Dimitrov thus became not just the head of the party or the father of the nation but a perfect synthesis of all Bulgarians.[21]

When Klement Gottwald, the head of the Czechoslovak Communist Party, died of a burst artery on March 14, 1953, just five days after attending Stalin's funeral in Moscow, it seemed to many like a final act of fealty toward his master. As they had with Dimitrov, the embalmers from the Lenin Mausoleum immediately set to work preserving the body of the lifelong alcoholic, and possible syphilitic. First, Gottwald's internal organs were removed and placed in glass jars, while the rest of his body was dressed in a military uniform, over two pairs of rubber suits. Only Gottwald's face and hands were exposed to the open air. These required frequent and meticulous interventions, including injections of paraffin and Vaseline, to keep them looking supple and fresh. Every night after the last visitors left the Prague mausoleum, Gottwald's body descended into a basement laboratory where these ablutions could be performed out of reach from prying eyes. Everything about this process—from the details of the embalming to the assistance proffered by Czechoslovakia's Soviet friends—was kept strictly top secret.

Despite—or possibly because of—this secrecy, rumors spread in Prague that all was not well with the body. A mere month after Gottwald's death, he was said to be putrefying and stank so horribly that he could only be approached while wearing a gas mask.[22] Later people became convinced that the leader was decaying by stages. First, Gottwald's feet turned black, then his legs. After that his whole ribcage had to be filled with asphalt. At this point, the entire body—by now unbearably noxious—had to be burned.[23]

None of this was true. According to the meticulous notes kept by its embalmers, in all the years Gottwald's body was on display, it suffered from no more than a slight discoloration of the palms. In the popular imagination, however, Gottwald's body became Czechoslovakia's version of *The Picture of Dorian Gray*. As the regime faltered, so too did the corpse. And indeed, even as his flesh remained inviolate, Gottwald's legacy suffered. In 1962, when Czechoslovakia belatedly broke with Stalinism as its governing ideology, the body was quietly cremated.

After the cremation, Gottwald's ashes were placed in a small columbarium within his mausoleum. After the fall of the Berlin Wall in 1989, the Czechoslovak Communist Party, finally out of power, decided that it was time to move their former leader to a normal cemetery. A historian associated with the mausoleum was supposed to take the urn and place it in a plot specially rented for this purpose. On the way from the mausoleum the historian stopped into a pub and forgot the ashes as he walked out.[24] Their current whereabouts remain unknown.

.   .   .

Cities rebuilt from the rubble of war; factories springing up out of the bare earth; brilliant leaders honored by a grateful populace into eternity: all of these were part of the dreamworld of High Stalinism. The reality was quite different. The Communist reality was supposed to be infinitely plastic, constantly advancing toward a golden future. Instead, all too often, it found itself stuck in the mud.

New housing developments in Muranów and Sztálinváros quickly became overcrowded and unsanitary. The blast furnaces of the new model cities could barely produce any steel for want of technical expertise and proper raw materials. Economic growth stalled or went into reverse. Agriculture, newly collectivized in much of the bloc, went into an especially steep decline.[25] In the early 1950s, as the promise of a lightning-quick transformation of society foundered, party leaders increasingly turned to accusations of sabotage and treason to explain their failings.

The summer of 1950 was a moment of particularly intense paranoia. War had just broken out in the Korean Peninsula. In Czechoslovakia, the second harvest of the first five-year plan, the centralized economic program guiding the development of the entire country, was just beginning. At the same time, in the far south and west of the country, close to the border with "imperialist" West Germany, a sinister assailant appeared in Czech fields: the potato bug.

The potato bug is native to North America, and the Czech Communist Party interpreted its appearance on Czech soil as a deliberate act of sabotage—practically an act of war. Government proclamations claimed that the insects were being dropped from planes flown by the U.S. Air Force. Not content to set Korean villages ablaze, these "gangsters in airplanes" were now also trying to spoil the hard-won crops of Czechoslovak farms.

Czech schoolchildren were quickly drafted to fight the war against these "six-legged ambassadors of Wall Street." Working in tightly coordinated skirmish lines, armed only with glass jars and keen eyes, Young Pioneers trapped and killed the imperialist enemy in great numbers. "Everyone into battle against the potato bug!" proclaimed banners.

In the Czech press, the potato bug turned into a metaphor, a symbol of all the homegrown enemies of socialism. One Prague newspaper wrote that the introduction of the insect pest was just the latest in a series of Western provocations, a chain of sabotage that culminated with the planting of agents at the highest levels of government.[26] The time was now ripe for these traitors to be unmasked.

The same year the potato bugs appeared in Czech fields, nearly every country in the Soviet Bloc staged show trials of alleged traitors, spies, and saboteurs. As in the great Stalinist show trials of the 1930s, the targets of these investigations were among the most prominent and powerful members of the Communist Party. Before he was put on trial, Rudolf Slánský was the second most powerful person in the Czechoslovak Communist Party. In Hungary, László Rajk had organized the very secret police that just a few years later arrested him. And when each of these tall trees fell, they pulled dozens of other people down with them.

The show trials were scripted like plays. Every question from the prosecutors, and every answer from the witnesses, was written out in advance. In Hungary, Mátyás Rákosi, the head of the Communist Party, personally drew up not only Rajk's indictment and the questions the judge asked him, but even Rajk's answers to those questions.[27] At some level, the accused understood their roles in this dance. When Rajk's trial was over, and he was sentenced to death by hanging, the head of the Hungarian secret police took him to a small room beside the court chambers and hugged him, telling him, "You were excellent, my dear Laci."[28]

As if they were episodes in a serial drama, the most exciting parts of the show trials were broadcast live on radio to the entire country. Work would stop while factory workers put their tools down to listen to the confessions of the accused. This could lead to strange situations, as the scripts used in the trials often collided with the bare facts of reality.

The novelist Péter Nádas described one such scene. In the Rajk trial, while one of the accused testified to Rajk's crimes, his father, mother, and young son listened at home. At one point, Rajk mentioned that in the course of a complicated plot to kill the leaders of the Hungarian party, orchestrated by the Yugoslav security services and the CIA, he had to excuse himself to attend his father's funeral. At this, the accused's son burst out:

> "Why did he say that? But he did not come home! Grandpa! Why? Why don't you answer? Grandpa, please answer me! Why did he say that? But you are alive, Grandpa?! Grandpa, please!" But the grandfather sat in dead silence. He did not say a word.[29]

Even a child could see through the obvious lies, but it was the grandfather who grasped the larger point. The purpose of the show trials was not to tell a convincing story about the state of the world but to show that no one but the party could determine the truth. The confession of the accused was the most important part, demonstrating the extent of the regime's power. Anyone could execute an opponent. Even framing someone for a crime was not difficult. But getting them to admit, seemingly of their free will, to something that was not only false but patently absurd—that took real mastery.

In Hungary, Bulgaria, and Albania, many of the victims of the show trials were accused of working with Josip Broz Tito, the leader of Yugoslavia and the arch-traitor of the moment. Unlike all the other Communist leaders in Eastern Europe, with the partial exception of Albania's Enver Hoxha, Tito had come to power without the help of the Soviet Red Army. His own Communist partisans had driven the Axis powers out of Yugoslavia. Although Tito had been a member of the Comintern and loyal Stalinist throughout the 1930s, he did not owe his position to Stalin and did not feel the need to consult him on his every decision. Simmering disagreements between the two led to a break in the summer of 1948, which culminated with a Soviet blockade of Yugoslavia's borders and calls for the Yugoslav people to overthrow Tito.

The split between Tito and Stalin shattered the unity of the Eastern

Bloc. The notion that Eastern Europeans could follow Tito's example and pursue their own path to Communism independently of the Soviet Union posed an immediate threat to Soviet hegemony over the region. Stalin consequently set his secret police chiefs to work hunting alleged Titoists in the leadership of all the Eastern European parties.

In Yugoslavia, this situation was reversed. The most suspect were those members of the Yugoslav Communist Party who might side with Stalin. There could be thousands of these internal enemies. But they weren't class enemies or fascists; they were party members, mostly seasoned partisans. Executing them would be a waste of precious human material for the building of socialism. Instead, they would have to be reformed.

The site of their reeducation was an island in the Mediterranean called Goli Otok, or "Bare Isle." Legend has it that the Croatian sculptor Antun Augustinčić, while scouting the Adriatic in search of quality stone, came across a particularly dismal islet that had once been home to a marble quarry. Sunbaked, treeless, and isolated, it looked like the perfect place for a prison. Augustinčić mentioned the idea to Croatia's minister of the interior, from whom it reached Tito's ear and was quickly approved.

In the end, the marble from the Goli Otok quarry proved to be unusable. It didn't matter, though. This was a place where human clay was to be sculpted, rather than stone. Prisoners carried quarried blocks down to the sea and then back up the hill, over and over. It was a task for Sisyphus.

On Goli Otok, at least officially, there were no jailers. The prisoners, who came from all corners of Yugoslavia, were mostly Communist Party members. They ran every aspect of their lives there, doing the cleaning, cooking, and construction work. They were both inmates and wardens, snitches and interrogators. They were also the torturers. Beating other prisoners was the only way to prove you had reformed. The moment prisoners arrived on the island from the mainland, they faced their first test: the *stroj*, or line. All the inmates already on the island arranged themselves in two rows while the new arrivals disembarked on shore. To chants of *"Ti-to!"* and *"Mar-ko!,"* the new prisoners ran barefoot for a kilometer and a half between a gauntlet of as many as four thousand men. Even former generals had to face this initiation by pain. Along with other Communist Party bigwigs, they then had to make a public accounting of the reasons for their fall.[30]

It would be easy to mock the atmosphere of paranoia that led to the Stalinist show trials and the creation of the hellish reformatory on Goli Otok. Nearly all those implicated in the trials were innocent, at least of the charges brought against them. So were many of those imprisoned on the Bare Isle. But even if the charges against prisoners proved unfounded, governments had reason to be cautious. Tito really was surrounded by Soviet spies, who suborned much of his private bodyguard.[31]

In the first years of the Cold War, international tensions ran high. Both the Communist and the anti-Communist blocs relied on covert means to advance their causes. By the late 1940s, Eastern Europe was teeming with secret agents and intelligence operations. Berlin in this period was perhaps the most spy-ridden city in history, while the forested border between Austria and Czechoslovakia became a giant staging ground for exfiltrations and infiltrations.[32] Some of the most ambitious Western-led operations involved ferrying anti-Communist exiles to their native countries by sea or dropping them from the air, as was done on several occasions in Albania.

In 1949's Operation Valuable, a group of Albanian partisans were supposed to spark an anti-Communist rebellion in the mountains. The effort proved a complete fiasco, a disastrous preview of the Bay of Pigs invasion. However, the idea of armed resistance against Communism was not in itself ridiculous. In many countries of the Eastern Bloc, anti-Communist guerrilla forces were a fact of life into the mid-1950s. Some of these groups were continuations of wartime resistance movements. Others were made up of fighters who had gone over to the Axis side and expected no quarter from the new Communist-led governments.

In the Baltic states, they were known as the Forest Brothers. In Romania, they were called *haiducs*. But by far the biggest such movement was in Poland. There after the war, many units of the Home Army, the vast underground partisan force that had opposed the Germans throughout their occupation, simply kept fighting long after peace was declared. Some of these soldiers joined a new organization, called Freedom and Independence (WiN), dedicated to pushing Soviet forces out of Polish territory. Others struck out on their own, retreated into the forests where they felt most secure, and operated in ways that suggested a robber band as much as a rebel army.

Usually, though, these insurgents had the support of the countryside. In much of Poland, a state of civil war existed well into the late 1940s. Ultimately the Communist security forces, armed with enormous advantages in manpower and a willingness to employ brutal methods, prevailed. Between 1945 and 1947, they managed to capture the leadership of four successive iterations or "commands" of WiN. Polish émigrés in the West, who looked to WiN as their last hope of a return to a free Poland, despaired.

And then something miraculous happened. In 1948 a fifth command of the resistance sprang up. When the emissaries of this new organization arrived in the West, after a difficult journey undercover across East Germany, they boasted that they had hundreds of armed men at their disposal, eager and ready to take up the fight against the Soviet occupiers.

For émigré Poles who had fought in the anti-Communist underground, this force was the answer to their prayers. Western spy agencies, especially the CIA, were delighted as well. They wanted allies on the ground in the event of a third world war, men who could be counted on to sabotage railways and rescue paratroopers, as well as help in the day-to-day work of spying on the enemy. WiN fit the bill perfectly. Over a nearly five-year span, the Americans rewarded the group with training, equipment, and money—over half a million dollars in total, delivered in gold.

The only hitch was that the whole thing was fake. The Fifth Command was a ruse, part of a top-secret Polish counterintelligence program code-named Operation Caesar. The Fifth Command was deliberately designed to deceive foreign intelligence services and entrap would-be saboteurs working against the workers' state. But many of the people caught up in its web never knew. In addition to their Western handlers, Polish couriers and soldiers in the Fifth Command were genuinely convinced that they were working to abolish Communist rule. They realized their mistake only when they were arrested—and often, not even then.

The Fifth Command's cover was blown in 1952, when Polish newspapers trumpeted the capture of agents parachuted into Poland from the West. Dozens of conspirators, drawn into the fictitious organization by provocateurs, faced life imprisonment or execution. Former double agents announced their pride in foiling a plot hatched by the "spittle-flecked" henchmen of reaction. To this day, no one knows who gave the order to dissolve the plot, though the main suspect is Stalin himself. It may have been connected to the election of Eisenhower that year, and been a way of warning the new administration about the strength of Soviet control in the satellite countries, though no one knows for sure.

Here the story of Operation Caesar intersects with my family's history in a small but tantalizing way. After the war, my grandfather (and namesake) Jakub Mikanowski worked for the same branch of state security—counterintelligence—that oversaw Operation Caesar. Jakub's path into the world of intelligence work was long and indirect. He spent most of the war underground, in the woods. After being captured by the Germans, he escaped outside Minsk, where he met a group of lost Soviet border guards. Together they crossed the German front lines near Smolensk. There his career as a soldier began. He enrolled in a course in diversionary tactics, followed by parachute school.

In the spring of 1942, Jakub was dropped back behind enemy lines in Belarus. He fought with the partisans in the Babruysk and Baranovichi woods. A terrible casualty rate among his superiors made his promotion swift. In a few months, he went from being head of a squad to leading a platoon. By November 1942, he was the commander of a company. That same month he applied for membership in the Communist Party.

He stayed fighting in the forest for almost two more years. During that time, the Belarusian woods were host to some of the worst atrocities committed during the whole war. A favorite tactic of the Nazi partisan hunters was to enter a village suspected of collaboration, round up all the peasants, lock them in a barn, and set it on fire. Jakub witnessed many of these terrors firsthand. With his partisan brigade, he personally freed several hundred Jewish prisoners from a transit labor camp. This deed later earned him a brief mention in the third (and in my opinion, best) volume of the *History of the Working Class of the Belarusian Workers' Republic*.[33] It also secured him a position in the security apparatus of the new Polish People's Republic. The secret police and interior ministry recruited heavily from the former partisan units. Their members were loyal, battle-tested, and used to operating in secret: perfect material for spies and spy-catchers.

For them, the war never ended. They went directly from fighting an underground war against Germany to fighting the Cold War against the West. The day victory was declared in Europe, my grandfather was still in Belarus, fighting remnants of General Andrey Vlasov's army— renegade Red Army troops who had sided with the Nazis. After that, he was assigned to be one of the hundreds of case officers manning the immense Operation Caesar. His signature is on some of the reports about it that were sent to the KGB's resident monitor for Polish affairs. Whether his involvement went deeper, I haven't been able to find out. The relevant sections of his personnel file were redacted long ago.

A family legend, though, may connect to the sad history of the Fifth Command. Sometime in the early 1950s, my grandfather's employer offered him a bonus. He could receive it in the form of either a car or a fur coat. In a decision whose infamy reverberated over the decades and became a byword for her foolish attraction to luxury, my grandmother Zofia told him to choose the fur coat.

Still, it was an enormous prize for the times. By way of comparison, one of the chief double agents involved in Operation Caesar was a man named Marian but whose operational code name was Artur. Artur did more than almost anyone else to recruit and then betray other members of the underground. For this, his reward was the following: a New Year's package containing four boxes of tea, two tins of sardines, one jar of fruit compote, one can of powdered cocoa, one can of powdered chocolate, and two nylon stockings.[34]

Two stockings—now *that* was luxury. Those were lean times in Poland. Food and fuel were still being doled out by ration cards. Goods tended to be meager. So why was my grandfather offered the coat or the car? My guess is that it had to do with the conclusion of Operation Caesar. The $500,000 in gold Polish counterintelligence intercepted over the course of the plot was the equivalent of some $10 million in today's money. The coat may have been a way of divvying up the spoils.

—

Not all the threats faced by Eastern Europe's security services consisted of spies and double agents. Some were wholly intangible, products of the Communist Party's long-standing struggle against religion. A totalitarian, atheist party-state could not abide any rival sources of authority, much less ones that bore the imprint of divine sanction. Miracles— such as the building of an apartment building in six days—had to be strictly secular, while those that seemed to come from Heaven had to be unmasked as frauds and otherwise repressed.

These two competing attitudes toward the sacred clashed most forcefully in the case of the so-called Číhošť miracle in Czechoslovakia. On December 11, 1949, in a small village chapel in the Moravian highlands, Father Josef Toufar, the parish priest, was preaching his Advent sermon. Suddenly a metal cross on the altar table behind him seemed to move of its own accord. As he was facing away from the altar, Toufar himself did not witness it himself, but twenty of his parishioners testified that they saw the cross incline, or "bow," three times, and then return to a standing position without anyone present touching it.[35]

News of this miracle spread, and within a few days the church became a place of pilgrimage for people from across Czechoslovakia. Rumors and prophecies, especially of an imminent war, attached themselves to the event. Toufar himself was full of foreboding. He knew the miracle meant danger for his parishioners. He didn't pretend to understand what had really taken place, but he was certain that he had nothing to do with it. He failed to foresee, however, that he would be made to shoulder the lion's share of the blame.

Czechoslovak State Security arrested Father Toufar on January 28, 1950. The order appears to have come from the uppermost echelons of the Czech Communist Party. Soon thereafter other, higher-ranking members of the Czech clergy were swept up in a far-ranging dragnet. It seems that the state was laying the groundwork for a grand show trial, in which the Catholic hierarchy was to be accused of plotting against the state at the very highest levels, reaching all the way to Rome.

The miracle at Číhošť would be a crucial piece of evidence at this trial. For the trial to have its desired effect, Father Toufar would have to admit that he had personally staged the miracle under orders from his superiors in the church. He refused. To force him to confess, members of the secret police deprived him of sleep and took turns beating him.

After four weeks, they finally succeeded; Father Toufar signed the document placed in front of him. Although the signature is so shaky that there is a question as to whether it is really his.

Next he was taken back to the church in Číhošť to demonstrate on camera how he had staged his deception. The footage still exists: Toufar's hands are broken and his teeth are missing, and he can barely stand on his swollen feet. Soon after filming ended, he collapsed. A day later, despite the intervention of the best Prague doctors, he was dead. The official cause was listed as a ruptured ulcer. His body was hidden away and later buried in a mass grave, where his bones were mingled with those of a circus elephant to throw prospective relic-seekers off the scent.

Missing its star witness, the show trial was called off. The rest of the accused clergy members received long prison sentences. Some were sent to work in uranium mines. In subsequent years, the Číhošť incident became a taboo subject in Czechoslovakia, except for a moment during the summer of 1968, when an investigation into the true circumstances of Toufar's death was briefly reopened.[36]

Since 1989, however, the church in Číhošť has once again become an object of pilgrimage, and beatification procedures have been started for Toufar. Central to them will be the question of the miraculous movement of the cross. Stalinist investigators were certain that it was a trick created by a pulley hidden inside the altar. However, they were never able to find evidence of such a device. Of course, the investigators never considered that the miracle could have been the work of God, just as the current investigators from the Vatican will be sure to deny any involvement on the part of the Devil.

Although the Číhošť miracle was deeply troubling to Communist authorities, it was a singular event, with no immediate successors. Things were different in Poland. There, miracles arrived in waves. Many involved icons of the Virgin Mary, which either spontaneously "renewed" themselves or suddenly began to weep. In the period from 1949 to 1950—the very height of the Stalinist terror—the secret police noted 280 separate occurrences of such apparitions.[37]

The most famous happened in Lublin, where on July 3, 1949, an icon of the Virgin Mary in the town cathedral began to shed tears. Within days, news of the miracle had spread across Poland. Pilgrims began to arrive from across the entire country. Many claimed to have been spontaneously healed by the crying Madonna. Soon the crowds grew so large, they could no longer be controlled. The mood among the pilgrims was intense. Thousands thronged to see the painting and make confession. Conversions were rife. A professor of philosophy at the Catholic University of Lublin recalled stacks of torn-up party membership cards piled on the altars. Even members of the Communist police prostrated themselves before the icon.[38]

A division of the Polish secret police was dispatched to observe the situation. The secret policemen studied the icon and determined that no artificial substance had been used to create the "tears." Nonetheless, they had the local press accuse the Catholic hierarchy of fabricating the miracle as a counterrevolutionary provocation. They closed the cathedral and bused in a group of workers from a shoe factory to hurl bricks at the remaining pilgrims. In the disorder that followed, a twenty-one-year-old female student was trampled to death. A police cordon blocked off the cathedral, and a special conference was called to condemn the actions of the church. Its slogan was "An End to Medieval Backwardness."

Still, the pilgrimages continued and increasingly became political protests aimed at the Communist authorities. The crowd alternated religious songs with slogans like "Down with Communism" and "Long Live the Clergy."[39] At one point, a rumor spread that pilgrims were being arrested in front of the convent of the Capuchins. Pilgrims streamed to the nearest militia station and pelted it with rocks. Militia and police surrounded them and arrested hundreds of people, jailing most of them underneath the Lublin Castle.

This action temporarily ended the frenzy in Lublin, but it also inspired a rash of new miracles nationwide. Some had witnesses and bore tangible evidence. Others existed only as rumors. One of the militiamen who arrested the Lublin pilgrims reportedly went blind afterward. Another suffered from a withered hand. Elsewhere, a Communist Party member who mocked the Virgin was said to have been turned into a pig.[40]

In spite of these troubling incidents, the Polish secret police proved fairly stalwart in combating the Virgin Mary's further manifestations in the people's republic. When She appeared in the form of an unearthly glow on the steeple of a church in the Muranów district of Warsaw, they painted the spire black with asphalt. When She appeared to a teenage girl in a pasture outside the village of Mazury, they arrested the girl. Then, when a myrtle bush appeared overnight on the spot where the Virgin had stood, they burned the bush. This didn't stop people from gathering the ashes and spreading them around their homes for protection.[41] Later, when the Virgin appeared to a different teenage girl in a field of sorrel outside the town of Zabłudów, police tried the same tactic again, surrounding the field where the vision had manifested and pouring quicklime over the sorrel.

Finally, tired of playing whack-a-mole with the Mother of God, the secret police began to compile what they had learned from twenty years of difficult combat, in a series of top-secret internal reports. Intended as guides for field officers, the reports covered topics such as how to deal with crowds, how to demolish illegal chapels, and what to do with the visionaries themselves. These publications catered to a uniquely Eastern European problem; they were handbooks for the suppression of miracles.

13

Socialism

Anna Musiałówna, *The Optimist.*
Queue for groceries, Warsaw, 1981.

E veryone remembered where they were the day Stalin died. When the "Gardener of Human Happiness" passed into the great beyond on March 6, 1953, the news was broadcast from every loudspeaker and radio in the Soviet Bloc. Hundreds of thousands of mourners poured into the streets, filling the main squares and grandest boulevards of Budapest, Warsaw, and Prague.

The countryside and factories grieved as well, in proper Stalinist style. Tens of thousands of workers and peasants immediately applied to join the Communist Party. At the No. 12 Glassworks in Tur, Poland, workers promised to "follow the line indicated by comrade Stalin and intensify their efforts on the production front," while in the village of Grzeczna Panna ("Polite Maiden"), farmers pledged to raise the yield of grain on each hectare of their land.[1] In the village of Ślesin, a seventy-two-year-old woman remarked publicly that it would have been much better if she had died in Stalin's place, since all she was doing was raising some young children, but Stalin, and his "immortal wisdom," was needed by "all the people of the world."[2]

The Hungarian poet György Faludy, interned in the notorious prison at Recsk, a miniature gulag on the Soviet model, where prisoners were starved and beaten to death while made to work in open-pit stone quarries, got word of Stalin's death a few days later than the rest of his countrymen. The prison barber came into his cell, hugging him and crying out, "The Caucasian bandit has at last departed from our midst!"[3]

Faludy had arrived at Recsk three years earlier, in 1950, sentenced for the crimes of returning to Hungary from abroad, being a writer, and not being a member of the Communist Party. The official reason for his conviction was that he was supposedly employed by American intelligence and had organized an uprising to overthrow the people's republic. Aware that resistance was futile, Faludy had confessed to the charge. His interrogator congratulated him and called on him, as a "man of imagination," to write a "really beautiful and credible confession."[4] Now he marveled as the camp guards apologized to their prisoners and nervously watched the skies for American planes.

Stalin's death was the first rumbling of a political avalanche. It took a few years to develop in full. A few months after Stalin's death, Hungary's leadership announced a general amnesty for political prisoners. Faludy was freed, along with everyone else in the camp at Recsk. Subsequent weeks saw strikes and workers' revolts erupt in Czechoslovakia, East Germany, and Bulgaria. But the real shock came in February 1956, when Nikita Khrushchev gave his "secret speech" to a closed gathering of the Soviet Communist Party. He accused Stalin of a bevy of crimes, including executing most of the Politburo in 1937 and leaving the Soviet Union unprepared for war with Germany in 1941. Although Khrushchev's talk was secret, its contents leaked out and quickly spread across the region. The disillusionment it produced in true believers was seismic. According to one Czech Communist, "It was as if you had told an Ursuline nun that there was no God and Voltaire was better than the Pope."[5]

Khrushchev's address proved to be the most significant speech of the twentieth century. In the long term, it marked the death of Stalinism as a method of rule across the region. With very few exceptions, the days of mass imprisonments and executions were now over. From now on, the iron fist of Communist power would have to wear a velvet glove. Its immediate consequences were equally drastic. In Poland, the secret speech led to massive protests and, ultimately, a change in the top party leadership. In Hungary, it sparked a revolution. For nearly a month in October and November 1956, the country was ruled from the streets, by protesters and workers' councils. In Budapest, crowds tore down a colossal bronze statue of Stalin and lynched secret policemen in front of their headquarters. It took a Soviet invasion, and weeks of bloody street fighting, to quash the uprising.

Once the Hungarian Revolution was put down, János Kádár, the head of the reestablished Hungarian Communist Party, made a tacit pact with the people: keep your heads down, never mention the uprising again, and enjoy a life of (relative) peace and prosperity. It was the start of a new era, nicknamed "Goulash Communism," heralding the direction of development in the region as a whole.

Across the Eastern Bloc, Communist governments relaxed their grip. Organized political opposition was still absolutely forbidden, but culture became increasingly open to influences from the West. In Czechoslovakia, where party hard-liners relinquished power only in 1962, the 1960s were a time of flourishing in cinema; it was the decade of Miloš Forman, Jiří Menzel, and Věra Chytilová. In Poland, a new generation of directors, including Andrzej Wajda and Roman Polanski, likewise found their voices in the thaw following 1956. With new art came new ideas, which quickly found an echo in politics. In 1968 Alexander Dubček, the newly chosen head of the Czechoslovak Party, announced a series of reforms that would restore local control over the economy and open parliament to multiparty rule. Crucially, he also lifted virtually all censorship in the country, inaugurating the brief period of openness celebrated as the "Prague Spring."

Dubček intended the changes as the adaptation of socialism to Czechoslovak circumstances or, in his phrase, "socialism with a human face." To the Soviet leadership, however, this sudden liberalization appeared as an existential threat. In August 1968 Brezhnev, Khrushchev's successor as head of the USSR, sent in tanks. As in Hungary in 1956, only raw military force could preserve the Soviet Union's hold over the "security zone" it had won for itself in the war.

After the invasion, many in Czechoslovakia feared a full-scale purge. What happened instead, however, was gradual, if perhaps equally insidious. The slow reestablishment of authority over society and culture came to be known, rather euphemistically, as "normalization."

In Poland, the Communist Party, faced with its own crisis of esteem, responded by scapegoating the country's few remaining Jews, most of whom were forced to emigrate in the summer of 1968. In Czechoslovakia, by contrast, the government's focus remained on subduing the existing opposition. Over a period of months and years, the various reform Communists, writers, intellectuals, and artists who had supported the Prague Spring were fired from their jobs, forbidden to publish or perform, and forced to work in menial occupations. Practically the entire intellectual elite of Czechoslovakia vanished from their places of employment and woke up to find themselves in factory basements, on the street spreading asphalt, or behind the wheel of a cab. Philosophers became bulldozer drivers. Editors became window washers. Literary scholars descended into sewers. It was a life of internal exile, of banishment without imprisonment.

In the 1950s, these same people would have simply disappeared, forced into prisons, work camps, and uranium mines, whose toxic conditions were considered a perfect fit for enemies of the people. In a 1978 essay, the Czech novelist and dissident Ludvík Vaculík summarized the difference between the two eras: "The fifties had their revolutionary cruelty as well as their selfless enthusiasm. . . . Today there is no sign of any enthusiasm and, except in the case of a few excesses, no particular cruelty. . . . Violence has become humanized."[6]

Stalinism eliminated its enemies. The socialist regimes that followed neutralized them instead. The philosopher Milan Šimečka called it the era of "civilized violence," in which the regime no longer tortured or starved people. Secret policemen didn't knock on doors at four in the morning. If someone had to be interrogated, it would occur at an appointed time, during normal office hours. If someone went to prison, they could expect to be treated according to the regulations. And when listening devices were installed in people's apartments, "it would be done without damage to the furniture."[7]

Forbidden, for the most part, from using beatings or torture, the Czech secret police, or StB, had to get creative in its methods of harassment. As a consequence, the 1970s were a golden age of dirty tricks. Leading Czech intellectuals woke up to find their private conversations— edited in the most unflattering possible light—broadcast on national TV. Bohumil Hrabal's birthday party was broken up, and Czechoslovakia's leading publishing houses no longer accepted his manuscripts.[8] After interrogations, Hrabal would ride tram number seventeen around Prague, back and forth, to prolong the moment of going home as long as possible, for as long as he wasn't home, the secret police couldn't summon him again.[9]

Marta Kubišová, one of the country's most popular singers, had her face pasted into pornographic photos, purportedly made in West Germany. The secret police then circulated these doctored images to concert promoters, newspaper editors, radio and TV stations, and her fellow singers, to make sure they knew not to cooperate with Kubišová or even speak her name out loud.[10] Thereafter Kubišová became a nonperson: the only work she could find was in a chicken-processing plant.

During a search of Ludvík Vaculík's apartment, the StB confiscated a clutch of photographs he had taken with his lover posing nude atop medieval tombstones. The secret police spent two years trying to use them to blackmail Vaculík to do what they wanted. When he refused for a final time, they published the photos in the newspaper and broadcast them on television. At the same time, they sent agents to Vaculík's wife, Madla, to tell her about his lover and pressure her to divorce him or, at the very least, inform on him. When Vaculíková refused, one of the agents snapped at her, "What are you—a saint?"[11]

The thing that made all these dirty tricks possible was surveillance, whose invisible ever-presence became a signal hallmark of this epoch. The StB kept constant pressure on dissidents through house searches, interrogations, and stakeouts. Relative to the size of the country, the opposition was small, while the secret police commanded enormous resources. As many as thirty agents might be tasked with tailing a single dissident who went on vacation. The secret police rented a flat across the street from the Vaculíks' Prague apartment so they could watch them full time. When the leading dissident playwright Václav Havel traveled to his country house to write, the secret police followed him on his walks, vandalized his car, and set up a special observation booth on stilts—apparently it looked just like a moon lander—so they could watch him while he was at home.[12]

But while the sheer manpower wielded by the StB was effective, the real breakthrough in surveillance was technological. Beginning in the 1960s, a new generation of electronic devices—listening devices, phone taps, and hidden cameras—allowed the bloc's security services to perform previously undreamed-of feats. In 1968 the inaugural issue of the Romanian secret police's in-house magazine, *Securitatea*, crowed about this beautiful new world in which agents could do things "that in the past were in the domain of the fantastic," such as eavesdropping on conversations through walls or keeping a tap running on a phone even after the receiver was hung up.[13]

It wasn't only Romania that benefited from this technological revolution. Even Albania, the most isolated and economically challenged member of the Eastern Bloc, embraced these new methods. At a time when a television cost eight months' salary, and personal tape recorders simply didn't exist, the Albanian secret police, or Sigurimi, had a galaxy of miniaturized electronic surveillance equipment at its disposal. Agents hid these bugs in handbags, broom handles, and handmade wooden pipes. They even manufactured some of their own.

All the signals and tapes recorded by these devices eventually made their way back to Tirana's House of Leaves, now a museum where visitors can step into old interrogation chambers and study the various clever disguises the Sigurimi devised for their listening devices. The House of Leaves, originally built as a villa for Tirana's first gynecologist, later became the Gestapo headquarters, then the center of the web that the Sigurimi wove over Albania. Thousands of hours of tape-recorded conversations and phone calls found their way to this comfortable manse, tucked away from the city center under the shade of spreading sycamores and palms.

But however much raw data Sigurimi intercepted, it was the *perception* that its eyes and ears were everywhere that was most important to its effectiveness. Even the most innocuous remark, such as complaining loudly about tomatoes in the market, or saying something positive about the West German soccer team, could land a person in jail for years.[14] Romanians learned to watch what they said at all times. This was true across the Eastern Bloc.

Typewriters struck Communist authorities as particularly dangerous to their security because they were one of the few means of mass communication remaining in private hands. The mid-1970s were the golden age of *samizdat*, or underground self-publishing, in Eastern Europe. Many leading writers in Czechoslovakia—including Vaculík—produced editions of their work by having it typed out in multiple copies using multiple pieces of carbon paper. The paper had to be onion-skin thin; even so, the eleventh and twelfth copies at the bottom of the stack would be barely readable and could often be purchased at a discount.[15]

In spite of their poor-quality paper and minuscule runs, *samizdat* editions were an important way for banned writers to stay in print. *Samizdat* printing was also the main way dissident writing circulated across the bloc. People read the latest essays by Václav Havel and Aleksandr Solzhenitsyn largely in homemade, typewritten copies. The secret police took notice. When Solzhenitsyn's 1974 essay "Live Not by Lies" began circulating in Kraków in the fall of 1977, the secret police summoned one of their most trusted secret informants inside the opposition to find out if he could recognize which of his friends' typewriters it had been written on.[16] After 1983 in Romania, all typewriters had to be registered at the local police office. Every year a postcard would summon you to the station to do a supervised typing test—three copies, without carbon.[17]

While informers could give the secret police a view of the inner workings of the dissident press, surveillance equipment let them monitor it continuously. By the early 1970s, there were so many bugs and cameras in the Vaculíks' Prague apartment building that the couple had to watch what they said at all times. From 1969 to 1989, if they had something important to communicate, they would write it in chalk on an erasable slate. If they wrote anything down on paper, they immediately flushed it down the toilet.[18]

In a world where prying ears were everywhere, toilets could serve as a much-needed refuge, or as an escape. (But not everywhere: the East German Stasi took the precaution of bugging public toilets, in addition to private boxes at the opera and Catholic confession booths.) Growing up in 1980s Romania, the literary scholar Cristina Vatulescu once heard one of her father's friends admit that "every night he went home, locked all doors and windows, hid in the bathroom, and ranted against the regime."[19] His rants probably weren't recorded, but it didn't matter—he was already doing precisely what the regime wanted. Its goal was not to convince its citizens that the regime was unconditionally good, but to scare them enough that they voiced their concerns only in private. Dissent existed, but it was hidden in a drawer or spoken in the isolation of a locked bathroom. As long as it stayed there, the regime was convinced that it could rule indefinitely.

The 1960s and '70s were also the great age of the file. Whole armies of informers, trackers, transcribers, and secretaries had a hand in compiling them—not just professionals but friends, lovers, even spouses. Their work was coordinated by agents and supervised by agent-generals. The Romanian political prisoner Belu Zilber joked that the production of files was "the first great socialist industry."[20]

Surveillance produced masses of paper, and files on dissident authors swelled to Tolstoyan lengths with Joycean levels of detail. In the process, secret policemen became apprentices in the gentle art of literary criticism. In their pursuit of Marin Preda, one of Romania's leading writers, Securitate agents interviewed his childhood friends, searching for past traumas and hidden motivations. They returned to add a story about Preda's "shock at accidentally seeing his father's genitals" to his file.[21] Meanwhile, other members of the team were hard at work analyzing the writer's relationship with his three ex-wives. Feeling unsure about their ability as readers of fiction, they hired a professional literary critic to suss out the various levels of meaning concealed in their target's novels.

After the Czech journalist Jiří Lederer was released from detainment in 1970, he was made to stop by a prison three or four times a week for detailed debriefings. Here he had to explain his articles sentence by sentence and clause by clause, while his interrogator asked him questions such as "What were you getting at with the comment in parentheses?" or "What did you want to suggest to the reader with those three periods?"[22]

Engaging with texts at such a granular level, the secret police could almost act as some writers' coauthors or editors. The Czech philosopher Karel Kosík felt that the StB had been a great help in his work, since by repeatedly seizing and destroying his manuscripts, they had forced him to reformulate his thoughts over and over again, allowing him to correct the flaws in his reasoning.[23] Ludvík Vaculík made individual secret policemen characters in his many feuilletons and works of autofiction. Lieutenant Colonel Noga, "a smallish man, well built, dark of skin and hair," whose faintly detectable accent betrayed his origins as a Moravian factory worker, is a recurring, and rather menacing, presence in Vaculík's *A Cup of Coffee with My Interrogator*. Vaculík's monthly interrogations with Major Fišer of the StB figure so prominently in his *A Czech Dreambook* that Vaculík felt obliged to share its contents, prepublication, with Fišer himself. The major returned the manuscript after a month, commenting that while he wasn't "a literary critic," he thought, based on what he had read so far, that Vaculík could "do better."[24]

In Poland, the secret police determined who could travel abroad, who was translated, and who won the most important literary awards. They made Andrzej Kuśniewicz, the author of urbane, melancholy, and now entirely forgotten novels set in the waning days of the Austro-Hungarian Empire, one of the most prominent writers of the 1970s and '80s. In return, Kuśniewicz told his handlers everything they wanted to know about what was going on in the literary world: who was upset about being overlooked for a prize, who was planning to emigrate, and who was talking to the opposition.[25]

But as much as the secret police smoothed the way for their chosen writers, they found it much easier to make life hell for those they saw as their enemies. Herta Müller has done more than perhaps any other Eastern European writer to describe the experience of living in the late socialist surveillance state. Her novels are works of subtle, suffocating paranoia. She wrote from experience. She grew up in the Banat, as a member of Romania's German-speaking Swabian minority. In college, she joined a literary group devoted to writing truthfully about the conditions they were living in. For her work in the literary underground, she was fired from her job as a technical translator in a factory. Her husband, also a poet, likewise lost his job. Later Müller was arrested for buying walnuts at an "exorbitant price"—meaning at the black market rate in one of Timişoara's bazaars. The Securitate offered to make life easier for her if she agreed to be a secret informant; she refused. The persecution grew worse.

By the end of the 1980s, Romania's secret police had some fifteen thousand active employees who knew how to make themselves seem omnipresent. The doorman of Müller's building recorded her comings and goings. Strangers seemed to let themselves in and out of her apartment. A truck knocked her off the road while she was riding her bicycle. Müller began to suspect that her friends were informing on her. She even began suspecting her husband. Her hair fell out in clumps. She was no longer worried about writing truthfully, or being published, or even staying above water. The battle for her, as she wrote at the end of *The Appointment*, became simply "how not to go mad."[26]

For all its brutality, and for all the suffering it inflicted, Communist rule in Eastern Europe, beginning in the 1950s, brought about a genuine revolution in people's lives. Across much of the region, it marked the final death of feudalism. Peasants, long tied to the land, left their farms for the first time in generations to try their hand at making a new life in freshly built factory towns. Big cities, ruined by the war, rose from the ashes in what felt like the blink of an eye. Modern conveniences, such as electricity, cinema, and the telephone, spread from the cities to the countryside. Housing, however modest, became available to nearly everyone who needed it.

Although life in the Eastern Bloc circa 1955 may not have been overly comfortable, it was entirely possible to enjoy the sense that major progress had been made. The promised land of full Communism, in which all social barriers melted away, had certainly not arrived, but equality— or at least *near* equality, in strictly material terms—was a fact. It was rare for anyone to have much more or much less than their neighbor. And life seemed to be improving all the time. Free schooling was available to everyone. Literacy rose to unprecedented heights, as did the availability of health care. Life expectancies approached those known in the West. Poverty—real, desperate poverty—and hunger were nearly relics of the past. Vacations to the mountains, to the sea, or to a country cottage were even becoming luxuries the majority of people could hope to enjoy. The vast touristic complexes in the Tatra Mountains of Poland and Slovakia, the Black Sea coast of Bulgaria, and Yugoslavia's Adriatic coast are a testament to this age of socialized recreation.

But a generation later enthusiasm for the new system was much harder to sustain. Growth sagged, and revolution settled into routine. The bold new world of socialism had transformed into a world of dull repetition. The Hungarian novelist György Konrád named this condition of unending stasis the "East European present tense."[27] Life moved very slowly. The moment children were born, parents, including mine, signed them up for waiting lists for apartments and cars. If they were lucky, the wait would take only thirty years.

The same few meager products were always for sale. Inferior goods ruled the market—that is, when they were available at all. It was a world of envelopes that wouldn't stick, pens that didn't write, and matches that wouldn't burn.

In these conditions of stasis and scarcity, "revolutionary" enthusiasm was hard to maintain. No one took ideology seriously anymore. Politics was known as a realm of deceit, of empty slogans and meaningless exhortations. By the late 1970s and early '80s, the tenets of Marxism-Leninism had undergone a process of total decay. Almost everywhere, except perhaps Albania—steadfastly militant thanks to its near-perfect isolation—they were perceived, in the words of one Romanian, as "a kind of amorphous burden."[28] Political training was a pure formality. Communist ideology—its slogans, its organizations, and their demands on one's time—combined to form a single oppressive nebula one had to somehow navigate in daily life.

In his essay "The Power of the Powerless," Václav Havel tells a story about an imaginary greengrocer who hangs a sign saying, WORKERS OF THE WORLD, UNITE! in his shop window. He doesn't believe this slogan, and the regime doesn't require him to believe it; it just wants him to show his obeisance by hanging up the sign. For Havel, this is a parable about life in "post-totalitarian society," where the regime maintained order by dictating public speech and crushing the free space reserved for individual expression. But as usual in Eastern Europe, the absurdity of reality outstripped that found in fiction. A real Bucharest greengrocer once put a note over the door that said, WE HAVE CABBAGE. Someone else quickly added a note below that read, A NEW VICTORY OVER CAPITALISM.[29]

In general, humor was a good barometer of what was really going on inside the people's democracies. Official propaganda depicted Romania's Nicolae Ceaușescu as a hero, a genius—practically a god. Privately, though, the diminutive, bouffant-haired, and perfectly megalomaniacal dictator was the butt of countless jokes. In one of them, Ceaușescu is on his way to Bucharest airport, when he spots a group of citizens standing in line. He orders his driver to stop and ask what they are waiting for.

> The whole motorcade pulls over, and soon the driver returns with the answer. "The people are waiting for bread." "My people should not have to wait for bread," thunders the concerned leader. "Let there be bread immediately!" Sure enough, a truck appears in no time and bread is distributed. Satisfied, Ceaușescu resumes his journey only to see another, longer line. Again he orders a halt, and dispatches the driver. "The people are waiting for eggs," he is told. "My people should not have to wait for eggs," he cries. "Bring my people eggs!" As before, a truck appears promptly, eggs are handed out, and Ceaușescu's motorcade continues on its way. Very soon, however, the President spots a third line, the longest yet. Again he stops, and sends the driver to investigate. "The people are waiting for meat." For a moment Ceaușescu is silent, but finally he speaks with the same authority as before. "Bring my people chairs!" he says.[30]

There was more than a grain of truth in this joke. To keep up the illusion that he was ruling over a happy and healthy country, blessed with the fruits of full socialism, Ceaușescu needed the help of thousands. He couldn't bear the sight of lines. If he visited a market or a store, it had to be brimming with food. If he visited a second one, the exact same goods would materialize there. Ceaușescu also couldn't stand to see churches or private homes, since these were signs of reaction. When he and his wife, Elena, went driving around Bucharest, all such signs of independent life had to be hidden behind scaffolding or wooden panels erected at the owners' expense. People living along the route of the motorcade had to take their laundry down, because it didn't "look nice."[31] If a foreign dignitary happened to be visiting, adoring crowds were summoned to cheer his progress, with plenty of Securitate agents interspersed through the masses to make sure there were no untoward outbursts.

Sometimes even nature would be made to participate in this all-pervasive charade. If Ceauşescu visited a field where the corn wasn't growing well, extra corn would be brought in and planted that same day to make the field appear fuller. The stage-masters had to be careful though: if they planted the extra corn too early, it would wither before the self-proclaimed "Genius of the Carpathians" arrived to inspect it.[32]

.   .   .

From the end of Stalinism onward, jokes about the regimes were part of life in the Eastern Bloc. The only place where they were noticeably absent was Albania.[33] There even innocuous remarks, like "I am eating bread with butter" or "I have no bread," might be interpreted as propaganda, depending on the emphasis with which they were said. One man received a sentence of twenty-three years in prison for telling a joke about Chairman Mao, then Albania's only major ally in the socialist world. Jokes about Enver Hoxha, Albania's ruler from the end of World War II until his death in 1985, weren't merely avoided—they were unthinkable.

For most of his years in power, Hoxha kept Albania sealed off from the rest of the world. Trips to Yugoslavia became impossible after his split with Tito in 1948. The Soviet Union became similarly off-limits after he broke off relations in 1960 because Hoxha didn't like how far Khrushchev was straying from the legacy of Stalinism. For Albanians, even having relatives abroad was a major demerit, one that could prevent them from getting an education or working in sensitive industries. Domestic travel was difficult as well, as private car ownership was illegal, making trips to the countryside an arduous undertaking.

Religion was another potential source of stigma. During a 1967 speech, Hoxha declared war on religious belief as the "opium of the masses." In the months that followed, he closed thousands of mosques, churches, and Sufi lodges. Some were adapted to other purposes: the beautiful King Mosque and Halveti lodge in Berat were turned, respectively, into a ping-pong parlor and a fruit market. Over two thousand other places of worship, including some of Albania's finest architectural treasures, were demolished outright.[34] With religion banned, the ancient cult of the saints went underground. Families continued to honor holy places covertly, by holding picnics nearby, for which the grave of the legendary proselytizer and wonder-worker Sarı Saltık in Krujë was a favorite spot.[35]

Hoxha did his best to keep his countrymen ignorant of their own traditions as well as of what was happening in the rest of the world. Even so, for a moment at the start of the 1970s, a breath of fresh air seemed poised to enter the sealed room of Albanian socialism. As the climate of nervous tension with both the Soviet Bloc and the West began to relax, hints of contemporary fashion began to appear on the streets of Tirana. Women cut their hair short, in bobs. Men began to wear their hair a bit longer, like the Beatles. Skirts rose, and sideburns dropped. New melodies hummed in the air. Many of them sounded Italian. Some even had a little bit of soul.

Most of those new songs had first been heard during the broadcast of the 1972 Song Festival. The festival was an annual event, put on by the state radio station. In previous years, it had featured rather staid songs in the socialist realist mode, paeans to the harvest or to resisting imperialism. Winning songs bore titles such as "Hero Teachers" and "The House Where the Party Was Born." The eleventh version of the festival was different. The stage looked more modern. There were no hammers and sickles as part of the decor. And the performances felt modern too.[36] The musicians tapped their feet, and the female singers swayed their hips. For the first time, the songs were catchy. People rushed to record them and share them with their friends and neighbors. Young people sang them on the street and copied the singers' clothes and style. Something new was clearly in the air. The title of the winning song, "When Spring Arrives," suggested that a Tirana version of the Prague Spring might be in the works. The Italian and Yugoslav press seized on the idea and announced the beginnings of an Albanian Thaw.

Everyone who could watched the eleventh Song Festival. Enver Hoxha was watching as well, and he didn't like what he saw. He had reason to be concerned. His heart was beginning to fail. The latest five-year plan was sputtering. And worst of all, China, Albania's only remaining ally, seemed to be softening toward the West. Just that year Chairman Mao had shaken hands with that capitalist warlord Richard Nixon. For Hoxha, this was a sign that it was time to close the window again.

On June 26, 1973, at the Fourth Plenum of the Central Committee of the Albanian Party of Labor, Hoxha announced his intentions. He denounced the importation into Albania of "poisonous bourgeois ideas," among them "long hair, extravagant dress, [and] screaming jungle music."[37] The counterattack was to begin immediately.

The party's first step was to expel the "internal and external enemies" of its youth leadership.[38] "Showing a foreign face" was one of the offenses punished met with expulsion. Students rushed to shave off their sideburns and get rid of any other decadent fashions they might possess. At Tirana airport, barbers waited for disembarking passengers, ready to trim the hair and shave the whiskers of foreigners whose appearance "violated the norms of socialist aesthetics."[39] Meanwhile, inside Albania, the purge rolled on, now extending to the leadership of the party itself. Between 1973 and 1975, eight ministers and 130 artists and intellectuals were dismissed from their jobs and either executed, exiled internally, or jailed. The purge began with the singers who performed in the festival, the head of the TV station that aired it, and the head of Ideology that allowed it to take place. The circle of those punished then expanded to include many of Albania's most prominent editors, poets, journalists, and theater directors, as well as the ministers of defense, central planning, and industry.

Most of these men, formerly the cream of the Albanian ruling apparatus, disappeared overnight from their regular lives, only to reappear in one of Albania's many prison camps. This sudden change of fortune did not necessarily dim their enthusiasm for Hoxha's rule. Some of Hoxha's top lieutenants, reunited at the notorious Ballsh prison, convinced themselves that their sentences were merely a test. They were certain that if they maintained vigilance against the class enemies and traitors in their midst, eventually they would be redeemed. Over the course of their internment, these "red pashas" would meet regularly to discuss Hoxha's collected works and convince themselves anew of his greatness. Whenever Hoxha appeared on TV, Dashnor Mamaqi, formerly the editor of the *Zëri i Popullit* newspaper, sighed, "How I miss that great man!"[40]

For many years after the fiasco of the song festival, it remained dangerous to show any signs of contact or familiarity with the West in Albania. Mari Kitty Harapi of Shkodër learned this the hard way, while she was still a teenager. Kitty had an aunt who had emigrated in 1945 and lived in Italy. This aunt was in the habit of sending care packages home, full of Italian clothes. Once Kitty asked her aunt for a pair of shoes, and she sent Kitty a pair of orange pumps.

As soon as she saw them, Kitty realized that her aunt didn't understand anything about what life was like in Albania anymore. In a country where "everything was the color of dust, ash, and dirt," these bright orange shoes, so unlike everything around them, would act like a red cape waved in front of a bull. Right away Kitty knew they would "summon the harpies." When she arrived at her factory for work the next day—she was forbidden to go to college because of her suspect class background—her boss suggested that the pumps might look better on her own feet, but Kitty refused to give them up. The next day she was fired for "imperialistic extravagance" in dress.[41]

However dangerous it might be, people still longed for contact with the world outside their borders. They went to great lengths to secure it. In the north of Albania, the Drin River would bring flotsam down from Yugoslavia, such as discarded Coca-Cola cans, plastic bottles, and makeup kits. People would fish them out and put them on their mantelpieces as trophies, or turn them into useful objects, like pen holders and television antennas.[42] One of the most sought-after items in the river were the soles of old shoes, which could be given to shoemakers and fitted to make shoes that were of better quality—and more stylish—than any available in the country.

Knowledge that they were forbidden made items from the West all the more desirable. Albanian children kept scrapbooks filled with fragments from this alternative reality: candy wrappers, advertisements, and packaging labels brought to their shores by the current. They called these collections *letra të bukura,* or "beautiful papers." Romanian children did the same. One Romanian woman, who used to receive food from relatives abroad as a child, remembered marveling at the "shining, swishing, golden or silvery" packages they came in. She used to keep these empty wrappers, "carefully and beautifully arranged," in a big coffee bag, where she could periodically inspect them and trade them with other girls in her class.[43]

Even my grandmother, in relatively open Poland, maintained this sort of shrine to the wonders of the West. In the TV room of her apartment, reserved for watching episodes of the prime-time oil-tycoon soap opera *Dynasty*, a set of wooden shelves housed the library of her treasures: decorative bottles of schnapps, empty containers of perfume, boxes of chocolate with pretty labels. The rest of the apartment was likewise full of cookie tins, clothes sent from New York in the 1970s, and ancient cans of food, all of which had never been used or worn, merely saved. I used to think these were a symptom of hoarding, a disorder common in those who lived through the hardships of the Great Depression and Second World War. But I came to realize that they represented something else entirely: they were tokens from another universe, a world of dreams that was close enough to touch, but forever out of reach.

Waiting, especially waiting in a queue, was one of the defining experiences of life under real socialism. This was especially true in less well-off members of the "Peace Bloc," like Romania and Albania, but also elsewhere during periods of economic crisis. In the early 1980s, the reintroduction of rationing turned Poland into a veritable land of lines. Virtually every available good became scarce. But this scarcity was itself unpredictable. If someone saw a long queue forming, they joined it. The longer the queue, the more desirable the goods being "thrown" onto the market appeared to be. A Polish sociologist, analyzing this era, reported seeing dozens of customers exiting a grocery store, beaming with happiness because they had managed to buy two blankets apiece. That same sociologist describes standing in line at a Warsaw butcher shop only to discover that the only item for sale was pig's knuckles. Despite not wanting them and never eating them, he bought two. The rest of the queue convinced him that his wife would be grateful, and that even if she wasn't, he could at least trade them away to someone else. This led him to formulate four fundamental laws of queueing, beginning with *The attractiveness of an article depends on the length of the queue.*[44]

The ubiquity of queuing led to the creation of new and rapidly evolving forms of social engagement. Housewives worked in teams of fifteen or more to cover all their necessary shopping. Neighbors pooled their resources, exchanging services—for instance, legal representation or carpentry work—for whatever goods any of them could get their hands on. Many workers spent the bulk of their day "on break," scouring the city for the basics of life. Managers in larger enterprises put more thought into their queueing. Like scouts in a well-run ant hive, first thing in the morning they would send out a pair of secretaries to look for promising delivery trucks or incipient lines. Then at midday, the remaining secretaries would go out together to try to bring back whatever they could for the office collective.[45]

A typical queue was a society in miniature. Usually, a queue would consist of two separate lines. One was made up of regular customers, and the other of privileged shoppers, those citizens who had some official claim to skipping to the head of the line. These included pregnant women, women with babies, the handicapped, war veterans, blood donors, and the elderly. The privileged shoppers didn't actually get to cut to the front. Rather, the two lines alternated, with a person from each taking a turn at the counter. In spite of these unwritten rules, a certain amount of abuse passed between the two lines, not least because many suspected that some of the privileged shoppers were in fact paid "standers," shopping for others, or cheaters, who borrowed a baby from someone else to stand in the shorter line.[46]

Queues for most items took at most a few hours, but for certain goods they could stretch much longer. For necessary but hard-to-procure items like children's shoes, people would queue for multiple days beginning as early as three a.m. One queue for color TVs in Kraków stood for ninety-six hours straight, with people sleeping in cars parked next to the line at night to keep their spots. Even this wasn't too bad, as waits for durable goods could at times stretch to almost cosmic dimensions. In the early 1980s, an American researcher observed a man waiting to receive an automatic washing machine who claimed he was 686th in line. This number had been issued to him by the queue committee, a spontaneous organization that arose in many such situations to maintain order during long waits. The unfortunate holder of this slip estimated that at the rate the line was moving, it would take him another five years to get his promised appliance.[47] Based on when this interview took place, his quest would have succeeded just as Communism ended and the washing machine itself became obsolete.

In Romania, the worst era of shortages came in the 1980s, shortly before the collapse of the socialist system as a whole. Like many other countries in the bloc, Romania had amassed a sizable amount of foreign debt trying to maintain living standards over the course of the 1970s. In 1982, Ceaușescu decided that he was going to pay off all $7 billion of it, at once, as quickly as possible. The only way to do so was to massively increase exports, primarily of food. To achieve this, Ceaușescu came up with some unique methods to make the most of what little meat remained in the country. After a visit to China, he suggested producing replacement sausages out of soybeans. The necessary technology and expertise were lacking, however, and the resulting product was soft, oily, and foul-smelling.

The other half of Ceaușescu's belt-tightening measures was to be a reduction of fuel imports. Soon enough, the country was cold and dark as well as hungry. To economize on electricity, streetlights stopped being lit, and bulbs over forty watts became impossible to obtain. Often, at six o'clock, the power was simply shut off. People in high-rise apartment buildings turned to old-fashioned kerosene lamps for light. To economize on gas, cities cut the gas supply for much of the day. The flow of gas was usually strongest at midnight, so the best time to cook was between two and five in the morning. To save money on fuel, they stopped heating buildings at all. The joke going around Bucharest was that it was colder indoors than outside.

With so much food earmarked for export, cities began running out of basic necessities. Sugar, eggs, oil, and butter were available only with ration cards. Getting milk, and especially baby formula, on which most working mothers relied because maternity leaves were very brief,[48] was usually a nightmare. Meat appeared and disappeared from stores according to mysterious patterns known only to an initiated few. At the height of the shortages, even potatoes became hard to obtain.

Systematic shortages resulted in a strange, funhouse-mirror economy that operated in parallel to the official one. Peasants came into the city to buy bread to feed to their pigs. City dwellers went to the countryside to bargain for paraffin. In this world of distorted goods and prices, gasoline, coffee, and cigarettes kept their value best. Each functioned effectively as a substitute currency. Kent cigarettes and coffee in particular were like gold. They could secure first-class sleeping car tickets, holiday lodgings, and hospital stays. Kents could even help someone get into Heaven. In the 1980s Romanian ethnographers noted that in some rural areas, relatives of the dead "would put packets of American Kent cigarettes in the coffin so the dead could pay the 'customs duty' on the way to the nether world."[49]

Coffee—real coffee—had less spiritual significance, but it was just as valuable. Most of what one could find in stores was a coffee substitute made from burnt chickpea flour called Nechezol. Actually, no one was really certain what it was made of: it might have contained barley, chestnuts, or chickpeas, probably with a small admixture of coffee to boot. Some people would sieve it before brewing, to get the bits of straw out.[50] Even coffee dregs were a treasure, to be used and reused again and again until they lost all their flavor.

Pure, natural coffee was almost too precious to use right away. One Romanian father managed to obtain a few dozen real coffee beans for his son. In those days, it felt as if time had reached a total standstill and socialism would last forever. The father was convinced that authentic coffee would soon disappear from his part of the world for good, so he kept his handful of beans safely hidden in a hermetically sealed container, as an inheritance for his little boy. He wanted to be sure that one day, when he was a grown man, his son would be able to have a single cup of real coffee and savor—just once—the smell of freedom.[51]

14

Thaw

Nicolae Ceauşescu comes down.
Cluj-Napoca, Romania, 1989.

A man is running to catch a train. The course of his life will
depend on whether or not he will make it. In one version,
the man, whose name is Witek, manages to catch the train.
Through a twisting series of events, he joins the Communist Party, loses
his girlfriend, and defuses a tense situation at a psychiatric hospital.
In a second version, as Witek is running down the train platform, he
slams into a railway guard, gets himself arrested, and joins the opposition. In the third version, Witek doesn't catch the train and he doesn't
slam into the guard. He finishes his medical studies, gets married, has
children, and avoids politics entirely. In the end, he gets on an airplane
to Paris that the two other versions of himself were meant to board but
couldn't—and he dies when it explodes just after takeoff.

This summary is the plot of Krzysztof Kieślowski's 1981 film *Blind*

Chance. It's an apt title, since for the past century or more, chance has played an outsize role in the lives of Eastern Europeans. Over the course of the twentieth century, countless lives were decided by what amounts to a coin flip: a missed train, an errant bomb, a slow departure, a line drawn arbitrarily on a map. I know countless such stories, from my extended family alone.

A woman misses a train in Siberia and falls deeply in love with a Soviet Army captain and marries him. He dies in battle, and she marries another man, in another country, who methodically destroys every trace of his predecessor. A son sends a horse cart back for his parents and baby brothers to take over the border. One brother comes, the rest stay. Only the brother who leaves survives. A man leaves from Warsaw to Minsk with three friends. The first one finds work as an electrician at the city opera and lives. The second starves to death in the Soviet Union. The third returns to Poland, where he is killed.

When the bombs start falling on Minsk two years later, two sisters begin walking east. They leave their father and brother behind. The brother is captured while driving a truck, escapes, and joins the partisans. The father, at work at a plant nursery outside town, is never seen or heard from again. The sisters survive the war, but they can never think of that day without weeping.

In my family, as for so many others, World War II was the pivotal moment. In its aftermath, people who otherwise never would have met were thrust together. In my family, that usually meant Jews getting together with Catholics. The daughter of dispossessed Polish-Hungarian aristocrats marries a Jewish counterintelligence officer; a Polish-Catholic girl from a radical nationalist family in the West marries a Communist shtetl boy from the East. Without those sudden, abrupt meetings, I and so many others wouldn't have been born.

Over and over again, the dice fly: two strangers meet on a beach by the Baltic Sea. A bayonet stab misses a woman hiding under dead bodies in a tramcar. A roofer falls off a roof to his death, leaving his daughter to be raised speaking German in Poland rather than Czech in Austria. A man sits in prison while hyperinflation destroys his fortune. A piece of shrapnel misses a heart by millimeters.

My own story begins with a roll of the dice that took place on the night of December 13, 1981. On that night at the stroke of midnight,

General Wojciech Jaruzelski—the prime minister of Poland, first secretary of the Polish United Workers' Party, and chairman of the Council of National Salvation—declared martial law. A nationwide curfew
went into effect immediately, and all gatherings were banned. But most
people didn't hear this news until the official announcement arrived at
six a.m. the following morning. During those first six hours of military
rule, riot troops and national police arrested thousands of opposition
leaders, trade union activists, intellectuals, artists, writers, actors, and
student demonstrators across Poland.

Imposing martial law was a desperate gamble on the part of the Polish government, an attempt to reimpose order on a society in the process of a total rebellion against Communist authority. The independent
trade union Solidarity was the primary instigator of this revolt. In fifteen
short months, Solidarity had grown from protesting local conditions
in a Gdańsk shipyard into a national movement with almost 10 million members—a shocking number in a country of less than 36 million
people. To have any hope of containing Solidarity, the police operation
would have to be swift and surgical—a decapitation performed before
the victim was even aware of the ax. It very nearly succeeded.

On the night martial law was declared, most of the leaders of Solidarity were attending a conference in Gdańsk. They were arrested in
their hotels before they could get home. A few who got away were
rounded up at the train station the next morning. Lech Wałęsa, its
leader, was brought to Warsaw in an army helicopter. He would remain
a prisoner of the state for most of the following year. Similar scenes
took place across Poland. People were awakened during the night by
squads of police, or they came home from parties to find the police at
their door. It was impossible to warn anyone else—first, because all the
arrests took place almost simultaneously, and second, because all the
phone lines in the country were cut just before midnight. In short, it
was a trap.

Almost six thousand people were arrested that first night. The few
people who managed to get away spent the next months and years in
hiding. When dawn finally broke, the country awoke to tanks in the
streets of all the major cities. Army units patrolled major streets. Police
swarmed around bus stops and train stations. Special squads of paratroopers surrounded radio transmitters, TV stations, and telephone

exchanges.[1] A famous photograph from that morning showed an armored personnel carrier in front of Warsaw's Cinema Moscow, whose marquee read APOCALYPSE NOW. The Coppola movie had just premiered in Poland. It really did seem like the end of the world. I was born exactly nine months later.

My parents had met a few months before, in Boston, at a screening of Krzysztof Kieślowski's *Camera Buff*. Both my mother and my father grew up in Warsaw, in apartments a five minutes' walk apart, but they didn't meet until they both separately relocated to the United States. My father was on a student visa that was set to expire in less than a year. My mother was visiting her aunt Jadwiga in Queens, New York. She was only supposed to stay six weeks. When Jaruzelski declared martial law, it was as if a castle gate dropped. Poland was closed. In the months that followed, Polish citizens had no way to leave the country, and for-eigners had nearly no way to get in. Return seemed futile, if not impossible. Once travel became possible again, everyone who could leave left.

Over the next eight years, over a million Poles emigrated to the West. Some left due to political persecution, but many more left to escape an economy in free fall. Those with any kind of technical education or higher degree were especially keen to leave a country that offered little employment, and where food and gas were once again being doled out with ration cards. Even before martial law, vinegar and matches were just about the only commodities you could buy without standing in line.[2]

And so I grew up in America, as an American, with Poland as a far-off place to be visited, a place where the stores had nothing and nothing ever worked. It seemed that it was going to stay that way for-ever. Like the Romanian with his coffee beans, sealed in a jar for his son to use in some distant future, my parents and many others felt that Poland and the rest of the bloc had entered a deep freeze that would last indefinitely. What no one knew or could guess was that the regime was already on its last legs.

Solidarity was the beginning of the end for Communist rule in Eastern Europe. The very existence of a mass organization of that size made the supremacy of the Communist Party appear hollow, while the fact that it was begun and led by workers made a mockery of the party's claims to act on behalf of the proletariat. Even those within the Communist Party felt this sudden implosion of their legitimacy. Every day hundreds of party members resigned. Three hundred thousand handed in their membership cards in the first year of Solidarity's existence alone. By July 1981, 20 percent of the party's own Central Committee were members of Solidarity.[3] The rot of demoralization had spread to the very top.

At two a.m. on the first night of martial law, an emergency meeting of the Sejm was called to ratify the army's emergency powers. During the debate, some deputies even called for abolishing *both* Solidarity *and* the Communist Party, thereby starting the country's politics afresh from a blank slate.[4] But this was impossible, as the leading role of the Polish Workers' Party was written into the constitution. Besides, many in the government feared that such a radical move might force the Soviet Union to intervene. Many Polish officers had taken part in the 1968 quelling of the Prague Spring by the Warsaw Pact nations. They worried that the Soviet Union and its allies might try to do the same unless Solidarity was brought under control. They also knew that they didn't have the legitimacy to impose their will purely by force. Resorting to violence on a mass scale would risk plunging the country into a civil war. Imposing martial law, therefore, was an act of desperation. It was intended as a firebreak, an attempt to stuff the genie of mass politics back into the bottle, while shedding as little blood as possible.

And indeed, no blood was shed that first night. The generals' gambit was that a bloodless coup would leave them in charge and the Soviets idling at the gates. But a few days later, riot police's storming of the Wujek Coal Mine in Silesia killed nine miners. The ploy had failed.

Only in Moscow was there a sense of relief. If the Polish party leaders were afraid of a Soviet incursion, the USSR leadership, as we now know, was equally afraid of having to intervene. Their empire in Eastern Europe was becoming ever harder to manage. Won by defeating Germany in World War II, it had served successively as an arena for plunder, a strategic buffer zone, and a captive economic market. It was also a persistent burden, as well as a spur for change.

The Soviet Union ruled over its satellite countries as a backseat driver. The results of this indirect rule were decidedly mixed. During Stalin's lifetime, the bloc was kept together through brute force. Extremes of violence could be used to pursue regime enemies, and when enemies were absent, they could be invented out of whole cloth. In the decades following the Great Leader's death, two great earthquakes shook the stability of the bloc: the armed revolution in Hungary in 1956, and the much more pacific opening of Czechoslovakia to independent media and rival political parties during the Prague Spring of 1968. Both uprisings resulted in military invasions led by the Soviet Union, but incorporated forces from the rest of the Warsaw Pact countries. In 1968, following the crushing of the Prague Spring, Leonid Brezhnev, the general secretary of the Communist Party of the Soviet Union from 1964 to 1982, made such interventions an official pillar of Soviet foreign policy. According to the so-called Brezhnev Doctrine, force would be used whenever a formerly socialist country threatened to cross over to the capitalist camp.

From 1945 on, the Soviet Union was consistent in using military power to maintain its empire in Eastern Europe. But over time the ferocity of these incursions decreased. In the 1950s, Soviet generals and KGB officers had supervised the outright elimination of anti-Communist partisans and other political enemies. The Soviet invasion of Hungary in 1956 claimed some three thousand lives. But the Warsaw Pact invasion of Czechoslovakia in 1968 cost only 137 lives. By the time Solidarity emerged in 1980, the Soviet leadership—bogged down in Afghanistan, and confronted with an opposition group whose membership reached into the millions—was desperate not to intervene at all.

Eastern Europe made the Soviet Union flinch, then pushed it toward its downfall. Most accounts of the Soviet Union's fall stress its inevitability. They argue that Communism was an impossible system, or they emphasize the role of international competition, in which the USSR could not outpace the United States militarily, while its economy could never provide a comparable standard of living to that of the West. A third approach points to the problem of succession: Soviet power lasted long enough to create one generation of leaders born into the system. Once that generation—with Brezhnev at its head—began to die out in the early 1980s, the Soviet Union as a whole was soon to follow.

While all these explanations have their merits, they are largely internal, taking no note of the Soviet Union's vast empire to its west. This is a grave error, for while Eastern Europe was acquired by the Soviets as a buffer zone, in the long term it proved to be a gate. It did not shield the USSR from Western influences; it ushered them into the tent.

In matters of economic and social reform, the satellites led, and the Soviet Union followed—albeit usually with a delay, and only after an intervening period of repression and retrenchment. Hungary, following 1956, became an example of a socialist economy that could deliver a relatively high standard of living. Czechoslovakia, during the brief flowering of the Prague Spring, showed that socialist leadership could conceivably coexist with a free press and a multiparty system. Polish Solidarity, although anti-Communist, paradoxically showed what a *real* worker-led social movement looked like.

The Soviet Union responded to these external stimuli in varying ways, exemplified by the successive reigns of Yuri Andropov and Mikhail Gorbachev at the head of the Soviet state. Andropov, who ruled for fourteen months from 1982 to 1984, was a member of the Brezhnevite old guard, with extensive experience in Eastern Europe. In 1956 he was the Soviet ambassador in Budapest and was instrumental in advocating the use of force to crush the revolution. In 1968, as head of the KGB, he recommended "extreme measures" to end the Prague Spring, which he was convinced was setting the groundwork for a "NATO coup" in Czechoslovakia. Andropov was the epitome of a hard-liner. And yet in 1981 he dissuaded Brezhnev from invading Poland. Andropov also promoted a cohort of reformers within the Communist Party, including the man who would undo most of his legacy—Mikhail Gorbachev.

Gorbachev came to power in 1985 after a brief interim period when the Soviet Union was led by the physically decrepit Konstantin Chernenko. Almost twenty years younger than Andropov, Gorbachev embodied a completely different attitude toward Eastern Europe. He admired Hungary's more flexible economy, and he had learned about the principles that informed the Prague Spring from one of its leaders, Zdeněk Mlynář, who had been Gorbachev's friend when they were both students at Moscow University in the early 1950s.

As general secretary, Gorbachev tried to revive the Soviet economy by importing some of the entrepreneurial nimbleness he had observed in Hungary and East Germany. He called this program *perestroika*, or "restructuring." Believing that reform could not succeed without an environment that was open to criticism, he paired perestroika with a policy of openness and transparency in state institutions, or *glasnost*. Both programs bore the imprint of previous Eastern European experiences. In 1987, when a Soviet foreign ministry spokesman was asked "what separated perestroika and glasnost from the Prague Spring," he answered: "Nineteen years."[5]

Glasnost and perestroika did not revive the Soviet economy. What they did, however, was remove fear as one of the primary supports of the Soviet system. For decades, Communist power in the Eastern Bloc sustained itself on fear. A Polish friend once told me that his most vivid memory during martial law was of seeing a policeman on a street in Warsaw and being immediately overcome by fear, for he knew that this "person could do whatever he wanted to me—arrest me, beat me, and there was nothing I could do about it."

A similar sense of helplessness in the face of arbitrary power infected the entire Eastern Bloc. Around 1987, though, it began to break, both in the satellite countries and in the Soviet Union itself. That year protesters in Soviet Estonia managed to block the opening of a massive, and ecologically catastrophic, phosphorite mine.[6] Their success spurred further action: demonstrations commemorating Estonia's annexation, and open calls for its renewed independence. Both strands of defiance came together in the 1988 Tallinn Song Festival, where three hundred thousand people gathered to sing folkloric and patriotic compositions, including the unofficial Estonian national anthem.[7]

Similar events were organized in neighboring Latvia and Lithuania. In Latvia, a rock opera based on the national epic *The Bear-Slayer* became the focal point for a revival of national sentiment. In Lithuania, people performed old war songs and pacifist chants as a way of commemorating their lost freedom. This was the beginning of the "Singing Revolution," which spread through all three Baltic countries and became their unique contribution to the emancipatory tsunami that swept through Eastern Europe between 1989 and 1991.

In Ukraine, the revolution was slower to get started. There in 1988 the blue and yellow flag of independence was still banned, regarded by Communist officials as a "fascist rag." Whoever had the temerity to fly it was swiftly reported to the police. But by 1989, attitudes had begun to shift dramatically. When a group of activists and ecologists mounted a rafting expedition down the Dniester River, local people "wept when they saw the blue and yellow flags on the catamarans," crying "lend us your flag!"[8]

Soon previously unimaginable scenes began to take place across the Soviet west. In 1990 in Ukraine, thirty thousand people, many of them in historical dress, gathered at the site of the old Zaporozhian Sich to commemorate the five-hundredth anniversary of the establishment of Cossackdom. The Communists held a competing event a few miles away, but it attracted only a tenth as many visitors.[9] At a political gathering near the Sich, one speaker reminded the crowd that the elections used to select Cossack hetmans three hundred years before were more democratic than those for the presidency of the USSR. Meanwhile in Soviet Moldova, hundreds of thousands of people gathered in Chișinău's Victory Square to demand that their alphabet be changed from Cyrillic to Latin script.

At this stage of rebellion, people in the Soviet republics concentrated their attention on the revival of national symbols and languages. As fear of reprisal ebbed, however, actual independence from the Soviet Union started to seem possible as well. On August 23, 1989, the fiftieth anniversary of the signing of the Molotov-Ribbentrop Pact that had doomed the Baltic nations to Soviet rule, 2 million people in Lithuania, Latvia, and Estonia gathered to form a human chain running all the way from Tallinn to Vilnius.

A few months later Ukrainians organized their own version of the "Baltic Way," with three hundred thousand participants forming a chain from Kiev to Lviv by way of Tarnopol and Ivano-Frankivsk. It was now January 20, 1990. The USSR still stood firm as a federation of fifteen socialist republics governed by the Communist Party, whose authority was being increasingly eroded by internal elections and other measures brought about by Gorbachev's reforms. But while the Soviet Union remained unified, its empire in Eastern Europe had slipped away.

Once again the crisis had begun in Poland. In the fall of 1988, General Jaruzelski's government, facing a renewed wave of strikes, coupled with mounting debts to foreign investors that it could not repay, decided it had no choice but to reach some kind of deal with the opposition. In exchange for ending the strikes, it offered to make Solidarity legal. But then the government went further, proposing a more complex power-sharing agreement. It offered Solidarity the option of participating in the elections for parliament to be held in June 1989. Solidarity would be allowed to compete for 35 percent of the seats in the lower house and 100 percent of the seats in the upper house. Some members of the Communist Party convinced themselves that they could use these "Gorbachev-style" elections to stay in power while giving themselves at least a partial mandate from society.[10]

This proved to be a disastrous mistake, rooted in hubris. But it was at least partially understandable. The terms of the deal guaranteed the Communists a majority in the lower house, and most people did not think it possible that the party could lose *every* seat that was up for grabs. In fact, that was precisely what happened. Despite having no control over the media, Solidarity won every contested seat but one, and in August 1989, Poland became the first country in Eastern Europe in forty years to have a non-Communist head of state.

While Solidarity was campaigning for office in Poland, Hungary was undergoing an invisible transformation of its own. Here the impetus for change did not come from a mass protest movement driven by civil society. Rather, the old regime simply gave up; in the words of the historian István Rév, it "melted like butter in late summer sunshine."[11] Reformers within the party led the way, first by edging the long-ruling party leader János Kádár out of power, then by offering to compete in free elections.

Sensing that anything that reminded people of Communist rule had little chance of success in these contests, the reformers changed their party's name from the Hungarian Socialist Workers' Party to the less-Communist-sounding Hungarian Socialist Party. This left the small rump of genuinely convinced Communists without a political home. Some of these true believers organized themselves around the remnants of the János Kádár Society—essentially, the former dictator's fan club—and announced that they were the true heirs of Hungary's Communists. During an October 1989 press conference, their leader, the Polish-born actor Roland Antoniewicz, announced that they were going to revive Stakhanovite labor competition in Hungary, rebuild the peasant-worker alliance, and emulate the great tradition set forth by other Communist leaders such as Jaruzelski, Ceaușescu, Kim Il-Sung, and Pol Pot. He concluded his speech by insisting that he was not mentally ill or under psychiatric care.[12]

By the end of the summer of 1989, Poland and Hungary were no longer under Communist rule. The rest of the Eastern Bloc was quick to follow. On November 9, East German authorities opened the Berlin Wall. The move was unintentional—the result of a bureaucratic blunder—but once it was done, there was no going back. A week later student protests shook Prague. At first, they drew a violent police response from the government, but a general strike on November 27 changed the situation. In quintessentially Czech fashion, this general strike was quite mild—it was only two hours long and was held at lunchtime so as not to interfere with work. Nonetheless, it succeeded in persuading the Czechoslovak government that it could no longer count on society's support. Two days later Communists in the federal assembly revoked the leading role of their party. Gustáv Husák, who had presided over the leaden years of normalization since the start of the 1970s, resigned from his presidency on December 10. Czechoslovakia was free.

At nearly the same moment, Bulgaria's Communist Party was likewise in the process of dissolving itself. No one wanted to die in the name of one-party rule anymore. More remarkably—especially given what had happened on Tiananmen Square that same year—no one seemed willing to kill for it either. In the absence of brute force, the Eastern European revolutions began to take on the appearance of a carnival. The world had gone topsy-turvy. In the Czech town of Olomouc, students dressed as policemen and party bureaucrats, and held a funeral for "Comrade Totalitarianism," just weeks after their peers had been beaten in the streets of Prague. In Sofia, Bulgaria, in 1989, police had opened fire on graffiti artists painting the slogan "We Support the Dissidents." A year later ten-year-olds marched down the street disguised as militiamen, while a soccer referee handed out red cards to the Communist Party.[13]

Truth became the slogan of the day. People demanded to know all the secrets that Communist authorities had hidden over the forty-five years of their rule. They also vowed to live more authentically themselves. Bank tellers in the Czech town of Trnava promised to tell each other "only truth" from the day of the revolution onward. Beer brewers in Prague told the world that they wanted to "live in truth."[14] Soon they would be able to vote for their truth as well. At the start of 1990, a group of concerned citizens in Pilsen created the "Friends of Beer Party," whose stated objective was to "decrease the price of beer while increasing its quality and consumption."[15]

Amid this general celebration, one country stood apart. Of all the revolutions of 1989, Romania's was by far the bloodiest and hardest fought. It began in mid-December, with demonstrations in Timişoara, the old capital of the Banat, led by the Hungarian-speaking pastor László Tőkés. Lacking any of his Czechoslovak peers' scruples, Ceauşescu ordered his security forces to fire on the protesters. Over a thousand Romanians lost their lives in the chaotic street fighting that followed.

However, the shoot-to-kill order only encouraged further protests, which now spread across the country. Hoping to shore up his support, Ceauşescu decided to stage a rally in Bucharest in front of his supporters. On the morning of December 21, 1989, he harangued a crowd of one hundred thousand from the balcony of the Central Committee with tales of fascist agitators and foreign provocateurs. Expecting applause, he was greeted instead with shouts of "Killer!," "Murderer!," and "Death to the criminal!" Decades of carefully staged performances had not prepared Ceauşescu for even the possibility of defiance. In front of everyone—and on live television—he faltered.

It was a fatal moment of weakness. The next day Ceauşescu and his wife, Elena, fled Bucharest by helicopter. Meanwhile the army and secret police panicked. Instead of trusting their survival to a new and possibly vengeful regime, they decided to seize the upper hand for themselves. The military forced the Ceauşescus' helicopter to land north of the city, after which members of the security forces arrested the couple. On Christmas Day 1989, a hastily arranged trial charged Nicolae and Elena with a litany of crimes against the state, including genocide of his fellow Romanians. After a few hours, the tribunal found them guilty and sentenced them to death by firing squad. Seven minutes later the Ceauşescus were dead.

With the demise of the "Genius of the Carpathians," Romania passed into the hands of the former Communist apparatchiks and secret police agents who had engineered his execution. In order to gain political credibility, they quickly rebranded themselves as the "National

Salvation Front" and took credit for the street protests that had helped instigate the Ceauşescus' downfall. In this way, the Romanian revolution was not a true transformation, but a continuation of previous arrangements under a new name. Still, it was a step on the path toward democratization.

In Albania, at the same time that the Ceauşescus were coming down, nothing had yet changed. Throughout 1989 and into 1990, the Communist Party remained firmly in charge. For decades, Albania had been the most isolated country in Europe. Having broken successively with Yugoslavia, the Soviet Union, and Mao's China, it could count only on North Korea and Cuba for support. Still, by the late 1980s, some slight cracks began to appear in Albania's neo-Stalinist facade. The Beatles could be heard on the radio, and following a 1987 decree, families could keep as many as two sheep in their homes, provided they were of the same sex, so they wouldn't breed.[16]

But these were only stray tufts of grass; the rest was concrete. Months after the fall of the Berlin Wall, Albanian authorities were building their own walls around Tirana's embassy quarter.[17] They were trying to prevent asylum seekers from gaining refuge from foreign embassies. Their efforts were thwarted, however, on July 2, 1990, when an Albanian mechanic and former political prisoner named Ylli Bodinaku drove his truck right through the cement wall surrounding the West German embassy. Over three thousand of Bodinaku's fellow countrymen followed him into the breach.

Still, it wasn't until February 1991 that student protesters pulled down the gigantic bronze statue of Enver Hoxha from Tirana's central Skanderbeg Square. The Enver Hoxha Museum, housed in a retro-futuristic pyramid designed by his daughter, was shuttered and turned into a conference center. The pyramid was later turned into a nightclub called the Mummy, and subsequently fell into a terrible state of disrepair. After many years spent being used as a canvas for graffiti and as a giant ramp for local skateboarders, the pyramid is currently in the process of being converted into an IT training center and technology hub.

The same year that the statues came down in Albania, the Soviet Union finally began to unravel for good. By the fall of 1991, Lithuania, Latvia, Estonia, Ukraine, Belarus, and Moldova had all declared their independence. Politics in this moment was as much about rewriting the past as it was about finding a path forward into the future. Across Eastern Europe, the early 1990s were a time of wandering corpses, of commemorations and condemnations, exhumations and reburials. History was being rewritten on the fly. Statues fell, and others were put up in their place. The long-exiled dead returned, while the old Stalinist mausolea were torn apart.

In Hungary, one of the first tasks of the new post-Communist epoch was to locate the remains of the victims of the 1956 revolution and give them a proper burial. A special commission finally located the unmarked graves where they had lain since their execution—and was surprised to discover that the victims' bones had been mixed with those of animals from the Budapest zoo. The remains of Prime Minister Imre Nagy, who had led Hungary throughout the uprising, and been executed in secret in its aftermath, were mixed in with those of a deceased giraffe.[18]

On June 16, 1989, the thirty-first anniversary of Nagy's execution, over two hundred thousand people attended his reburial, making it one of the largest public demonstrations of that revolutionary year. Symbolically, this was the moment when the country's Communist past was put to rest. It was also the coming-out party for the young student politician Viktor Orbán, whose speech that day helped launch his national career. Hungary's gradual turn toward the right was also signaled by another reburial, that of the interwar dictator, Miklós Horthy, who had led the country into a disastrous alliance with Hitler. Horthy had died in exile in Portugal in 1957, and his will stipulated that he was not to be brought back to Hungarian soil until the last Russian soldier had left. He was finally buried in his hometown of Kenderes in 1993.

While Hungary found new homes for past heroes, Bulgaria exorcized its demons by tearing down old shrines. In 1990 Georgi Dimitrov's family removed his body from its lavish Stalinist-era mausoleum and had it quietly cremated. Nine years later the mayor of Sofia decided to destroy the mausoleum itself. However, the demolition team misplaced the explosives, and after the first blast the monument, which had been built by shock brigades in just six days, was still standing, with barely a scratch on it. It withstood the next two explosions as well, developing at most a slight lean. Only the fourth explosion managed to bring the marble structure down. Sadly, the blast was so massive that it devastated much of the surrounding square as well.

If toppling old monuments signaled the start of a new era, in Belarus the discovery of forgotten martyrs sparked a new sense of collective identity. In 1988 two amateur archaeologists announced the discovery of several mass graves at Kuropaty, in the woods on the edge of the Minsk city limits. The graves contained hundreds of bodies, nearly all of which had been shot through the head. The excavations also turned up numerous small objects—mugs, clothes, shoes, toothbrushes, combs, and coins—that mostly dated to the late 1930s. It quickly became clear that these were the remains of executions committed during the Great Purge of 1937–38—the high point of Stalinist terror—and concealed ever since.

Within weeks of the announcement of the discovery, the Kuropaty grave field became a site of spontaneous pilgrimage. Tens of thousands of Belarusians marched onto what had until then been an empty field surrounded by barbed wire, holding aloft signs reading "We'll not forget! We'll not forgive!" Riot police dispersed some of these marches using tear gas, but the remembrance marches nonetheless initiated the first major protest movement in modern Belarusian history. As one of the discoverers of the burial site later wrote, "Kuropaty marked the beginning of the collapse of communism" in the republic.[19]

In Yugoslavia as in Belarus, the fall of Communism coincided with the return of the hitherto unacknowledged dead. But while the commemoration of past crimes helped Belarus find its identity, in Yugoslavia, it helped to tear the state apart.

Socialist Yugoslavia had been built on an act of mutual forgetting. The country was created in the midst of war. A partisan army, organized by the Communist Party and led by General Josip Broz Tito, had managed to beat back the Axis occupation with only minimal help from abroad. In the official narrative, this army included representatives from all of Yugoslavia's many peoples. Its victory belonged to everyone. "Brotherhood and Unity" became the most frequently repeated slogan of the federal state.

Unfortunately, the truth was rather darker. Inside the Kingdom of Yugoslavia, which lasted from 1918 to 1941, World War II was very nearly a war of all against all. In Croatia, a fascist puppet government—the

Ustaše—openly collaborated with the Nazis. Its police conducted mass executions of Serbs, Jews, Muslims, and Roma at the concentration camp in Jasenovac. In Bosnia-Herzegovina, Muslims fought Serbs, while Serbs committed reprisal killings against Muslims and Croats. Within Serbia, pro-royalist and pro-Communist Serbs waged a deadly guerrilla war against one another. In the course of this fratricidal war, thousands of people were killed in cold blood. Their bodies were buried in shallow graves or dumped into some of the innumerable caves that dot the country's landscape.

For the duration of Tito's rule, the details of these killings were covered by a code of silence. They belonged to memory, but not to history. But as Communists lost their grip on power at the end of the 1980s, this history returned to haunt the present. Just as scurvy can cause old wounds to reappear on the body and bleed anew, the very land began to disgorge its dead. In Croatia, caverns filled with dead bodies appeared on the cover of popular news magazines. In Serbia, the skeletons of three thousand "victims of the Ustaše" were unearthed from Herzegovinian caves and brought to Belgrade, to be buried in an immense public funeral presided over by the patriarch of the Serbian Orthodox Church.[20] The lines of coffins and mourners stretched for a kilometer and a half across downtown.

Some of Yugoslavia's nationalist reburials reached deeper into the past. In 1987 the body of Prince Lazar, the fallen hero of the Battle of Kosovo, began a tour of the Serbian, Orthodox monasteries in Serbia, Bosnia-Herzegovina, Croatia, and Kosovo, which was at this point an Albanian-majority autonomous province within Serbia, but one with powerful emotional resonance for Serbs. The places visited by Prince Lazar's skeleton were likewise parts of an imaginary greater Serbia, whose borders were delimited by the presence of both the living and the dead, according to the principle "Serbian land is where Serbian bones are."[21]

Today, however, it is no longer necessary to descend into caverns or monastery crypts to find the bodies of the martyred dead. Bones litter the landscape of the former Yugoslavia. Old mines are full of them. They turn up buried under rubbish heaps and floating in wells. In some places, people pull bones out of the soil along with potatoes.[22] They are then left to wonder who they belong to. A neighbor? A friend? A husband who came back from Germany in 1992 and immediately disappeared? Or a brother who was driven away as a prisoner of war and never came home again?

Between 1991 and 1995, Yugoslavia tore itself apart. Four years of war shattered the country and left over one hundred thirty thousand people dead. It was the first major conflict on European soil since the end of World War II. It also marked the return of ethnic cleansing to the continent, as belligerents on all sides used mass killings and expulsions to create "ethnically pure" territories that they could then claim as their own.

Bosnia-Herzegovina, home to a mixed population of Muslims, Croats, and Serbs, in which no group held an absolute majority, was the most diverse of all the Yugoslav republics. Its very diversity left it open to territorial claims by its neighbors. As Serbs fought to create a greater Serbia and Croats a greater Croatia, Bosnians—and especially Bosnia's Muslims, who had no one else to fight for them—found themselves trapped in the middle of a three-way war. In the span of a few years, a whole way of life, a pattern of mutual tolerance reaching back to the end of the Middle Ages—one of the last stands of the old, pre-twentieth-century Eastern Europe—vanished. Or rather, it was murdered in the name of nationalism. Today, thirty years later, the scars of this violence still lie heavy on the land. I've been to villages in the Republika Srpska, the Serbian-controlled half of Bosnia-Herzegovina, in which the houses people abandoned in 1991–92 have stayed completely empty. Trees now grow out of collapsed roofs, and moss covers the floors. In these haunted places, it feels as if the killings ended only yesterday.

Since the Yugoslav wars began, people have wondered why the end of Communism brought about such bloodshed there and nowhere else. The paradox deepens when one considers that of all the Eastern European countries, Yugoslavia enjoyed one of the highest living standards and was by far the most open to the West. Beginning in the 1960s, Yugoslavs could easily travel to Italy to shop and to Germany for work. In the 1980s an economic crisis brought on by a too-large debt burden took some of the shine off the Yugoslav economy. Still, heading into 1990, it was a place that had enjoyed forty-five years of peace and seemed like a model for using local autonomy to forge unity out of diversity.

What went wrong? One answer is that Yugoslavia suffered from a crisis of legitimacy. As time went on, especially following Tito's death in 1980, the state's constituent republics grew in importance relative to the federal state. As in the Soviet Union, the local units that made up Yugoslavia seemed to many of their inhabitants to be more meaningful than the country as a whole. The republics' leaders, meanwhile, were busy jockeying for power in a world that was swiftly leaving Communism behind. With the party dwindling in relevance, they needed a new source of authority. They found it by exploiting ethnic grievances. The Serbian leader Slobodan Milošević first came to prominence in 1987 by giving a speech in defense of Serbian rights in Kosovo, a fiery address that culminated with the phrase "No one will ever beat a Serb again!"[23] Meanwhile the Croatian leader Franjo Tudjman, a former major general obsessed with Croatian military greatness, revived much of the symbolism of the collaborationist Ustaše regime, further stoking Serbian fears. He also forced Serbs in Croatia to switch from Cyrillic to Latin script, an action that drew particular resentment.[24] Soon, the two sides were at each other's throats.

But why did a quarrel between republics turn into a deadly war of neighbor against neighbor? How could people who had known each other their whole lives suddenly turn against each other? Here propaganda provides a crucial piece of the puzzle. Under Tito, Yugoslavia had had eight television stations—one for each of the six republics, plus two for the autonomous regions of Vojvodina and Kosovo—all of which cooperated to create a single common broadcast.[25] The rule, in those years, was that one was permitted to criticize the nationalism of one's own republic, but not that of one's neighbors.

By the early 1990s, the different stations produced competing broadcasts that spent most of their time attacking their sister republics. Radio Television Belgrade was especially vehement, bombarding its viewers with dire reports of Croatian and Bosnian Muslim aggression. When civil war broke out in 1991, many Serbs, especially those living in Bosnia and Croatia, were convinced that they were about to be slaughtered by "Ustaše hordes" and "Muslim jihadis."

Propaganda could turn neighbors into enemies; it could also absolve combatants of their crimes. After Serbian forces shelled a Sarajevo market in May 1992, killing twenty-six civilians in a breadline, Bosnian Serb television reported that Muslims had done it to themselves in order to frame the Serbs.[26] When Serbian forces struck the market again two years later, the same station likewise claimed that the event had been staged.[27] In this environment, any lie, no matter how outlandish, became believable. Wild rumors circulated in the media. One claimed that Muslims were feeding live Serbian babies to the lions at the Sarajevo zoo.[28]

By the time this bizarre story began circulating, the lions in the Sarajevo zoo were already a memory. Just months into Sarajevo's four-year-long siege, the zoo ran out of food. Someone shot the giraffes, ponies, and buffaloes. The lions, tigers, leopards, and pumas slowly starved, eating their mates as they succumbed in turn. By October 1992, only a single bear, a black female, was left alive. Volunteers braved sniper fire to keep her fed with bread and apples, the only food they had on hand, but by November she too was dead.[29]

In Sarajevo, during the years of siege, time passed differently. Food for the starving city had to be delivered by air—there is now a mocking monument to the famously unpalatable canned beef included in the international relief airdrops. Even burying the dead meant risking death. Ten gravediggers died at the Lion Cemetery alone, while Sarajevo's Jewish cemetery—a beautiful place, perched on a hillside with a view of the Austro-Hungarian part of the city, and long used as a lover's lane—became a snipers' nest.[30]

But while Sarajevo was enduring the perpetual winter of the blockade, the rest of Eastern Europe was experiencing a sudden thaw. The early 1990s were a springtime for capitalism. In many places, people greeted its arrival with unrestrained—and unrealistic—enthusiasm. During a 1990 demonstration in Sofia, next to banners calling for "Bread, Peace, and Freedom!" an echo of Lenin's slogan "Peace, Land, Bread," some more hopeful protesters held aloft signs predicting "Free today—Rich tomorrow!"[31]

Most of these hopes for immediate wealth were quickly dashed. The pattern of change was remarkably uniform. Virtually everywhere old government controls on the economy were swiftly dismantled, while privatization of state property progressed at a startling rate. Apartments and homes suddenly gained private owners. Jobs disappeared. Farm cooperatives were shuttered. Most of the shipyard workers who had brought the Polish Communist Party to its knees by protesting in Gdańsk and sparking the Solidarity movement lived long enough to see their workplaces sold for scrap. The same would eventually prove true for much of the rest of the region's heavy industry.

All this restructuring resulted in skyrocketing unemployment, combined with breathtaking inflation. Everywhere, the accumulated gains of entire lifetimes were melting into the air. Especially for the old, it was a time of terrible dislocation. Many longed for a return to the old days, when employment was predictable and the state took care of their health and welfare. Now suddenly doctors expected cash, while cash seemed to lose value by the day. It only took a brief taste of the chaos of the free market to make the past seem like a lost golden age. In the words of one Hungarian farmworker, "János Kádár tried for 30 years to make people love communism, and he failed completely; but the present government has succeeded in just two years!"[32]

For others, though—especially the young—the nascent market economy opened the way to undreamed-of pleasures. In August 1989 a young Polish journalist wrote in his diary that something incredible had happened to him: he had gone into a store and bought three pounds of Canadian bacon without yelling, without fighting, without queuing. "I am twenty-three years old," he wrote, "and for the first time in my life I have my very own ham." A few months later he bought his first kiwi-fruit. He recorded his impressions of his first taste: "on the outside, it looks like a potato. On the inside—ecstasy."[33]

New flavors spurred new desires, which could be satisfied only by plunging headfirst into the world of commerce. Most Eastern Europeans were accustomed to living with illicit trade. Years of privation had taught them that the best strategy for survival was to keep one foot in the socialized workforce and the other in the black market. For instance, a generation of Polish alpinists, who in the 1980s were among the best Himalayan mountain climbers in the world, financed their expeditions through this combination of activities. Two or three months a year they worked painting chimneys and smokestacks at some of the country's largest factories. They spent the rest of the year in India and Nepal, where they made most of their money by smuggling whiskey and sheepskin coats back to Poland.[34]

The end of Communism spelled the demise of this kind of in-between lifestyle. (It also coincidentally put an end to the great age of Polish mountaineering.) Now everyone had to fight for a living. The first businesses were focused entirely on primitive accumulation, usually of foreign currency. Currency exchanges and pawnshops quickly occupied every available bit of space in Eastern Europe's capitals. Meanwhile, every large private apartment seemed to have turned into an antique store, and every patch of unoccupied sidewalk into a bazaar selling old medals and icons.

After a year or two, when a basic appetite for liquid assets had been met, this incipient commerce shifted toward the satisfaction of higher needs. During the great era of orthodontists and travel agents, everyone who could either fixed their teeth or took their first Mediterranean vacation. At the same time, gambling and other forms of speculation became ever more attractive. By 1993 the stock market, founded only a year or two earlier, had become a national obsession. I remember watching people lined up before dawn on a cold December morning to buy shares in a Silesian bank, just as they previously would have lined up for toilet paper or sausages.

International trade offered another avenue to quick cash. The early 1990s were the golden age of the long-distance hauling trade in Eastern Europe. Most traders were private individuals who trafficked in whatever they could personally carry across borders. Clothes were the backbone of this industry. Fueled by the region's insatiable appetite for cheap apparel, in a few short years the Tuszyn Market, built on an anonymous stretch of roadway outside Łódź, Poland, grew into one of the largest outdoor markets in all of Europe.[35] Customers converged from all directions in search of affordable clothes, especially undergarments: lacy, furry, and kinky for the Germans; cheap-as-could-be for the Belarusians and Lithuanians; plain and sturdy for the Russians—though the Russians made sure to switch the labels so they could pass the Polish bras off as Italian made—when they returned home.

These two currents of trade—personal transport and local manufacture—converged most spectacularly in one location: the Stadium of the Tenth Anniversary in Praga, across the river from Warsaw. The stadium had originally been built to host sporting events and Communist Party ceremonies. Over time it acquired the appearance of a well-weathered meteor crater and the ambience of a forgotten airstrip.

But then at the start of the 1990s, its top levels were taken over by an impromptu open-air market nicknamed the Jarmark Europa, or Europe Bazaar. The mood became one of sheer pandemonium.

When I visited it in 1993, the Jarmark was the largest bazaar in Europe. At its apex, it was home to an estimated $1 billion in legal trade annually, and a further $3 billion in illegal transactions. It was where all the other open-air markets in Poland got their goods, where wholesalers from Moscow and Leningrad went to renew their supplies, and where half of Bulgaria got its clothes. Its reach stretched out across Eurasia, from Germany to North Korea. Everything was for sale at the Jarmark. One could buy bathroom fittings, musical instruments, pirated software, and bootleg cassette tapes. I went in winter and left with an imitation-down coat and an excellent Soviet Army–issue monocular. Had I known more and been a bit older, I could have purchased items of a more illicit nature, for the Jarmark was one of Eastern Europe's greatest clearinghouses for illegal activity of all kinds, from prostitution to fraud. There you could purchase drugs, counterfeit goods, and specialized weapons, from submachine guns to high explosives. Supposedly, you could even order an execution for hire.[36] Most of the trade at the Jarmark wasn't criminal, however; it was simply a matter of survival. On its periphery, migrant Roma from Romania sold scavenged pots, Bulgarian men played the accordion, and old women from the outskirts of Warsaw hawked mismatched socks, individual shoes, and old combs. It was hard to fathom that anyone would want to purchase any of these orphaned objects, while the idea that one could make a living selling seemed beyond imagining.

To survive doing this kind of trade required luck. In search of it, many traders turned to a supernatural source. Starting at some point in the mid-1990s, stall-holders at the Jarmark commonly placed a picture of a "Jew with a Penny" in their stalls. Usually, the picture showed a bearded man in Hasidic dress holding up a gold coin. Sometimes it was an actual oil painting; more often it was merely a photocopy. Most people in the West regarded these images as simple anti-Semitic caricatures, but in fact they were something rather different: they were charms, whose purpose was to multiply cash. A whole body of folklore sprang up on the nascent internet about how the charm was supposed to work. If one kept a "Jew with a Penny" at home, it was to be pointed away from the door so that money would enter the home and not leave it. A coin slipped behind the picture frame made its powers stronger, but on the Sabbath, it was best to turn the picture facedown, to give the Jew his day of rest.[37]

Poles weren't the only ones to look for supernatural assistance in navigating the stormy waters of the nascent market economy. The coming of capitalism was a moral as well as an economic revolution. A generation that had been raised to believe that productive labor was the only acceptable source of wealth suddenly had to adapt to a world of rampant speculation, where money could mate and multiply as if by magic. Few could say exactly how this was supposed to work, but the prospect of immense gains was too great to resist.

As a consequence of this uncertainty, in many Eastern European countries, pyramid schemes and other dubious investment ventures ballooned to immense size. Between 1992 and 1994, as many as half of Romanian households placed money in one scheme called Caritas, which promised an eightfold return in just three months. For a time, it worked. Caritas's founder, the former accountant Ioan Stoica, became Romania's most popular man. Church leaders celebrated him for devising a homegrown solution to the problem of global capitalism. His beneficiaries hailed him as "a saint," "the Pope," "a messiah," and "the prophet."[38]

When the inevitable end came for Caritas in 1994, its collapse was also interpreted in religious terms. Remorseful creditors told tales of cursed money and houses infected by poltergeists. For others, Caritas's malign origin had been obvious all along. As one woman explained to a visiting American anthropologist, "Caritas must be the work of the devil: money can't give birth!"[39] Many Romanians lost their savings to Caritas, but thanks to judicious government intervention, its fall did not trigger wider unrest. In Albania, the collapse of an even vaster network of pyramid schemes in 1997 triggered a civil war that cost more than two thousand lives and precipitated an outflux of refugees even greater than the one that accompanied the fall of Communism six years before.

Growth, dislocation, chaos: this was the Poland I remember from childhood. I learned about the fall of Communism through the television news, but I lived through hyperinflation myself. When I think of those years, my mind always turns to my mother's nanny, Julcia. After her father died when she was seven, Julcia became my mother's main caregiver. She arrived in Warsaw from the tiny village of Nowa Pecyna and went to work for my mother's family after another family threw her out. Long after my mother and her sister left Poland, Julcia stayed with my grandmother. When I would visit, she would offer me honey for my colds in between trips to pray at the church on Savior Square.

Over the years, the apartment Julcia shared with my grandmother made up most of her world. She kept her life savings in a Danish butter-cookie tin with windmills on the lid. She had no next of kin, so when she died in 1993, we opened it up. It was full of old coins and bills gathered over the decades. Ballooning inflation had stripped them of most of their value. Taken together, they were worth almost nothing—maybe a penny, maybe less.

That value could simply evaporate shocked eleven-year-old me. The idea that you could prepare for the future appeared then as yet another Eastern European mirage. Now it seems merely to sit at the end of a long line of family losses: the estates somewhere in western Lithuania, the brownstone in Warsaw, a fortune in German marks kept somewhere near Poznań, and my great-grandfather's butterfly collection, turned into a fine yellow dust by a bomb in the First World War. All seem contained in that blue tin box. To me, it symbolizes not just the era of transition but the capriciousness of history itself.

Epilogue

Great Kurultáj. Bugac, Hungary.

The shift from socialism to capitalism left deep scars across Eastern Europe. Some of them were physical: children born during the transition grew up to be, on average, a centimeter shorter than those born a few years before or after.[1] Similar decreases in height have otherwise been observed only as a consequence of major famines and wars. Other scars were psychological. During the transition, several Eastern European countries—notably Hungary and the Baltic republics—reported some of the highest rates of suicide in the world.[2] Although those rates declined following a peak in the mid-1990s, for the quarter-century following the fall of the Berlin Wall, Eastern Europe continued to lag sharply behind the West in terms of overall life satisfaction.

This so-called "transition happiness gap" was one of the most robust and frequently confirmed findings in all of social science.[3] Or it was until around 2016, when the effect started to wane. The reason for this seems twofold: Eastern Europeans grew happier as their nations recovered from the 2008 recession, while at the same time Western happiness decreased. By 2018, however, the gap had vanished entirely, as people in Eastern Europe reported a degree of life satisfaction that put them on a par with Turkey, Cyprus, and Greece. Eastern Europe was a gray place no longer.

And yet despite all this happiness, joy has not been a major part of the region's political life. The story of the past decade in much of Eastern Europe has been one of increased polarization and receding or embattled democracy. In several countries (Hungary, Belarus, Serbia), the state has effectively been captured by a single ruler or political party. Other nations have seen the development of deep social fissures, either between ethnicities (Bosnia-Herzegovina), political orientations (Poland), or a combination of both (Ukraine).

Until recently, Ukraine's divisions seemed especially stark. These were at once regional and generational, pitting a Russian-speaking east and south against a Ukrainian-speaking west, and an older generation that looked back fondly on the stability granted by the Soviet Union against a younger cohort that pinned its hopes on joining the rest of Europe. During the Revolution of Dignity, or Maidan Revolution, of 2014, led by members of this second group, protesters managed to oust Viktor Yanukovych, the country's lavishly corrupt, pro-Russian president. A subsequent Russian invasion robbed Ukraine of the Crimean Peninsula as well as the territory around Donetsk and Luhansk in the country's far east. The ensuing war in the Donbas claimed some thirteen thousand dead over the following seven years. While this was a huge price in lives, it had the effect of rallying Ukrainian society around a common enemy. Just how far this unification had progressed became evident during the Russian invasion of 2022, when Ukrainians put up an armed resistance far in excess of anything anticipated by Moscow—or the rest of the world, for that matter.

War forged Ukraine into a nation, but its nationhood came at the cost of its territorial integrity. The rest of Eastern Europe has largely managed to avoid armed conflict, at least since the Kosovo war of 1999 in the former Yugoslavia, but it has not been safe from internal dissension. Politics in much of the region has grown ever more contentious with time. Paradoxically, this increase in tension has occurred even as these same nations have successfully tackled many of the biggest challenges facing them as they emerged from the revolutions of 1989. The current era of partisan squabbling comes on the heels of two decades of hard-won victories in economics and diplomacy, as an era of difficult compromises has been replaced with a scramble for power.

Although the pain of the transition was great, since then most countries in the region have successfully developed market economies and mostly functioning democracies. Geopolitically, the scale of change has been equally impressive. Estonia, Latvia, Lithuania, Poland, Czechia, Slovakia, Hungary, Slovenia, Croatia, Romania, and Bulgaria have all joined the European Union. All the same countries, plus Albania, Montenegro, and North Macedonia, have also joined NATO. Only Serbia, Bosnia-Herzegovina, Kosovo, Belarus, Ukraine, and Moldova remain outside both organizations.

Nineteen eighty-nine proved to be one of the most deeply transformative revolutions in recent history. The scale of what has been accomplished in the intervening years is immediately visible on a visit to any of the region's larger cities, especially for anyone who remembers Eastern Europe as it was in the 1980s and early '90s. But this progress has also been sharply unequal, as vast stretches of countryside, and sometimes whole nations, have been left far behind the pace set by the newly glittering capital cities.

The sheer scale of these changes left many Eastern European countries riven by deep divisions of generation and class. The view confronting the young and old, the urban and the rural, has rarely seemed more different. The resulting crisis of identity has led many Eastern Europeans to look to history for answers to the question of who they really are in a suddenly globalized world. But history is never singular; it always provides multiple narratives with which to explain the present. In the political vacuum left by the end of Communism, the choice of which story to go with became immensely important. As the heroic phase of Eastern Europe's transition has come to an end, politics have shifted into a never-ending series of battles about the past.

Many Eastern European nations face an odd predicament. They possess a surplus of history, but a deficit of useful narrative. That is, plenty of things have happened *to* them, but not enough has been done *by* them to establish a deeply rooted sense of shared destiny. In much of the region, national sovereignty has tended to be brief, partial, or intermittent. Empire, and the struggle against it, has tended to be the leading story, while opportunities to develop national mythologies independent of their influence have tended to be rather sparse.

Decades of life in the Soviet Bloc slowed the process of narrative-building even more, as histories had to be rewritten to accord with Communist norms. Much of what had been established as national canon in the interwar period had to be scrapped, while the history of the Second World War was obfuscated or told through a narrowly pro-Soviet lens. This left many contentious episodes either untold or unmentionable. This was why the revolutions of 1989 were accompanied by a great unearthing of buried histories. People cast around for new pasts as a way of making up for lost time. Recovering lost graves and reclaiming banished or forgotten heroes was a way of drawing boundaries around new states; it also helped to fracture some old ones.

The years that followed the transition saw the demise of several states and the emergence of a host of brand-new ones. The Soviet Union fell apart, as did Yugoslavia and Czechoslovakia. Slovakia, Slovenia, Croatia, Bosnia, Macedonia, and Belarus all became independent entities for the first time in well over half a millennium. Ukraine, which had enjoyed a long history of autonomy and several flickering moments of independence reaching back to the seventeenth century, started a new life as a modern state. Its borders encompassed territory that had previously belonged to the Habsburg, Ottoman, and Russian empires.

What to do with such a complex and fragmented inheritance? For many countries, the first task was to establish a new point of origin. Because recorded history began with the arrival of Christianity in much of the region, many twenty-first-century nationalists have had to reach back a thousand years or more in search of a national progenitor.

In recent years, some Slovaks have seized on Svatopluk I of Great Moravia, who reigned from 871 to 894, as a national ancestor. In 2010 the ruling SMER party erected a huge bronze statue of Svatopluk, "King of the Ancient Slovaks," in front of Bratislava Castle; this despite the fact that he was neither Slovak, nor—probably—a king.[4] Belarus, similarly in need of a recognizable founding father, has turned to

Vseslav the Sorcerer, the famously cruel wizard-prince of Polotsk, who may or may not have been a werewolf.[5] Pre-Christian religious traditions have likewise seen a revival. This trend has been especially strong in Latvia and Lithuania, where paganism as an organized faith lasted the longest, but it also has equivalents across the Slavic world. These neopagan movements go by a variety of names—Romuva, Rodnovery, Svetoary—and are highly syncretic, imaginative reconstructions of otherwise vanished traditions.

Building national mythologies requires a certain melding of opposites. Invaders and assimilators, resistance leaders and collaborators, rulers and ruled—all have to find their place in the total picture. But while this is true of virtually every Eastern European nation, none has pursued a more eclectic approach to its past than the Republic of Macedonia.

For as long as Macedonians have considered themselves a separate people, outsiders have claimed ownership over parts of their identity. Greeks think the name "Macedonia" belongs to their own northern provinces. Many Bulgarians consider the Macedonian language no more than a dialect of Bulgarian. Others have laid claim to its territory. Macedonia's inclusion in Yugoslavia for most of the twentieth century was predicated on Macedonians belonging to a larger community of "South Slavs."

Amid this welter of competing stakes, Macedonia has embarked on a boldly maximalist approach to defining its history. Beginning in 2011, Macedonia has become home to one of the most profuse, and confounding, historical displays in Europe. The capital of Skopje is now crowded with hundreds of statues commemorating every conceivable aspect of Macedonia's past. Classical heroes stand next to Byzantine emperors, Serbian despots jostle with Communist politicians. Albanians, who make up about 25 percent of Macedonia's population, have their own pantheon of famous figures, located by the old Ottoman bazaar. Perhaps the most surprising thing about the Skopje assemblage is that it includes monuments not just to individuals but to whole categories of people. There are statues honoring beggars, shoppers, and businesswomen. Mothers receive an entire fountain, decorated with massive sculptures depicting the four phases of motherhood. It shares a neighborhood with monuments to street musicians and clowns.

Odd as it is to witness, this view of the past—and present—at least has the virtue of being inclusive. Sadly, the story of this big-tent approach to history has an awkward coda. The Skopje 2014 initiative, which called for a citywide facelift in addition to construction of all the new monuments, proved to be cripplingly expensive. It was also shoddily done. Large cracks have appeared in many of the city's brand-new neoclassical facades and ostensibly marble pavements.

Meanwhile politics have intervened to further complicate the initiative's message. In 2018, Macedonia signed the Prespa Agreement, which allowed it to join NATO. One of the conditions for membership was changing its name from Macedonia to North Macedonia. This provision was a concession to Greece, which has long claimed the name "Macedonia" for itself. Greece also lays claim to the legacy of ancient Macedonia, the homeland of Alexander the Great. One of the provisions of the Prespa Agreement required North Macedonia to renounce any connection between itself and the fourth-century B.C. kingdom. Since many Macedonian heroes had already been commemorated by the Skopje 2014 initiative, many of the statues now bear disclaimers notifying passersby that they have nothing to do with North Macedonia per se, but rather belong to the "cultural and historic heritage of the entire world." A giant statue of Alexander the Great on horseback, which still dominates the main downtown esplanade, has been renamed, generically, *An Equestrian Warrior.* The battle for a usable past rages on.

Blessed with a long tradition of independence and autonomy, Hungary has not had to defend itself from rival claimants on its identity as has Macedonia. Nonetheless, its approach to the past has been similarly expansive. With their unique language, so unlike any other in Europe (Finnish and Estonian are only distant relatives), Hungarians have felt themselves to be the odd man out among Eastern European peoples. This has long been a point of pride, as well as a source of some confusion. Beginning in the Middle Ages, chroniclers connected the ninth-century arrival of the nomadic Magyar tribes—ancestors to today's Hungarians—to previous onslaughts carried out by the Avars and Huns.

In the nineteenth and twentieth centuries, scholars and intellectuals expanded this somewhat tenuous connection into an elaborate theory of quasi-racial kinship. They claimed that Hungarians belonged to a vast brotherhood of peoples that they named the "Turanians" as a counterpoint to the Germanic and Slavic ethnic groupings. Turanians included a bevy of other former or current nomads, everyone from Turks to Kazakhs and Mongols. In the interwar years, promoting a specifically Turanian identity became associated with movements on Hungary's extreme right. For this reason, under Communism, public reference to Turanism was almost completely forbidden, but since Communism's end, it has made a spectacular comeback.

Today people in Hungary celebrate their nomadic past in a variety of ways. Some practice paganism or shamanism as a religion. Others, seeking a more authentic embodiment of the past, have taught themselves the ancient ways they feel they have lost. They practice "shamanic drumming" and send their children to special summer camps where they can learn mounted archery. One now finds road signs—as well as a great many tattoos—written in ancient Hungarian runes. Even malls are getting in on the action: one major shopping center in Budapest is surrounded by boulders carved with ancient patterns borrowed from Kazakhstan, Mongolia, and other stops on the great steppe road that brought the Magyars from Inner Asia to their present home by the Danube.

All these strains of nationalist-nomadic revivalism converge in an annual celebration called the Great Kurultáj. This event, which shares a name with the convocations that were once used by the Mongols to select their khans, is held every August on a patch of *puszta* grassland two hours south of Budapest. There, over the course of a long weekend, thousands of Hungarians camp in yurts and sample the music and cuisine of Eurasia's twenty-three Turkic "tribes." Full choirs of shamanic drummers provide the music; food vendors sell Mongolian dumplings as well as classic Hungarian dishes like cabbage rolls, goulash, and *lángos*.

A gigantic, grim-faced portrait of Attila the Hun, flanked by rows of horsehair banners and tribal flags, presides over the assembly. Beneath it, visitors can learn how to wield a recurve bow, and gape at archaeological exhibits showing the deformed, alien-like skulls of the ancient Huns. Every day mounted riders gather in the central arena to re-create great moments of early Magyar history, such as the slaughter of the Bavarians, the pillaging of the Pannonians, and the massacre of the Moravians. In doing so, they are reenacting the founding moment of

Hungarian statehood, the Honfoglalás, or "Conquest of the Home-land." This event has been celebrated in Hungary with vast sculptural assemblages and painted panoramas since the turn of the nineteenth century. The supposed one-thousandth anniversary of the conquest in 1896 was the occasion for a particularly lavish outpouring of national sentiment.

In today's world, however, it is not enough to win a country by right of arms; a nation also needs a moral basis for its existence. In contemporary Eastern Europe, that basis is usually provided by a victory over fascism or Communism. Hungary has opted for a third option, choosing to portray homegrown fascists *and* local Communists as if they were exactly the same thing—and foreign imports to boot. The best place to see this radical new vision of history in action is at the House of Terror in Budapest. Formerly the home of the Stalinist secret police, and before that of their fascist-era equivalent, this handsome building on Budapest's most fashionable street is now a museum that purports to unveil the buried, secret history of Hungary's criminal past. This is the poisoned legacy Hungary's current government claims to have finally, and heroically, supplanted.

Visitors are treated to a multimedia exploration of the darkest periods of Hungary's history. Designed by a master set designer, the exhibits feel like dioramas culled from the mind of David Lynch. The House of Terror is a haunted house of twentieth-century history, with Volga sedans (the "Black Marias" of the secret police) and fascist interrogators playing the role of zombies and werewolves. Visits conclude with a slow ride down an elevator to basement dungeons—the former torture chambers and isolation cells used to break prisoners.

Built with an infusion of government cash, the House of Terror is meant to convey a specific political message: that the morally repugnant Communists were just as bad as the fascist Arrow Cross, and that neither had anything to do with the "real" Hungary. This idea has also been written into the nation's laws. When Viktor Orbán and his party Fidesz rewrote the Hungarian constitution in 2011, they inserted a preamble that declares that from March 19, 1944, to May 2, 1990, Hungary, as an independent entity, simply did not exist.[6] For the duration of those forty-six years, it was wholly in the possession of a foreign power. In this way, the new constitution complements the House of Terror. Both perform a sort of political exorcism, excising those parts of the country's history that its current rulers consider illegitimate.

In Poland, by contrast, nation-building has focused on elevating those who were formerly cast out. For centuries, Poland's national memory has been structured around moments of defeat and suffering. The chief twentieth-century contributions to this canon of national sacrifice are the massacre of over twenty thousand Polish army officers by the Soviet secret police at Katyń in 1940 and the failed Warsaw Uprising of 1944. Discussion of both events was suppressed under Communism, a prohibition that served only to heighten their power as objects of fascination and reverence. In 2010 President Lech Kaczyński and almost a hundred other Polish political and military dignitaries died in a plane crash on their way to Smolensk in Russia to pay their respects on the seventieth anniversary of Katyń.

In recent years, the ruling Law and Justice Party has added a third pillar of national commemoration: the *żołnierze wyklęci*, the "accursed soldiers." These anti-Nazi partisans didn't put down arms at the end of the war but instead kept fighting against Communism. Gradually eliminated by the Stalinist security services and later condemned as "bandits," they have now been resurrected as Poland's greatest heroes. Their faces have become a ubiquitous sight in Poland, portrayed on giant murals and postage stamps. The accursed soldiers have also become a favorite of historical reenactors, who organize marches and races across the countryside in full partisan costume.

Poland's embrace of its armed anti-Communist resistance is part of a region-wide trend. In Lithuania, Latvia, and Estonia, the equivalent honors fall to the Forest Brothers, who battled the Red Army following the Soviet occupation of 1945. Romania, Albania, and Czechia likewise have networks of museums dedicated to commemorating the "crimes of totalitarianism." No country, however, has gone further than Poland in melding history with politics. A whole network of government institutions—chief among them, the Institute of National Memory— and civil society organizations exist to promote a certain view of Polish history and keep it alive.

I experienced the extent of this "reenactment complex" firsthand one day in August 2021, while on a visit with my wife and cousin to Góra Kalwaria, a small town thirty-five kilometers outside Warsaw. I was there to see the synagogue of the Ger Rebbes, Ger being the Yiddish name for the town. Between the late nineteenth century and the Second World War, the Ger dynasty, descendants of the most learned of the Kotzker Rebbe's disciples and inheritors of his spiritual authority, attracted the largest following of any Hasidic group in all of Poland. They were so popular that a special rail line was built to manage the crush of pilgrims making their way from Warsaw to see their rabbis every holy day.

Today Góra Kalwaria is a sleepy outer suburb, beloved as a pit stop by local cyclists. Its Jewish past lies largely dormant. The Ger synagogue, under the protection of Warsaw's Jewish community, is an empty husk of rain-rotted brick and officially marked: "derelict"—dangerous to enter. Birch saplings sprout from its facade. In the course of inspecting the ruin, I was surprised to hear Jazz Age ballads drift across the synagogue's abandoned courtyard. Turning the corner to Góra Kalwaria's main square, I came upon the source of the music—a big band, dressed entirely in fashion from the early 1920s.

The square was full of soldiers in uniform—the old blue-gray khakis of the first Polish army, and the dark olive fatigues of their Russian opponents from the Polish-Bolshevik war of 1920. Some of the soldiers on both sides appeared to be children. Others were old men. Artillery pieces and vintage machine guns littered the square. Toddlers played with replica rifles, while nurses tended to those acting the part of the wounded. Across the square, woman Bolsheviks in black leather riding boots strolled along the boulevard, sampling various flavors of ice cream. Everyone seemed to be enjoying themselves, and no one seemed to be fighting. A bit disappointed, I asked one of the young Chekists if the Russians were going to attack. Putting down her ice cream cone, she told me that of course they would; "the battle will begin at four o'clock."

Six months later, in February 2022, the battle began in earnest. Russia invaded Ukraine with the full force of its mechanized army. Their military entered a country that had been struggling for over thirty years to create its own version of a usable past.

Since Ukraine's independence in 1991, it has proven difficult to create a unified story for the country as a whole. Various regions of Ukraine differ not just in ethnicity and language, but in memory. They inherited different pasts from different empires. Ukraine's east had been part of the Soviet Union from its inception, and part of the Russian Empire before that. It felt close to its former home and tended to be ambivalent about a strictly Ukrainian nationalism defined along ethnic lines. Until 1939, Ukraine's far west had been a part of Poland; before that, it belonged to the Habsburg empire and Polish-Lithuanian Commonwealth. It was here, away from Russian rule, that Ukrainian national consciousness developed most fully in the late nineteenth and early twentieth centuries. In more recent times, this part of the country regarded the Soviet Union as an oppressor, and looked back fondly to the Cossack Hetmanate of the seventeenth century as the wellspring of its independence.

In recent decades, the Holodomor, the deadly famine of 1932 to 1934 that claimed some 3.9 million Ukrainian lives, has emerged as a defining event for Ukraine's national consciousness.[7] But even there, regional differences have shaped the perception of this tragedy. Although eastern Ukraine was more affected by the Great Famine than the west, the west tended to feel its legacy more deeply.[8]

Russia's attack swept away most of these distinctions and divisions. Confrontation with a real enemy has a way of solidifying a shared identity in a way that no amount of memory politics or play-acting can. Ukraine's different versions of national memory may diverge, or even contradict one another, but they are also subject to revision and open to change. The same cannot be said of the vision of Ukrainian history promoted by Russia and the Kremlin. Like many national mythologies, it too is a patchwork of different eras and epochs. It borrows the idea of the "gathering of Rus"—the program for the annexation of all East Slavic lands—from the reign of Ivan III in fifteenth-century Muscovy. Its diminution of the Ukrainian language as a dialect, and its people as "Malorossiyans," or "little Russians," descends from the late czarist era. So does the project for a "New Russia" along the Black Sea coast. Finally, the framing of the war as a campaign of denazification, waged against "fascists" and "neo-Nazis," is a perverse repurposing of Soviet propaganda from World War II.

But while the sources of this Russian story span the better part of a millennium, the message is always one of total negation. It says that

Ukraine did not exist in the past, should not exist in the present, and will not exist in the future.

Soon after the invasion of Ukraine began, the Belarusian intellectual Ihar Babkou described the ensuing conflict as "a war for diversity. A war between Central Europe and Eastern Europe."[9] I am inclined to agree, with the qualification that Babkou's Central Europe coincides with the Eastern Europe described in this book. This Eastern Europe is a land of small countries, wedged between great powers. (Put otherwise, it is Central Europe without Germany, or Babkou's Eastern Europe without Russia). It is a place that has long been dominated by empires, but it has not, for the most part, inherited an imperial frame of mind. Since the close of the nineteenth century, its politics have been dominated by nationalisms of various stripes. Its history, by contrast, has been shaped most by the clash of feuding ideologies. But that is only the story of the past hundred or so years. Eastern Europe has a longer history and older traditions to draw on in formulating its future. Largely neglected by historians, there was an Eastern Europe that existed alongside the structures imposed by empire and independent of the hopes fostered by nationalism.

This was a world of multiple faiths and languages, in which many parallel truths lived beside one another. It was a place of shared saints and intersecting stories, where folk cures and prophecies passed among neighbors, and sacred heroes donned one another's clothes. It coalesced gradually in the centuries following the introduction of monotheism— the three great religions of the Book—and the decline of paganism, which itself never disappeared completely but simply refashioned itself as the background of all later folk belief.

This Eastern Europe was not a conscious creation, but the product of open spaces and centuries of benign neglect. This was not a place where different peoples deliberately chose to live side by side, but where they did so out of long and practiced habit, enshrined more by custom than by law. Inequality—especially of class—was part of the bedrock below its foundations. But despite its not being built around principles of universal rights, this order did have its own considerable advantages. Chief among them were plurality and multiplicity—truly impressive virtues, especially if one knows what followed in their wake.

For Eastern Europe, the twentieth century was a century of barely interrupted cataclysms. The old ties that bound people together dissolved, only to be replaced with murderous aggression. As rival armies flooded into the region from east and west, neighbor killed neighbor. When the wars ended, mass expulsions and population transfers unraveled what was left of the old Eastern European tapestry.

Like a house built on top of a lava flow, the history of my family, and that of so many others, was founded on these catastrophes. If not for them, I wouldn't exist. Across the twentieth century, my ancestors included downwardly mobile aristocrats from Lithuania of Hungarian descent, illiterate peasants from the Polish heartland, patriotic Catholic bookbinders, Orthodox Jewish farmers, and Communist seamstresses. It took two consecutive, world-destroying wars for these people to meet. If it had not been for the fall of empires, the collapse of feudalism, and the rise of Communism, the various mésalliances and exchanges of status that went into their relationships would have been not only impossible, but inconceivable.

Today, even the memory of an older, more inclusive way of life seems to be ebbing away. And yet that too makes sense, as Eastern Europe is one of the world's great homelands of forgetting. Travel anywhere in this vast half-continent, and you are apt to come across abandoned temples, untended graves, and vanished sepulchers; foreign gods and other peoples' dead.

Every now and again, bits of this submerged past bubble to the surface, like flotsam from Atlantis. I've seen it in the scattered pagan groves and the ancient, honored oaks of Latvia and Lithuania, and in the particolored bits of string tied around the shrine to Koyun Baba in the woods above Babadag, Romania; in ghost signs written in Polish, Yiddish, and German in Lviv, Komarno, and the rest of Ukrainian Galicia; in overgrown caravan trails leading to the Vlach metropolis of Voskopojë, and in the shattered steps of the Armenian cathedral in Dumbrăveni. And finally, I've seen it in my paternal grandfather's native shtetl, Zambrów, where hardly a stone in the Jewish cemetery remains standing, but where the forests still harbor the wild fruits of his childhood: the "Little Diaspora Apples," whose dark juice could be used for writing the Torah; the sweet, red Rosh Hashanah apples that ripened every year in time for the new year; and the little green Kol Nidre pears that ripened a week later for Yom Kippur and fed the poorest of the poor.

To me, these fruits are memorials as much as any monument or tomb. They are fragments of a vanished world, an Eastern Europe characterized by endless diversity, whose emblems were the kaleidoscope, the chessboard, and the microcosm. Here, many peoples and faiths and languages lived together, arranging themselves in a loose symbiosis, whose bonds were nonetheless strong enough to last for centuries. It was not always a peaceful or happy world, or one devoid of prejudice. But however humble or haphazard, the mere possibility of coexistence constitutes a kind of ramshackle utopia. For Europe to have a future as a whole, it would be best not to lose sight of its promise, even as we remember the tragedy of its demise.

Acknowledgments

The road to writing this book, starting almost twenty years ago, has been a long one. Along the way, I've incurred many debts, only a fraction of which I can list here. Some of the first were to my teachers. At Princeton, Caryl Emerson introduced me to the delights of Eastern European fiction. Michael Cook taught me to think comparatively and take the wider view. John McPhee made me contemplate writing as a craft. Daniel Mendelsohn introduced me to the practice of criticism. Anthony Grafton was a model of everything a humanist, and a teacher, can aspire to be. He also read a full draft of the manuscript at a critical time, providing comments and suggestions with his usual deftness and generosity.

The Berkeley History Department has been my intellectual home for longer than I care to remember. The many friendships I made there made it a magical place to study and grow as a scholar. Margaret Lavinia Anderson made the nineteenth century come alive, and instructed me in the subtle art of teaching undergraduates. David Frick opened up Eastern Europe's neglected early modern period. István Rév inspired me in his writing and teaching to look at the twentieth century in all its moral and philosophical complexity. John Connelly has been a patient mentor and friend for years and years, and I have profited immensely from his seemingly bottomless wellspring of knowledge.

The community around the *kroužek*, Berkeley's Eastern European history working group, has been an especially stimulating one. Many ideas in this book come from conversations with its many participants and presenters, among them David Beecher, Sarah Cramsey, William Hagen, Lee and Gosia Hekking, Mark Keck-Szajbel, Harrison King, Pawel Koscielny, Andrej Milivojevic, Brandon Schechter, Agnieszka Smelkowska, Thomas Sliwowski, and Victoria Smolkin. Outside the History Department, a class on criticism taught by Greil Marcus encouraged me to look beyond academia and begin writing for a popular audience.

This book had its original genesis in an essay that first appeared in *The Los Angeles Review of Books.* I am tremendously grateful to Boris Dralyuk for editing that initial piece, and a subsequent one on Islam in Eastern Europe, and to Evan Kindley for making the connection. A grant from the Robert B. Silvers Foundation provided much-needed help while writing the book itself. *Harper's Magazine* provided support for reporting from Hungary. Doe Library on Berkeley's campus kept me supplied with a galaxy of precious materials—a service they maintained during the difficult days of the pandemic. Before the pandemic hit, many chapters were first drafted in the inviting sanctum of Souvenir Coffee on Claremont Avenue. In Portland, I benefited from the hospitality of Jean Sammis and Thom Fahrbach, and Jay and Mary Harris.

Many good friends have contributed to make this book inestimably better than it would have been without them. Frances and Randy Starn both read the whole manuscript at an early stage, providing invaluable insights and commentary—as well as many nights of delightful conviviality. I have been talking to Linda Kinstler about Eastern Europe for almost as long as I have been working on the book. Her thinking and reporting have been an inspiration. I also owe her for introducing me to the splendors of Riga. Albert Wu read a very late draft on very short notice and amended and improved it with his trademark humanity.

I am eternally grateful to Michelle Kuo for connecting me with my agent Sam Stoloff, who took on the hard work of turning a pie-in-the-sky proposal into a reality; my thanks go out to him and everyone at the Frances Goldin Literary Agency for their continued support. Thanks as well to Carrie Plitt and her team at Felicity Bryan Associates on the other side of the Atlantic. At Pantheon, Maria Goldverg saw what this book could be at the outset and guided me all the way to the finish line. Lisa Kwan shepherded the manuscript through every phase of production with great patience. At Oneworld, Cecilia Stein nudged, shaped, and molded the text in a thousand ways, making it better in every case. Rida Vaquas provided additional editing, catching errors with her eagle eye. My thanks also go to Pantheon's design department, which prepared the maps, and to its production team, led by the redoubtable Nicole Pedersen, who saved me from countless blunders, and earned themselves a case of the finest Moldovan champagne for all their hard work.

My greatest thanks and my deepest debts go to my family. Thanks first to Ryan Bresnick and Jessica Saia for being game travel companions across the backroads of Ukraine and Romania, and for innumerable acts of kindness before and since. Thanks also to Marc and Anna Bresnick, and Angela and Gene Espinoza, for welcoming me into their family.

In Poland, my cousin Maria Zawadzka and her husband, Ignacy Strączek, were perfect hosts and partners in many adventures across the Polish countryside. Ignacy's father, Tomasz, opened his home to me and generously shared his expertise on all things Balkan. In Warsaw, Anna Gren shared memories and family history. Her mother, my aunt Ewa Gren, dug up old family photos, put me up at her inn outside Zambrów, and joined me on an unforgettable trip through Lithuania. I owe much of my interest and passion for family history to her.

My parents, Piotr Berman and Sabina Mikanowska, nurtured my appetite for learning of every kind from childhood. Together, they inculcated a love for language and the past that has stayed with me my entire life. It has been my privilege to share some of their stories here.

Since I first met her nine years ago, my wife, Nik Bresnick, has heard about every version of this book, from essay to proposal to final draft. In that time, she has edited countless drafts and accompanied me on journeys everywhere from Lviv to Tirana. Nik has been a sounding board, a travel companion, an adviser, and a provider—in short, my North Star. She is my great love and the woman of my life. I feel grateful to have been able to share this adventure with her and hope dearly that there will be many more to come.

Notes

Prologue

1. Czesław Miłosz, *Native Realm: A Search for Self-Definition*, trans. Catherine R. Leach (New York: Farrar, Straus & Giroux, 1968), 20.
2. Cristian Mungiu, "The Legend of the Party Photographer," a segment in the omnibus film *Tales from the Golden Age* (Romania, 2009).
3. Robert Elsie, *A Biographical Dictionary of Albanian History* (London: I.B. Tauris, 2013), 292–93.

1. Pagans and Christians

1. Pliny the Elder, *The Natural History*, 37.11.
2. Aleksander Bursche, "Circulation of Roman Coinage in Northern Europe in Late Antiquity," *Monnaie et espace* 17, no. 3–4 (2002): 121–41.
3. The major exceptions are the Hungarians and Romanians, speakers of Finno-Ugric and Romance languages respectively, and the Balts—Lithuanians and Latvians, principally—who have their own language family, distantly related to Slavic. On the fringes of the region, Estonian is closely related to Finnish, and Albanian, although Indo-European, belongs to a group all its own.
4. Lucian Musset quoted in Florian Curta, *The Making of the Slavs: History and Archaeology of the Lower Danube Region, c. 500–700* (Cambridge: Cambridge University Press, 2011), 74.
5. Florin Curta, "The Slavic Lingua Franca (Linguistic Notes of an Archeologist Turned Historian)," *East Central Europe* 31, no. 1 (2004): 144.
6. Robert Bartlett, "Reflections on Paganism and Christianity in Medieval Europe," *Proceedings of the British Academy* 101 (1998): 69.
7. Kate Brown, *A Biography of No Place: From Ethnic Borderland to Soviet Heartland* (Cambridge, Mass.: Harvard University Press, 2005), 227.

8. Ebo and Herbordus, *The Life of Otto, Apostle of Pomerania, 1060–1139*, trans. Charles H. Robinson (London: Macmillan, 1920), 80.

9. Kurt Villads Jensen, "Sacralization of the Landscape: Converting Trees and Measuring Land in the Danish Crusades Against the Wends," in *The Clash of Cultures on the Medieval Baltic Frontier*, ed. Alan V. Murray (London: Routledge, 2020), 145.

10. Kaspars Kļaviņš, "The Significance of the Local Baltic Peoples in the Defence of Livonia (Late Thirteenth–Sixteenth Centuries)," in Murray, *Clash of Cultures*, 338.

11. Andrzej Buko, *Bodzia: A Late Viking-Age Elite Cemetery in Central Poland* (Leiden: Brill, 2014).

12. Marek Jankowiak, "Dirhams for Slaves: Investigating the Slavic Slave Trade in the Tenth Century," Medievalists.net, 2012.

13. Alternatively, "pumpkins." Martin Rady, "The Gesta Hungarorum of Anonymus, the Anonymous Notary of King Béla: A Translation," *Slavonic and East European Review* 87, no. 4 (2009): 692.

14. Dmitri Obolensky, *The Byzantine Commonwealth: Eastern Europe, 500–1453* (London: Weidenfeld & Nicolson, 1971), 88–91.

15. Peter Brown, *The Rise of Western Christendom: Triumph and Diversity, A.D. 200–1000* (Malden, Mass.: Wiley-Blackwell, 1996), 318.

16. Marvin Kantor, *The Origins of Christianity in Bohemia: Sources and Commentary* (Evanston, Ill.: Northwestern University Press, 1990), 146.

17. Richard Fletcher, *The Barbarian Conversion: From Paganism to Christianity* (Berkeley: University of California Press, 1999), 428.

18. Ryszard Grzesik, "Święty Wojciech w środkowoeuropejskiej tradycji hagiograficznej i historycznej," *Studia Źródłoznawcze* 40 (2002): 43–56, at 49.

19. Speros Vryonis, Jr., "The Byzantine Legacy in Folk Life and Tradition in the Balkans," in *The Byzantine Legacy in Eastern Europe*, ed. Lowell Clucas (New York: Columbia University Press, 1988), 124.

20. Éva Pócs, *Fairies and Witches at the Boundary of South-eastern and Central Europe* (Helsinki: Suomalainen tiedakatemia, 1989), 25.

21. Carlo Ginzburg, *The Night Battles: Witchcraft and Agrarian Cults in the Sixteenth and Seventeenth Centuries*, trans. John and Anne Tedeschi (London: Routledge & Kegan Paul, 1983), 30.

22. Carlo Ginzburg and Bruce Lincoln, *Old Thiess, a Livonian Werewolf: A Classic Case in Comparative Perspective* (Chicago: University of Chicago Press, 2020), 16.

23. Éva Pócs, *Between the Living and the Dead*, trans. Szilvia Rédey and Michael Webb (Budapest: Central European University Press, 1998), 136.

24. Ibid.

25. Beata Wojciechowska, "The Remembrance of the Deceased in the Traditional Polish Culture of the Middle Ages," in *Cultures of Death and Dying in*

Medieval and Early Modern Europe, ed. Mia Korpiola and Anu Lahtinen (Helsinki: Helsinki Collegium for Advanced Studies), 38.

26. Jan Louis Perkowski, *Vampire Lore: From the Writings of Jan Louis Perkowski* (Bloomington, Ind.: Slavica, 2006), 394.

27. Ibid., 213.

28. Tomasz Wiślicz, "The Township of Kleczew and Its Neighbourhood Fighting the Devil (1624–1700)," *Acta Poloniae Historica* 89 (2004): 74.

29. Thomas M. Bohn, "Das Gespenst von Lublau: Michael Kaspereks/Kaspareks Verwandlung vom Wiedergänger zum Blutsauger," in *Vampirismus und magia posthuma im Diskurs der Habsburgermonarchie*, ed. Christoph Augustynowicz and Ursula Reber (Vienna: LIT Verlag, 2011), 147–61.

2. Jews

1. Nathaniel Deutsch, *The Jewish Dark Continent: Life and Death in the Russian Pale of Settlement* (Cambridge, Mass.: Harvard University Press, 2011), 49.

2. "Ibrāhīm ibn Ya'qūb on Northern Europe, 965," in *Ibn Fadlān and the Land of Darkness: Arab Travellers in the Far North*, trans. Paul Lunde and Caroline Stone (London: Penguin Classics, 2012), 162–68.

3. Haya Bar-Itzhak, *Jewish Poland: Legends of Origin, Ethnopoetics and Legendary Chronicles* (Detroit: Wayne State University Press, 2001), 33.

4. Gershon David Hundert, *Jews in Poland-Lithuania in the Eighteenth Century* (Berkeley: University of California Press, 2006), 3.

5. Nathan Hanover, *Abyss of Despair* (London: Routledge, 1983), xiii.

6. Adam Teller, *Rescue the Surviving Souls: The Great Jewish Refugee Crisis of the Seventeenth Century* (Princeton, N.J.: Princeton University Press, 2020).

7. Menashe Unger, *A Fire Burns in Kotsk: A Tale of Hasidism in the Kingdom of Poland*, trans. Jonathan Boyarin (Detroit: Wayne State University Press, 2015).

8. Jiří Langer, *Nine Gates to the Chassidic Mysteries* (New York: Behrman House, 1976), 257.

9. David Assaf, ed., *Journey to a Nineteenth-Century Shtetl: The Memoirs of Yekhezkel Kotik* (Detroit: Wayne State University Press, 2002), 285.

10. Dr. Yom-Tov Levinsky, ed., *The Zambrów Memorial Book: In Memory of a Martyred Community That Was Exterminated*, trans. Jacob Solomon Berger (Mahwah, N.J.: Jacob Solomon Berger, 2016), 22.

11. Glenn Dynner, *Yankel's Tavern: Jews, Liquor, and Life in the Kingdom of Poland* (New York: Oxford University Press, 2013), 22.

12. Kacper Pobłocki, "Niewolnictwo po polsku," *Czas Kultury* 3 (2016): 60–69.

13. Levinsky, *Zambrów Memorial Book*, 272–74.

14. Judith Kalik, "Fusion vs. Alienation: Erotic Attraction, Sex, and Love Between Jews and Christians in the Polish-Lithuanian Commonwealth," in

Kommunikation durch symbolische Akte. Religiöse Heterogenität und politische Herrschaft in Polen-Litauen, ed. Yvonne Kleinmann (Stuttgart: Franz Steiner Verlag, 2010), 157–70.

15. Hundert, *Jews in Poland-Lithuania*, 144.

16. Moshe Rosman, *Founder of Hasidism: A Quest for the Historical Ba'al Shem Tov* (Berkeley: University of California Press, 1996), 120.

17. Marcin Wodziński, "Dybbuk. Z dokumentów Archiwum Głównego Akt Dawnych w Warszawie," *Literatura Ludowa* 36, no. 6 (1992): 19–29.

18. Hanna Węgrzynek, "Shvartse Khasene: Black Weddings Among Polish Jews," in *Holy Dissent: Jewish and Christian Mystics in Eastern Europe*, ed. Glenn Dynner (Detroit: Wayne State University Press, 2011).

19. Levinsky, *Zambrów Memorial Book*, 357–58.

20. Ibid., 289–90.

3. Muslims

1. Chantal Lemercier-Quelquejay, "Un condottiere lithuanien du XVIe siècle: Le prince Dimitrij Višneveckij et l'origine de la *Seč* zaporogue d'après les archives ottomanes," *Cahiers du Monde Russe et Soviétique* 10, no. 2 (1969): 257–79.

2. Robert Dankoff and Sooyong Kim, ed. and trans., *An Ottoman Traveler: Selections from the Book of Travels of Evliya Celebi* (n.p.: Eland, 2001), 170–71.

3. Catherine Wendy Bracewell, *The Uskoks of Senj: Piracy, Banditry and Holy War in the Sixteenth-Century Adriatic* (Ithaca, N.Y.: Cornell University Press, 2015), 182.

4. Safet HadžiMuhamedović, *Waiting for Elijah: Time and Encounter in a Bosnian Landscape* (New York: Berghahn Books, 2018), 135.

5. Halil Inalcik, *The Ottoman Classical Age, 1300–1600*, trans. Norman Itzkowitz and Colin Imber (London: Weidenfeld & Nicolson, 1973), 147.

6. Machiel Kiel, *Art and Society of Bulgaria in the Turkish Period* (Assen, Netherlands: Van Gorcum, 1985), 85.

7. Malcolm, *Rebels, Believers, Survivors: Studies in the History of the Albanians* (New York: Oxford University Press, 2020), 90.

8. Vlajko Palavestra, *Legends of Old Sarajevo*, trans. Mario Suško and William Tribe (Zemun: Most Art, 2000), 35.

9. Malcolm, *Rebels, Believers, Survivors*, 56.

10. Sara Kuehn, "A Saint 'on the Move': Traces in the Evolution of a Landscape of Religious Memory in the Balkans," in *Saintly Spheres and Islamic Landscapes: Emplacements of Spiritual Power Across Time and Place*, ed. D. Ephrat et al. (Leiden: Brill, 2021), 121. In addition to tombs, Sarı Saltık's followers also honored his footprints and other magical traces of his corporeal being. These shrines have continued to multiply to the present day. In 2008, believers discovered one of his footprints near the Albanian port of Sarandë; it has since become the focus of a major Bektashi shrine.

11. Elizabeta Koneska, "Shared Shrines in Macedonia," *East European Folklife Center*, no. 2 (Winter 2013), dev.eefc.org.

12. Another tradition claims that this Koyun Baba was a local shepherd, whose sheep managed to discern the hidden location of Sarı Saltık's grave in Babadag (Kuehn, "A Saint 'on the Move,'" 122–23).

13. Paulina Dominik, "Where Is the Deputy of Lehistan?" *Polonia Ottomanica* (2014), poloniaottomanica.blogspot.com.

14. Dariusz Kołodziejczyk, *Ottoman-Polish Diplomatic Relations (15th–18th Centuries): An Annotated Edition of 'Ahdnames and Other Documents* (Leiden: Brill, 2000), 134.

4. Heretics

1. Florentina Badalanova Geller, *Qur'ān in Vernacular: Folk Islam in the Balkans* (Berlin: Max Planck Institute, 2008), 1.

2. Ibid., 3.

3. Florentina Badalanova Geller, "The Bible in the Making: Slavonic Creation Stories," in *Imagining Creation,* ed. Markham J. Geller and Mineke Schipper (Leiden: Brill, 2007), 252.

4. Stanisław Vincenz, *Zwada* (Warsaw: Instytut Wydawnicy PAX, 1981), 484.

5. Michał Rozmysł, "Rubaszna mitologia, czyli huculskie kłopoty z sacrum," *Myszliciel* no. 4/5 (2013): 23–24.

6. Nikolay Antov, *The Ottoman "Wild West": The Balkan Frontier in the Fifteenth and Sixteenth Centuries* (Cambridge: Cambridge University Press, 2018), 114.

7. A millennium later many of these doctrines—especially the idea of earth being the work of a sloppy and inattentive, if not out-and-out depraved, creator—resurfaced in the works of Czesław Miłosz, Emil Cioran, and Bruno Schulz.

8. Dimitri Obolensky, *The Bogomils, a Study in Balkan Neo-Manichaeism* (Cambridge: Cambridge University Press, 1948), 137.

9. A. A. Zaliznyak, Yanin V. L., "Novgorodskij kodeks pervoi chetverti XI v. — drevneishaya kniga Rusi," *Voprosy yazykoznaniya* 5 (2001): 3–25. Much remains unclear about this startling discovery.

10. H. C. Erik Midelfort, *Mad Princes of Renaissance Germany* (Charlottesville: University of Virginia Press, 1996), 134.

11. Angelo Maria Ripellino, *Magic Prague,* trans. David Newton Marinelli (Berkeley: University of California Press, 1993), 76.

12. Annemarie Jordan Gschwend, "The Emperor's Exotic and New World Animals: Hans Khevenhüller and the Habsburg Menageries in Vienna and Prague," in *Naturalists in the Field: Collecting, Recording and Preserving the Natural World from the Fifteenth to the Twenty-First Century,* ed. Arthur MacGregor (Leiden: Brill, 2018), 76–103.

13. Lee Hendrix, "Natural History Illustration at the Court of Rudolf II," in

Rudolf II and Prague: The Court and the City, ed. Eliška Fučíková (Prague Castle Administration, 1997), 162.

14. R.J.W. Evans, *Rudolf II and His World: A Study in Intellectual History, 1576–1612* (Oxford: Clarendon Press, 1973), 32.

15. Katarzyna Brezina, "Gabinet Osobliwości Hieronima Floriana Radziwiłła w Białej," *Studia Podlaskie* 7 (Białystok, 1997), 5–20.

16. Adam Teller, *Money, Power and Influence in Eighteenth-Century Lithuania: The Jews on the Radziwiłł Estates* (Stanford, Calif.: Stanford University Press, 2016), 207.

17. R.J.W. Evans, *The Making of the Habsburg Monarchy, 1550–1700: An Interpretation* (Oxford: Clarendon Press, 1979), 361.

18. Paweł Maciejko, *The Mixed Multitude: Jacob Frank and the Frankist Movement, 1755–1816* (Philadelphia: University of Pennsylvania Press, 2011), 218.

19. Ibid.

20. Sent into exile after his conversion, Zevi died in 1676. His burial place in Ulcinj, in what is now Montenegro, soon became a place of pilgrimage for his followers. However, as often happens in Eastern Europe with figures of popular, but not official, esteem, his tombs had a way of multiplying. Berat, in Albania, also claims to be home to Zevi's tomb. The two sites are a study in contrasts. In Berat, the false messiah rests in a beautiful square, between a fine old mosque and a sumptuously decorated Sufi lodge. In Ulcinj, he is buried behind a locksmith's shop next to a parking lot. Scholars consider this latter location to have the stronger claim on being genuine.

5. Empires

1. Noel Malcolm, *Kosovo: A Short History* (New York: HarperPerennial, 1999), 46.

2. Dimiter Angelov and Judith Herrin, "The Christian Imperial Tradition—Greek and Latin," in *Universal Empire: A Comparative Approach to Imperial Culture and Representation in Eurasian History*, ed. Peter Fibiger Bang and Dariusz Kołodziejczyk (Cambridge: Cambridge University Press, 2012), 160.

3. Peter Brown, *The World of Late Antiquity* (New York: W.W. Norton, 1989), 184.

4. Halil Inalcik, *The Ottoman Empire: The Classical Age, 1300–1600*, trans. Norman Itzkowitz and Colin Imber (London: Weidenfeld & Nicolson, 1973), 29.

5. Caroline Finkel, *Osman's Dream: The History of the Ottoman Empire* (New York: Basic Books, 2005), 129.

6. "Captain Milosh and Ivan Kosanchich," in *The Battle of Kosovo: Serbian Epic Poems*, trans. John Matthias and Vladeta Vuckovic (Athens: Ohio University Press, 1987), 36.

7. Lester J. Libby, Jr., "Venetian Views of the Ottoman Empire from the Peace of 1503 to the War of Cyprus," *Sixteenth Century Journal* 9, no. 4 (1978): 103–26.

8. Bertrandon de La Brocquière, *The Travels of Bertrandon de La Brocquière, to Palestine*

and His Return from Jerusalem Overland to France, During the Years 1432 & 1433…, trans. Thomas Johnes (n.p.: Hafod Press, 1807), 292.

9. Virginia Aksan, "The One-Eyed Fighting the Blind: Mobilization, Supply, and Command in the Russo-Turkish War of 1768–1774," *International History Review* 15, no. 2 (1993): 221–38.

10. Jason Goodwin, *Lords of the Horizons: A History of the Ottoman Empire* (New York: Picador, 1998), 72.

11. Virginia H. Aksan, "Feeding the Ottoman Troops on the Danube, 1768–1774," *War and Society* 13, no. 1 (1995): 1–14.

12. Aksan, "One-Eyed Fighting the Blind," 232.

13. "The Man Who Lost One Thousand Eggs to the Tax Officials on His Way to Istanbul," in *19th Century Macedonian Folktales*, ed. Marko Cepenkov (Sydney: Macquarie University School of Modern Languages, 1991), 177.

14. Walter Zev Feldman, *Klezmer: Music, History, and Memory* (New York: Oxford University Press, 2016), 356.

15. Nina Ergin, "The Albanian Tellâk Connection: Labor Migration to the Hamams of Eighteenth-Century Istanbul, Based on the 1752 İstanbul Hamâmları Defteri," *Turcica* 43 (2011): 231–56, at 234.

16. Dariusz Kołodziejczyk, "Between Universalistic Claims and Reality: Ottoman Frontiers in the Early Modern Period," in *The Ottoman World*, ed. Christine Woodhead (London: Routledge, 2013), 216.

17. Dariusz Kołodziejczyk, *The Ottoman Survey Register of Podolia (ca. 1681)* (Cambridge, Mass.: Harvard University Press, 2004), 1.

18. Ibid., 28.

19. Dariusz Kołodziejczyk, "The 'Turkish Yoke' Revisited: The Ottoman Non-Muslim Subjects Between Loyalty, Alienation, and Riot," *Acta Poloniae Historica* 93 (2006): 184.

20. Virginia H. Aksan, *An Ottoman Statesman in War and Peace: Ahmed Resmi Efendi, 1700–1783* (Leiden: Brill, 1995), 78.

21. Dariusz Kołodziejczyk, "Khan, Caliph, Tsar and Imperator: The Multiple Identities of the Ottoman Sultan," in *Universal Empire: A Comparative Approach to Imperial Culture and Representation in Eurasian History*, ed. Peter Fibiger Bang and Dariusz Kołodziejczyk (Cambridge: Cambridge University Press, 2012), 191.

22. Once freed, the hetman, whose name was Wincenty Gosiewski, was assassinated by his own troops as part of a complicated plot whose true instigator remains unknown. Suspicion fell variously on the Radziwiłłs, the Sapiehas, and the Habsburg emperor. But the perpetrators, arrested (with my ancestor's help) in an ambush, never revealed the truth. In 1665 the mutineers were brought to Warsaw, where they were tortured with fire, beheaded, and then drawn and quartered in the Old Town Square, while members of parliament (then in session) watched.

23. Nikolai Gogol, *Taras Bulba,* trans. Peter Constantine (New York: Modern Library, 2004), 28.

24. Andreas Kappeler, *The Russian Empire: A Multiethnic History,* trans. Alfred Clayton (New York: Routledge, 2001), 64.

25. Stanisław Łubieński, *Pirat Stepowy* (Wołowiec: Wydawnictwo Czarne, 2012), 14. Freed under an amnesty, he became a monk and chose to remain in his monastery-prison, where he lived to the age of 112. He is now considered a saint by the Orthodox Church.

26. Richard Pipes, "Iurii Samarin's Baltic Escapade," *Journal of Baltic Studies* 42, no. 3 (2011): 316.

27. Kappeler, *Russian Empire,* 76.

28. Magdalena Wilkołaska-Karpierz, "Porównanie relacji pamiętnikarskich z zesłania na Syberię Fiodora Dostojewskiego i Szymona Tokarzewskiego," *Przestrzenie Teorii* 11 (2009): 239–52.

29. Wojciech Lada, *Pożytki z Katorgi* (Wołowiec: Wydawnictwo Czarne, 2019), 8.

30. The borders of the Pale shifted over time. At times, it included parts of the former Cossack Hetmanate but excluded some of its cities, like Kiev.

31. S. Ansky, *The Enemy at His Pleasure: A Journey Through the Jewish Pale of Settlement During World War I,* trans. Joachim Neugroschel (New York: Henry Holt, 2004), 261.

32. Mary Antin, *The Promised Land* (1912; reprint n.p.: CreateSpace, 2016), 14.

33. Eda Kalmre, "The Saga of the Voitka Brothers in the Estonian Press: The Rise and Fall of a Heroic Legend," *Folklore* 29 (2005): 103.

34. Jacob Marateck, *The Samurai of Vishogrod: The Notebooks of Jacob Marateck,* ed. Shimon and Anita Wincelberg (Philadelphia: Jewish Publication Society, 1976), 148.

35. Antin, *Promised Land,* 15.

36. R.J.W. Evans, *The Making of the Habsburg Monarchy, 1500–1700: An Interpretation* (Oxford: Clarendon Press, 1979), 447.

37. Joseph Roth, *The Emperor's Tomb,* trans. John Hoare (Woodstock, N.Y.: Overlook Press, 2002), 61.

38. Joseph Roth, "The Bust of the Emperor," in *The Collected Stories of Joseph Roth,* trans. Michael Hofmann (New York: W. W. Norton, 2002), 228–29.

39. András Gerő, *Emperor Francis Joseph, King of the Hungarians* (n.p.: East European Monographs, 2001), 214.

40. Martin Pollack, *Cesarz Ameryki: Wielka ucieczka z Galicji* (Wołowiec: Wydawnictwo Czarne, 2017), 192.

41. Martin Pollack, *Po Galicji* (Wołowiec: Wydawnictwo Czarne, 2017), 116.

42. Bruno Schulz, *Sanatorium Under the Sign of the Hourglass,* trans. Celina Wieniewska (New York: Mariner, 1977), 60–61.

43. Gerő, *Emperor Francis Joseph,* 196.

44. Ibid., 207.

45. István Deák, *Beyond Nationalism: A Social and Political History of the Habsburg Officer Corps, 1848–1918* (New York: Oxford University Press, 1990), 44.

46. Józef Wittlin, *Salt of the Earth* (London: Metheun & Co., 1940), 216.

47. Deák, *Beyond Nationalism,* 47.

48. Miklós Bánffy, *The Phoenix Land,* trans. Patrick Thursfield and Katalin Bánffy-Jelen (London: Arcadia, 2003), 11.

49. Deák, *Beyond Nationalism,* 203.

50. Gunther E. Rothenberg, *The Army of Francis Joseph* (West Lafayette, Ind.: Purdue University Press, 1999), 220.

6. Peoples

1. Eleanor Perényi, *More Was Lost: A Memoir* (1946; reprint New York: New York Review Books, 2016), 16.

2. Ibid., 94.

3. Ibid., 61.

4. Jerzy Stempowski, *W Dolinie Dniestru: Pisma o Ukrainie* (Warsaw: Biblioteka Więzi, 2014), 6; translated by the author.

5. Quoted in Nora Berend, *At the Gates of Christendom: Jews, Muslims and "Pagans" in Medieval Hungary, c. 1000–c. 1300* (Cambridge: Cambridge University Press, 2001), 40.

6. David Frick, *Kith, Kin, and Neighbors: Communities and Confessions in Seventeenth-Century Wilno* (Ithaca, N.Y.: Cornell University Press, 2013), 97.

7. David Rechter, *Becoming Habsburg: The Jews of Austrian Bukovina, 1774–1918* (Oxford: Littman Library of Jewish Civilization, 2013), 59.

8. In 1940, following the Molotov-Ribbentrop Pact, Jahn's players and staff were deported to Germany, along with the rest of Bukovina's Germans. The club found a new home near Stuttgart, where it now plays in the ninth division.

9. Florin Faje, "Romania," in *The Palgrave International Handbook of Football and Politics,* ed. Jean-Michel De Waele et al. (Cham, Switzerland: Palgrave Macmillan, 2018), 252.

10. Czernowitz's student fraternities (really dueling clubs) operated along similar lines but with much more fraternal feeling. There were separate associations for nationalist Germans, Catholic Germans, Romanians, Ukrainians, Poles, and Jews, as well as some pan-Austrian ones. However, despite being predicated on conflict (their members fought each other with swords), according to one of their former members, these fraternities did more to unify students than divide them. In his words, the Czernowitz duelers were "the first Europeans," having mastered the "art" of cohabitation long before

it became a "measure of European maturity." Hans Prelitsch, cited in Cristinia Florea, "City of Dreams, Land of Longing: Czernowitz and Bukovina at the Crossroads of Empires" (Ph.D. diss., Princeton University, 2016), 104.

11. Yudel Flior, *Dvinsk: The Rise and Decline of a Town* (Johannesburg: Dial Press, 1965).

12. Thomas C. Hubka, *Resplendent Synagogue: Architecture and Worship in an Eighteenth-Century Polish Community* (Waltham, Mass.: Brandeis University Press, 2003), 43.

13. Alexander Granach, *From the Shtetl to the Stage: The Odyssey of a Wandering Actor* (Abingdon, U.K.: Routledge, 2017), 7.

14. Miklós Bánffy, *They Were Counted*, vol. 1 of *The Transylvanian Trilogy*, trans. Patrick Thursfield and Katalin Bánffy-Jelen (New York: Everyman's Library, 2013), 196.

15. Maruta Lietiņa Ray, "Recovering the Voice of the Oppressed: Master, Slave, and Serf in the Baltic Provinces," *Journal of Baltic Studies* 34, no. 1 (2003): 7.

16. M. P. Dragomanov, *Notes on the Slavic Religio-Ethical Legends: The Dualistic Creation of the World*, trans. Earl W. Count (Bloomington: Indiana University Press, 1961), 136.

17. Virginia H. Aksan, *An Ottoman Statesman in War and Peace: Ahmed Resmi Efendi, 1700–1783* (Leiden: Brill, 1995), 78.

18. Conrad Ozog, "Scottish Merchants in Poland, 1550–1750," *Journal of the Sydney Society for Scottish History* 3 (1995): 53–75.

19. Alina Cała, *Wizerunek Żyda w polskiej kultury ludowej* (Warsaw: Oficyna Naukowa, 2005), 14.

20. Dragica Mugoša, "Ulcinj et ses Noirs," *Au Sud de l'Est* 6 (2010): 110–13. As recently as 2010, seven self-identified Afro-Albanians remained in Ulcinj. Some of their descendants now live in Serbia and Sweden. The main reminder of their centuries-long presence in the port at present is a mural of the well-known photographer Rizo Šurla on the steps leading to the Small Beach.

21. Mikhail Kizilov, *The Sons of Scripture: The Karaites of Poland and Lithuania in the Twentieth Century* (Berlin: Walter de Gruyter, 2015), 4.

22. Ibid., 163.

23. Ibid., 227.

24. As the story of the Karaites shows, the connection between Judaism as religion and Jewishness as ethnicity could be complex. The Szekler Sabbatarians, another Eastern European isolate, followed the same passage between the two types of identity, but in reverse. The Sabbatarians began life as an anti-Trinitarian Protestant sect in seventeenth-century Transylvania. Its members were all Szeklers, or members of Transylvania's Magyar-speaking minority. Avid readers of the Bible, they became convinced that

they should follow Jewish law, at least as set down in the Old Testament. They kept kosher and avoided work on the Sabbath. Though ostensibly Christian, their religious observance came to resemble Judaism so much that the Sabbatarians were often mistaken for Jews, and persecuted as such. When Hungary emancipated its Jews in 1867, many Sabbatarians converted to Judaism to gain legal protection. By World War II, the two groups were increasingly hard to distinguish. As a result, many Szekler Sabbatarians were sent to work in Jewish ghettos and perished in the concentration camps. Today, the Sabbatarians' main center, the village of Bözödújfalu, sits under a lake, having been flooded during the completion of a reservoir project in 1988. Gábor Győrffy et al., "Back to the Origins: The Tragic History of the Szekler Sabbatarians," *East European Politics and Societies* 32 (2018): 566–85.

7. Wanderers

1. Peter Paul Bajer, *Scots in the Polish-Lithuanian Commonwealth, 16th to 18th Centuries: The Formation and Disappearance of an Ethnic Group* (Leiden: Brill, 2012), 138.

2. Wayne S. Vucinich, "Transhumance," in *Yugoslavia and Its Historians: Understanding the Balkan Wars of the 1990s*, ed. Norman M. Naimark and Holly Case (Stanford, Calif.: Stanford University Press, 2003), 68.

3. Ibid., 73.

4. Frederick Anscombe, "Albanians and 'Mountain Bandits,'" in *The Ottoman Balkans, 1750–1830*, ed. Frederick Anscombe (Princeton, N.J.: Princeton University Press, 2006), 100.

5. Louis Ginzberg, *The Legends of the Jews*, trans. H. Szold (Philadelphia: Jewish Publication Society of America, 1925), 5:202–35; and I. Omar, "Khidr in the Islamic Traditions," *Muslim World* 83 (1993): 279–94.

6. Hirsz Abramowicz, *Profiles of a Lost World: Memoirs of East European Jewish Life Before World War II*, trans. Eva Zeitlin Dobkin, ed. Dina Abramowicz and Jeffrey Shandler (Detroit: Wayne State University Press, 1999), 90.

7. Ahmet T. Karamustafa, *God's Unruly Friends: Dervish Groups in the Islamic Later Middle Period, 1200–1550* (Oxford: Oneworld, 2006), 14.

8. Ibid., 19.

9. Ibid., 72.

10. Natalie O. Kononenko, *Ukrainian Minstrels: Why the Blind Should Sing* (New York: Routledge, 2015), 70.

11. Ibid., 71.

12. Ibid., 4.

13. Elena Mariushkova and Vesselin Popov, *Gypsies in the Ottoman Empire: A Contribution to the History of the Balkans* (Hertfordshire, U.K.: University of Hertfordshire Press, 2001), 15.

14. Elena Mariushkova, "Gypsy Slavery in Wallachia and Moldavia," in *Nationalisms Today*, ed. Tomasz Kamusella and Krzysztof Jaskulowski (Oxford: Peter Lang, 2009), 91.

15. Jerzy Ficowski, *Demony Cudzego Strachu* (Warsaw: Ludowa Społdzielnia Wydawnicza, 1986), 23. Yaron Matras, *Romani: A Linguistic Introduction* (Cambridge: Cambridge University Press, 2002), 27.

16. Among some Western Roma, this word is used more generally to mean "foreigner." Yaron Matras, *I Met Lucky People: The Story of the Romani Gypsies* (London: Allen Lane, 2014), 110.

17. Lech Mróz, *Roma-Gypsy Presence in the Polish-Lithuanian Commonwealth, 15–18th Centuries* (Budapest: Central European University Press, 2016), 93.

18. Ibid., 111.

19. Ibid., 92.

20. Jerzy Ficowski, *Cyganie na Polskich Drogach* (Warsaw: Wydawnictwo Nisza, 2013), 80.

21. Mariushkova and Popov, *Gypsies in the Ottoman Empire*, 85.

22. Viorel Achim, *The Roma in Romanian History* (Budapest: Central European University Press, 2004), 53.

23. Ibid., 33.

24. Mariushkova, "Gypsy Slavery in Wallachia and Moldavia," 8.

25. Achim, *Roma in Romanian History*, 92.

26. Ibid., 98.

27. Mariushkova and Popov, *Gypsies in the Ottoman Empire*, 85.

28. Jerzy Ficowski, *Cyganie w Polsce* (Warsaw: Wydawnictwo Interpress, 1989), 31.

29. Heinrich von Wlislocki, *Aus dem inneren Leben der Zigeuner* (Berlin: E. Felber, 1892), 182.

30. Ibid., 202.

31. Angelika Kuźniak, *Papusza* (Wołowiec: Wydawnictwo Czarne, 2013), 33.

32. Ibid., 61.

33. Ibid., 80–82.

34. Ficowski, *Cyganie na Polskich Drogach*, 340.

35. Ibid., 351.

8. Nations

1. Christopher Clark, *The Sleepwalkers: How Europe Went to War* (New York: HarperCollins, 2013), 65.

2. Ibid., 66.

3. Vladimír Macura, *The Mystifications of a Nation: "The Potato Bug" and Other Essays on Czech Culture*, trans. and ed. Hana Pichová and Craig Cravens (Madison: University of Wisconsin Press, 2010), 8.

4. Vladimír Macura, "Problems and Paradoxes of the National Revival," in

Bohemia in History, ed. Mikuláš Teich (Cambridge: Cambridge University Press, 1998), 188.

5. Josef Kajetán Tyl, quoted in Vladimír Macura, "Problems and Paradoxes of the National Revival," in *Bohemia in History*, ed. Mikuláš Teich (Cambridge: Cambridge University Press, 1998), 190.

6. Jan Fellerer, "Ukrainian Galicia at the Crossroads: The 'Ruthenian Alphabet War' of 1834," in *Studien zur Sprache und Literatur bei den Slawen: Gedenkschrift für George Y. Shevelov*, ed. Andrii Danylenko and Serhii Vakulenko (Munich: Verlag Otto Sagner, 2012), 114.

7. Robert Auty, "Orthographical Innovations and Controversies Among the Western and Southern Slavs During the Slavonic National Revival," *Slavonic and East European Review* 46, no. 107 (1968): 328.

8. Aurelija Tamošiūnaitė, "Defining 'Lithuanian': Orthographic Debates at the End of the Nineteenth Century," *Written Language and Literacy* 18, no. 2 (2015): 320.

9. Giedrius Subačius, "Lithuanian Language: An Inconvenient Uniqueness," *Passport Journal* 2 (2019): 109.

10. Łukasz Sommer, "Ile znaczeń pomieści jedna litera? Problematyczna obecność igreka w języku estońskim," in *Tożsamość tekstu, tożsamość literatury*, ed. Paweł Bem, Łukasz Cybulski, and Maria Prussak (Warsaw: Instytut Badań Literackich PAN, 2016), 191.

11. Robert Elsie, *Albanian Alphabets: Borrowed and Invented* (London: Centre for Albanian Studies, 2017), 53.

12. R.J.W. Evans, *Austria, Hungary, and the Habsburgs: Central Europe c. 1683–1867* (New York: Oxford University Press, 2008), 110.

13. Pavlína Rychterová, "The Manuscripts of Grünberg and Königinhof: Romantic Lies About the Glorious Past of the Czech Nation," in *Manufacturing a Past for the Present: Forgery and Authenticity in Medievalist Texts and Objects in Nineteenth-Century Europe*, ed. János M. Bak, Patrick J. Geary, and Gábor Klaniczay (Leiden: Brill, 2015), 16.

14. R.J.W. Evans, "'The Manuscripts': The Culture and Politics of Forgery in Central Europe," in *A Rattleskull Genius: The Many Faces of Iolo Morganwg*, ed. Geraint H. Jenkins (Cardiff: University of Wales Press, 2009), 58.

15. David Cooper, *Mystifications and Ritual Practices in the Czech National Awakening* (Seattle: National Council for Eurasian and East European Research, 2012), 12.

16. Evans, "'Manuscripts,'" 62.

17. Czesław Miłosz, *The History of Polish Literature* (Berkeley: University of California Press, 1983), 203.

18. Marcel Cornis-Pope and John Neubauer, *History of the Literary Cultures of East-Central Europe: Junctures and Disjunctures in the 19th and 20th Centuries*, vol. 4, *Types and Stereotypes* (Amsterdam: Benjamins, 2010), 25.

19. Ibid., 112.

20. Marko Juvan, "The Poetic Sacrifice: Cultural Saints and Literary Nation Building," *Frontiers of Narrative Studies* 4, no. 1 (2018): 158–65.

21. Cornis-Pope and Neubauer, *History of Literary Cultures*, 49.

22. Orest Subtelny, *Ukraine: A History* (Toronto: York University Press, 1988), 235.

23. Karel Šíma, Tomáš Kavka, and Hana Zimmerhaklová, "By Means of Singing to the Heart, by Means of Heart to the Homeland," in *Choral Societies and Nationalism in Europe*, ed. Krisztina Lajosi and Andreas Stynen (Leiden: Brill, 2019), 202.

24. Bradley Woodworth, "Patterns of Civil Society in a Modernizing Multi-ethnic City: A German Town in the Russian Empire Becomes Estonian," *Ab Imperio* 2 (2006): 147–48.

25. Gunther E. Rothenberg, *The Army of Francis Joseph* (West Lafayette, Ind.: Purdue University Press, 1998), 130.

26. Miklós Bánffy, *They Were Counted*, vol. 1 of *The Transylvanian Trilogy*, trans. Patrick Thursfield and Katalin Bánffy-Jelen (New York: Everyman's Library, 2013), 590.

27. In 2013 scholars found what may be a second Old Prussian poem, written on the margins of yet another medieval manuscript. This poem deals with a maiden, a drinking horn, and a holy linden tree. See Stephan Kessler and Stephen Mossman, "Ein Fund aus dem Jahre 1440: Ein bisher unbekannter Text in einer baltischen Sprache," *Archivum Lithuanicum* 15 (2013): 511–34.

28. Kevin Hannan, "The Lachian Literary Language of Óndra Łysohorsky," *Slavic and East European Journal* 40, no. 4 (1996): 728.

9. Moderns

1. Janina z Puttkamerów Żółtowska, *Inne czasy, inni ludzie* (London: Wydawnictwo Polska Fundacja Kulturalna, 1998), 28.

2. Ibid., 127.

3. Tom Sandqvist, *Dada East: The Romanians of Cabaret Voltaire* (Cambridge, Mass.: MIT Press, 2006), 233.

4. Eugenie Fraser, *The House by the Dvina: A Russian Childhood* (New York: Random House, 2011), 157.

5. Bánffy, *Transylvanian Trilogy* (New York: Everyman's Library, 2013), 44.

6. Béla Zombory-Moldován, *The Burning of the World: A Memoir of 1914*, trans. Peter Zombory-Moldován (New York: New York Review Books, 2014), 12.

7. Bertram Wolfe, "War Comes to Russia," *Russian Review* 22, no. 2 (1963): 126.

8. István Deák, *Beyond Nationalism: A Social and Political History of the Habsburg Officer Corps, 1848–1918* (New York: Oxford University Press, 1990), 191.

9. Alexander Watson, *The Fortress: The Great Siege of Przemysl* (London: Allen Lane, 2019), 76. By the end of 1914, total Austro-Hungarian casualties exceeded 850,000.

10. R.J.W. Evans, "Language and State Building: The Case of the Habsburg Monarchy," *Austrian History Yearbook* 35, no. 1 (2004): 18.

11. Piotr Szewc, *Ocalony na Wschodzie: z Julianem Stryjkowskim Rozmawia Piotr Szewc* (Montricher, Switzerland: Editions Noir sur Blanc, 1991), 31.

12. Deák, *Beyond Nationalism*, 184.

13. Eleanor Perényi, *More Was Lost: A Memoir* (1946; reprint New York: New York Review Books, 2016), 116.

14. Gyula Krúdy, *Krúdy's Chronicles: Turn-of-the-Century Hungary in Gyula Krúdy's Journalism*, ed. and trans. John Bátki (Budapest: Central European University Press, 2000), 252.

15. Dezső Kosztolányi, *Anna Édes*, trans. George Szirtes (New York: New Directions Books, 1991), 1.

16. Orest Subtelny, *Ukraine: A History* (Toronto: York University Press, 1988), 359.

17. T. J. Clark, *Farewell to an Idea: Episodes from a History of Modernism* (New Haven, Conn.: Yale University Press, 1999), 237.

18. After Stalin purged Bukharin in 1937, the street was renamed yet again, this time for "Truth." Aleksandra Semenovna Shatskikh, *Vitebsk: The Life of Art* (New Haven, Conn.: Yale University Press, 2007), 27.

19. Peter Demetz, *The Air Show at Brescia 1909* (New York: Farrar, Straus & Giroux, 2002), viii.

20. Geoffrey Wawro, *A Mad Catastrophe: The Outbreak of World War I and the Collapse of the Habsburg Empire* (New York: Basic Books, 2014), 232.

21. S. Ansky, *The Enemy at His Pleasure: A Journey Through the Jewish Pale of Settlement During World War I*, ed. and trans. Joachim Neugroschel (New York: Henry Holt, 2002), 182.

22. Isaac Babel, *1920 Diary* (New Haven, Conn.: Yale University Press, 2002), 18.

23. K. S. Malevich, *Essays on Art: 1915–1933*, ed. Troels Andersen, trans. Xenia Glowacki-Prus and Arnold McMillin (New York: George Wittenborn, 1971), 1: 122.

24. Zółtowska, *Inne czasy*, 50.

25. Stefan Zweig, *The World of Yesterday: An Autobiography*, trans. Anthea Bell (1943; reprint Lincoln: University of Nebraska Press, 1964), 23.

26. Danilo Kiš, *Garden, Ashes*, trans. William J. Hannaher (New York: Harcourt, 1975), 122.

27. "Ich, Anna Csillag—ein k.k. Marketingstar," Biographie des Monats, n.d., oeaw.ac.at.

28. Josef Greiner, *Das Ende des Hitler-Mythos* (Vienna: Amalthea-Verlag, 1947), cited in *Poemas del Río Wang*, riowang.blogspot.com.

10. Prophets

1. Jerzy Stempowski, *W dolinie Dniestru: Pisma o Ukrainie* (Warsaw: Biblioteka Więzi, 2014), 22.

2. Robert Gerwarth, *The Vanquished: Why the First World War Failed to End, 1917–1923* (London: Allen Lane, 2016), 150.

3. Paul Hanebrink, *A Specter Haunting Europe: The Myth of Judeo-Bolshevism* (Cambridge, Mass.: Harvard University Press, 2018), 70.

4. István Deák, "Hungary," in *The European Right: A Historical Profile*, ed. Hans Rogger and Eugen Weber (Berkeley: University of California Press, 1965), 384.

5. Ibid., 385.

6. Eugen Weber, "Romania," in *The European Right: A Historical Profile*, ed. Hans Rogger and Eugen Weber (Berkeley: University of California Press, 1965), 519.

7. Roland Clark, *Holy Legionary Youth: Fascist Activism in Interwar Romania* (Ithaca, N.Y.: Cornell University Press, 2015), 78.

8. Ibid., 79.

9. Radu Ioanid, *The Sword of the Archangel: Fascist Ideology in Romania*, trans. Peter Heinegg (Boulder, Colo.: Eastern European Monographs, 1990), 141.

10. Marta Petreu, *An Infamous Past: E. M. Cioran and the Rise of Fascism in Romania*, trans. Bogdan Alden (Chicago: Ivan R. Dee, 2005), 40.

11. Roland Clark, *Holy Legionary Youth: Fascist Activism in Interwar Romania* (Ithaca, N.Y.: Cornell University Press, 2015), 139.

12. Mihail Sebastian, *Journal 1935–1944: The Fascist Years*, trans. Patrick Camiller (Lanham, Md.: Rowman & Litttlefield, 1998), 78.

13. Ibid., 337.

14. Weber, "Romania," 538.

15. Aleksander Wat, *My Century: The Odyssey of a Polish Intellectual*, ed. and trans. Richard Lourie (1977; reprint New York: New York Review Books, 2003), 18.

16. Ibid.

17. Deák, "Hungary," 366.

18. Wat, *My Century*, 11.

19. Ibid., 4.

20. Bruno Jasieński, *The Legs of Izolda Morgan: Selected Writings*, trans. Soren Gauger and Guy Torr (Prague: Twisted Spoon Press, 2016), 59.

21. Bruno Jasieński, *I Burn Paris*, trans. Soren Gauger (Prague: Twisted Spoon Press, 2017), 297.

22. Ibid., 304.

23. Marci Shore, *Caviar and Ashes: A Warsaw Generation's Life and Death in Marxism, 1918–1968* (New Haven, Conn.: Yale University Press, 2006), 106.

24. Panaït Istrati, *Kyra Kyralina*, trans. Christopher Sawyer-Lauçanno (Northfield, Mass.: Talisman House, 2010), 3.

25. Stelian Tanase, "The Renegade Istrati," trans. Alistair Ian Blyth, *Archipelago* 10–12 (n.d.), archipelago.org.

26. Ibid.

27. Panaït Istrati, "Final Exchange with Romain Rolland," trans. Mitchell Abidor, marxists.org.

28. Włodzimierz Pawluczuk, *Wierszalin: Reportaż o końcu świata* (Kraków: Wydawnictwo Literackie, 1974).

11. War

1. Árpád von Klimó, *Remembering Cold Days: The 1942 Massacre of Novi Sad and Hungarian Politics and Society, 1942–1989* (Pittsburgh: University of Pittsburgh Press, 2018), 68.

2. Romania actually possessed Bessarabia and Bukovina until 1939, when it was forced to surrender them to the Soviet Union as part of the Molotov-Ribbentrop Pact. As a result of this deal between Nazi Germany and the USSR, the Soviet Union also claimed eastern Poland in 1939 and Lithuania, Latvia, and Estonia in 1940. The Nazis subsequently conquered all these territories in 1941, only for the Red Army to retake them in 1944–45.

3. John Connelly, *From Peoples into Nations: A History of Eastern Europe* (Princeton, N.J.: Princeton University Press, 2020), 486.

4. Mihail Sebastian, *Journal 1935–1944: The Fascist Years*, trans. Patrick Camiller (Lanham, Md.: Rowman & Littlefield, 1998), 315–16.

5. Ota Pavel, *How I Came to Know Fish*, trans. Robert McDowell and Jindriska Badal (New York: New Directions, 1991), 96.

6. Jiří Weil, *Life with a Star*, trans. Rita Klimova and Roslyn Schloss (Evanston, Ill.: Northwestern University Press, 1998), 179.

7. The Slovak government formed by the Catholic priest Joseph Tiso might more accurately be described as clerical-authoritarian, but it followed many of the same racial policies as Croatia's outrightly fascist Ustaše.

8. Edward Dębicki, *Ptak umarłych* (Warsaw: Bellona, 2007), 99.

9. Jacek Leociak, *Tekst wobec zagłady: O relacjach z getta warszawskiego* (Wrocław: Wydawn. Leopoldinum Fundacji dla Uniwersytetu Wrocławskiego, 1997), 93.

10. Jacek Leociak, *Text in the Face of Destruction: Accounts from the Warsaw Ghetto Reconsidered* (Warsaw: Żydowski Instytut Historyczny, 2004), 76.

11. RING. I/470. Mf. ŻIH—786; USHMM—17. RING. I (first part of the

Ringelblum Archive, unearthed in 1946). Mf. (Microfilm) ŻIH (Żydowski Instytut Historyczny Warszawie). USHMM (United States Holocaust Memorial Museum). Further information on this document can be found in eds. Robert Moses Shapiro and Tadeusz Epsztein, *The Warsaw Ghetto Oyneg-Shabes-Ringelblum Archive: Catalog and Guide* (Bloomington: Indiana University Press, 2009), 122.

12. A report compiled by the underground government, investigating the participation of Polish police officers in the execution of Jews, completes the picture: "The execution was even worse than the previous one: the victims, badly tied to the poles wriggled themselves and resisted, the execution was carried out in two rounds, so a part of the condemned were waiting for the execution of the sentence on the first round. The police shot badly, the first time they gave two volleys, at the second execution—three. In both cases the condemned ones had to be finished off." Sylwia Szymanska-Smolkin, "Fateful Decisions: The Polish Policemen and the Jewish Population of Occupied Poland, 1939–1945," Ph.D. diss., University of Toronto, 2017, 110.

13. Dr. Yom-Tov Levinsky, ed., *The Zambrów Memorial Book: In Memory of a Martyred Community That Was Exterminated*, trans. Jacob Solomon Berger (Mahwah, N.J.: Jacob Solomon Berger, 2016), 74.

14. Ibid., 104.

15. Jan Grabowski, *Hunt for the Jews: Betrayal and Murder in German-Occupied Poland* (Bloomington: Indiana University Press, 2013).

16. Joanna Tokarska-Bakir, *Okrzyki Pogromowe* (Wołowiec: Wydawnictwo Czarne, 2012), 21.

17. Jan Grabowski, *Rescue for Money: Paid Helpers in Poland, 1939–1945* (Jerusalem: Yad Vashem, 2008), 36.

18. Jan Tomasz Gross and Irena Grudzińska Gross, *Golden Harvest: Events at the Periphery of the Holocaust* (New York: Oxford University Press, 2012), 77.

19. Anna Bikont, "Zagłada Żydów ze wsi Strzegom," *Gazeta Wyborcza*, December 4, 2014.

20. Gross and Gross, *Golden Harvest*, 83.

21. This makes it the highest casualty rate of any country in Europe, followed by Lithuania at 90 percent, Czechoslovakia 85 percent, Greece 80 percent, Austria 77 percent, Hungary 75 percent, Latvia 75 percent, Yugoslavia 73 percent, Romania 47 percent, and Bulgaria 10 percent. Albania's Jewish population, only a few hundred strong in 1939, actually increased over the course of the war, as the country took in refugees from Germany and elsewhere.

22. This isn't as crazy as it sounds with the benefit of hindsight. In the fall of 1939, things in the Soviet zone were hardly great, and no one knew for sure what the future held. My mother's uncle Turnowski crossed the border in 1939 as well, with two of his friends. One died of hunger in Minsk, while the other, sick with tuberculosis, returned to the German zone on his own.

23. Tokarska-Bakir, *Okrzyki Pogromowe*, 161.

24. Ibid., 146.

25. Ibid., 145, 169–70.

26. Alina Cała, *Wizerunek Żyda w polskiej kulturze ludowej* (Warsaw: Oficyna Naukowa, 2005), 196.

12. Stalinism

1. Beata Chomątowska, *Stacja Muranów* (Wołowiec: Wydawnictwo Czarne, 2012), 11.

2. The Polish term *szybkościowiec* is a coinage from the Stalinist era that has not survived to the present day.

3. Chomątowska, *Stacja Muranów*, 11.

4. Ibid., 241.

5. Vincas Krėvė-Mickevičius, "Conversations with Molotov," *Lituanus* 11, no. 2 (Summer 1965), lituanus.org.

6. Sigrid Rausing, *Everything Is Wonderful: Memories of a Collective Farm in Estonia* (New York: Grove Press, 2014), 83.

7. Soviet mass deportations from the Baltic states continued after the war, encompassing some 90,000 people in 1949 alone.

8. Bradley Abrams, *The Struggle for the Soul of the Nation: Czech Culture and the Rise of Communism* (Lanham, Md.: Rowman & Littlefield, 2005), 12.

9. John Connelly, *Captive University: The Sovietization of East German, Czech and Polish Higher Education, 1945–1956* (Chapel Hill: University of North Carolina Press, 2000), 118.

10. Milan Kundera, *The Joke* (1967; reprint London: Faber & Faber, 1992), 31.

11. Bohumil Hrabal, *Mr. Kafka and Other Tales from the Time of the Cult*, trans. Paul Wilson (New York: New Directions, 2015), 139.

12. Ibid., 19.

13. Ibid., 73.

14. Katherine Lebow, *Unfinished Utopia: Nowa Huta, Stalinism and Polish Society, 1949–56* (Ithaca, N.Y.: Cornell University Press, 2013), 74.

15. Zora Rusinová, "The Embodiment of Communist Utopia: Socialist Realism in Slovakia, 1948–1956, in *A Reader in East-Central-European Modernism*, ed. Beáta Hock et al. (London: Courtauld Institute, 2019), 416.

16. Pavel Janáček, "From Literature Censored by Poets to Literature Censored by the Party: Censorship in the Czech Literary Culture of 1945–1955," in *Socialist Realism in Central and Eastern European Literatures Under Stalin: Institutions, Dynamics, Discourses*, ed. Evgeny Dobrenko and Natalia Jonsson-Skradol (London: Anthem Press, 2018), 64.

17. This became the subject of Hrabal's novel *Too Loud a Solitude*, which he self-published in 1976.

18. Michał Jan Bednarczyk, "Cały kraj serdecznie wita swego pierwszego obywatela. Przebieg obchodów 60. rocznicy urodzin Bolesława Bieruta na łamach Trybuny Ludu," *Annales Universitatis Mariae Curie-Skłodowska sectio F—Historia* 69, nos. 1–2 (2014): 65.

19. Balázs Apor, *The Invisible Shining: The Cult of Mátyás Rákosi in Stalinist Hungary, 1945–1956* (Budapest: Central European University Press, 2017), 165.

20. Ibid., 157.

21. Tania Vladova, "Heritage and the Image of Forgetting: The Mausoleum of Georgi Dimitrov in Sofia," in *Heritage, Ideology, and Identity in Central and Eastern Europe: Contested Pasts, Contested Presents,* ed. Matthew Rampley (Newcastle, U.K.: Newcastle University Press, 2012), 144.

22. Luděk Vacín, "Náš pracující lid nedal setlíti tělu Klementa Gottwalda—příspěvek k dějinám pražského mauzolea," *STUDIE securitas imperii,* n.d., ustrcr.cz.

23. Jan Kužník, "Pátrejte s námi po stopách Gottwaldovy mumie," iDnes.cz, November 7, 2005.

24. Ibid.

25. John Connelly, *From Peoples into Nations: A History of Eastern Europe* (Princeton, N.J.: Princeton University Press, 2020), 555.

26. Vladimír Macura, *The Mystifications of a Nation: The "Potato Bug" and Other Essays on Czech Culture,* ed. and trans. Hana Píchová and Craig Cravens (Madison: University of Wisconsin Press, 2010), 57.

27. István Rèv, "In Mendacio Veritas," *Representations 35* (Summer 1991), 9.

28. István Rèv, "The Truth Is the Whole," unpublished manuscript.

29. Rèv, "In Mendacio Veritas," 11.

30. Ivo Banac, *With Stalin Against Tito: Cominformist Splits in Yugoslav Communism* (Ithaca, N.Y.: Cornell University Press, 1988), 250.

31. Connelly, *From Peoples into Nations,* 538.

32. John Le Carré, "The Madness of Spies," *The New Yorker,* September 29, 2008.

33. P. T. Petrikov, Instytut historyi (Akademiia navuk Belaruskaĭ SSR), *Istoriia rabochego klassa Belorusskoĭ SSR v chetyrekh tomakh,* vol. 3 (Minsk: Nauka i tekhnika, 1984), 209.

34. Piotr Lipiński, *Kroków siedem do końca* (Wołowiec: Wydawnictwo Czarne, 2020), 259.

35. Tomáš Petráček, "The First and Second Life of Father Josef Toufar (1902–1950) and Shifts in Interpretations of Modern Czech History," *Kirchliche Zeitgeschichte* 29, no. 2 (2016): 358.

36. The 1968 investigation forms the backdrop for Josef Skvorecky's novel *The Miracle Game.*

37. Agnieszka Halemba and Konrad Siekierski, "Apparitions of the Mother of God in Soviet Poland in the Early Years of the Cold War," in *Cold War Mary:*

Ideologies, Politics, Marian Devotional Culture, ed. Peter Jan Margry (Leuven, Belgium: Leuven University Press, 2021), 196.

38. Maciej Krzywosz, *Cuda w Polsce Ludowej: studium przypadku prywatnego objawienia maryjnego w Zabłudowie* (Białystok: Instytut Pamięci Narodowej, Oddział w Białymstoku, 2016), 98.

39. Ibid., 106.

40. Dariusz Jarosz, "Pogłoski jako wyraz świadomości potocznej chłopów w Polsce w latach 1949–1956," *Dzieje Najnowsze* 25, no. 3 (1993): 53.

41. Halemba and Siekierski, "Apparitions of Mother of God," 199.

13. Socialism

1. Katarzyna Maniewska, "Toast na cześć…Reakcje społeczne na śmierć Józefa Stalina i kampania propagandowa wokół uroczystości żałobnych w województwie bydgoskim w marcu 1953 r.," *Dzieje najnowsze* 48, no. 2 (2016): 117.

2. Ibid., 120.

3. György Faludy, *My Happy Days in Hell* (1962; reprint New York: Penguin Classics, 2010), 510.

4. Ibid., 313.

5. Jonathan Bolton, *Worlds of Dissent: Charter 77, The Plastic People of the Universe, and Czech Culture Under Communism* (Cambridge, Mass.: Harvard University Press, 2012), 279.

6. Ludvík Vaculík, *A Cup of Coffee with My Interrogator: The Prague Chronicles of Ludvík Vaculík,* trans. George Theiner (London: Readers International, 1987), 51.

7. Bolton, *Worlds of Dissent,* 80.

8. Bohumil Hrabal, *Gaps,* trans. Tony Liman (Evanston, Ill.: Northwestern University Press, 2011), 122.

9. Mariusz Szczygieł, *Gottland: Mostly True Stories from Half of Czechoslovakia,* trans. Antonia Lloyd-Jones (New York: Melville House, 2014), 144.

10. Ibid., 138.

11. Bolton, *Worlds of Dissent,* 240.

12. Ibid., 230.

13. Katherine Verdery, *Secrets and Truths: Ethnography in the Archive of Romania's Secret Police* (Budapest: Central European University Press, 2014), 165.

14. Małgorzata Rejmer, *Błoto słodsze niż miód* (Wołowiec: Wydawnictwo Czarne, 2018), 144.

15. Bolton, *Worlds of Dissent,* 104.

16. Ewa Zając and Henryk Głębocki, ed., *"Ketman" i "Monika"—Żywoty równoległe* (Warsaw: Instytut Pamięci Narodowej, 2005), 184.

17. "Typewriter," *Martor: The Museum of the Romanian Peasant Anthropological Review* 7 (2002): 181.

18. Bolton, *Worlds of Dissent*, 239.

19. Cristina Vatulescu, *Police Aesthetics: Literature, Film, and the Secret Police in Soviet Times* (Stanford, Calif.: Stanford University Press, 2010), 52.

20. Verdery, *Secrets and Truths*, 63.

21. Vatulescu, *Police Aesthetics*, 48.

22. Bolton, *Worlds of Dissent*, 84.

23. Vaculík, *Cup of Coffee*, 10.

24. Bolton, *Worlds of Dissent*, 250.

25. Joanna Siedlecka, "Oporów moralnych nie zdradzał," *Rzeczpospolita*, April 7, 2007.

26. Herta Müller, *The Appointment*, trans. Philip Boehm (New York: Picador, 2002), 214.

27. George Konrád, *The City Builder* (Champaign, Ill.: Dalkey Archive Press, 2007), 82.

28. "Political," *Martor* 7 (2002): 123.

29. "Queue," *Martor* 7 (2002): 138.

30. Robert Cochran, "'What Courage!': Romanian 'Our Leader' Jokes," *The Journal of American Folklore* 102, no. 405 (1989): 259–274, at 264.

31. "Facade," *Martor* 7 (2002): 63.

32. "Visit," *Martor* 7 (2002): 185.

33. Shannon Woodcock, "The Absence of Albanian Jokes About Socialism, or Why Some Dictatorships Are Not Funny," in *The Politics and Aesthetics of Refusal*, ed. Caroline Hamilton et al. (Newcastle upon Tyne, U.K.: Cambridge Scholars, 2007), 55.

34. Valbona Bezati, "How Albania Became the World's First Atheist Country," *Balkan Transitional Justice*, August 28, 2019.

35. Nathalie Clayer, "Saints and Sufis in Post-Communist Albania," in *Popular Movements and Democratization in the Islamic World*, ed. Masatoshi Kisaichi (London: Routledge, 2006), 36.

36. Rejmer, *Błoto słodsze niż miód*, 30.

37. Idrit Idrizi, "Magic Apparatus and Window to the Foreign World? The Impact of Television and Foreign Broadcasts on Society and State-Society Relations in Socialist Albania," in *Television Beyond and Across the Iron Curtain*, ed. Kirsten Bönker, Julia Obertreis, and Sven Grampp (Newcastle upon Tyne, U.K.: Cambridge Scholars, 2016), 238.

38. Shannon Woodcock, *Life Is War: Surviving Dictatorship in Communist Albania* (Bristol, U.K.: Hammeron Press, 2016), 117.

39. "On the Introduction of Foreign Citizens in the People's Republic of Albania," Instruction no. 7, April 25, 1975. Violations of socialist aesthetics included "men with hair like women," "exaggerated sideburns," "irregular

beards," and "inappropriate clothing." Women were forbidden to wear "mini and maxi skirts."

40. Rejmer, *Błoto Słodsze niż miód*, 193.
41. Ibid., 103.
42. Woodcock, *Life Is War*, 98.
43. "Collection," *Martor* 7 (2002): 45.
44. Zbigniew Czwartosz, "On Queueing," *European Journal of Sociology* 42, no. 1 (2001): 183–84.
45. Joseph Hraba, "Consumer Shortages in Poland: Looking Beyond the Queue into a World of Making Do," *Sociological Quarterly* 26, no. 3 (1985): 399–400.
46. Leszek Dzięgiel, *Paradise in a Concrete Cage: Daily Life in Communist Poland: An Ethnologist's View* (Kraków: Arcana, 1998), 34.
47. Hraba, "Consumer Shortages in Poland," 393.
48. Jill Massino, "From Black Caviar to Blackouts: Gender, Consumption, and Lifestyle in Ceaușescu's Romania," in *Communism Unwrapped: Consumption in Cold War Eastern Europe*, ed. Paulina Bren and Mary Neuburger (New York: Oxford University Press, 2012), 248.
49. "Cigarettes," *Martor* 7 (2002): 42.
50. "Nechezol," *Martor* 7 (2002): 109.
51. Ibid.

14. Thaw

1. Gabriel Meretik, *Noc generała* (1989; reprint Warsaw: Dowody na Istnienie, 2014), 179.
2. John Connelly, *From Peoples into Nations: A History of Eastern Europe* (Princeton, N.J.: Princeton University Press, 2020), 703.
3. Meretik, *Noc generała*, 56.
4. Ibid., 83.
5. Connelly, *From Peoples into Nations*, 731.
6. Henri Vogt, *Between Utopia and Disillusionment: A Narrative of Political Transformation in Eastern Europe* (New York: Berghahn Books, 2005), 22.
7. Guntis Šmidchens, *The Power of Song: Nonviolent National Culture in the Baltic Singing Revolution* (Seattle: University of Washington Press, 2014), 244.
8. Padraic Kenney, *A Carnival of Revolutions: Central Europe 1989* (Princeton, N.J.: Princeton University Press, 2002), 271.
9. Andrzej Łomanowski, "Mołojecka Sława," *Gazeta Wyborcza*, August 12, 1990.
10. Gale Stokes, *The Walls Came Tumbling Down: Collapse and Rebirth in Eastern Europe* (New York: Oxford University Press, 2011), 123.
11. István Rév, *Retroactive Justice: Prehistory of Post-Communism* (Stanford, Calif.: Stanford University Press, 2005), 30.

12. Małgorzata Takacs, "Nowy przywódca węgierskich komunistów: 'Nie jestem chory psychicznie,'" *Gazeta Wyborcza*, October 15, 1989.

13. Marian Orlikowski, "Inna Sofia," *Gazeta Wyborcza*, May 18, 1990.

14. James Krapfl, *Revolution with a Human Face: Politics, Culture and Community in Czechoslovakia, 1989–1992* (Ithaca, N.Y.: Cornell University Press, 2013), 42.

15. "Party Brews in Czechoslovakia," Associated Press, February 13, 1990.

16. Małgorzata Rejmer, *Błoto słodsze niż miód* (Wołowiec: Wydawnictwo Czarne, 2018), 303.

17. "Mur w Tiranie," *Gazeta Wyborcza*, March 8, 1990.

18. Rév, *Retroactive Justice*, 27.

19. Serguei Alex Oushakine, "Postcolonial Estrangements: Claiming a Space Between Stalin and Hitler," in *Rites of Place: Public Commemoration in Russia and Eastern Europe*, ed. Julie Buckler and Emily D. Johnson (Evanston, Ill.: Northwestern University Press, 2013), 304.

20. Robert M. Hayden, "Recounting the Dead: The Discovery and Redefinition of Wartime Massacres in Late- and Post-Communist Yugoslavia," in *Memory, History and Opposition Under State Socialism*, ed. Rubie S. Watson (Santa Fe: School of American Research Press, 1994), 179.

21. Katherine Verdery, *The Political Lives of Dead Bodies: Reburial and Postsocialist Change* (New York: Columbia University Press, 2000), 18.

22. Wojciech Tochman, *Like Eating a Stone: Surviving the Past in Bosnia*, trans. Antonia Lloyd-Jones (New York: Atlas, 2008), 103.

23. Stokes, *Walls Came Tumbling*, 233.

24. Misha Glenny, *The Fall of Yugoslavia: The Third Balkan War* (New York: Penguin, 1992), 12.

25. Marie-Janine Calic, *A History of Yugoslavia* (West Lafayette, Ind.: Purdue University Press, 2019), 478.

26. Mladen Vuksanović, *From Enemy Territory: Pale Diary* (Ann Arbor: University of Michigan Press, 2004), 103.

27. Hikmet Karcic, "How Denial of Bosnian War Crimes Entered the Mainstream," *Balkan Transitional Justice*, June 30, 2020.

28. This particular lie enjoyed much credence for a time. A Bosnian Serb spokeswoman even brought it up in talks with the visiting head of the UNHCR. David Rieff, *Slaughterhouse: Bosnia and the Failure of the West* (New York: Simon & Schuster, 1995), 99.

29. John F. Burns, "Sarajevo Journal: In the Zoo's House of Horrors, One Pitiful Bear," *New York Times*, October 16, 1992.

30. Zlatko Dizdarević, *Portraits of Sarajevo*, trans. Midhat Ridjanović, ed. Ammiel Alcalay (New York: Fromm International, 1994), 87.

31. Marian Orlikowski, "Inna Sofia," *Gazeta Wyborcza*, May 18, 1990.

32. Chris Hann, "Notes on the Transition in Tázlár," *Cambridge Journal of Anthropology* 15, no. 3 (1991): 1–21, at 17.

33. Mariusz Szczygieł, ed., *20 lat nowej Polski w reportażach według Mariusza Szczygła* (Wołowiec: Wydawnictwo Czarne, 2009), 9–12.

34. Bernadette McDonald, *Freedom Climbers: The Golden Age of Polish Mountain Climbing* (Seattle: Mountaineers Books, 2013), 58.

35. Piotr Lipiński and Michał Matys, *Niepowtarzalny urok likwidacji* (Wołowiec: Wydawnictwo Czarne, 2018), 39.

36. Roch Sulima, "The Laboratory of Polish Postmodernity: An Ethnographic Report from the Stadium-Bazaar," in *Chasing Warsaw: Socio-Material Dynamics of Urban Change Since 1990*, ed. Monika Grubbauer and Joanna Kusiak (Frankfurt am Main: Campus Verlag, 2012), 252.

37. Ewa Tartakowsky, "Le Juif à la pièce d'argent," *La Vie des idées*, January 10, 2017.

38. Katherine Verdery, "Faith, Hope, and *Caritas* in the Land of the Pyramids: Romania, 1990 to 1994," *Comparative Studies in Society and History* 37, no. 4 (1995): 625–69, at 653.

39. Ibid., 656.

Epilogue

1. Alícia Adserá et al., "Transition, Height and Well-Being," EBRD Working Paper no. 24, European Bank for Reconstruction and Development, September 15, 2019.

2. Kairi Kõlves, "Suicide Rates and Socioeconomic Factors in Eastern European Countries After the Collapse of the Soviet Union: Trends Between 1990 and 2008," *Sociology of Health and Illness* 35, no. 6 (2013): 956–70.

3. Sergei Guriev and Nikita Melnikov, "Happiness Convergence in Transition Countries," *Journal of Comparative Economics* 46, no. 3 (2018): 683–707.

4. Weronika Gogola, *UFO nad Bratysławą* (Wołowiec: Wydawnictwo Czarne, 2021), Kindle, chapter titled "Słowacki król, przed którym drżał świat."

5. Henadz Sahanovich, "The Heritage of the Grand Duchy of Lithuania in the Belarusian Policies of Memory Under the Lukašenka Regime," unpublished paper presented at the 13th Annual Session of Warsaw East European Conference, Warsaw, July 18–21, 2016. Some scholars contend that Vseslav was merely a shape-shifter who could assume the form of a wolf. See Carlo Ginzburg and Bruce Lincoln, *Old Thiess, a Livonian Werewolf: A Classic Case in Comparative Perspective* (Chicago: University of Chicago Press, 2020), 135–38.

6. Hungary's Constitution of 2011, constituteproject.org.

7. This estimate comes from the work of a team of Ukrainian demographers, who estimate 3.9 million direct losses from the famine in Soviet Ukraine, and an additional 0.6 million indirect ones. O. Rudnytski, N. Levchuk, O. Wolowyna, and P. Shevchuk, "Famine Losses in Ukraine in 1932 and 1933 Within the Context of the Soviet Union," in *Famines in European Economic History: The Last Great European Famines Reconsidered*, ed. Andrew G. Newby, Declan Curran, and Lubomyr Luciuk (Abingdon, U.K.: Routledge, 2015), 168.

8. Andreas Kappeler, "From an Ethnonational to a Transnational Ukrainian History," in *A Laboratory of Transnational History: Ukraine and Recent Ukrainian Historiography*, ed. Georgiy Kasianov and Philipp Ther (Budapest: Central European University Press, 2009), 55.

9. Ihar Babkou, "Of Fish and People," *Eurozine*, April 20, 2022, eurozine.com.

Index

Page numbers in *italics* refer to captions.

Illustration Credits

Page 3: Photograph by Leopold Węgrzynowicz. Collection of Seweryn Udziela Ethnographic Museum of Kraków.

Page 22: Drawing by Nik Bresnick. Collection of the Princeton University Art Museum.

Page 23: Collection of the Museum of Photography in Kraków.

Page 34: Drawing by Zygmunt Gloger, from *Budownictwo drzewne i wyroby z dzrewa w dawnej Polsce*, vol. 1 (Warsaw: 1907). Wikimedia Commons.

Page 42: balkanmuslims.tumblr.com.

Page 59: Drawing by Nik Bresnick.

Page 60: Photograph © Piotr Lisiecki. Courtesy of Piotr Lisiecki.

Page 66: Photograph by Jens Mohr. Courtesy of Skokloster Castle, Sweden, in cooperation with Wikimedia Sverige.

Page 79: Collection of the British Museum, London.

Page 107: Designed by Koloman Moser for the sixtieth anniversary of the emperor's reign, 1908. Author's collection.

Page 109: *(left)* Photograph by the American Red Cross. Library of Congress, Washington D.C.; *(right)* photograph courtesy of Foto Fortepan, donated by GGAABBOO.

Page 123: *(left)* Collection of the Ethnological Archive of the Museum of the Romanian Peasant, Bucharest; *(right)* Varka Michadiuk, from the village of Ptushichi, near Babruysk. Photograph by Isaak Serbov. Collection of the Vilnius University Library.

Page 129: Photograph by the Atelier Adler. Collection of the Ethnological Archive of the Museum of the Romanian Peasant, Bucharest.

Page 148: Photograph © Tadeusz Rolke. Courtesy of Agencja Agora SA.

Page 150: Postcard from Vinohrady, Prague. Author's collection.